McGraw-Hill
ENGLISH

Authors

Elizabeth Sulzby
The University of Michigan
Marvin Klein
Western Washington University
William Teale
University of Texas at San Antonio
James Hoffman
University of Texas at Austin

Literature Consultant

Sylvia Peña
University of Houston

Contributing Authors

Lois Easton
Arizona Department of Education
Henrietta Grooms
Tyler ISD, Texas
Miles Olson
University of Colorado
Arnold Webb
Research for Better Schools, Philadelphia, Pennsylvania

McGraw-Hill School Division
New York   Oklahoma City   St. Louis   San Francisco   Dallas   Atlanta

Grateful acknowledgment for permission to reprint copyrighted material, illustrations, and photographs appearing in this book is made on page 494 of this book, which is hereby made a part of this copyright page.

ISBN 0-07-064269-9

McGraw-Hill School Division
1200 Northwest 63rd Street
Oklahoma City, Oklahoma 73116-5712

3 4 5 6 7 8 9 0   8 9 7 6 5 4 3 2 1 0

CONTENTS

A Letter to the Student   12

PART ONE • Connections   16

UNIT 1

Composition • Personal Narrative

What Do You Know?   18

PLANNING

Thinking   Thinking About Personal Narratives   19
Literature   "The Committee" by Ellen Conford
Narrowing a Topic   26
Main Idea and Topic Sentence   28
Using Supporting Details   30

COMPOSING
Writing a First Draft   32

REVISING
Speaking/Listening   Discussing a First Draft   33
Sentence Style   Combining Sentences for Style   34

PROOFREADING
Mechanics   Punctuating Sentences   36
Spelling   Checking Spelling/Writing a Final Copy   38

PRESENTING
Speaking/Listening   Sharing Your Personal Narrative   39

◆ CONNECTIONS
Poetry   The Literature Connection: Sentences   40
The Writing Connection: Sentences   41

Grammar • Sentences I

What Is a Sentence?   42
Complete Subjects and Predicates   44
Simple Subjects and Predicates   46
Finding Subjects in Sentences   48
Sentences with *Here* and *There*   50
Study Skills   Dictionary Skills   52
Speaking/Listening   Language in Action
     A Group Discussion   54
History of Language
     A History of the English Language   56
Test   Unit Review   57

UNIT 2

Composition • Biographical Sketch

What Do You Know? 60

PLANNING

Thinking
Literature

Thinking About Biographical Sketches 61
  "Eleanor Roosevelt: First Lady of the World" by Doris Faber
Preparing for an Interview 66
Conducting an Interview 68

COMPOSING
Writing a First Draft 70

REVISING

Speaking/Listening
Sentence Style

Discussing a First Draft 71
Sentence Variety 72

PROOFREADING

Mechanics
Spelling

Punctuating with Commas 74
Checking Spelling/Writing a Final Copy 76

PRESENTING

Speaking/Listening

Sharing Your Biographical Sketch 77

◆ CONNECTIONS

Poetry

The Literature Connection: Nouns 78
The Writing Connection: Nouns 79

Grammar • Nouns

Common and Proper Nouns 80
Singular and Plural Nouns 82
Possessives 84
More About Possessives 86

Mechanics
Vocabulary
Life Skills

Abbreviations 88
Using a Thesaurus 90
Language in Action
  Reading a Newspaper 92

Study Skills

Test Taking
  Studying for a Test 94

Test
Cooperative Activity
Test

Unit Review 95
Making All the Connections 98
Cumulative Review 102

UNIT 3

Composition · Book Report

What Do You Know?   106

PLANNING

Thinking   Thinking About Book Reports   107
Literature   Book Report on *A Wrinkle in Time* by Madeleine L'Engle
Finding a Book in the Library   110
Introductions and Summaries   112
Supporting an Opinion with Facts   114

COMPOSING
Writing a First Draft   116

REVISING

Speaking/Listening   Discussing a First Draft   117
Sentence Style   Combining Sentences for Style   118

PROOFREADING

Mechanics   Punctuating Titles of Written Works   120
Spelling   Checking Spelling/Writing a Final Copy   122

PRESENTING

Speaking/Listening   Sharing Your Book Report   123

◆ **CONNECTIONS**
Poetry   The Literature Connection: Verbs   124
The Writing Connection: Verbs   125

Grammar · Verbs I

Action Verbs   126
Linking Verbs   128
Main and Helping Verbs   130
Present, Past, and Future Tenses   132
Perfect Tenses   134
Principal Parts of Regular Verbs   136
Principal Parts of Irregular Verbs   138
More Irregular Verbs   140
Vocabulary   Prefixes and Suffixes   142
Life Skills   Language in Action
    Reading a Bus Schedule   144
History of Language
    Words from French   146
Test   Unit Review   147

UNIT 4

Composition · Letters

What Do You Know?   150

PLANNING

Thinking   Thinking About Letters   151
Literature   *Letters to Horseface* by F. N. Monjo
   Planning a Business Letter   154

COMPOSING

Writing a First Draft   156

REVISING

Speaking/Listening   Discussing a First Draft   157
Sentence Style   Combining Sentences for Style   158

PROOFREADING

Mechanics   Punctuating a Letter   160
Spelling   Checking Spelling/Writing a Final Copy   162

PRESENTING

Speaking/Listening   Sharing Your Business Letter   163

COMPOSING

Writing a Friendly Letter   164

◆ **CONNECTIONS**

Poetry   The Literature Connection: Verbs   166
   The Writing Connection: Verbs   167

Grammar · Verbs II

Direct Objects   168
Indirect Objects   170
Transitive and Intransitive Verbs   172
Predicate Nouns and Adjectives   174
Vocabulary   Word Roots   176
Life Skills   Language in Action
   Filling Out Forms   178
Study Skills   Test Taking
   Following Test Directions   180
Test   Unit Review   181
Cooperative Activity   Making All the Connections   184
Test   Cumulative Review   188

UNIT 5

Composition · Descriptive Writing

What Do You Know?　　194

PLANNING
Thinking　Thinking About Descriptive Writing　　195
Literature　　*The Endless Steppe* by Esther Hautzig
　　and ''Metamorphosis'' by May Sarton
　Organizing Sensory Details　　200
　Using Precise Details　　202
　Using Figurative Language　　204

COMPOSING
Writing a First Draft　　206

REVISING
Speaking/Listening　Discussing a First Draft　　207
Sentence Style　Avoiding Repetition　　208

PROOFREADING
Mechanics　Using Commas and Semicolons　　210
Spelling　Checking Spelling/Writing a Final Copy　　212

PLANNING
Poetry　Learning about Poetry　　213
Poetry　Tanka and Acrostic Poems　　216

COMPOSING AND REVISING
Poetry　Writing a Poem　　218

PRESENTING
Speaking/Listening　Sharing Your Descriptive Writing　　219

◆ **CONNECTIONS**
Poetry　The Literature Connection: Pronouns　　220
　The Writing Connection: Pronouns　　221

Grammar · Pronouns

Subject Pronouns　　222
Object Pronouns　　224
Using Pronouns Correctly　　226
Pronouns and Antecedents　　228
Possessive Forms of Pronouns　　230
Vocabulary　Homophones and Homographs　　232
Life Skills　Language in Action
　　Giving Directions　　234
　History of Language
　　Words from Place Names　　236
Test　Unit Review　　237

UNIT
6

Composition · Research Report

| | **What Do You Know?** | 240 |

PLANNING

Thinking	Thinking About Research Reports	241
Literature	"The End of Pompeii"	
	Organizing a Research Report	244
	Using Reference Materials	246
	Understanding the Parts of a Book	248
	Taking Notes in Your Own Words	250
	Making an Outline	252

COMPOSING

| | Writing a First Draft | 254 |

REVISING

| Speaking/Listening | Discussing a First Draft | 255 |
| Sentence Style | Using Transition Words | 256 |

PROOFREADING

| Mechanics | Punctuating a Bibliography | 258 |
| Spelling | Checking Spelling/Writing a Final Copy | 260 |

PRESENTING

| Speaking/Listening | Sharing Your Research Report | 261 |

◆ CONNECTIONS

| Literature | The Literature Connection: Adjectives | 262 |
| | The Writing Connection: Adjectives | 263 |

Grammar · Adjectives

	Adjectives	264
	Proper Adjectives	266
	Predicate Adjectives	268
	Comparisons with Adjectives	270
	Irregular Comparisons	272
	Prepositions and Adjective Phrases	274
Vocabulary	Synonyms and Antonyms	276
Speaking/Listening	Language in Action	
	Giving an Oral Report	278
Study Skills	Test Taking Skills	
	Planning Your Time	280
Test	Unit Review	281
Cooperative Activity	Making All the Connections	284
Test	Cumulative Review	288

Composition · Persuasive Essay

What Do You Know?   294

PLANNING
Thinking   Thinking About Persuasive Essays   295
Literature   "I Have a Dream" by Dr. Martin Luther King, Jr.
                  Supporting an Opinion   300
                  Structuring a Persuasive Essay   302

COMPOSING
                  Writing a First Draft   304

REVISING
Speaking/Listening Discussing a First Draft   305
Sentence Style   Revising for Order of Presentation   306

PROOFREADING
Mechanics   Using Apostrophes and Hyphens   308
Spelling   Checking Spelling/Writing a Final Copy   310

PRESENTING
Speaking/Listening Sharing Your Persuasive Essay   311

◆ **CONNECTIONS**
Poetry   The Literature Connection: Adverbs   312
                  The Writing Connection: Adverbs   313

Grammar · Adverbs

                  Adverbs   314
                  Comparisons with Adverbs   316
                  Adverb or Adjective?   318
                  Adverb Phrases   320
                  Avoiding Double Negatives   322
Vocabulary   Context Clues   324
Life Skills   Language in Action
                      Recognizing Propaganda   326
                  History of Language
                      Animal Words   328
Test   Unit Review   329

UNIT 8

Composition · Story

What Do You Know?   332

PLANNING

Thinking   Thinking About Stories   333
Literature   "Raymond's Run" by Toni Cade Bambara
Creating Characters   348
The Parts of a Story   350

COMPOSING
Writing a First Draft   352

REVISING

Speaking/Listening   Discussing a First Draft   353
Sentence Style   Combining Sentences for Style   354

PROOFREADING

Mechanics   Punctuating Conversation   356
Spelling   Checking Spelling/Writing a Final Copy   358

PRESENTING

Speaking/Listening   Sharing Your Story   359

◆ CONNECTIONS

Poetry   The Literature Connection: Sentences   360
The Writing Connection: Sentences   361

Grammar · Sentences II

Prepositional Phrases   362
Conjunctions and Interjections   364
Compound Subjects   366
Compound Predicates   368
Compound Sentences   370
Mechanics   Avoiding Run-on Sentences   372
Vocabulary   Denotation and Connotation   374
Speaking/Listening   Language in Action
   Giving a Speech   376
Study Skills   Test Taking
   Answering Essay Questions   378
Test   Unit Review   379
Cooperative Activity   Making All the Connections   382
Test   Cumulative Review   386

RESOURCES
Resources Table of Contents   392
Thesaurus   393
Writing Handbook   417
Grammar and Mechanics Handbook   437

INDEX   486

A Letter to the Student

You are at the beginning of a new school year. You are meeting many new people, including your teacher and classmates. This book is also new—at least to you.

As the authors of *McGraw-Hill English,* we want you to know the reasons we wrote this book as we did. We planned this book so that you can make the best possible use of your time.

We feel confident that you will learn to write better this year. In the book, you will follow a clear step-by-step plan to complete each writing assignment. You will also learn how knowing about grammar helps you to write better.

To help you get the most from this book, you will need to keep three types of journals or logs:

◆ **a personal journal**—where you will record your thoughts and feelings on almost any subject throughout the year. You may use your notes to find topics for writing assignments. This journal is for your eyes only.

◆ **a spelling log**—where you will record the words you misspelled in your writing. Keep it in a special place in order to review the words before each new writing assignment.

◆ **a learning log**—where you will write about the lessons that were most difficult for you and how you learned them, or the skills you grasped most easily. By reviewing your learning log, you can do better the next time.

Above all, remember that we have thought about you while writing each page of this book. Please let us know if we have helped you in improving your writing and language skills.

The Writing Process

English: Write a business letter. Due Wednesday.
      Reminder: Book report due next Thursday.
Social Studies: Research report on American presidents.
      Due Tuesday.
Science: Complete report on lab experiment. Due
      Monday.

Do these homework assignments sound familiar to you? This book will help you write reports, stories, and other assignments for all your subjects. However, your writing does not begin when you put pencil to paper. Good writing starts long before that.

In each unit, you will complete your own work by following a step-by-step plan called the *writing process*. Here, briefly, are the steps:

Planning

- First, you must know the features of the type of writing you will do. You will read a literature model of that type.
- Next, you must know your purpose for writing and your audience.
- Then, choose a topic that interests you and that you know something about.
- Then, take notes, make lists, draw a chart, or plan an outline to help you organize your ideas.

Choose a topic you *care* about.

Composing

♦ Use your plan to write a first draft. Include any new ideas you get while writing, even if they are not in your notes.

> Do not worry about making mistakes at this point. Later you will have the chance to go back and correct them.

Revising

♦ Have a partner read your draft. Discuss how you may make your writing clearer or more interesting. Revise your work for content.
♦ Revise your draft for style or organization. Decide where to combine sentences or move them around to make your writing read better. Add details or take out unnecessary words.

> Now is the time to make your draft say *exactly* what you want it to say. Focus on your message.

Proofreading/Writing a Final Copy

♦ Read over your draft for errors in punctuation, capitalization, and spelling.
♦ Write a final copy, making all your changes in content, style, and proofreading.

> It takes a little time to check mistakes, but it's *important*. Those tiny errors can really get in the reader's way.

Presenting

♦ Find interesting ways to share your work with other people.

> People write to communicate. Here's *your* chance!

The more you practice the writing process in this book, the easier it will be to do each new assignment. Your writing will improve steadily throughout the year.

Our Approach to Grammar

Some students like to study grammar; others do not. We have organized this book for both kinds of students. We will explain how we did it.

First, we asked ourselves these questions: What is easy about grammar for students your age, and what is not? We wrote special tests to help us find out. We gave them to students all over the country. The results provided us with valuable information. It helped us plan our grammar lessons.

Every grammar lesson has a section called Strategy. This section gives you a hint to help you understand the grammar skill being taught. Using our test results, we wrote strategies that focus on areas students find difficult in grammar.

The instruction and exercises are divided into **A** and **B** sections. Use the **A** part of the instruction to help you with the **A** part of the exercises; do the same with the **B** parts.

We know that you may sometimes wonder if there is a good reason to study grammar. In this book, we show how grammar can help improve your writing.

We hope you will find this book the most interesting and helpful English book you have ever used. We worked hard to make it right for you!

PART ONE

Connections

You are part of my city,
my universe, my being.
If you were not here
to pass me by,
a piece would be missing
from my jigsaw-puzzle day.

Margaret Tsuda

You make **connections** all the time—with friends and family, with classmates at school, and with the world around you. There are many reasons that people need to make connections. Our lives are enriched through communication and cooperation with others. In these units, consider how connections have helped you to grow and better understand yourself.

UNIT 1

Personal Narrative

◆

Sentences I

What Do You Know?

"What have you been up to?"

When someone asks you this question, how do you answer it? You probably tell the person about one of the more interesting things you have done recently—a trip to a movie or something exciting that happened to you at school. Whenever you share an experience of your own, you are telling a **personal narrative**. You tell about the event, and you also tell how you feel about the event.

Personal narratives can be shared in many ways. You may tell them over the telephone, or you may share them with friends at school. You may write them in a letter or in a diary you keep. A personal narrative is a good way of making connections with others.

Thinking About Personal Narratives ◆

What Is a Personal Narrative?

A personal narrative has these characteristics:

- ◆ It tells about a real or imaginary incident that happened to the writer or narrator.
- ◆ It usually describes the events in the order they happened.
- ◆ It mentions the time, place, and people involved.
- ◆ It is told from the writer's or narrator's point of view and uses words such as *I, me,* and *my.*
- ◆ It relates the writer's or narrator's thoughts and feelings about the experience.

Long ago, people would sit around a campfire and tell each other about the experiences of the day. These narratives provided a means by which traditions of the culture were passed along. Later, people began to write down their personal experiences.

The personal narrative can take many forms. Christopher Columbus's journal of his voyage in 1492 and Anne Frank's diary are two examples of personal narratives. Many poets, journalists, and historians have used personal narratives to inform or entertain.

Discussion

1. Describe an interesting experience that happened recently to you or to someone you know.
2. Describe an interesting experience you have recently told friends about.
3. How did you share the experience with your friend—in person, by telephone, or in writing?

19

Reading a Personal Narrative

This selection is about Dorrie, a sixth grader who works on a committee for a class project—a newspaper about books the class has read. In this personal narrative, Dorrie is the narrator, or teller of the story. She tells how she and her committee worked on the newspaper and how she felt when she first saw it in print.

The Committee
by
Ellen Conford

The narrator states the main idea. The other characters are introduced.

Charles and I began typing up the stories. Time was running out and even as we began to type up our final copies for the printer, we kept thinking of new ideas for articles.

TOM SAWYER HOLDS PAINT-IN
Youngsters Flock to Take Part
in Street Beautification Project

Serena drew picture after picture, till she had one for almost every story we'd written. Then we made up captions for them: "Little Women who want to do their bit for the soldiers. Meg, Jo, Beth and Amy knit stockings for the Union cause."

The Wednesday before Book Week we met at my house and made our final choices of articles and pictures. We did a rough layout, as my father had explained, to get an idea of where we'd put everything, and how the paper would look when it was finished.

On Thursday morning, my father took all our material to the office with him. The printers were going to set up the galleys, and he would bring the proofs home in the afternoon.

That day the committee had its final meeting. We had to proofread everything to check for mistakes and correct the few we found. Then we had to cut stories out of the long sheets of paper that were the galley proofs and paste them onto a dummy sheet the same size as our newspaper.

When it was finally done, my father checked it over one last time while we slumped, exhausted, on the living room floor.

The place is introduced. Events are told in time order.

"This is a fine job," he announced at last.

"Thank goodness!" Serena sighed with relief.

Haskell gave a tired cheer, and slapped hands with Charles.

"Now how many copies should I make up?" my father asked.

"I never thought of that," I realized. "I guess one for everybody in the class, and an extra one for Mrs. O'Neill."

"You know, once the type is set it's as easy to make a hundred as it is to make twenty-five," he said.

"Then why don't we make enough for the whole school?" Serena suggested eagerly. "Mrs. O'Neill wants to display the projects and have the other classes come in and see them. She said we would do things the whole school could enjoy."

"So you'll need about a thousand?"

"Will that be too expensive?" I worried.

"No, it's all right," he assured me. "With the free advertising you gave me, it's worth it."

On the front page in a little box, we had set up a plug for my father's paper. It read: "The *Book Week Leader* is grateful to the *Brockton Center Leader* for printing this special edition. For news of the *real* world, read the *Leader* every Thursday."

I couldn't wait for school to be over on Friday. My father was going to bring the finished paper home with him, and I was a nervous wreck all day, wondering how it would turn out. Until the *Book Week Leader* was safely printed and handed out to everyone, I couldn't really work up too much excitement for anything else.

My father came home just before dinner and I flung myself at him when he was barely over the threshold.

"Let me see it! Did it come out okay? *How does it look?*"

"Here," he said, handing me a bunch of papers. "See for yourself. I think it came out beautifully."

The narrator explains her feelings.

My mother came up behind me and reached for a copy. "I've been waiting all day for this. Oh, Dorrie! It's beautiful!" She sat down on the couch and began to read it. She turned the pages eagerly. Every once in a while she smiled or laughed, and pointed out something she especially liked to my father.

It *was* beautiful. It looked just like the *Leader*, but it had only four pages. *Book Week Leader* was in the same kind of type my father uses for *Brockton Center Leader* on the top of the front page. Serena's pictures had come out perfectly.

I smiled as I re-read the stories and headlines that I already knew practically by heart.

R. CRUSOE LOST AT SEA
TORNADO RIPS HOUSE FROM KANSAS FARM
Girl, Dog, and House Vanish During Killer Storm
QUICK-THINKING YOUNGSTER PLUGS DIKE
Saves Holland from Flood Disaster

"Oh, it's gorgeous, gorgeous!" I cried. "Isn't it? Oh, it's just the way I pictured it. No, it's *better!*"

Understanding What You've Read

Write your answers on a separate sheet of paper.

1. Where does the personal narrative take place?
2. What characters are involved in the narrative?
3. In what order are the events presented?
4. What words are clues that this is a personal narrative?
5. What are the writer's feelings about her experience?
6. How might the story have been different if Dorrie's father hadn't worked at a newspaper?

Writing Assignment

In the personal narrative that you read, the main character helped put together a class newspaper. Imagine that you have been asked to write a personal narrative of one paragraph for a school newspaper. In the coming lessons, you will learn how to develop your own narrative, step by step. You will describe a memorable experience you have had and will describe your feelings about it. As part of the writing process, you will have a classmate listen to your ideas and make suggestions.

Your **audience** will be your teacher and the other students in your class. Your **purpose** will be to describe a personal experience and your feelings about it.

What can I write about?

Choose a Topic

Think of three topics that you might like to write about. Select topics from this list, or provide others of your own.

team sports	holidays
neighbors	summer adventures
school events	class trip

List your three choices, and save them for the next lesson.

Narrowing a Topic

In your personal narrative, you should focus on a single experience that you can cover in one paragraph. If you merely list a group of related experiences, your narrative will be too general. To avoid this, you must narrow your general topic down to one specific incident that you can describe in detail.

One way to narrow a topic is by **clustering**. Write your general topic on a sheet of paper. Then write related subjects beneath the general topic to get more ideas. Below is a cluster that one writer used for the topic of animals. Notice that the farther away from the starting point you get, the narrower the topic becomes.

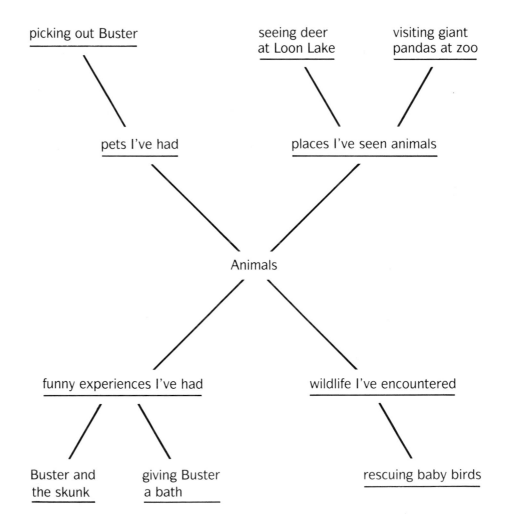

Practice

A. Write which topic is the narrowest of each group.
1. food, breakfast, nutrition
2. sports, the ninth inning, baseball
3. vitamins, health, diet
4. libraries, atlases, reference books
5. pines, trees, evergreens
6. pets, terriers, dogs
7. waterways, the Mississippi, rivers
8. carrots, vegetables, gardens
9. photographs, hobbies, developing film

B. For each broad topic draw a cluster diagram to narrow the topic to a single experience.
10. entertainment
11. relatives
12. transportation
13. achievements
14. after-school jobs
15. weather

Narrow Your Topic

   Look back at the list you made of three topics. Use clustering to narrow each topic down to a specific experience that you can cover in detail. Circle the experience you would like to write about. Save your choice for the next lesson.

Main Idea and Topic Sentence

As you know, a paragraph is a group of sentences with one **main idea**, or central thought. In some paragraphs, the main idea is stated by a **topic sentence**. In other paragraphs, the main idea is clear without being stated by a topic sentence. In your personal narrative, you will state the main idea of your paragraph by writing a topic sentence. Look at the examples below.

> **Topic:** The first day I went ice-skating
> **Main Idea:** It was a sport that was difficult for me.
> **Topic Sentence:** The first day I went ice-skating, I knew it was a sport at which I would never excel.

Writing a topic sentence for your paragraph will help you decide what details to include in your narrative.

Since the topic sentence of your paragraph will be at the beginning of your narrative, the sentence should be as interesting as possible. It should grab the readers' attention and make them want to read further. Here are two topic sentences that could introduce a personal narrative. Which do you prefer?

> **Topic Sentence:** I received a phone call from the actor Rhett Sinclair.
> **Topic Sentence:** Receiving a phone call is an everyday happening, unless, of course, it's from a famous movie star like Rhett Sinclair.

The second topic sentence is much more appealing. It makes readers want to read further to find out why Rhett Sinclair called the writer.

Practice

A. Read each topic and main idea. Write an interesting topic sentence that states the main idea.
  1. Topic: My eleventh birthday
     Main Idea: I received a big surprise.
  2. Topic: The day my dog Brewster came home smelling horrible
     Main Idea: I decided that his skunk-chasing days were over.
  3. Topic: My visit to Aunt Sylvia's house
     Main Idea: Her house was neat until I showed up.
  4. Topic: Exploring the attic on a rainy day
     Main Idea: I discovered hidden treasures.

B. Read each pair of sentences. Write the sentence that is better as the topic sentence for a paragraph.
  5. **a.** Baby-sitting for a talking parrot was interesting.
     b. Baby-sitting is an ordinary experience, unless it's for a talking parrot with a sense of humor.
  6. **a.** Climbing Ridgehorn Mountain was an exciting adventure that brought my father and me closer together.
     b. My Dad and I climbed Ridgehorn Mountain.
  7. **a.** I'll never forget the family picnic.
     b. The family picnic, which turned into the family laugh-in, was an unforgettable experience.
  8. **a.** Our class trip made the news.
     b. We expected to have fun on our class trip, but we never thought we'd make the evening news.

Write Your Topic Sentence
   Look at the experience you chose to write about in the previous lesson. Decide what your main idea will be. Then write a topic sentence that states your main idea in an interesting way. Save your work for the next lesson.

Using Supporting Details

The topic sentence in a paragraph states the main idea. Other sentences in the paragraph give **supporting details** about the main idea. Supporting details are facts or examples that support the main idea. You should include only those details that relate directly to the topic sentence. Do not include details that stray from the main idea.

In a narrative paragraph, supporting details are usually arranged in **sequence**, or the order in which they occurred. One student decided to write about her first airplane trip. She began by writing a topic sentence: *My first flight was an experience I will never forget*. Then she listed some details about the experience.

--- Took a cab to the airport with Mom and Dad
--- Checked our bags and bought some magazines to read
--- My mother and father subscribed to two magazines
--- Went inside the jet and took our seats; I got to sit by the window since it was my first plane ride
--- From the air, the world was like a yard full of toys!
--- Once we landed, I couldn't wait for the plane ride home

The details are listed in the order in which they occurred. However, the third detail does not belong in the paragraph. Subscribing to two magazines does not support the idea that the writer's first flight was an unforgettable experience.

Practice

A. Read the topic sentence below. Then write only the details that support it.

> **Topic Sentence:** Music is supposed to be soothing, but when I practice the violin, it has the opposite effect.

1. I set up my music stand as usual, took out my violin, and began to play.
2. The tuba is a beautiful instrument to play.
3. At the first few notes, my dog began to bark.
4. The howling dog caused my baby sister to cry.
5. I want to play my violin with Itzhak Perlman someday.
6. I put the dog in the basement, hoping he'd be quieter.
7. The sound of his howling came up through the ventilator.
8. Finally, my violin and I moved to the garage, where there was some peace and quiet.

B. Read the topic sentence and the details that follow. Then write the details in a logical order.

> **Topic Sentence:** When I flung a bottle with a message into the ocean last summer, little did I realize I would get a reply.

1. I tore open the letter and discovered it was from an English girl named Marian.
2. I made sure the cork was on tight, and then I threw the bottle in the ocean.
3. I was bored stiff one day last summer.
4. I decided to write a message and put it into a bottle.
5. Then, a few days ago, Mom said there was a letter for me.
6. She had found the bottle on a beach in Dover, England.
7. Soon I had forgotten all about the bottle and the message.
8. Now Marian and I are pen pals and are planning to meet.

Organize Your Details

Look at the topic sentence you wrote for your personal narrative. List details that will help support your main idea. Then rewrite the details in the order in which they occurred. Save your work for the next lesson.

Writing a First Draft

Read the first draft of the personal narrative below. The writer wasn't worried about making it perfect. It will be changed later.

When I walked out of the house that morning, I had no idea that I would have to reunite a family of birds. At first, I saw only the mother bird. She was perched on a bush. She was chirping in fright. Then I saw two baby birds hopping around beneath the bush. They probably had been trying out their wings. They had maniged to land on the grassy lawn. They could not fly back to thier nest in the small tree nearby. I started toward them, intending to pick them up. Suddenly, something I'd read flashed through my mind. Never touch baby birds with your bare hands. If you do, the mother bird might smell you're scent and reject the babies. What could I do? I rushed into the house and brought back a large box of sterelized cotton. Then I got a crate from the garage. I placed the crate next to the small tree. Using the cotton, I carryed the first bird to the tree, stepped onto the crate, and placed the bird back in the nest. Then I did the same thing with the second bird. When I had finished, I stood back and waited. In a few moments, the mother bird flew back to the nest. She began to sing. Everything was fine again.

Write Your First Draft

If you wish, start by discussing your narrative with your teacher. If you prefer, work on your own. Begin with the topic sentence you wrote. Then refer to your list of details. Continue your paragraph by writing detail sentences that tell about the events in order. Mention the people involved, as well as the time and place of the experience. Tell how you felt about what happened. Write on every other line so that you will have room for changes later. Save your work.

Discussing a First Draft

After completing your first draft, look for ways to improve it. One way is by discussing it with a classmate.

Discussion Strategy

If you do not completely understand something your partner has written, ask for an explanation before making your comments. You may have misunderstood the ideas your partner is trying to express.

Use the Content Checklist to discuss with your class the draft on the previous page.

Content Checklist
- ✔ Does the narrative tell about an interesting experience that happened to the narrator?
- ✔ Does the narrative mention the characters, time, and place of the experience?
- ✔ Are the events told in the order in which they occurred?
- ✔ Does the narrative indicate the narrator's feelings about the experience?

Revise Your First Draft for Content

To the Reader: Cover up the topic sentence on your draft. Then exchange papers with a classmate. Read your partner's personal narrative and say what you think the main idea is. Then compare it with the topic sentence. If your statements are not similar, discuss ways to improve the topic sentence and other parts of the draft so the main idea is clearer. Use the Content Checklist for help.

To the Writer: Listen to your partner's suggestions. Then revise your draft for content. Save your work.

Combining Sentences for Style

In the narrative about the baby birds, some of the sentences are short and choppy. The writer could improve the draft by combining sentences.

Sentences with the same subject may be combined. Use *and* to show that one subject did two different actions. Use *or* to show that one subject can do either of two actions.

The bird flapped its wings. The bird cried.
The bird flapped its wings and cried.
The bird will fly away. The bird will stay.
The bird will fly away or will stay.

Sentences with the same action may be combined. Use *and* to show that two different subjects did the same action. Use *or* to show that either subject might do the same action.

My brother saw the birds. I saw the birds.
My brother and I saw the birds.
He will rescue them. I will rescue them.
He or I will rescue them.

Here is how the writer combined some of the sentences in the first draft.

These sentences are about the same subject.

> She was perched on a bush. ~~She~~ ,and was chirping in fright.
>
> Then I got a crate from the garage, and I placed the crate next
>
> to the small tree.
>
> In a few moments, the mother bird flew back to the nest.
> and
> ~~She~~ began to sing.

Practice

Combine each pair of sentences. Make a single sentence using the words *and* or *or*. Write your new sentence.

1. Dad saw a puppy in an animal shelter. I saw a puppy in an animal shelter.
2. A kitten would make a nice pet. A puppy would make a nice pet.
3. The puppy wagged its tail. The puppy barked.
4. Dad brought the puppy home. I brought the puppy home.
5. My sister will take turns walking the puppy. I will take turns walking the puppy.
6. Tomorrow, my sister will wash the puppy in the garage. Tomorrow, I will wash the puppy in the garage.
7. The puppy chases most of the balls we throw. The puppy catches most of the balls we throw.
8. My mother will let the puppy sleep indoors on an old blanket. My father will let the puppy sleep indoors on an old blanket.

Revising Checklist
✔ Have I included all the features of a personal narrative?
✔ Where can I combine sentences by using the words *and* or *or*?

Can I combine any sentences?

Revise Your Narrative for Style
Check for the items on the Revising Checklist. Combine any short sentences that tell about the same subject or action. Mark the changes on your draft. Save your work for the next lesson.

APPLY STEP BY STEP

35

Punctuating Sentences

As a writer, you are in charge of the kinds of sentences you create. Your end punctuation helps the reader know whether you are making a statement, giving a command, asking a question, or showing emotion. It's your choice!

Here are rules for punctuation and capitalization.

Rule	Example
Indent the first word in a paragraph.	Suddenly something that I had once read flashed across my mind.
Capitalize the first word in a sentence.	Then I got a sturdy old crate from the garage and placed it next to the tree.
Use a period (.) at the end of a statement or a command.	Next morning, it was business as usual. Never touch baby birds with your bare hands.
Use a question mark (?) at the end of a question.	How could I help the birds?
Use an exclamation mark (!) at the end of a statement or a command showing strong emotion or surprise.	There they were on my front lawn and too young to fly! Leave those birds alone!
Capitalize the name of a particular person, place, or thing.	I considered calling Anne Lopez, the vet at Brookville Hospital, for advice.

Practice

Write the sentences below. Add end punctuation to show how you want readers to understand each sentence. Use capital letters where necessary. Indent the first sentence.

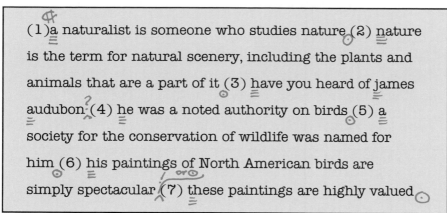

(1) a naturalist is someone who studies nature (2) nature is the term for natural scenery, including the plants and animals that are a part of it (3) have you heard of james audubon (4) he was a noted authority on birds (5) a society for the conservation of wildlife was named for him (6) his paintings of North American birds are simply spectacular (7) these paintings are highly valued

Proofreading Marks

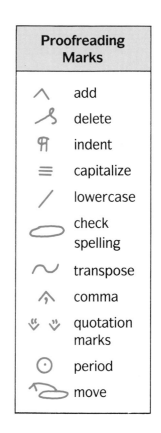

∧	add
⚡	delete
¶	indent
≡	capitalize
/	lowercase
⬭	check spelling
∼	transpose
∧	comma
❝ ❞	quotation marks
⊙	period
↰⊃	move

Proofreading Checklist

- ✔ Did I indent the first word of the paragraph?
- ✔ Did I capitalize the first word of each sentence?
- ✔ Did I capitalize the names of particular people, places, and things?
- ✔ Did I end each sentence with the correct punctuation?

APPLY STEP BY STEP

Proofread Your Personal Narrative

Check for correct punctuation and capitalization. Use the Proofreading Checklist. Make corrections on your draft. Save your work.

Checking Spelling/Writing a Final Copy ◆

Spelling Strategy

When you proofread, always check for spelling errors.

◆ Circle each word you think may be misspelled.
◆ Using a dictionary, look up the spelling you think is correct.
◆ If the word is not listed, try another spelling. Keep checking until you find the correct spelling in the dictionary.

Here is a portion of the revised and proofread narrative.

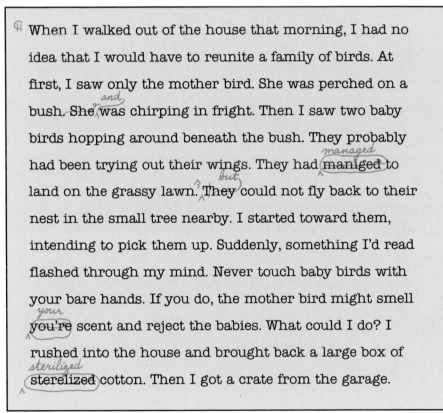

¶ When I walked out of the house that morning, I had no idea that I would have to reunite a family of birds. At first, I saw only the mother bird. She was perched on a bush. She *and,* was chirping in fright. Then I saw two baby birds hopping around beneath the bush. They probably had been trying out their wings. They had *managed* (maniged) to land on the grassy lawn. *but,* They could not fly back to their nest in the small tree nearby. I started toward them, intending to pick them up. Suddenly, something I'd read flashed through my mind. Never touch baby birds with your bare hands. If you do, the mother bird might smell *your* you're scent and reject the babies. What could I do? I rushed into the house and brought back a large box of *sterilized* (sterelized) cotton. Then I got a crate from the garage.

Check Your Spelling

Use the proofreading marks to correct errors in spelling. Begin your spelling log.

Write a Final Copy

Write a neat, final copy of your narrative. Proofread your work. Keep your final copy.

Sharing Your Personal Narrative ◆

Speaking/Listening Strategy

Speak loudly and clearly while reading aloud. Add laughter or pauses where they seem natural. If you are in the audience, listen closely to learn the speaker's thoughts and feelings about the experience.

Choosing a Way to Share

After writing a neat, final copy of your narrative, share it with classmates. Here are several ways to share your work.

Reading Aloud Read your narrative aloud to classmates. To give your story an added "personal touch," pretend you are telling the story over the telephone to a friend or relative.

Presenting a Radio Show Produce an imaginary radio show called "Have I Got a Story For You." Have a classmate act as moderator and introduce speakers on the show. Along with other "guests" on the program, present your narrative. You may want to include sound effects for your "radio audience." Then answer questions about your narrative posed by the moderator.

Compiling a Magazine Put your narrative together with your classmates' narratives into a class magazine entitled *That's Life!* Make copies so that each student can have a copy.

Share Your Narrative

Choose the way you prefer to share your narrative. Present it and discover your audience's reaction.

Begin a Learning Log

Answer these questions in your learning log.

- ◆ What part of my narrative do I like best?
- ◆ What did I enjoy most about writing my narrative?
- ◆ What will I do differently in the next narrative I write?

The Literature Connection: Sentences

Have you ever tried to communicate with a person who speaks no English? Because you don't share a language, you probably had difficulty understanding each other. Language is our connection, or way of communicating, with other people.

In writing, problems arise when writers don't write clearly. Unclear sentences make readers strain and struggle for understanding. They seem to be speaking in a language you don't know. You feel frustrated and confused. The poem below describes a person trying to communicate with a bird. Note how difficult communication is when an unknown language is spoken.

The Peabody Bird
by
Rachel Field

Peabody! Peabody! Peabody!
Why do you call that name
Over and over and over?
Is it sort of a game
That you play by yourself
The whole day through?
Is it someone you want?
I wish I knew.

Peabody! Peabody! Peabody!
From fir top or leafy spray,
It's a long name and a queer name
For a bird like you to say.
Can't you forget for a single hour?
They are either lost or dead.
Couldn't you look for someone else?
And wouldn't I do instead?

Discussion

1. How many words does the bird know?
2. How are the languages of the speaker and the bird different?
3. What do you imagine the word *Peabody* means to the bird?
4. What other birds or animals make distinct sounds? Describe the "words" you hear them say.

The Writing Connection:
Sentences

In your own writing, you are in control. In the scenes you describe, you determine the effect of every word, every sound, and every action. Here are some examples of how you might interpret sounds in your writing.

When an owl says "hoot," it means "the moon is up."
When a frog says "ribbit," it means "a snake is near."

Activity

Complete the following sentences. Look at the sentences and the picture above for ideas. Then explain what each animal sound means. The first three have been started for you.

- When the wolf says "gr-r-r," it means "_____."
- When the leopard says "purr-r-r," it means "_____."
- When the snake says "s-s-s-s," it means "_____."
- When the fox says "_____," it means "_____."
- When the hyena says "_____," it means "_____."
- When the chimp says "_____," it means "_____."

What Is a Sentence?

A **sentence** is a group of words that expresses a complete thought. A sentence begins with a capital letter and ends with an end mark.

A. There are four different kinds of sentences.

Type of Sentence	Purpose	End Mark	Example
declarative	gives information	.	The Mississippi River once held our nation together.
interrogative	asks a question	?	Does the river lead to the Gulf of Mexico?
imperative	gives a command or makes a request	. or !	Please open the window. Stop! Look there!
exclamatory	shows surprise or strong feeling	!	How wide the river is at St. Louis! What a huge tanker that is!

B. A **fragment** is a group of words that does not express a complete thought. The meanings of fragments may be clear in conversation, but fragments are never used in formal writing.

The roar of the river. Took a steamboat down the river.

What about the roar of the river? *Who* took a steamboat?

Strategy

If you are not sure whether a group of words is a sentence or a fragment, read it aloud to yourself or to a friend. If it confuses you or seems incomplete, it is probably a fragment.

Check Your Understanding

A. Write the letter that identifies each sentence.
   1. What a large steamboat that is!
      a. imperative   **b.** interrogative   **c.** exclamatory
   2. Was Mark Twain born near the Mississippi?
      a. declarative   **b.** interrogative   **c.** imperative

B. Write the letter that identifies each group of words.

   3. Barges carried cargo.
      a. sentence   **b.** fragment

   4. Is the longest river in the entire United States.
      a. sentence   **b.** fragment

Practice

A. Identify each sentence as declarative, interrogative, imperative, or exclamatory. Then write the sentence, using the correct end mark.

   5. Does the Missouri River flow into the Mississippi
   6. How muddy the river is today
   7. Much American folklore centers on the river
   8. Read that story by Mark Twain

B. Write each group of words. If it is a sentence, write sentence. If it is a fragment, write fragment.

   9. Early explorers sailed up the Mississippi River.
   10. Paddled canoes into the wilderness.
   11. Many settlers on the Mississippi.
   12. The river was often busy.

C. Mixed Practice Read each group of words. If it is a sentence, write it with the correct end mark. If it is a fragment, rewrite it as a sentence and add an end mark.

   13. Mail traveled on the Mississippi River
   14. Does the river flow more than 2,300 miles
   15. Grew on the river's shores
   16. How did early explorers cross the great river
   17. What a mighty river it is
   18. Many of our greatest cities
   19. Look at those enormous cotton fields
   20. What lured settlers down the Mississippi was new land

Apply: Work with a Partner

Write three sentences about famous rivers. End each sentence in three different ways. For example: *The Nile is the world's longest river. The Nile is the world's longest river? The Nile is the world's longest river!* Then exchange papers with a classmate, and discuss how the meaning of the sentence changes.

Complete Subjects and Predicates

A. Every sentence can be divided into two parts. One part of a sentence is the complete subject.

The **complete subject** is all the words that tell who or what the sentence is about. It can be one or more words.

In the sentences below, the complete subjects are in red.

> Every school should have its own newspaper.
>
> The newspapers in our city publish excellent articles.
>
> They greatly affect public opinion.

B. The other part of a sentence is the complete predicate.

The **complete predicate** is the verb and all the other words that tell what the subject does, has, is, or is like.

In the sentences below, the complete predicates are in blue.

> Thousands of daily newspapers exist.
>
> *The New York Times* is one of the largest papers.
>
> People have been printing newspapers for 1,200 years.

Strategy

Some people have trouble recognizing these forms of *be* as verbs: *am*, *is*, *are*, *was*, and *were*. When you see any one of these verbs in a sentence, it is often the first word in the complete predicate.

Check Your Understanding

A. Write the letter of the complete subject in each sentence.
1. Newsrooms are often very busy places.
   a. Newsrooms are   **b.** Newsrooms
   c. very busy places
2. Many large newspapers employ foreign correspondents.
   a. newspapers   **b.** foreign correspondents
   c. Many large newspapers

BULLETIN

NOVEMBER IS

B. Write the letter of the complete predicate in each sentence.

    3. Many novelists start their careers as journalists.

        a. Many novelists   **b.** start

        c. start their careers as journalists

    4. Newspapers provide both facts and opinions.

        a. provide   **b.** provide both facts and opinions

        c. Newspapers

Practice

A. Write each sentence. Underline the complete subject.

    5. Newspapers can unite the members of a community.

    6. They provide information and entertainment.

    7. Articles in newspapers tell events in detail.

    8. Investigative reporters write long articles.

B. Write each sentence. Underline the complete predicate.

    9. Many people buy more than one newspaper each day.

   10. Newspapers contain advertisements for many products.

   11. Editorials express the opinions of the newspaper.

   12. News articles describe some events very thoroughly.

C. Mixed Practice Write each sentence. Underline the complete subject once and the complete predicate twice.

   13. Some newspapers publish morning and afternoon editions.

   14. A German printer published the first European newspaper in 1609.

   15. Many newspapers circulate throughout the world.

   16. Some large cities publish newspapers in many languages.

   17. Editors of large newspapers work under great pressure.

   18. The history of newspapers is an interesting topic.

   19. Newspapers and pamphlets played an important role.

   20. Such leaders as Benjamin Franklin and Thomas Paine frequently wrote newspaper articles about their views.

Apply: Work with a Group

Work with three other students. Write five fragments about newspapers or about a topic of your choice. Leave out either the complete subject or the complete predicate in each. Exchange papers with other members of your group and complete one another's sentences. Then compare the completed sentences.

45

Simple Subjects and Predicates

◆

A. The complete subject of a sentence contains a simple subject.

The **simple subject** of a sentence is the main word or group of words in the complete subject.

The simple subject is a noun or a pronoun. Below, each complete subject is in red; each simple subject is underlined.

The first woman cabinet member was Frances Perkins.

She served under President Franklin D. Roosevelt.

Notice that sometimes, as in the second sentence, the complete subject is the same as the simple subject.

B. The complete predicate of a sentence contains a simple predicate.

The **simple predicate** of a sentence is the main word or group of words in the complete predicate.

The simple predicate is always a verb or a verb phrase. In each sentence below, the complete predicate is shown in blue, and the simple predicate is underlined.

Frances Perkins labored for workers' rights.

She was a supporter of the rights of women and children.

She had worked many years on behalf of the work force.

The simple predicate can be more than one word. How many words make up the simple predicate in the third sentence?

Strategy

Some simple predicates have more than one word. The simple predicate below has three words.

Perkins's work has been inspiring women for years.

Check Your Understanding

A. Write the letter of the simple subject in each sentence.
  1. Frances Perkins lived in Massachusetts.
      a. Frances Perkins   **b.** lived   **c.** Massachusetts
  2. Her name was originally Fannie Cordalie Perkins.
      a. Her   **b.** name   **c.** Fannie Cordalie Perkins

46

B. Write the letter of the simple predicate in each sentence.

   3. She kept her maiden name after her marriage.
       a. She   **b.** kept   **c.** after her marriage
   4. Perkins had lived in Illinois before her move east.
       a. had   **b.** had lived in Illinois   **c.** had lived

Practice

A. Write each sentence. Underline the simple subject.
   5. Young Frances spent time with the poor in Illinois.
   6. The 27-year-old woman went to Philadelphia in 1907.
   7. She headed an important city organization.
   8. Philadelphia was her home for only two years.

B. Write each sentence. Underline the simple predicate.
   9. Perkins became secretary of the New York Consumer's League.
   10. She accomplished much during her tenure.
   11. She had worked for the passage of important labor laws.
   12. She was an investigator for a statewide commission.

C. Mixed Practice Write each sentence. Underline the simple subject once and the simple predicate twice.
   13. Perkins discovered many unsafe working conditions.
   14. Several New York governors appointed her to important posts.
   15. One of the governors was Franklin D. Roosevelt.
   16. He was President of the United States from 1932 to 1945.
   17. Perkins impressed Roosevelt.
   18. He made her his secretary of labor.
   19. Former Secretary of Labor Frances Perkins will be remembered for a long time.
   20. The long career of Frances Perkins would be remarkable even without her role as the first woman cabinet member.

Apply: Learning Log

What was the hardest part of this lesson for you? In your learning log, write a plan that will help you understand that part better.

47

Finding Subjects in Sentences ◆

The complete subject is not always the first word or group of words in a sentence.

A. An **imperative sentence** gives a command or makes a request. In an imperative sentence, *you* is understood to be the subject. The word *you* is not written in the sentence, however.

(You) Join a club at your school.

B. An **interrogative sentence** asks a question. In an interrogative sentence, the complete subject often comes between parts of the predicate. To help you identify the complete subject more easily, rewrite each interrogative sentence as a declarative sentence.

Does the group accept students? (interrogative)

The group does accept students. (declarative)

Is the new club interesting? (interrogative)

The new club is interesting. (declarative)

Strategy

Because some imperative sentences are short, they may look like sentence fragments. Here's a way to tell the difference between the two. Read the group of words in question. Is the subject understood to be *you*? If it is, the sentence is imperative.

Check Your Understanding

A. Write the letter of the simple subject in each sentence.
   1. Join a club today.
       a. (You) **b.** Join **c.** club **d.** today
   2. Choose from among many different kinds of clubs.
       a. Choose **b.** kinds **c.** clubs **d.** (You)

B. Write the letter of the simple subject in each sentence.
   3. Do you belong to a club?
       a. Do **b.** you **c.** belong **d.** club
   4. Do some clubs meet at your school?
       a. do **b.** clubs **c.** meet **d.** school

Practice

A. Write each sentence. Underline the simple subject. If the subject is *you*, write *(You)*.

    5. Join your local 4-H club.

    6. Work for the good of your community.

    7. Learn about food, health, animals, and safety.

    8. Share your skills with others.

B. Write each sentence. Underline the simple subject.

    9. Do some clubs help women?

    10. Do the letters represent *head, heart, hands,* and *health*?

    11. Has this group improved community life?

    12. Does your school support student clubs?

C. Mixed Practice Write each sentence. Underline each simple subject. If the subject is *you*, write (You).

    13. Meet people with similar interests.

    14. Has the Rotary Club helped businesses succeed?

    15. Subscribe at the membership office.

    16. Is she a member of the National Organization of Women?

    17. Find out about projects in your school.

    18. Please post a list of candidates for club officers.

    19. Does the League of Women Voters provide information for voters?

    20. Distribute the advertisements for the car wash tomorrow morning.

Apply: Test a Partner

Write five interrogative sentences you might ask a member of a club you are thinking of joining. Or write five interrogative sentences about a topic of your choice. Exchange papers with a classmate and rewrite each other's sentences as declarative sentences. Underline the simple subject in each sentence. Then check each other's papers.

Sentences with *Here* and *There*

In a sentence that begins with *here* or *there*, the complete subject usually appears later in the sentence.

A. The word *here* is not the subject of any of the sentences below. If a sentence begins with *here*, rearrange the words to find the simple subject.

Here is	Williamsburg.	→	Williamsburg	is here.
Here are	many tourists.	→	Many tourists	are here.
Here is	a link to our past.	→	A link to our past	is here.

B. The word *there* is not the subject of any of the sentences below. You can find the simple subject in sentences like these by rearranging the words.

There is	a shop from 1700.	→	A shop from 1700	is there.
There are	many houses.	→	Many houses	are there.
There is	the wigmaker.	→	The wigmaker	is there.

Strategy

When a pronoun is the subject of a sentence that begins with *here* or *there*, the pronoun usually comes before the verb.

Here comes the tour guide. ⟶ Here she comes.

There is the old capitol. ⟶ There it is.

Check Your Understanding

A. Write the letter of the simple subject in each sentence.
   1. Here is the old town hall.
      a. Here   **b.** old   **c.** town   **d.** town hall
   2. Here is the original governor's palace.
      a. Here   **b.** is   **c.** original   **d.** palace

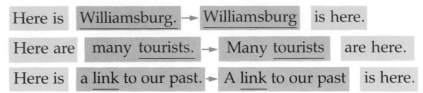

50

B. Write the letter of the simple subject in each sentence.

    3. There are the members of the fire brigade.

        a. There   **b.** members   **c.** fire   **d.** brigade

    4. There is a little antique shop.

        a. There   **b.** little   **c.** antique   **d.** shop

Practice

A. Write each sentence. Underline the simple subject.

    5. Here is the oldest home in Williamsburg.

    6. Here are the blacksmiths in their shop.

    7. Here is the cloth weaver's house.

    8. Here are Williamsburg's original boundaries.

B. Write each sentence. Underline the simple subject.

    9. There are craftsworkers from the blacksmith's shop.

    10. There is the barrel maker.

    11. There is the town's cabinetmaker.

    12. There is the seat of the Town Council.

C. Mixed Practice Write each sentence. Underline the simple subject.

    13. Here is a woman in colonial dress.

    14. Here is the home of Virginia's first newspaper.

    15. There is the first courthouse in Williamsburg.

    16. There is the village's busiest street.

    17. Here is the site of the original market square.

    18. There is Williamsburg's oldest tavern.

    19. There's a wall from 1633.

    20. Here we are at the end of our tour.

Apply: Journal

Imagine you are conducting a tour of a historic site or of your hometown. Write five sentences in your journal about places to see. Begin each sentence with *Here* or *There*.

Dictionary Skills

guide words

scatter / **scholar**

scat•ter (skat′ər) *v.* **1** throw in all directions; sprinkle. **2** separate and go in different directions; *The birds scattered when we appeared.*

scat•ter•brain (skat′ər brān′) *n.* a thoughtless, silly person.

scat•ter brained (skat′ər brānd′) *adj.* thoughtless and silly.

pronunciation   part of speech   definition

sched•ule (skej′ül) *n.* **1** a written list. **2** a timed plan for doing something. —*v.* **1** make a schedule of. **2** arrange for a certain time: *schedule an appointment.*

scheme (skēm) *n.* **1** a plan of action. **2** a plot: *a scheme to steal the jewels.* **3** an organized framework: *a color scheme.* —*v.* devise plans; plot.

syllables

example sentence

example phrase

entry words

Pronunciation Key

a back	**i** it	**oi** coin	**ch** child		a in about
ā cage	**ī** ice	**ou** out	**ng** sing		e in taken
ä far	**o** dot	**u** cup	**sh** she	**ə =**	i in pencil
e let	**ō** open	** u̇** put	**th** thin		o in lemon
ē equal	**ô** order	**ü** rule	**t̶h** that		u in circus
er term			**zh** measure		

Abbreviations for Parts of Speech

n.	noun	*adj.*	adjective
v.	verb	*adv.*	adverb

A. A dictionary tells what words mean and how they are used. **Entry words** are listed alphabetically and divided into **syllables.** The **pronunciation** follows. A separate **pronunciation key** shows what the symbols in the pronunciation sound like. Heavy and light **accent marks** show which syllables to stress. The entry word's part of speech is abbreviated.

B. One or more **definitions,** or meanings, are given for each entry word. Sometimes an **example sentence** or **phrase** is given. When a word has several meanings, each one is numbered. If a word can be used as more than one part of speech, the definitions for each part of speech are numbered separately.

Strategy

If you are not sure how to spell a word that you want to find in the dictionary, try to sound it out. Watch for silent letters such as the *k* in *knight* or the *g* in *gnat.*

Check Your Understanding

A. Write the letter of the correct answer. Use the sample dictionary page.

   1. Which symbol shows the sound of the *u* in *schedule*?

     a. u   **b.** ü   **c.** ū   **d.** ō

52

2. How many syllables are there in *scatterbrained*?
   a. one   **b.** two   **c.** three   **d.** four

B. Write the letter of the correct answer. Use the sample dictionary page.

   3. How many meanings does the entry word *scatter* have?
   a. one   **b.** two   **c.** three   **d.** four

   4. Which parts of speech can the word *schedule* be?
   a. noun, adjective   **b.** verb, adverb   **c.** noun, verb

Practice

A. Use the sample dictionary page to answer these questions.

   5. What is the pronunciation of the entry word *schedule*?
   6. Which syllable is accented in the entry word *scatter*?
   7. How many syllables does *schedule* have?
   8. Which part of speech is *scatterbrain*?

B. Use the sample dictionary page to answer these questions.

   9. Which entry word has exactly two meanings?
   10. Which entry words can be used as either verbs or nouns?
   11. Which meaning of *scheme* fits this sentence? Most daily worries are petty in the big *scheme* of things.
   12. How many meanings does *scheme* have as a verb?

C. Mixed Practice   Use the sample dictionary page to answer these questions.

   13. What is the entry word for this pronunciation: skēm?
   14. Which entry word has three meanings as a noun?
   15. How many words shown on the page can be nouns?
   16. Would the word *school* appear on this page?
   17. Which entry word has an *e* pronounced the same way as the *e* in *let*?
   18. How many meanings does *schedule* have as a noun and a verb?
   19. Write an example sentence for *scatterbrain*.
   20. Write an example sentence using *scheme* as a verb and *schedule* as a noun.

Apply: Work with a Group

   With your group try to guess the English word that has the most meanings listed in the dictionary. Ask your teacher to write each group's choice on the chalkboard. Then consult a dictionary, and count the number of meanings for each choice. Were you familiar with all the meanings of your word?

Language in Action

A Group Discussion

Your class wants to put on a play. All of you must decide which play to perform. You have a group discussion to choose one. Maybe the teacher will ask you to lead the discussion. What do you do?

People have group discussions to share ideas and to solve problems. Group discussions should be calm and constructive. Here are some tips about participating in group discussions.

◆ Be prepared to participate. Think about what you want to say before the discussion begins.

◆ Listen to what other people say. Consider their opinions.

◆ Don't be wordy. Say what you have to say simply and quickly.

◆ Don't interrupt. Raise your hand when you have something appropriate to say. If you're afraid you'll forget what you want to say, write it down.

◆ Keep to the topic. You may be tempted to say something funny and interesting that doesn't really relate to the subject. Save it until the discussion is over.

◆ You may disagree with someone. Say so politely and pleasantly. Never raise your voice.

Here are some tips for leading a group discussion.

◆ Open the discussion. State the topic to be discussed, and ask if anyone has something to say.

◆ Call on people. Make sure that everyone has a chance to speak. If someone interrupts, ask that person to let the speaker finish.

◆ Make sure the discussion stays on the topic.

◆ Remain fair. Don't favor any one viewpoint.

◆ Take notes. Summarize what people said.

◆ If a decision is needed, take a vote.

◆ Close the discussion, and state what was decided.

Practice

Read the following group discussion. On a separate sheet of paper, list what some people did wrong. Number each item.

Teacher: Jesse, would you lead the discussion?

54

Jesse:	Um, OK. The question is: What play should we pick for our class play? Does anyone have any ideas? Ho-il?
Ho-il:	We could do *Oliver!*
Luz:	How about *The Sound of Music?*
Jesse:	No, I don't like that play. Roger?
Roger:	I like *Heidi.*
Ho-il:	No way! That's a stupid play. Let's do *Oliver!*
Jesse:	Debbie?
Debbie:	I've never seen *Oliver!*, but I—
Richard:	It's really good. The—
Jesse:	Richard, please let Debbie finish. Then it'll be your turn.
Richard:	Sorry.
Debbie:	Anyway, I've never seen a play of *The Sound of Music,* but I loved the movie.
Jesse:	Richard?
Richard:	I just wanted to say that I think *Oliver!* is a really good play.
Jesse:	Monique?
Monique:	I saw the movie of *The Sound of Music,* too, and I really liked it. I loved the part where they're singing at the concert, and—
Jesse:	Excuse me, Monique, but we should talk about that after the discussion is over. Does anyone have any other suggestions? No? OK. Ho-il suggested *Oliver!*, Luz likes *The Sound of Music,* and Roger wants to do *Heidi.* Has everybody seen or read all three? No? OK. I suggest that we all go to the library and read them and then continue the discussion in a couple of days. Is that OK with everyone? OK. The discussion is over.

Apply

Have a group discussion in your class. Ask your teacher to suggest a topic and to pick a discussion leader.

HISTORY OF LANGUAGE

Old English (449—1050)

There were three main contributors to Old English: Englisc, Latin, and Old Norse. Englisc was spoken by European tribes who invaded Britain in the fifth century. Latin was spoken by the Romans who ruled most of Europe, including Britain, until the fifth century. Old Norse was spoken by Vikings who invaded Britain between 750 and 1050. Old English was a blend of words from all three groups, Englisc, Roman, and Viking.

Middle English (1050—1475)

The Norman invasion in 1066 was the turning point between Old and Middle English. William the Conqueror, leading an army from Normandy, France, invaded England. During the next 300 years, the Normans ruled, and thousands of French words entered the English language.

Modern English (1476 to the present)

The Renaissance and improved communication served as the main influences on Modern English. When the printing press was invented, books became available to ordinary people. Printed books led to standardized spelling, grammar, and punctuation.

At the same time, transportation was improving. British sailors brought back words from the places they visited, and they were gradually incorporated into everyday speech. The process continues today. Cars, trains, and planes let people travel easily from country to country. Radio, television, and records transmit language from place to place. English words enter foreign languages, and foreign words enter English.

Activity

Write the list of influences on English. Next to each one, write when it was important—in Old, Middle, or Modern English.

1. the Norman invasion
2. the Vikings
3. Roman rulers
4. the printing press
5. airplanes
6. the radio

56

UNIT REVIEW

Personal Narratives (page 19)

1. List at least three characteristics of a personal narrative.

Narrowing a Topic (pages 26–27)

Write the name of the topic in each group that would be narrow enough for a brief personal narrative.

2. School, My Education, The Last Day of Summer Vacation

3. Rebuilding Our Porch, Carpentry, The Importance of Architectural Detail

4. Friendship, My Best Friend, Our Camping Trip

Topic Sentence and Supporting Details (pages 28–31)

Read the topic sentence and the numbered sentences below. Then, write only the sentences that give supporting details for the topic sentence.

Topic Sentence: Most people like to ride on ferris wheels, but after yesterday, I decided I'd rather build models of them at home.

5. My uncle Charlie took me to Coney Island for the day.

6. Immediately, he suggested a ride on the giant ferris wheel.

7. Uncle Charlie was visiting from California.

8. During the first part of the ride, I enjoyed looking down and seeing the people below grow tinier and tinier.

9. Up, up, we went—higher and higher.

10. By the time we reached the top, I had shut my eyes, and I refused to open them until my feet touched the ground again.

11. "That was fun," he said. "Let's try the roller coaster next."

12. He must have seen my expression, because we stopped for lunch next.

13. Uncle Charlie once took me to the circus, too.

Punctuating Sentences (pages 36–37)

Write the sentences below. Add end punctuation to show how you want the reader to understand each sentence. Use capital letters where needed.

14. my family and I moved to vermont last summer

15. the moving van delivered someone else's furniture

16. Where was our own furniture

17. a family in minnesota had received all of our belongings

18. Boy, I hope we never have to move again

What Is a Sentence? (pages 42–43)

Read each group of words. If it is a sentence, write it with the correct end mark. If it is a fragment, rewrite it as a sentence, and add an end mark.

19. Where is the dog
20. Is outside
21. Let him in, please
22. I don't see him
23. Where did he go

24. Oh no, the doghouse is empty
25. That silly dog
26. Then where is he
27. Over there
28. Wow, he scared us

Complete Subjects and Predicates (pages 44–45)

Write each sentence. Underline the complete subject once and the complete predicate twice.

29. Icebergs are blocks of fresh-water ice.
30. Icebergs split from much larger glaciers.
31. These mammoth blocks of ice move through the oceans.
32. They can travel thousands of miles.
33. Some icebergs are bigger than islands.
34. Such large blocks of ice roam the polar seas.
35. They stray into busy water lanes sometimes.
36. People on ships avoid these huge white ghosts.
37. Such an iceberg sank the great ship *Titanic*.
38. These giants look like majestic mountains.

Simple Subjects and Predicates (pages 46–47)

Write each sentence. Underline the simple subject once and the simple predicate twice.

39. The first inhabitants of the North American continent were Native Americans.
40. They made their difficult journey to this continent more than 10,000 years ago.
41. These early explorers were probably hunters.
42. They traveled in small tribes.
43. Many such tribes existed.
44. The Native Americans came from Asia originally.
45. These hunters had followed the migrations of animals.
46. Many different animals had been their food source.
47. The first Americans may have crossed into North America on a stretch of dry land.
48. Scientists have called this ancient land bridge between North America and Asia Beringia.

Finding Subjects in Sentences (pages 48–49)

Write each sentence. Underline each simple subject. If the subject is understood to be *you*, write (You).

49. Have you read many interesting books about the United States of America?

50. Is Alaska the largest state?

51. Find out the name of the smallest state.

52. Do you know the capital of our state?

53. Write the names of three state capitals.

54. Read the Constitution.

55. Did thirteen states ratify it?

56. Visit the Green Mountain State.

57. Learn the name of the most populous state.

58. Was Hawaii the last state in the Union?

59. Research the geography of Montana.

60. Does the map show the state of Hawaii?

61. Can you locate the capital of Nebraska?

62. Tell us the name of the capital of Ohio.

Sentences with *Here* and *There* (pages 50–51)

Write each sentence. Underline the simple subject.

63. Here is our new home.

64. There are the curtains for the windows.

65. There is the old fireplace in the living room.

66. Here is the largest bedroom.

67. There are the bushes in our backyard.

---

ruffian | rumpus

ruf fi an (ruf′i ən), *n.* rough, brutal fellow; a bully.
ruf fle (ruf′əl), *v.* **1** make rough; cause to lose the flatness or evenness of: *The frightened bird ruffled its feathers when it saw the cat.* **2** disturb; annoy; disquiet: *Our late arrival ruffled our host.* **3** draw into folds or pleats, *n.* a frill: *Instead of a collar, her new dress has a ruffle of lace around the neck.*

ru ler (rü′lər), *n.* **1** a person who governs or reigns; a sovereign. **2** strip of wood, metal, etc. that is often marked with inches or the like and used to draw and measure straight lines.
rul ing (rül′ing), *n.* decision made by an authority: *the ruling of the court. adj.* **1** governing; having authority: *the ruling classes.* **2** most widely held: *The ruling sentiment of the town is in favor of the new mayor.*

Dictionary Skills (pages 52–53)

Use the sample dictionary page to answer these questions.

68. How many words shown on the page can be nouns?

69. What is the meaning of *ruffle* when used as a noun?

70. Which meaning of *ruler* names a common object?

71. How many meanings does the word *ruling* have as an adjective?

72. Would the word *run* appear on this page?

73. Would the word *rue* appear before or after this page?

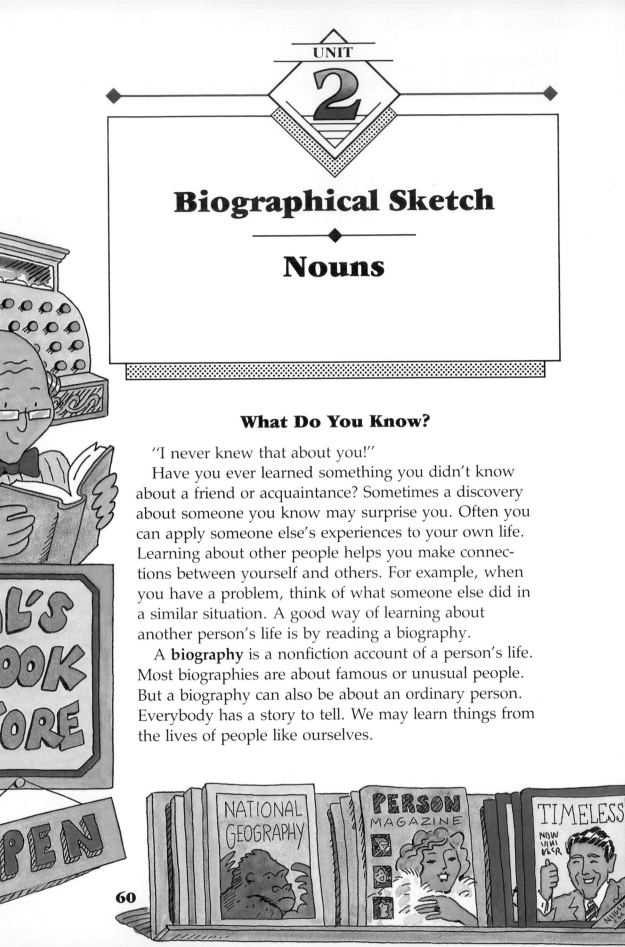

UNIT 2

Biographical Sketch

◆

Nouns

What Do You Know?

"I never knew that about you!"

Have you ever learned something you didn't know about a friend or acquaintance? Sometimes a discovery about someone you know may surprise you. Often you can apply someone else's experiences to your own life. Learning about other people helps you make connections between yourself and others. For example, when you have a problem, think of what someone else did in a similar situation. A good way of learning about another person's life is by reading a biography.

A **biography** is a nonfiction account of a person's life. Most biographies are about famous or unusual people. But a biography can also be about an ordinary person. Everybody has a story to tell. We may learn things from the lives of people like ourselves.

AL'S BOOK STORE

OPEN

NATIONAL GEOGRAPHY

PERSON MAGAZINE

TIMELESS

Thinking About Biographical Sketches

A **biographical sketch** has these characteristics:

◆ It gives information about the life of a real person.
◆ It usually tells important dates in the person's life.
◆ It describes the person's most important achievements.
◆ It tells what events shaped the person's life.

A biographical sketch is written to share information about a person's life. Because it is brief, it highlights the important facts in a person's life and focuses on what made that person special. He or she may have made a noteworthy contribution to the world, may have developed unique or original ideas, or may have led an exciting or unusual life.

Biographical sketches can be found in several places. Encyclopedias include many biographical sketches about famous people in the world. Newspapers and magazines often carry stories of people who are in the news. These short biographical descriptions give readers the background information they need to understand the news better. There are also books that contain collections of biographical sketches about various people.

Discussion

1. What new things have you found out about someone you know?
2. What were some of the important events in that person's life?
3. How did those events make a difference in the person's life?

Reading a Biographical Sketch

Read the following paragraphs from a biographical sketch about Eleanor Roosevelt. The first part describes the influences of her childhood and tells of her marriage to Franklin Delano Roosevelt, who became President in 1933. The second part describes her life after President Roosevelt's death in the spring of 1945.

Eleanor Roosevelt:
First Lady of the World
by
Doris Faber

Information is about a real person.

Events that shaped the person's life are described.

Though she was born into a wealthy and influential New York City family (her uncle was President Theodore Roosevelt), Eleanor Roosevelt's childhood was not storybook perfect. Before she turned ten, she was orphaned. She then joined the busy household of her kindly but distant grandmother. Thinking herself plain and unattractive, she was a shy girl who never quite felt she belonged. Her life changed when she was sent to boarding school in England. Eleanor thrived at school, where she became known for her intelligence and sensitivity to others. When she returned to the U.S. at the age of 17, she brought with her a new air of self-confidence. At the time of her marriage to Franklin Delano Roosevelt, Eleanor was showing the signs of leadership and compassion that would distinguish her later on. Though naturally shy, she soon plunged into public life, first campaigning for her husband, and eventually working for causes of her own. Franklin's election to the presidency gave Eleanor her biggest chance yet to work for the country and the principles in which she believed.

Important dates are noted.

In the autumn of 1945, soon after her sixty-first birthday, Mrs. Roosevelt received a telephone call from the White House. President Truman wanted to appoint her to represent the United States at the first meeting of the new United Nations in London. By now the war had ended—and how could she refuse? For she and Franklin both had been strongly convinced that only an effective international organization could guarantee a lasting peace.

Mrs. Roosevelt spent the rest of her life striving to promote the cause of peace. "The First Lady of the World," President Truman would call her.

She retired from the U.N. when she was nearly seventy, but she still did not stop speaking and traveling. She went to Russia and Japan, to Israel and India, visiting peasants and prime ministers, always spreading the message that world peace depended on international friendship.

At home, Eleanor Roosevelt had more political influence than any other woman in American history. Would she have acquired such power if the man she married had not become an outstanding president?

Probably not. For Franklin Roosevelt had undoubtedly opened a great opportunity to her. But her own energy and amazing capacity to keep on learning surely were almost as significant. Fifteen years after F.D.R.'s death, his widow's word carried so much weight that a young man named John F. Kennedy came to seek her approval before he began campaigning for the presidency in 1960.

By then, Mrs. Roosevelt's health had begun failing. Yet she kept writing and speaking two more years—until a complicated blood disease made her enter a hospital. Shortly after her seventy-eighth birthday, on November 7, 1962, this world-famous woman died.

Her funeral in Hyde Park was attended by President Kennedy and also by two former presidents, Truman and Eisenhower, as well as a future president, Lyndon Johnson. Yet a man who had twice lost to Eisenhower in presidential elections spoke the most moving words about Eleanor Roosevelt after her death.

"She would rather light a candle than curse the darkness," said Adlai Stevenson. "And her glow has warmed the world."

Person's influence is noted.

Understanding What You've Read

Write the answers to these questions.

1. Where did Eleanor receive her education?
2. Who asked Mrs. Roosevelt to go to the first meeting of the United Nations?
3. What were two important events that helped shape Mrs. Roosevelt's life?
4. How do you think Eleanor's experiences at school helped her overcome her shyness?
5. Why do you think John F. Kennedy sought her advice?
6. If you could have met Mrs. Roosevelt, what questions might you have asked her?

Writing Assignment

It can be fun to research the facts of another person's life. Imagine that you have been hired to write a biographical sketch for a *Who's Who* of your community. The person you write about could be someone you know who has made contributions to your community. The person could be a friend or acquaintance whom you would like to learn more about. You will be writing your biographical sketch step by step. You will learn how to interview the person in order to get the information you need. You will also learn how to organize the information into a sketch of two or three paragraphs.

Your **audience** will be your classmates. Your **purpose** will be to tell about the life of the person you think is special. You will show your readers how the person you have chosen is interesting or unusual.

Choose a Person to Interview

Choose a special person that you know in your neighborhood or town. Choose a person whose life interests you, a person who has an interesting job or hobby, or a person who has made a valuable contribution to the community.

Make a list of several people in case your first choice is not available to be interviewed. Save your work for the next lesson.

Preparing for an Interview

Conducting an interview is one way of obtaining interesting facts about a person for a biographical sketch. An **interview** is a meeting at which one person asks specific questions of another person in order to obtain information. Conducting a good interview requires planning and preparation.

To prepare for the interview, think carefully about what you want to learn from the person. Why are you interviewing this particular person? What is it about him or her that interests you? Decide on the main points you want to include.

For a biographical sketch, you might want to cover the following main points.

- What does the person do that is special?
- How did the person begin doing this?
- What are the person's accomplishments so far?
- What are the person's plans for the future?

It is important to ask questions that will give you the most information. Ask questions that require more than simple "yes" or "no" answers. Questions that begin with *what, when, where, who, why,* and *how* will give you more detailed responses. Which of these two questions will result in more information?

> Did you enjoy writing when you were younger?
>
> How did you become interested in writing?

The first question can be answered "yes" or "no." The second question requires a more specific answer. The second question is a better one to use in an interview.

You may wish to write your questions on index cards or on a sheet of paper. Whichever way you choose, leave room to write the response.

Some interviewers use a tape recorder to record the person's responses. Before you use a recorder, you must get the person's permission.

When were you born?

Where did you go to school?

Why did you choose that school?

What were your best subject

Practice

A. A student decided to interview Lucy Grant, a woman whose special job was to caption film and television programs for deaf people. Below are some questions that the student asked during the interview. Read each question and decide whether it is useful or not useful in getting information. Write whether you think the question is good or bad and explain why.

1. When and where were you born?
2. Do you like your work?
3. How did you become interested in helping deaf people?
4. What are your favorite foods?
5. Why do you think it is important to do something that helps other people?
6. What kind of training did you have to get in order to do this job?
7. What other related jobs have you had?
8. Did you find any of your early life experience helpful for this career?

B. Choose one of the following jobs. Write three questions you might ask when interviewing a person who does this job.
   a. a firefighter   **b.** a teacher   **c.** a film director

Prepare for Your Interview

Call the person you have chosen to interview. Arrange a time and a place for the interview. Think carefully about why you want to interview this person and what main points you wish to include. Then make a list of questions to ask.

When you have finished writing your questions, look them over. Make sure you haven't repeated any questions or haven't forgotten to ask something important. Then arrange your questions in a logical order so that your interview will flow smoothly. Make sure your questions relate to your subject and that they don't jump back and forth from one main idea to another. Save your work for the interview.

Conducting an Interview

During the interview, it is important to be polite when you ask your questions and to listen carefully to the answers. Because you will not be able to remember detailed answers, you must take notes. If you have the person's permission to use a tape recorder, you will still need to take notes from the recording.

When taking notes, you should **paraphrase,** or express in your own words, what the person says. However, be sure to take accurate notes on dates, places, and other important facts. Read the interview and the notes below to see how the interviewer took notes.

Interviewer: How did you become interested in helping deaf people?

Answer

Lucy Grant: That's a good question. Well, my younger brother, Bobby, was born deaf. I saw the types of problems he faced every day. He overcame many of them. But there was something he couldn't share with everybody else, something that connects people with the rest of the world. He couldn't enjoy television. I really wanted to help him.

Notes
Younger brother born deaf.
LG saw the problems he faced.
He overcame many.
He couldn't enjoy TV.
LG wanted to help him.

Notice that the interviewer wrote down only the most important details from the interview. The interviewer also used abbreviations and shorthand in order to write the information faster. The notes are clear enough, however, to be used as a source of facts for writing the biographical sketch.

Sometimes the person being interviewed will say something that you want to write word for word. You can use a **direct quote,** or the exact words that the person said. When you write a quote, use quotation marks to separate those words from the rest of the text. To make sure those words are accurate, read them back to the person you are interviewing.

During the interview, questions may occur to you as a result of what the other person says. Such questions, if they are brief and to the point, can help you get additional information.

Practice

The following sentences are responses to interview questions. On a separate piece of paper, write the notes you would take in this interview.

1. I guess I should start at the beginning. I was born in Baltimore, Maryland, back in 1898. Like most small children, I danced a lot to music, but my real lessons began when I was five.

2. There weren't any ballet companies in Baltimore in those days; so when I finished high school, I decided to open my own dance school.

3. I became interested in teaching dance to blind people after reading a newspaper article on the subject. I spoke with the headmistress of a school for blind people, and she asked me to teach there.

4. Teaching dance to blind people may seem like a difficult task. Yet the students were so enthusiastic that teaching them was easy. Because these students couldn't see, my instructions had to be precise. I found that using images such as "float like a butterfly" didn't work. The students had no image of a butterfly.

5. Often I physically moved a dancer's arms to show how the movement should flow. Usually, the music helped the dancer move in a particular way. Sometimes I asked the dancers to think about a certain feeling, such as happiness or anger, to elicit certain movements.

Conduct the Interview

- Be on time for the interview. Take two sharpened pencils, your organized list of questions, and extra paper.
- Ask follow-up questions to explore or clarify a point.
- Take accurate notes. Read direct quotes back to the person.
- After the interview, go over your notes. Add important points that you remember.
- Save your work for the next lesson.

Writing a First Draft

Read the first draft of the biographical sketch below. The writer wasn't worried about making it perfect. It will be changed later.

Lucy Grant has a special interest in deaf people and their problems. Her younger brother was born deaf. Lucy watched him and saw that he could not enjoy television shows because he could not hear the sounds. She decided to do something about it. That decision in the end benifited a great number of people.

Lucy was born on March 23, 1960, in Tulsa, Oklahoma. She studied television video and film in college. She worked at Live Wood a summer camp for deaf children during her vacations. She then worked with a Chicago company that put captions, or subtitles, on television shows. Part of every television signal is reserved for these captions. You need a speshal attachment to see them on your TV set.

Lucy took a job adding captions to American films in 1983. Matilda and Happy Times are among the films she captioned. She has worked since 1986 for a company that captions television shows for the deaf. Lucy says, "I'm glad my job is one that helps others and I feel that I get as much out of it as I put into it."

Write Your First Draft

Before beginning to write, you may want to discuss your ideas with a classmate or your teacher. Listen to any suggestions they may have.

Which facts from the interview should I include in my biographical sketch?

♦ Review your notes from the interview.
♦ Decide what main ideas to include in the biographical sketch.
♦ For each main idea, select the facts that support your point. Remember that you may not be able to use everything in your notes.
♦ Arrange the main ideas and the supporting facts in a logical order.
♦ For each of your main ideas, write one paragraph based on the information in your notes.

Discussing a First Draft

When you complete your first draft, look for ways to improve it. One way is by discussing it with classmates.

Discussion Strategy

Remember to make kind and helpful comments. Avoid just giving criticism. If you can, suggest a different way to write parts you think could be improved. For example, instead of saying, "This doesn't make sense," say, "Maybe this phrase would present your idea more clearly."

Use this Content Checklist to discuss with your class the biographical sketch on the previous page.

Content Checklist
- ✔ Does the sketch give information about the life of a real person?
- ✔ Does it tell important dates in the person's life?
- ✔ Does it describe the person's most important achievements?
- ✔ Does it tell what events shaped the person's life?

Revise Your First Draft for Content

To the Reader: Exchange papers with a classmate. Read your partner's biographical sketch. Find the main ideas. Look for the details that support each main idea. Use the Discussion Strategy and the Content Checklist for help.

To the Writer: Listen to the suggestions made by your partner. Then revise your first draft for content. Save your work.

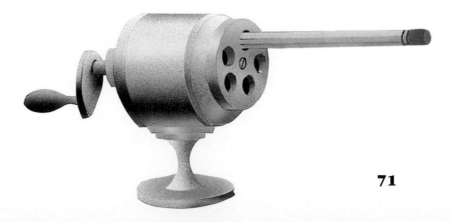

Sentence Variety

Read through the first draft on page 70. Notice that every sentence begins with a subject. A good writer knows that if every sentence begins the same way, the writing will seem drab and dull. Varying the word order in sentences helps make your writing lively and interesting.

One way to vary sentences is to begin with **phrases,** or groups of words, that tell *when*. Look for the phrase that tells *when* and move it to the beginning of the sentence. Use a comma to separate the phrase from the rest of the sentence.

She worked at a summer camp for deaf children during her vacations.	During her vacations, she worked at a summer camp for deaf children.
She has worked since 1986 for a company that captions television shows for the deaf.	Since 1986, she has worked for a company that captions television shows for the deaf.

Phrases that tell *where* can also be used to begin a sentence.

She studied television, video, and film in college.	In college, she studied television, video, and film.

Parts of the predicate of a sentence may often be used to begin the sentence.

You need a special attachment to see them on your TV set.	To see them on your TV set, you need a special attachment.

As you change the word order in a sentence, be aware of how the stress of the sentence changes.

Lucy took a job adding captions to American films in 1983.	In 1983, Lucy took a job adding captions to American films.

In the first sentence, Lucy's job of captioning films is stressed because that information is given first. The second sentence stresses the year in which Lucy took the job. You may use word order to help stress the important ideas in your sentences.

Practice

Rewrite each sentence, varying the word order.

1. Albert Schweitzer was born in 1875 in Alsace, Germany.
2. He studied science, music, and religion during his twenties.
3. He became a famous organ player and an expert on the composer J.S. Bach after graduating.
4. Schweitzer was well-known by the age of 30.
5. In 1902, Schweitzer became a principal at the University of Strasbourg.
6. He studied medicine at the University from 1905 to 1913.
7. He built a hospital in Africa because of his desire to help people.
8. To raise money for the hospital, he gave benefit concerts with the Paris Bach Society.
9. Schweitzer was awarded the 1952 Nobel Peace Prize for his humanitarian work.
10. He used the $33,000 that came with the prize to finance his hospital and establish a leper colony.

Revising Checklist
- ✔ Have I included all the characteristics of a biographical sketch?
- ✔ Where can I combine sentences? (p. 34)
- ✔ Where can I vary word order for sentence variety?

Revise Your First Draft for Style

Check the items on the Revising Checklist. Vary the word order in at least three of your sentences so that your writing will have a variety of sentences. Mark the changes on your draft. Save your work for the next lesson.

How can I vary my sentences to keep my biographical sketch interesting?

Punctuating with Commas

After revising your biographical sketch, make a proofreading check for punctuation and capitalization. While proofreading, check to see that you have used commas correctly. Commas help make sentences clearer by separating words and letting the reader know where to pause. Here are some rules for punctuating with commas.

Rule	Examples
Use a comma to separate three or more words in a series.	She studied television, video, and film in college. Lucy's job is challenging, important, and rewarding.
Use a comma before the conjunction *and*, *or*, or *but* in a compound sentence.	I'm glad my job is one that helps others, and I feel that I get as much out of it as I put into it. Lucy's brother wanted to enjoy television shows, but he couldn't hear the sound.
Use commas to set off words that interrupt.	That decision, in the end, benefited a great number of people. The captions, by the way, are viewed with the aid of a special device.
Use commas to set off introductory phrases that begin sentences.	In 1983, Lucy took a job adding captions to American films. As part of her work, Lucy puts subtitles on television shows.
Use commas to set off phrases that explain or clarify nouns.	She worked at Live Wood, a summer camp for deaf children, during her vacations. Lucy was inspired by someone special, her younger brother.

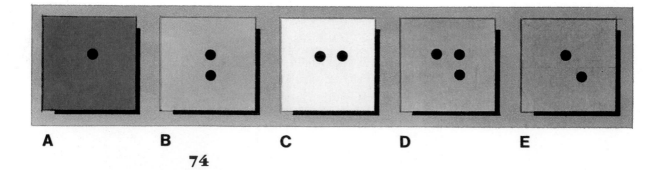

A   B   C   D   E

Practice

Write the sentences below. Use the rules on the previous page to punctuate with commas.

1. Louis Braille a Frenchman created a system of writing for the blind.
2. At the age of three Braille was blinded in an accident.
3. The braille system uses a code of raised dots on paper to indicate letters punctuation and numerals.
4. Louis Braille incidentally also developed a way to write music for blind people.
5. Braille's method was not accepted at first but people soon began to recognize its value.
6. A braillewriter a special machine works like a typewriter.
7. Because of Braille's system blind people are now able to read many books and magazines.
8. Braille is read by gently running your fingers over the raised dots and the code is very easy to learn and remember.

Proofreading Checklist
✔ Did I indent the first word of each paragraph? (p. 36)
✔ Is each sentence capitalized and punctuated correctly? (p. 36)
✔ Did I use commas correctly?
✔ Is each one of my sentences a complete thought?

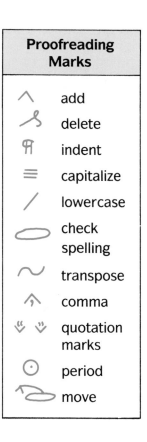

Proofreading Marks

∧	add
✄	delete
¶	indent
≡	capitalize
/	lowercase
◯	check spelling
∼	transpose
∧	comma
⌄ ⌄	quotation marks
⊙	period
↪	move

Proofread Your Biographical Sketch

Check for correct capitalization, punctuation, and grammar. Use the Proofreading Checklist. Use the proofreading marks to make corrections on your paper. Save your work for the next lesson.

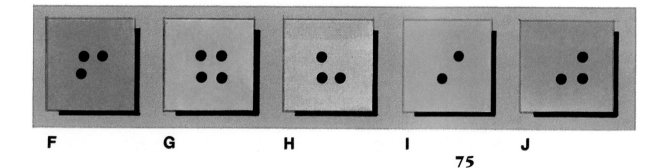

F   G   H   I   J

Checking Spelling/Writing a Final Copy

Spelling Strategy

You may learn to spell a word in three different ways. Find the method that works best for you.

♦ Speak the word aloud. Listen to the sounds.
♦ Visualize the word. Picture the letters in your mind.
♦ Write the word. Practice making the letters.

Here is part of the revised and proofread biographical sketch.

Lucy was born on March 23, 1960, in Tulsa, Oklahoma. She studied television video and film in college. She worked at Live Wood a summer camp for deaf children during her vacations. She then worked with a Chicago company that put captions, or subtitles, on television shows. Part of every television signal is reserved for these captions. You need a special attachment to see them on your TV set.

Lucy took a job adding captions to American films in 1983. Matilda and Happy Times are among the films she captioned. She has worked since 1986 for a company that captions television shows for the deaf. Lucy says, "I'm glad my job is one that helps others and I feel that I get as much out of it as I put into it."

Check Your Spelling

Use the proofreading marks to correct errors in spelling on your paper. Use the Spelling Strategy. Add any misspelled words to your learning log. Then write a clean, neat, final copy of your biographical sketch. Proofread your work to make sure there are no mistakes. Keep your final copy.

Sharing Your Biographical Sketch

Speaking/Listening Strategy

As you speak, watch your audience to make sure you are not speaking too quickly or too slowly. While you are listening to a classmate read, think of questions you may wish to ask about his or her presentation.

Choosing a Way to Share

Here are some ways to share your biographical sketch with your class.

Reading Aloud   Read your biographical sketch aloud to classmates. Read as though you are talking to them about a friend or a relative that you would like them to meet. Try to speak as you would to friends.

Presenting a Skit   Perform your biographical sketch as a skit. Act out an event that you think changed the person's life. You may wish to have a few of your classmates play the people who were important to the person in your biographical sketch.

Making a Book   Put your biographical sketch together with your classmates' into a book you might entitle *Who's Who in Our Town*. If possible, make copies of the book so that each student can have a copy.

Share Your Biographical Sketch

Choose one of the ways to present your biographical sketch to your classmates.

Add to Your Learning Log

- Am I satisfied with my biographical sketch? Why or why not?
- Which part of doing the sketch was easiest for me? What was hardest?
- What could I do differently next time?

The Literature Connection: Nouns ◆

Writers sometimes use imaginary words to describe imaginary things. Imaginary words allow writers to connect their imaginations to the real world.

Whether they identify real or imaginary things, names are important. The words that name people, places, or things are called **nouns.** All nouns name things that exist in real or imagined worlds.

What is the difference between a real and an imaginary noun? Consider this sentence: *Jason went to the store.* The words *Jason* and *store* name real people and things. However, now consider this sentence: *Jason bought a zlabgrot there.* What is a *zlabgrot*? It is an imaginary noun the writer has invented.

The writer of this poem invents imaginary words by combining real words. As you read the poem, try to identify which real words she used to create her imaginary words.

Eletelephony
by
Laura E. Richards

Once there was an elephant
Who tried to use the
    telephant—
No! no! I mean an elephone
Who tried to use the
    telephone—
(Dear me! I am not certain
    quite
That even now I've got it
    right.)

Howe'er it was, he got his
    trunk
Entangled in the telephunk;
The more he tried to get it
    free,
The louder buzzed the
    telephee—
(I fear I'd better drop the
    song
Of elephop and telephong!)

Discussion

1. Which words in the poem name real things?
2. Which words in the poem have been invented by the author?
3. Suppose the elephant was trying to communicate by telegram instead of by telephone. Can you invent some words by joining parts of the words *elephant* and *telegram* to describe this?

The Writing Connection: Nouns

Many words in our language are combinations of two other words. For example, *smog* is made from *smoke* and *fog*. In your own writing, you may want to make up your own "combination" words. Can you guess what two words the underlined combination words below were made from?

> We had buffalamb for dinner on Thanksgiving. Buffalamb comes from a combination of buffalo and lamb. In the future, people might borrow books from a libramat. Libramat comes from a combination of library and automat.

Activity

Write five combination words of your own. Use each in a sentence. Then explain where the parts of each combination word come from. Use the picture above for ideas. An example has been provided.

> We saw the strange heliballoon hovering in the sky.
>
> *Heliballoon* is a combination of *helicopter* and *balloon*.

Common and Proper Nouns

A **common noun** names any person, place, thing, or idea. A **proper noun** is the name of a particular person, place, thing, or idea.

A. A common noun begins with a lowercase letter. You have learned about idea nouns such as *truth*, *purpose*, and *adventure*. Words related to time are also idea nouns. Some of these are *day*, *occasion*, and *summer*.

B. Some proper nouns have more than one word. Each important word is capitalized. Words such as *the*, *and*, *of*, or *by* are not capitalized unless they begin a book or movie title.

Type	Common Nouns	Proper Nouns
person	man, woman, doctor, professor	Ellery, Susanna, Doctor Jane Kulp, Professor Keller
place	country, town, bay, river, park	France, Croton-on-Hudson, Bay of Fundy, Yellowstone River, Badlands National Park
thing	ship, bridge, organization, painting	*Calypso,* London Bridge, the Wilderness Society, the *Mona Lisa*
idea	mischief, quality, year, holiday	Wednesday, July, 1492, Thanksgiving Day

Strategy

Sometimes it is hard to tell if a noun that names a thing is a proper noun. If you aren't sure, ask yourself: Does it name something famous? If it does, the noun is probably a proper noun.

Common noun: the gold bridge
Proper noun: the Golden Gate Bridge

Check Your Understanding

A. Write the letter of the answer that lists the common noun or nouns in each sentence.
1. Over the years, Jacques Cousteau has had many adventures.
   a. Jacques, Cousteau   **b.** many, years
   c. years, adventures
2. On one occasion, his crew caught two seals in Africa.
   a. crew, Africa   **b.** two, seals   **c.** occasion, crew, seals

B. Write the letter of the proper noun or nouns in each sentence.

    3. Cousteau has shown how humans can help animals.

        a. Cousteau   **b.** Cousteau, humans, animals

        c. humans, animals

    4. His crew found the seals near the Cape of Good Hope.

        a. crew, seals   **b.** Cape of Good Hope   **c.** crew

Practice

A. Write each sentence. Underline the common nouns.

    5. At that time, the crew named one seal Pepito.

    6. The intelligence of the seals impressed Cousteau.

    7. One day the animals performed tricks for the crew.

    8. In spring, Pepito frequently clapped his flippers.

B. Write each sentence. Capitalize the proper nouns.

    9. The ship departed from seal island.

   10. st. helena was the first port of call.

   11. The governor of the island visited the *calypso*.

   12. The doctor, dr. millet, helped at the local hospital.

C. Mixed Practice Write each sentence. Underline the common nouns. Capitalize the proper nouns where necessary.

   13. The cousteau society helps many expeditions.

   14. pepito almost escaped from the *calypso*.

   15. The name of the other seal was christobald.

   16. raymond coll and pepito became friends.

   17. The seals swam in the ocean with the divers all summer.

   18. In may, the crew removed the harnesses from the seals.

   19. They didn't try to escape from the *calypso* and its crew.

   20. They had developed an affection for the divers.

Apply: Journal

In your journal, write five sentences about a pet you have or would like to have. Use as many nouns as you can in your sentences. Make sure that you write only complete sentences.

Singular and Plural Nouns

A **singular noun** names one person, place, thing, or idea. A **plural noun** names more than one person, place, thing, or idea.

A. You form the plurals of most nouns by following these rules.

Singular Form	Rule	Examples
most nouns	Add s.	habit → habits lock → locks gnat → gnats
nouns ending in s, ss, ch, sh, x, or z	Add es.	bus → buses loss → losses latch → latches dish → dishes box → boxes waltz → waltzes
nouns ending in vowel + y	Add s.	tray → trays monkey → monkeys toy → toys
nouns ending in consonant + y	Change y to i, add es.	study → studies fly → flies diary → diaries

B. For other nouns, there is no rule to follow. You must remember how to form the plural.

Singular Form	Rule	Examples
some nouns ending in f or fe	Change f or fe to ve. Add s.	leaf → leaves half → halves wife → wives knife → knives shelf → shelves loaf → loaves
other nouns ending in f or fe	Add s.	chief → chiefs reef → reefs safe → safes belief → beliefs café → cafés cliff → cliffs
most nouns ending in vowel + o	Add s.	patio → patios rodeo → rodeos radio → radios video → videos
most nouns ending in consonant + o	Add es.	mosquito → mosquitoes tomato → tomatoes potato → potatoes echo → echoes
other nouns ending in consonant + o	Add s.	solo → solos poncho → ponchos alto → altos photo → photos cello → cellos auto → autos
a small group of nouns	irregular spelling changes	goose → geese child → children man → men woman → women mouse → mice tooth → teeth ox → oxen crisis → crises emphasis → emphases
a small group of nouns	spelling remains the same	series → series offspring → offspring trout → trout moose → moose deer → deer salmon → salmon sheep → sheep

Strategy

You can form the plurals of most nouns that end in a consonant + *o* by adding *es*. Many of the words that do not follow this rule are words related to music (piano ⟶ pianos).

82

Check Your Understanding

A. Write the letter of the correct plural form of each noun.
1. crutch   **a.** crutchs   **b.** crutches   **c.** crutchis
2. hobby   **a.** hobbies   **b.** hobbis   **c.** hobbys

B. Write the letter of the correct plural form of each noun.
3. tomato   **a.** tomatoes   **b.** tomatos
      c. tomati
4. series   **a.** serial   **b.** serieses
      c. series

Practice

A. Write the plural form of each singular noun.

5. fox	**8.** turkey	**11.** berry
6. bush	**9.** pickle	**12.** grass
7. peach	**10.** waltz	**13.** bus

B. Write the plural form of each singular noun.

14. chief	**17.** sheep	**20.** wife
15. potato	**18.** photo	**21.** emphasis
16. rodeo	**19.** solo	**22.** video

C. Mixed Practice Write each sentence. Use the plural form of each noun in parentheses.
23. (Series) of (study) have shown that many social (animal) cannot survive on their own.
24. (Elephant) are intelligent (creature).
25. (Whale) communicate over long (distance) using (echo).
26. (Owl) and (bat) spend their (day) resting.
27. (Goose) fly (hundred) of (mile) yearly.
28. (Salmon) return to (stream) at the end of their (life).
29. Do (animal) tell (story) about (hero) to their (offspring) just as (human) do for their (child)?

Apply: Test a Partner

Write a list of 20 nouns you think are the hardest to pluralize. Exchange your list with a classmate, and write the plural forms of your classmate's nouns. Compare your answers with those of your classmate.

Possessives

A **possessive** is a word that tells who or what owns or has something.

A. Many nouns can be changed into possessives. Notice the possessive form for each underlined noun in the chart.

	Owner		What Is Owned		Possessive	What Is Owned
The	plane	has	passengers.	the	plane's	passengers
	Jasu	owns	luggage.		Jasu's	luggage
The	visit	has	an end.	the	visit's	end
	Scotland	has	hills.		Scotland's	hills

B. To form the possessive of a singular noun, add *'s*. Do this even if the singular noun ends in *s*.

Charles has brothers.   Charles's brothers
   ↑   ↑
singular noun   possessive

The guide has answers.   the guide's answers
Tess owns a camera.   Tess's camera
Kim Wu has a friend.   Kim Wu's friend

Strategy

When we use possessives while talking, we don't have to worry about the apostrophe. In writing, however, it is important to place the apostrophe correctly. Always use an apostrophe when forming the possessive of a noun.

singular owner	+	's	=	possessive

Check Your Understanding

A. Write the letter of the phrase that shows the correct use of the possessive.

  1. Luz takes a trip.
    a. Luz's trip   **b.** Luz trip's   **c.** Luzs trip's
  2. The woman owns cars.
    a. the womans car's   **b.** the car's woman
    c. the woman's cars

B. Write the letter of the possessive for the noun in parentheses.

   3. Scotland has some of (Europe) loveliest scenery.

      a. Europes   **b.** Europe's   **c.** Europes'   **d.** Europes's

   4. A tour (bus) passengers viewed the Scottish Highlands.

      a. bus'   **b.** buses   **c.** bus's   **d.** bus'es

Practice

A. Write a sentence to tell what is possessed.

Example: Joan's pencil⟶Joan has a pencil.

   5. Glasgow's library   **7.** the nation's long history
   6. Scotland's national poet   **8.** the country's artists

B. Write each sentence. Use the noun in parentheses as a possessive.

   9. One of the (country) basic social units is the clan.
  10. A (member) kilt is the badge of his clan.
  11. Each (kilt) plaid pattern identifies a clan.
  12. After Queen (Elizabeth) death, Scotland and England were united.

C. Mixed Practice Read the first sentence. Then use the possessive form of the noun in parentheses in the second sentence.

  13. Ben Nevis is the tallest (mountain) in Scotland. The _____ peak is 4,406 feet above sea level.
  14. Robert Louis (Stevenson) was a famous Scottish writer. _____ best-known work is *Treasure Island*.
  15. Heather is a Scottish (flower). The _____ color is purple.
  16. A visit to Scotland would be an ideal (class) trip. A _____ visit should include all of the historic sights.
  17. (Loch Ness) is a lake in Scotland. A legendary monster in the lake has made _____ name famous.

Apply: Work with a Partner

Can you figure out the answer to this riddle?

   "My brother's mother's father's son is my neighbor. What relation is my neighbor to me?"

Try to use possessives to write your own riddle. Exchange riddles with a classmate, and solve each other's riddles.

More About Possessives

A. A **plural possessive** shows ownership by more than one owner.

	Owner	What Is Owned		Possessive	What Is Owned
The	photographers	own	cameras.	the	photographers'	cameras
The	children	have	a party.	the	children's	party

If a plural noun ends in *s*, add only an apostrophe (') to form the possessive.

The girls have pictures.   the girls' pictures
    ↑   ↑
plural noun   possessive

If a plural noun does *not* end in *s*, add an apostrophe and an *s* ('s) to form the possessive.

The women have a team.   the women's team

B. Remember to add *'s* to form the possessive of singular nouns.

The camera has a strap.   the camera's strap
The gallery has exhibits.   the gallery's exhibit

Strategy

Be careful not to confuse plural nouns with plural possessives. Plural nouns do *not* have an apostrophe; plural possessives *do*.

Plural noun: the tourists (no apostrophe)
Singular possessive: the tourist's photo album
Plural possessive: the tourists' portraits

Check Your Understanding

A. Write the letter of the correct possessive.
1. Some companies develop (customers) photos in one hour.
    a. customers'   **b.** customer's   **c.** customers's
2. Parents often have their (children) photographs taken.
    a. children'   **b.** childrens'   **c.** children's

B. Write the letter of the correct possessive.

3. A (photographer) job is not an easy one.
   a. photographer's   **b.** photographers   **c.** photographers'
4. Sports photos capture a (player) concentration.
   a. players   **b.** player's   **c.** players'

Practice

A. Write each sentence. Use each noun in parentheses as a possessive.

5. The first (cameras) exposure times were measured in hours.
6. Dentists use X-ray photos to check your (teeth) alignment.
7. Several (women) photo contests have been set up.
8. (Slides) colors are much better than those of prints.

B. Write each sentence. Use each noun in parentheses as a possessive.

9. George (Eastman) camera was mass-produced.
10. A (candidate) photo appears on campaign buttons.
11. Photos bring our (world) wonders closer to us.
12. One famous photo shows a woman shearing a (sheep) wool.

C. Mixed Practice   Write each sentence. Use each noun in parentheses as a possessive.

13. The (magazine) photo spread won an award.
14. (Children) photos often capture the joy of childhood.
15. Museum exhibits display (photojournalists) works.
16. Many (amateurs) photos have won awards.
17. A (press) capabilities limit the quality of newspaper photos.
18. A photo essay on (deer) habitats can be interesting.
19. A photo of a (lioness) cubs makes a good picture.
20. Ansel (Adams) photos are among the (world) best.

Apply: Learning Log

Which rule for forming possessives gives you the most trouble? In your learning log, write that rule and 10 examples of how it is applied. Then write a hint to help you remember it.

Abbreviations

An **abbreviation** is a shortened form of a word. Many abbreviations begin with a capital letter and end with a period.

A. The chart below lists some common abbreviations.

Titles		Addresses			
Mr.	a married or unmarried man	St.	Street	Dr.	Drive
Ms.	a married or unmarried woman	Rd.	Road	Blvd.	Boulevard
Mrs.	a married woman	Ave.	Avenue	Rte.	Route
Dr.	doctor	Pl.	Place	Terr.	Terrace
Prof.	professor Jr. Junior	Apt.	apartment	Hwy.	Highway
Pres.	president Sr. Senior	P.O.	Post Office	Ct.	Court

Business		Nations	
Co.	Company	U.K.	United Kingdom
Inc.	Incorporated	U.S.A.	United States of America
Ltd.	Limited	U.S.S.R.	Union of Soviet Socialist Republics

Government Agencies	International Organizations
EPA Environmental Protection Agency	OAS Organization of American States
USPS United States Postal Service	UN United Nations

Time	Days and Months
a.m. midnight to noon (before noon)	Mon. Tues. Wed. Thurs. Fri. Sat. Sun.
p.m. noon to midnight (after noon)	Jan. Feb. Mar. Apr. Aug. Sept. Oct. Nov. Dec.

B. Some titles or addresses and most dates contain more than one part. Commas are usually used to separate the parts. Here are some examples:

Thurs., Jan. 15, 1988   Dr. Manuel Narvaez, UN

Prof. Lisa J. Gonzales, OAS   The Think-Tech Co., Inc.

Strategy

You may use abbreviations when addressing envelopes, labeling charts and maps, and taking notes. You should *not* use abbreviations when writing complete sentences in letters, reports, and stories. Titles such as *Mr.* and *Dr.*, however, are usually abbreviated.

Check Your Understanding

A. Write the letter of the correct abbreviation.

    1. Incorporated

        a. inc.   **b.** Inc.   **c.** Inco.

    2. Union of Soviet Socialist Republics

        a. U.O.S.S.R.   **b.** U.SSR   **c.** U.S.S.R.

B. Write the letter of the correct abbreviation.

    3. Professor J. Smythe, Environmental Protection Agency

        a. Prof. J. Smythe, EPA   **b.** Pr. J. Smythe, EP

        c. Pr. J.S., EPA

    4. 27 Robin Drive, Apartment 2D

        a. 27 Robin Dr., Apart 2D   **b.** 27 Robin Dr., A. 2D

        c. 27 Robin Dr., Apt. 2D

Practice

A. Write each item. Abbreviate the underlined part.

    5. President Anne Wharton

    6. Post Office Box 15

    7. Organization of American States

    8. Environmental Protection Agency

B. Write each item. Abbreviate the underlined part.

    9. 101 Loeb Place, Manhattan

   10. Doctor Malcolm Glass, Junior

   11. Sunday, November 10, 1987

   12. 10:30 in the morning

C. Fill in the blanks by writing the abbreviations or the full words.

Full Words	Abbreviations
13. Penny-Loafers, Incorporated	_____
14. The Lincoln Company, Limited	_____
15. _____	2:30 p.m., Thurs.
16. Professor Lynn Yokoe, Apartment 8J	_____
17. _____	U.S.A.
18. 10 Downing Street, London, United Kingdom	_____
19. 5:30 in the morning, Monday, February 12	_____

Apply: Work with a Group

   Write an invitation for a graduation party, listing the date, time, and place. Write the names and addresses of five people you will invite. Use abbreviations.

Using a Thesaurus

A **thesaurus** is a book of synonyms and antonyms. A **synonym** is a word that has the same or almost the same meaning as another word. An **antonym** is a word that has the opposite or almost the opposite meaning as another word.

A. The thesaurus at the back of this book on pages 393–416 is an example of one kind of thesaurus. It lists words alphabetically, as does a dictionary. It also lists some synonyms and antonyms for each entry word. Look at the sample entry below.

part of speech   example sentence

entry word ⟶ **give** *v.* They will give free samples of the new cheese.
Synonyms: grant, issue, bestow, donate, furnish,   ⟵ synonyms
contribute, sacrifice, relinquish, endow, render.
antonyms ⟶ *Antonyms:* take, seize, repossess.

B. A thesaurus can help you choose words that express the exact shade of meaning you want to convey. Read the sentence below.

Ms. Calavida <u>gives</u> clothing to the thrift store.

Using the sample entry above, you can find the more precise word *donates* to replace *gives*. Can you find a more exact word to replace *gave* in this sentence?

Sabrina also <u>gave</u> her efforts to the cause.

What antonym could replace *give* in this sentence?

What did he <u>give</u> as a prize?

Strategy

It is important to use words correctly when you write. Be sure that you know the exact meaning of each synonym or antonym that you choose from a thesaurus. If you're not sure, look up the word in a dictionary.

Check Your Understanding

A. Write the letter that answers each question below. Use the sample entry for *give*.

   1. What part of speech is the word *give*?

     a. noun   **b.** adjective   **c.** verb   **d.** adverb

   2. How many synonyms are listed for *give*?

     a. three   **b.** five   **c.** ten   **d.** fourteen

B. Write the letter of the word that correctly completes each sentence.

    3. Governors sometimes (synonym for *give*) pardons to certain people.
        a. sacrifice **b.** grant **c.** endow **d.** contribute

    4. The police officers (antonym for *give*) the stolen items.
        a. seize **b.** repossess **c.** render **d.** issue

Practice

A. Use the thesaurus on pages 393–416 to answer each question.

    5. How many synonyms are listed for *guide*?

    6. Which words are antonyms for *worried*?

    7. What part of speech is the entry word *valley*?

    8. What part of speech is the second entry for *make*?

B. Write each sentence. Use the thesaurus to replace each underlined word with a synonym (*S*) or an antonym (*A*).

    9. Telephone messages <u>go</u> through special wires. (*S*)

    10. Modern telephone wires are placed <u>above</u> ground. (*A*)

    11. People can <u>tell</u> each other news over the telephone. (*S*)

    12. Many people were <u>calm</u> about the invention of the telephone. (*A*)

C. Mixed Practice Write your own sentences as indicated below. Use the thesaurus on pages 393–416.

    13. a sentence with a synonym for the word *careful*

    14. a sentence with an antonym for the word *ugly*

    15. a sentence with a synonym for the word *suggest*

    16. a sentence with an antonym for the word *change*

    17. a sentence with a synonym for the word *winning*

    18. a sentence with an antonym for the word *happy*

    19. a sentence with an antonym for the second entry for the word *like*

    20. a sentence with a synonym for the two entries for the word *hard*

Apply: Work with a Group

Write several sentences from a newspaper or reading selection. Take turns replacing at least one word in each sentence with a synonym that fits the sense of the sentence. Then discuss how the new word changes the sentence.

Language in Action

Reading a Newspaper

Imagine that you're talking to a friend on the phone. He tells you that there is an article about your aunt, who is the mayor, in the Sunday paper. You want to read it, and so you buy the paper. But the Sunday edition is very long. How do you find what you want to read?

Thousands of newspapers are published in this country every day. Some are local, small-town papers. Some are read throughout the country, even throughout the world. Some newspapers are published daily, and others are published weekly. But all of them are usually organized in the same way. Here's how the various parts, or sections, of a newspaper are divided.

- **The News Section** This section contains stories about important current events. They are factual accounts of recent events. Large newspapers carry stories about events around the world. They also report events that have taken place across the country and in the areas in which the newspapers are published. Local newspapers generally focus on news in their immediate areas. This provides coverage of events that are not reported in larger papers.

- **The Feature Section** This section contains articles about people or places in the news. For example, a feature article might include details about the early life of a politician or a TV star. The feature section also contains articles about architecture, cooking, movies, and other fields of special interest. Comics and crossword puzzles are often found in the feature section.

- **The Sports Section** You can easily figure out what kinds of articles are found in this section. A large paper carries stories about major league teams and world-class athletes. A local paper reports on local minor league teams, as well as high school and junior high school teams in the area.

Practice

On a separate sheet of paper, write the name of the section of the newspaper in which each item can be found.

1. a column about chess
2. an article about the City Council meeting yesterday
3. a story about a movie actress, which includes details about how she started her career
4. an article about the high school tennis championships
5. a story about the latest styles in men's suits
6. an article about the U.S. Open golf tournament
7. an article about the results of yesterday's elections
8. an article about the Super Bowl
9. an interview with a famous author
10. an article about cleanup efforts after yesterday's hurricane
11. an article about the British prime minister's conflicts with Parliament
12. a story about last night's Islanders–Maple Leafs game
13. an article about last night's school board meeting
14. a story about rare and valuable stamps
15. a story about the high school football game last Saturday
16. a story on how a crossword-puzzle writer creates his puzzles
17. an article on last night's World Series game
18. an article on a protest march that took place yesterday
19. an interview with a collector of oddly shaped lamps
20. a story about a new drive-in zoo that opened last month
21. an article about last week's pro bowling championship
22. a story about the results of last night's heavy rains
23. a story about a major trade between two baseball teams
24. an article with a local boy who has won fifty dance contests
25. a story about a new tax bill passed by Congress yesterday

Apply

Find a copy of a newspaper, and read it. Locate the news section, the feature section, and the sports section. Make a list of three articles that appear in each section. Briefly describe what each article is about.

TEST TAKING

Studying for a Test

In order to do well on tests, it is very important that you prepare by studying. Here are some steps to follow when studying for a test:

♦ Listen carefully, and take notes when your teacher tells what the test will cover and which materials to review.
♦ Make sure you have all the books, worksheets, handouts, notes, old tests, and other materials you need to review for the test.
♦ Find a quiet, well-lit place to work. You will need a table or desk that is large enough so that you can spread out all review materials.
♦ Plan on spending an adequate amount of uninterrupted time for studying. Pick a time when you don't have something important to do and when there will be no distractions.
♦ Set up a study system that works best for you. Here are several ways you can study.
   Reread the material that is going to be tested.
   Outline the review material as you study.
   Think of questions that might be asked on the test, and think of the best answers for them.

Practice

Read each item. Then write how each student's study habits can be improved.
1. Gerry studies in the living room where his sister is watching TV.
2. Carey studies by glancing over her textbook 10 minutes before the test.
3. Sherri knows there will be a test tomorrow, but she doesn't know what it will be about.

Apply: Learning Log

Decide which information from this lesson was most helpful to you. Write the information in your learning log.

UNIT REVIEW

Biographical Sketches (page 61)

1. List at least three characteristics of a biographical sketch.

Preparing for and Conducting an Interview (pages 66–69)

Read each question below. Write whether you think the question is good or bad for an interview you might conduct with an architect. If you think a question is not good, explain why.

2. How did you become interested in architecture?

3. What are your favorite animals?

4. Do you remember your first job?

5. What buildings are you proudest of having designed?

6. How many brothers and sisters do you have?

7. What new projects are you working on now?

Sentence Variety (pages 72–73)

Rewrite each of the following sentences to vary the word order so that the subject does not come first in the sentence.

8. I planned to attend medical school at first.

9. I joined a drama club in my first year at college.

10. I became stagestruck by my second year there.

11. I found my true goal to everyone's delight.

Punctuating with Commas (pages 74–75)

Rewrite each of the following sentences, adding commas wherever they are needed.

12. Elsa Wooton a jazz musician was born in Michigan in 1944.

13. By 1950 she was playing the trumpet.

14. She also learned to play the piano the clarinet and the saxophone.

15. Her band is called Rhythmatism and it is constantly on tour.

16. Elsa Wooton's talents at long last are becoming widely known.

17. This book tells about Wooton and it also contains biographies of other jazz greats.

18. The book also discusses Duke Ellington a popular jazz singer and song composer.

19. One of his songs "Take the A Train" became a standard jazz favorite very quickly.

20. Around the world Ellington is a jazz legend.

Common and Proper Nouns (pages 80–81)

Write each sentence. Underline the common nouns, and capitalize the proper nouns.

21. bombay is the largest port in india.

22. The city is an important port on the arabian sea.

23. bombay remains the financial center of india.

24. The city occupies an island on the western coast of india.

25. About eight million people live in the busy port.

26. The nation of great britain ruled india until the middle of this century.

27. bombay once served as the headquarters of the british east india company.

28. The island fell into the hands of britain 300 years ago.

29. bombay is now a lively port and a colorful city in independent india.

30. bombay has many museums, libraries, and theaters.

Singular and Plural Nouns (pages 82–83)

Write the plural form of each singular noun.

31. watch

32. belief

33. salary

34. emphasis

35. echo

36. leaf

37. clock

38. cattle

39. video

40. boy

41. salmon

42. poncho

43. half

44. piano

45. deer

46. holiday

Possessives (pages 84–85)

Decide which noun in the first sentence should be a possessive. Write that noun as a possessive in the second sentence.

47. A library is a storehouse of treasures. A _____ collection can be enjoyed by everyone.

48. Universities have libraries for their students. A _____ library must serve many different student needs.

49. Harvard has a very large library. In fact, _____ library is the world's largest university library.

50. The Folger Library in Washington houses only the works of Shakespeare. All of _____ plays can be found there.

51. The town of Ross has an interesting library. _____ library is in an old lighthouse.

More About Possessives (pages 86–87)
Write each sentence. Use each noun in parentheses as a possessive.

52. Many American (settlers) homes were built as part of the Homestead Movement.

53. Some city (workers) jobs did not pay well.

54. Country (farmers) lives were also poor.

55. Many thousands of acres of the (government) land were given to these people.

56. Each (person) plot of land was five acres.

57. A (family) job involved land development.

58. Today, many (people) homes are in cities.

59. Workers repair some of the (city) buildings.

60. They help improve many (children) lives.

61. A (neighborhood) homes are important assets.

Abbreviations (pages 88–89)
Write each item. Abbreviate the underlined part.

62. Organization of American States

63. Ludy Company, Incorporated

64. 1312 Rye Boulevard

65. Tuesday, October 30, 1962

66. Environmental Protection Agency

67. XYJ Limited

68. Doctor Hoody

69. United Nations

70. Professor Vera Levine

71. United Kingdom

Thesaurus Skills (pages 90–91)
Use the thesaurus on pages 393–416 to answer these questions.

72. Write two synonyms for the word *crease*.

73. Write an antonym for the word *smooth*.

74. What part of speech is the word *order* in the thesaurus?

75. Write two antonyms for the word *threat*.

76. Write four synonyms for the word *information*.

77. What part of speech is the word *goal* in the thesaurus?

78. Write an antonym for the word *hill*.

79. Write a synonym for the word *family*.

80. What part of speech is the word *artistic*?

81. Write a synonym for the word *memory*.

MAKING ALL THE
CONNECTIONS

You and several classmates will now write a news feature together as a group. What you have learned about describing people and events will help you in your writing.

You will do the following in your news feature:

- Write about a subject you feel will interest readers.
- Describe a newsworthy person, place, or event.
- Use a casual, or informal, style in your writing.
- Include your opinions as well as facts about the subject, if you wish.

Reading a News Feature

Read this news feature about a person who felt a strong connection to folk music.

The first sentence introduces the subject and catches the reader's attention.

People are always surprised to learn how Moses Asch almost single-handedly preserved the best of America's folk music. A son of Polish-born writers does not seem a likely person for such a venture. But in 1923, when Moses was 18, he became fascinated by a rare book of cowboy songs. About ten years later, Asch set up a small recording studio in New York City. He recorded anything that interested him, from Native American music, blues, and jazz to the songs of rural workers. He located, encouraged, and recorded some of the finest American folk singers, such as Woody Guthrie. Performers knew they had a friend in Moses Asch.

Facts about the person's life are given.

The writer's opinions may be included.

Although few of the albums recorded by Asch's company sold more than 500 copies, Asch never let a single one of the 2,200 titles go out of print. "Do you get rid of the letter *Q*," he used to say, "just because people don't need it very often!" Today, we can all be

Quotations may be included.

98

grateful to Moses Asch, because the music he refused to let disappear is now a priceless part of American history. The original recordings are preserved in the Smithsonian Institution. From this legacy will come new records for future generations.

The importance of the person's work is emphasized.

Speaking and Listening

Your teacher will assign you to a group. Choose a discussion leader. Talk about these questions:

1. Why do you think the writer of this news feature thought people might be interested in the subject?
2. What can you learn about American folk music from the picture at the top of this page?
3. What are some facts you learned from the feature?
4. What do you think the writer's opinion is of Moses Asch?

Thinking

Brainstorming

Choose one person in your group to take notes as you discuss the following questions. Save the notes.

1. What person connected with music or art do you think would make a good subject for a news feature? The person can be someone you know or someone you have heard about.
2. Why would this person be a good subject? What is newsworthy about the person?
3. What facts about the person's life would you include?
4. What opinions do you have about the person's accomplishments?

Organizing

It is easier to use the information you have gathered for a news feature if you put the facts into a chart. Look at the chart below. It organizes the details that were used to write the news feature about Moses Asch.

With your group, look at the notes you took in the brainstorming session. Make a chart like the one below. Have one group member fill in the chart with the details needed to write your news feature.

Subject	Why Newsworthy	Facts	Opinions
Moses Asch	preserved American folk music	son of Polish-born writers	was devoted friend to performers
		intrigued by rare book of cowboy songs, 1923	
		had recording studio in New York, 1930s	recordings now priceless part of American history
		kept all titles in print	
		originals now in Smithsonian	deserves our gratitude for his work

Writing a News Feature

Imagine that you and the other members of your group have been asked to write a news feature about a musician, a dancer, an artist, or some other creative person. Your group will write two paragraphs about this person. Use your chart to help you.

Planning

- Review your chart. Add any new details that occur to you.
- Discuss how your first paragraph will introduce the subject and include details about the person's life.
- Discuss how the second paragraph will add information about the person. Try to include a quotation by or about the person.
- Organize the information you have collected into an outline. The first section will describe the person's life. The second section will tell about the person's accomplishments. Agree with your group on the main idea and the details for each section. Try to include some opinions in each section.

Composing

- Work with your group to write the news feature. Choose one member to write down the first draft as all members of the group make suggestions. Tell the note taker to skip lines so that the group can make corrections.
- Decide on the exact wording of the attention-getting introductory sentence and the topic sentence of your first paragraph. Then agree on the exact wording for each detail sentence.
- Decide on the wording for the topic sentence and the detail sentences in the second paragraph. Try to end with a statement that points out the person's importance.

Revising

- With your group, read over the news feature, sentence by sentence. Try to think of ways to improve the content and make your feature more interesting.
- Check that you have included both main ideas. Be sure that all details and opinions have been included in a smooth, logical order.
- Have one group member make the changes on the first draft.

Proofreading

Proofread your feature as a group. Have one member make the corrections on the first draft. Use these questions:

- Does each sentence have a subject and a predicate?
- Does each sentence have correct end punctuation?
- Are proper nouns capitalized correctly?
- Are possessive nouns written correctly?
- Are all words spelled correctly?

Presenting

- Choose one member of the group to write a neat, final copy of your news feature.
- Ask your teacher to choose a time for each group to read its feature to the class. Select one member from your group to do this.
- Put your news feature up on a class bulletin board. You may wish to add an illustration to your feature.

CUMULATIVE REVIEW

A. Write the letter of the correct end punctuation for each sentence. *(pages 36–37)*

1. Where are you going
   a. .   **b.** ?   **c.** !

2. It is now two o'clock
   a. .   **b.** ?   **c.** !

3. How late it is
   a. .   **b.** ?   **c.** !

4. Try to be on time
   a. .   **b.** ?   **c.** !

B. Write the letter of the term that identifies each sentence or group of words. *(pages 42–43)*

5. Birds require special care.
   a. sentence   **b.** fragment

6. Are sensitive to changes.
   a. sentence   **b.** fragment

7. Learn more about the care of birds.
   a. declarative   **b.** interrogative   **c.** imperative   **d.** exclamatory

8. Have you cared for any other pets?
   a. declarative   **b.** interrogative   **c.** imperative   **d.** exclamatory

C. Write the letter of the term that identifies the underlined part in each sentence. *(pages 44–47)*

9. Charles Dickens <u>was</u> one of England's greatest novelists.
   a. complete subject   **c.** complete predicate
   b. simple subject   **d.** simple predicate

10. This former <u>journalist</u> wrote chapters for monthly publication.
    a. complete subject   **c.** complete predicate
    b. simple subject   **d.** simple predicate

11. <u>His vivid characters</u> bring the books to life.
    a. complete subject   **c.** complete predicate
    b. simple subject   **d.** simple predicate

D. Write the letter of the subject in each sentence. *(pages 48–51)*

12. Here is the paper.
    a. Here   **b.** is   **c.** paper

13. Read it to me.
    a. it   **b.** me   **c.** (You understood)

14. Did you read this story?
    a. Did   **b.** you   **c.** story

15. There is our mayor!
    a. There   **b.** is   **c.** mayor

E. Write the letter of the sentence that is *not* punctuated correctly. *(pages 74–75)*

16. **a.** Ms. Sitomer the sixth-grade teacher organized a science fair.
    b. It was, by the way, a great success.
    c. Students, parents, and teachers all enjoyed it.
17. **a.** Adrienne built a volcano, and Linda researched solar energy.
    b. At the end of the fair, the judges awarded prizes.
    c. Ralph Jane and Kathleen all won awards.

F. Write the letter of the proper noun in each group of words. *(pages 80–81)*

18. **a.** dam   **b.** Boulder Dam   **c.** hydroelectricity
19. **a.** community   **b.** city   **c.** Tucson
20. **a.** team   **b.** player   **c.** Babe Ruth
21. **a.** Washington Monument   **b.** monument   **c.** memorial

G. Write the letter of the correct plural form of each singular noun. *(pages 82–83)*

22. rodeo   **a.** rodeoes   **b.** rodeos   **c.** rodei
23. cliff   **a.** cliffes   **b.** clives   **c.** cliffs
24. emphasis   **a.** emphasises   **b.** emphases   **c.** emphasis
25. child   **a.** childs   **b.** children   **c.** childrens

H. Write the letter of the correct possessive form of each noun. *(pages 84–87)*

26. writer   **a.** writers'   **b.** writer'   **c.** writer's
27. players   **a.** players's   **b.** player's   **c.** players'
28. Bess   **a.** Bess'   **b.** Bess's   **c.** Bess'es
29. men   **a.** mens'   **b.** men's   **c.** men'

I. Write the letter of the correct abbreviation for each word. *(pages 88–89)*

30. Thursday   **a.** Thurs.   **b.** Thur.   **c.** Thurs
31. Incorporated   **a.** Inc.   **b.** inc.   **c.** Incorp.
32. President   **a.** Pr.   **b.** Pres.   **c.** Presid.
33. Post Office   **a.** p.o.   **b.** PO   **c.** P.O.

J. Write the letter of the answer to the following questions about a dictionary and a thesaurus. *(pages 52–53, 90–91)*

34. Which of the following words would appear on a dictionary page with the guide words *federal/feed?*
    a. feeble   **b.** fed   **c.** feedback   **d.** feast
35. Which of the following does *not* appear in a thesaurus entry?
    a. antonyms   **b.** synonyms   **c.** entry word   **d.** definition

PART TWO

Marvels

To see the world in a grain of sand
And a heaven in a wild flower
Hold infinity in the palm of your hand
And eternity in an hour.

from "Auguries of Innocence"
by William Blake

Marvels are everywhere for people with the imagination to appreciate them. Writers of science fiction and fantasy create marvels all the time. However, the marvels in our own realistic world can be just as fascinating to explore. In these two units, focus on the marvels—both real and imaginary—that fascinate you the most.

Book Report

◆

Verbs I

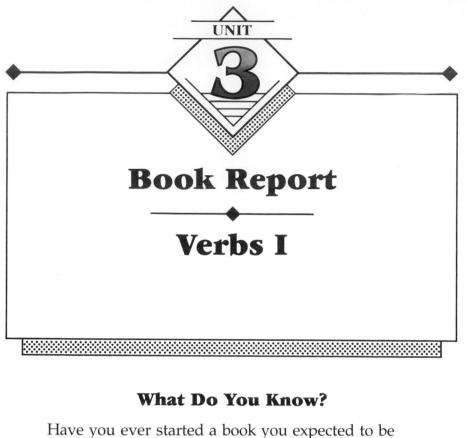

What Do You Know?

Have you ever started a book you expected to be good, only to wind up tossing it aside after a chapter or two? There are millions of books to read. How can you tell which ones *you* might like? You might look for books by authors you've enjoyed before. You might ask friends and classmates what they've read lately. Or you might choose a book after reading a classmate's book report.

A book report summarizes a book and gives the writer's opinion of it. Such a report helps you decide whether you would like to read the book yourself. When *you* write a book report, your opinion will help others decide whether or not to read the book.

Thinking About Book Reports

What Is a Book Report?

A **book report** has these characteristics:

- It names the title and author of the book.
- It identifies the main characters and the setting.
- It summarizes the story without giving away the ending.
- It tells why the writer of the book report liked or disliked the book.

Book reports and reviews are popular because most people want to know a little about a book before they decide whether or not to read it. After all, there are a lot of books out there! You want to choose the ones that you will most enjoy reading.

There are several good reasons for doing a book report. One is to help others decide whether to read a book. Another is that a book report helps you understand the book better. Summarizing the story on paper helps you shape your ideas about the plot and characters clearly. Also, writing your own opinion of the book helps you know better what you really think of the story.

Discussion

1. Think of some of the books you have read. What helped you decide to read those particular books?
2. Which of the books would you most strongly recommend to your classmates?
3. What kinds of things help make a book interesting reading for you?

107

Reading a Book Report

Read this book report. Look for details that might help a reader decide whether or not to read the book.

Can you imagine traveling through millions of miles of space in just a flash? *A Wrinkle in Time* by Madeleine L'Engle tells about a family from a typical New England town who suddenly find themselves in outer space, battling alien forces.

The story opens with Meg Murry, her brother, and her mother having a snack in the kitchen of the Murrys' house while a thunderstorm rages outside. An unusual woman, Mrs. Whatsit, is blown in by the storm. She has astonishing news. Meg's father, a physicist who disappeared some time ago, is being held prisoner on the planet Camazotz. With the help of Mrs. Whatsit, Meg and her companions use a super-fast method of space travel to journey through a "wrinkle in time" in hopes of rescuing Meg's father. What follows is an exciting, suspenseful story as Meg and her fellow travelers struggle against enormous odds.

This is the kind of book you won't want to put down until it is over. Something new happens on almost every page. The characters travel to places you will never read about in any other book, and they have adventures no other author has ever thought of. The story will transport you along with the characters to distant planets. You don't have to like science fiction to love this story, though. It is a story about people, not rockets and machines. It is exciting because it makes impossible events seem as though they could really happen. I highly recommend this book.

The title and author are identified.

The setting and plot are described.

The main characters are named.

Important events are summarized.

The writer's opinion of the book is stated.

Reasons are given to support each opinion.

Understanding What You've Read

Write the answer to each question below.

1. Where does the story take place?
2. What news does Mrs. Whatsit bring?
3. What is the goal of the main characters in the book?
4. What kind of person do you think Mrs. Whatsit is?
5. Why has the reviewer not revealed the story's ending?
6. What details of this report might convince someone to read the book?

Writing Assignment

Imagine that you are working on a committee to choose new books for your school. You are asked to write a three-paragraph book report on a book you would recommend. The first paragraph will introduce the book. The second paragraph will summarize the story. The third paragraph will offer your opinion of the book.

Your **audience** for the report will be other committee members who need to know whether others will enjoy the book as much as you did. Your **purpose** will be to convince the other committee members to order the book.

What books have I especially enjoyed reading?

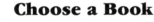

Choose a Book

Think of some books that you have read and enjoyed. Consider kinds of books that you particularly enjoy, such as mysteries, science fiction, stories set in other countries, or books by a favorite author. Make a list of titles. Then choose the one book you would most like to report about. Save your choice for the next lesson.

Finding a Book in the Library

It is easy to find a book in the library if you know how the books are arranged. **Fiction books,** which tell stories made up from an author's imagination, are located in a special section. They are arranged alphabetically according to the author's last name. **Nonfiction books** give facts and information. They are located in another section of the library. **Reference books** such as encyclopedias, atlases, and dictionaries have their own section.

You can use the card catalog or the computer listing in your local library to help you locate a book. A **card catalog** is an alphabetical card file that lists all the books in the library. Fiction books have an author card and a title card. Nonfiction books usually have a subject card as well as author and title cards. Study the information on the cards for a nonfiction book:

Author Card
author's name
book title

Schlein, Miriam.   599
Giraffe: The Silent Giant.   SCH

call number

Title Card
book title
author's name

Giraffe: The Silent Giant   599
Schlein, Miriam.   SCH
Giraffe: The Silent Giant

Subject Card
subject
author's name
book title
publisher
pages,
illustrations

ANIMALS—GIRAFFES   599
Schlein, Miriam.   SCH
Giraffe: The Silent Giant.
New York: Four Winds Press, 1976.
58 p. illus.

Dewey Decimal System

000—099	General References (encyclopedias, periodicals)
100—199	Philosophy and Psychology
200—299	Religion
300—399	Social Sciences (economics, law, education)
400—499	Language
500—599	Pure Sciences
600—699	Technology and Applied Sciences
700—799	Arts and Recreation
800—899	Literature
900—999	History and Geography

Notice that each card has a code number, or **call number,** in the top right corner. Most nonfiction books have these numbers based on the **Dewey Decimal System.** This system assigns a call number to each book according to its subject. The call number appears on the spine of the book and on the catalog card. Nonfiction books are shelved according to these call numbers. To find a book with the call number 514.88, for example, go to the shelves labeled 500-599.

You can also use the catalog cards to find fiction books. You can use a book's title card to find out the author's name. To find out what books an author has written, look at the card under that author's name.

Practice

A. Refer to the catalog card below to answer the questions. Write your answers on a separate sheet of paper.

Sign of the Beaver, The.
Speare, Elizabeth George.
    The Sign of the Beaver.
Boston: Houghton Mifflin Company, 1983.
    135 pp.

---

   1. What type of catalog card is this?
   2. What is the title of the book?
   3. Who is the author of this book?
   4. Where in the library would you find the book?
   5. How could you find out if there are other books by this author?

B. For each subject below, tell which Dewey Decimal System category and call numbers you would use to find a nonfiction book on the subject. Use the Dewey Decimal numbers on the opposite page. Write your answers on a separate sheet of paper.

   6. life in ancient Rome
   7. the ideas of the Greek philosopher Aristotle
   8. the work of the famous artist Picasso
   9. the latest computer technology
  10. a description of the English language
  11. an analysis of American literature
  12. a description of economic theories

Find and Reread Your Book

Use the card catalog or computer listing in your library to locate the book you chose for your report. Then skim or quickly reread the book to refresh your memory. Take notes on the characters, the setting, and events. Also note the important events. Save your notes for the next lesson.

PLANNING
Introductions and Summaries

Did you notice that the book report about *A Wrinkle in Time* uses a special method to get the reader's attention? The very first sentence of the report is a question that startles the reader and introduces the book in an interesting way. The second sentence not only names the title and author but also tells what the book is about. Together the two sentences provide a strong introduction for the report.

Compare the two introductions below.

A Wrinkle in Time is by Madeleine L'Engle. The story is about a family from New England that travels through space.	Can you imagine traveling through space in just a flash? *A Wrinkle in Time* by Madeleine L'Engle tells about a family from New England who suddenly find themselves in outer space, battling alien forces.

The introduction at the right grabs the reader's attention. The reader of the report wants to know more about the book.

The introduction is the first paragraph of the book report. In the second paragraph, you will summarize the main events of the story. A **summary** does three things. It names the characters, it tells about their problem or their goal, and it describes how the characters try to solve their problem or reach their goal.

To help you write a summary, you can begin with a **story map.** A story map lists the important details you will want to include in your summary.

This story map lists the setting, the characters, and the details of the plot for the book *The Wheel on the School*. Notice that the outcome section does not reveal the story's ending.

SETTING:	Shora, a small Dutch fishing village	
CHARACTERS:	Lina, her five schoolmates, and the other villagers	

PLOT: Problem	Solution Attempts	Outcome
Storks no longer have places to build their nests build their nests in Shora.	Lina and her classmates look everywhere for a wagon wheel to attach to the roof.	Lina finally finds a wheel. The villagers help put it up and wait to see if the storks come back.

112

Practice

A. Read the following two introductions for a book report. Choose the one you think is better, and tell why you chose it.

    1. *The Wizard of Oz* is a famous book by L. Frank Baum. The book tells about the fantastic adventures of a girl named Dorothy, who is carried off by a cyclone and travels to the imaginary land of Oz.

    2. Not everyone gets whisked away by a cyclone and lands in a far-off, magical place. But that is exactly what happens to Dorothy Gale, the main character in *The Wizard of Oz*, by L. Frank Baum.

B. Look at the story map for a book report on *The Wizard of Oz*. Use the map to write a short summary paragraph for the report.

SETTING:	the imaginary land of Oz	
CHARACTERS:	Dorothy Gale (a girl from Kansas), the Scarecrow, the Tin Woodsman, the Cowardly Lion, the Wizard, the wise Queen Glinda	

PLOT: Problem	Solution Attempt	Outcome
A cyclone has carried Dorothy from Kansas to Oz. Dorothy wants to get back home.	Dorothy searches for the Emerald City to seek help from the Wizard. Along with the Scarecrow, the Tin Woodsman, and the Cowardly Lion, she finds the Wizard, but he does not help them.	Dorothy finally reaches Glinda, who may be able to help her get home.

Plan an Introduction

    Reread the notes you took on your book, and think of ways to introduce the book to other readers. Write down ideas you might use for an introduction. Save your notes.

Make a Story Map

    Use the notes you took to make a story map for your book. Include the setting, characters, and the plot categories. Save your story map for the next lesson.

Supporting an Opinion with Facts

In the last paragraph of a book report, you tell the reader your opinion of the story. An **opinion** is what a person thinks about something. When you express your opinion, you express your personal view. Each person's opinion is unique. An opinion cannot be proved and checked, but it can be supported with specific facts and examples. A **fact** is a piece of information that can be proved true and that can be checked.

Read the following sentences:

It is a lovely day.
The sky is cloudless.
The temperature is in the mid-70s.
There is a soft breeze blowing.

The first sentence is an opinion. It really means "I believe that it is a lovely day." The other three sentences are facts. They are statements that can be checked for accuracy and supply reasons that support the opinion "It is a lovely day." By using facts to support your opinion, you are more likely to convince people to agree with your view.

Which of the facts below support the following opinion?

Opinion: *A Wrinkle in Time* is a thrilling, action-packed book.
Fact: It tells how Meg and her companions travel through space to find Meg's long-lost father.
Fact: It tells how Meg risks her life to rescue her brother.
Fact: It describes the life of an American family from a typical New England town.

All three statements are facts. However, only the first two support the idea that the book is an action-packed thriller. The fact that the book tells about an American family is not related to this idea.

As you write your book report, be aware of when you are stating facts and when you are stating opinions. Always support your opinions with facts that relate to the opinion.

Practice

A. Read each statement below. Decide which statements are facts and which are opinions. Write your answers on a separate sheet of paper.

1. *The Incredible Journey* is an interesting book.
2. It tells how two dogs and a cat traveled across the Canadian wilderness in search of their masters.
3. The book describes how the animals communicated with one another.
4. The book is incredibly exciting.
5. The book tells how the dogs and the cat fought off wild animals.
6. You will love this book.

B. Read both opinions below. Choose the one you agree with, and support it with two facts.

Opinion: Dogs are useful to people.
Opinion: Cats are easy to care for.

Support Your Opinion with Facts

Think about the book you are planning to write about. Write down your opinion about the book. Under each opinion, list details and examples from the story that support your opinion. Save your notes for the next lesson.

Writing a First Draft

Read the first draft of a student's book report. The writer wasn't worried about making it perfect. It will be changed later.

Why have all the storks left town? This is the question that confronts Lina and her friends in Meindert Dejong's book, The wheel on The School. This story, set in the little Dutch fishing village of Shora, tells what happens when many people join together to get something done.

One of the children, Lina, decides to write a school composition about storks. She finds that storks inhabit the neighboring towns. There are no storks in Shora. Lina decides to find out why. Her classmates decide to help her. Lina learns that many years before, storks had nested in the village. Then a violent storm came. The storm blew down all the trees in town. After that, the storks stopped coming. Lina figures out that the roofs are too steep for the storks, so she and her friends go hunting for something the storks can nest on. Their search is full of disappointments, some dangers, and a few laughs. Finally, they stumble across a wheel. The villagers put it on the roof of the school. Will the storks return to Shora? Will they stay away? Read the book to find out!

This book is worth reading because it's lively and interesting. It has a lot of information about the Dutch people and their customs, as well as about storks. The characters are likeable and admirable. They believe in their dream and work hard together to achieve it. I like the book because it is so full of hope. In the story, Lina's wonder and curiosity help make things happen.

Write Your First Draft

If you wish, start by discussing your ideas with your teacher or a classmate. Then use your notes to write your report. In the introduction, include the title and author of the book and information to interest the reader. Then use your story map to help summarize the plot. Don't give away the ending. Finally, give your opinion of the book, and back it up with facts and examples.

Discussing a First Draft

After completing your first draft, seek ways to improve it. One way is by discussing it with a classmate.

Discussion Strategy

When having a discussion, keep to the topic being discussed. For example, focus on ways to improve the book report instead of discussing other books you have read that have a similar plot.

Use the Content Checklist to discuss with your classmates the book report on the previous page.

Content Checklist
- ✔ Does the report name the title and the author of the book?
- ✔ Does the introduction attract the reader's attention?
- ✔ Does the report tell about the characters and the setting?
- ✔ Does the report summarize the main events of the story without giving away the ending?
- ✔ Does the report give the writer's opinion of the book?
- ✔ Are the writer's opinions clearly stated and backed by facts from the book?

Revise Your First Draft for Content

To the Reader: Exchange papers with a classmate. As you read your partner's book report, see if you have any trouble following the story line. If so, discuss ways to improve the draft so that the events can be more clearly described. Use the Content Checklist for help.

To the Writer: Discuss your partner's suggestions. Then revise your first draft for content. Save your work.

Combining Sentences for Style

    The book report draft you read could be improved by combining the sentences. Notice that a comma is used after the first part of the new, combined sentence.

    Sentences with related ideas may be combined with *and*.

> Lina searched for a wheel. Her friends helped her.
> Lina searched for a wheel, <u>and</u> her friends helped her.

    Sentences with contrasting ideas can be combined with *but*.

> Lina searched for storks in Shora. There were none.
> Lina searched for storks in Shora, <u>but</u> there were none.

    Sentences that state a choice can be combined with *or*.

> Lina could write a report. She could do a project.
> Lina could write a report, <u>or</u> she could do a project.

    Sometimes the same sentences can be combined with different words, depending on the meaning you want them to have.

> The storks left Shora, <u>and</u> they returned the next summer.
> The storks left Shora, <u>but</u> they returned the next summer.

    Here is how the book report writer combined sentences. Notice that a repeated noun can be replaced with another word.

These sentences express related ideas.

These sentences state a choice.

> Lina learns that many years before, storks had nested in the village. Then a violent storm came. ~~The storm~~ *and it* blew down all the trees in town. After that, the storks stopped coming. Lina figures out that the roofs are too steep for the storks, so she and her friends go hunting for something they can nest on. Their search is full of disappointments, some dangers, and a few laughs. Finally, they stumble across a wheel. *and,* The villagers put it on the roof of the school. Will the storks return to Shora? *or,* Will they stay away? Read the book to find out!

Practice

Combine each pair of sentences. Make a single sentence using the word *and*, *but*, or *or*. Write your new sentence.

1. Meg Murry wonders where her missing father is. No one knows where to find him.
2. Meg meets Mrs. Whatsit. Charles Wallace introduces Meg to Mrs. Which.
3. Charles wants to travel in space. Meg does not.
4. Meg can journey to find her father. She can stay behind.
5. Mrs. Whatsit takes the Murrys into space. They travel through a wrinkle in time.
6. The Murrys reach the planet Uriel. They learn more about Mrs. Whatsit.
7. The Murrys get to the planet Camazotz at last. Escaping is harder than they had planned.
8. Will the Murrys succeed in their rescue? Will their plan fail?

◆————————————————————————————◆

Revising Checklist
- ✔ Have I included all the characteristics of a book report?
- ✔ Where can I vary word order for sentence variety? (p. 72)
- ✔ Where can I combine sentences by using the word *and*, *but*, or *or*?

◆————————————————————————————◆

What sentences can I combine to make my writing smoother?

APPLY STEP BY STEP

Revise Your First Draft for Style

Check for the items on the Revising Checklist. Combine short sentences with *and*, *but*, or *or*. Mark the changes on your draft. Hold on to your work for the next lesson.

Punctuating Titles of Written Works ◆

A book report must include the complete title of the book. It is important to punctuate and capitalize titles correctly. Here are some rules for punctuating and capitalizing titles.

Rule	Example
Capitalize the first word, the last word, all important words, and other words over five letters long in the titles of written works.	The Sign of the Beaver The Wheel on the School Journey Toward Freedom
Underline the titles of books, plays, magazines, newspapers, and other larger works.	The Tower by the Sea (book) Hamlet (play) Computer Weekly (magazine) The Elmwood Times (newspaper)
Use quotation marks for the titles of articles, short stories, poems, chapters of books, songs, and other short works.	"How to Build a Boat" (article) "Paw-Paw" (short story) "The Moth" (poem) "Madeline Saves the Wedding" (chapter) "Home on the Range" (song)
When a title in quotation marks appears at the end of a sentence, the period goes inside the quotation marks. When a title appears in the middle of a sentence, the comma also goes inside the quotation marks.	I just read "Friendship." Can you sing "The Star Spangled Banner"? I just love the poem "Actions"! The story "The Telltale Heart," by Edgar Allen Poe, is very famous.

Practice

Write each sentence below, adding the correct capitalization and punctuation.

1. Madeleine L'Engle is the author of several books, including a swiftly tilting planet.
2. A play called the front page earned a Pulitzer Prize for Ben Hecht and Charles MacArthur.
3. A study in scarlet, a book by Arthur Conan Doyle, marked the first appearance of Sherlock Holmes.
4. Sidney Paget illustrated a Sherlock Holmes story called a case of identity for strand magazine.
5. The catbird seat, a short story by James Thurber, was first published in 1942 by a famous magazine, the new yorker.
6. Do you know what comic strips appear in the greenlawn gazette?
7. To find out about knitting, you might read a chapter called knitting an afghan in the book arts and crafts.
8. Eve Merriam wrote a poem called out of the city.
9. Who knows the lyrics to the song blue skies?
10. My favorite book is alice in wonderland.

Proofreading Checklist
✔ Did I indent the first word of each paragraph? (p. 36)
✔ Did I capitalize the first word in each sentence? (p. 36)
✔ Did I capitalize the names of specific people, places, and things? (p. 36)
✔ Did I end each sentence with the right punctuation? (p. 36)
✔ Did I capitalize and punctuate the book title correctly?
✔ Did I write plural nouns and possessives correctly?

Proofread Your Draft
Check for correct capitalization and punctuation in your book report. Use the Proofreading Checklist above. Make corrections on your draft. Save your work for the next lesson.

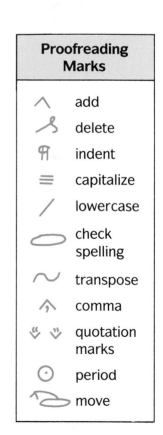

Proofreading Marks	
∧	add
⅄	delete
¶	indent
≡	capitalize
/	lowercase
◯	check spelling
∼	transpose
⌃	comma
⌄ ⌄	quotation marks
⊙	period
⌒	move

Checking Spelling/Writing a Final Copy ◆

Spelling Strategy

If a long word is difficult for you to spell, break it into syllables. The spelling may then become easier.

Examples: spontaneous   spon ta ne ous
           trigonometry   trig o nom e try

Here is part of the revised and proofread book report.

Why have all the storks left town? This is the question that confronts Lina and her friends in Meindert Dejong's book, The wheel on The School. This story, set in the little Dutch fishing village of Shora, tells what happens when many people join together to get something done.

One of the children, Lina, decides to write a school composition about storks. She finds that storks inhabit the neighboring towns. *but* There are no storks in Shora. Lina decides to find out why. *and* Her classmates decide to help her. Lina learns that many years before, storks had nested in the village. Then a violent storm came. *and it* The storm blew down all the trees in town. After that, the storks stopped coming. Lina figures out that the roofs are too steep for the storks, so she and her friends go hunting for something *the storks* they can nest on. Their search is full of disappointments, some dangers, and a few laughs. Finally, they stumble across a wheel. *and* The villagers put it on the roof of the school. Will the storks return to Shora? *or* Will they stay away? Read the book to find out!

Check Your Spelling

Use the proofreading marks to correct errors in spelling. Apply the Spelling Strategy.

Write a Final Copy

Write a neat, final copy of your book report. Be sure to proofread your work. Keep your final copy.

Sharing Your Book Report

Speaking/Listening Strategy

When you are reading aloud, speak clearly and carefully so that your audience can hear everything you say. When you are listening, be quiet and attentive. Don't disturb others.

Choosing a Way to Share

After you make a neat, final copy of your book report, share it with classmates. You may do it in several ways.

Presenting a Book Review Program Take turns presenting an imaginary book report program on TV. Have each member of a three-person panel present his or her book report and then compare and contrast the three books in a panel discussion.

Making the Book "Speak" As part of your book report presentation, choose an especially interesting, funny, or exciting passage from the book, and read it aloud to the class. Hearing something from the book will make your classmates even more curious to read the rest of the story for themselves.

Making a Class Book Report File Put all of your classmates' book reports into a folder. Arrange them alphabetically by title. Put the folder in the school library so that the students can read a book before they take it out.

Share Your Book Report

Choose the way you prefer to share your book report. Present it and discover your audience's reaction.

Add to Your Learning Log

Answer these questions in your learning log.

- How well did my book report present my opinions about the book?
- What was the most difficult part of writing the report?
- When I write my next book report, what might I do differently to make it interesting to readers?

123

The Literature Connection: Verbs

In good writing, each sentence is like a separate picture or photograph. Some "pictures" are clear; others are blurry. Action words, or *verbs*, are words that can help give sentences a sharp "focus."

There are many verbs you can use. Each verb describes a different action. The actions can be mental or physical, real or imagined.

Picture this activity in your mind: Brenda walked to the library. The verb walked gives you some idea of the action, but you could form a sharper image in your mind with a more specific verb such as skipped, strolled, raced, or strode.

In the poem that follows, ordinary verbs are used to describe extraordinary, marvelous things. As you read the poem, try to picture each movement that the dream woman makes.

The Dream Woman
by
Patricia Hubbell

Early in the morning
Before the lights are on,
The dream woman scurries
Uptown and down.
Leaping in my window
She rushes to my bed,
Grasps at my dream
And wrings it from my
  head.

Quickly, quietly, she stuffs it
  in her bag,
Snaps shut the clasp
And runs from my side.
Out at the window,
Down a film of air,
The dream woman hurries
Lest the dawn appear.

Discussion

1. Which verbs in the poem show that the dream woman is in a hurry?
2. Which verbs show the dream woman's other actions in the poem?
3. What will the dream woman do with the dream after emptying it out of her bag? Think of some verbs that describe what you think she might do.

The Writing Connection: Verbs

In the poem "The Dream Woman," the woman "scurries" and "rushes" with the dream she has taken. There are many words you may use to describe the way people run. As a careful writer, you should choose the most accurate words possible to name the way you see people or animals moving. Read these examples.

The early-morning runner <u>jogged</u> around the track.

The marathon runner <u>sped</u> around the track.

The tired horse <u>loped</u> around the track.

Activity

The picture above shows different subjects moving in various ways. Write a sentence that describes the way each person or animal is moving. Be sure to use a verb that precisely identifies each subject's action. A sample sentence is given.

A woman late for work <u>dashes</u> for the bus.

Action Verbs

A **verb** is a word that expresses action or helps to tell what the subject is or is like. An **action verb** expresses action and tells what a subject does.

A. Many action verbs describe physical actions.

> Composers usually play several instruments.
> Young Mozart jumped and ran like other children.
> He also performed on the piano.

Sometimes an action verb expresses physical action, even though you cannot picture real action or change.

> Mozart fits our picture of a creative genius.
> His parents waited for his musical development.
> Mozart's mother stood proudly beside her son.

B. Some action verbs express mental actions or show ownership.

> Leopold Mozart noticed his son's talent. (mental action)
> New audiences will like Mozart's music. (mental action)
> Modern pianos have 88 keys. (ownership)
> Wolfgang possessed remarkable ability. (ownership)

Strategy

If you are not sure whether a verb is an action verb, ask yourself if the subject does or owns something. Remember that not all actions are physical. Mental activity is also a kind of action.

Check Your Understanding

A. Write the letter of the action verb in each sentence.
1. Mozart wrote his first symphony at age seven.
   a. wrote   **b.** first   **c.** seven
2. He lived in Salzburg, Austria, until age 25.
   a. He   **b.** lived   **c.** until

B. Write the letter of the action verb in each sentence.

    3. Young Wolfgang enjoyed a happy childhood.

        a. Young   **b.** enjoyed   **c.** happy

    4. The boy had a brilliant sister.

        a. boy   **b.** had   **c.** brilliant

Practice

A. Write each sentence. Underline the action verb.

    5. Mozart gave a concert for the king.

    6. He composed a special opera for the king.

    7. The king sat in a place of honor.

    8. Leopold Mozart accompanied his son to the concert.

B. Write each sentence. Underline the action verb.

    9. Operas have both words and music.

   10. Mozart's opera had great charm.

   11. The king and his court ignored Mozart's brilliant music.

   12. Only a few people liked the performance.

C. Mixed Practice Write each sentence. Underline each action verb. Write whether it shows *physical action*, *mental action*, or *ownership*.

   13. Mozart played the piano at the age of three.

   14. His family always valued his abilities.

   15. The composer heard his music in his own head.

   16. He copied the notes afterward.

   17. Mozart possessed extraordinary musical ability.

   18. Most of his pieces have perfect form.

   19. Many people have heard his beautiful melodies.

   20. His music will enjoy wide popularity for many years.

Apply: Work with a Partner

Write five sentences about music or another topic of your choice. Replace the verbs in your sentences with blank spaces, and exchange papers with a classmate. Then fill in the blanks in the sentences. Exchange your papers again to see how your partner has completed your sentences.

Linking Verbs

Not all verbs express actions. A **linking verb** connects the subject of a sentence with words that describe or identify it. Linking verbs usually help to tell what the subject is or is like.

A. The most common linking verbs are forms of the verb *be*: *am, is, are, was,* and *were.*

Function of Verb	Example
identify subject	The machines <u>are</u> our computers.
describe subject	They <u>were</u> uncommon until recently.

B. Many other verbs can serve as linking verbs. Some of these are verbs that involve the senses, such as *look, sound, smell, taste, feel, seem,* and *appear.* Others express change or a lack of change, such as *become, remain, grow, stay,* and *turn.* Whether a verb is an action verb or a linking verb depends on how it is used in the sentence.

Action: The first computers <u>appeared</u> in the 1940s.
Linking: They <u>appeared</u> strange to many people.

Strategy

You may not be sure whether a verb other than a form of *be* is an action verb or a linking verb. Try substituting the word *seem* in its place. If the sentence still makes sense, the verb is probably a linking verb.

Computers <u>look</u> futuristic. Computers <u>seem</u> futuristic.

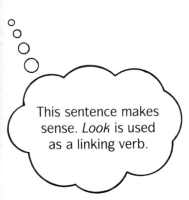

This sentence makes sense. *Look* is used as a linking verb.

Check Your Understanding

A. Write the letter of the linking verb in each sentence.
1. The first computers were enormous machines.
    a. computers   **b.** were   **c.** enormous
2. They are much smaller today.
    a. are   **b.** smaller   **c.** today

B. Write the letter of the term that describes each underlined verb.

   3. The woman turned the computer monitor around.
   a. action verb   **b.** linking verb
   4. Bulky vacuum tubes became impractical for computers.
   a. action verb   **b.** linking verb

Practice

A. Write each sentence. Underline the linking verb.

   5. The first digital computer was ENIAC.
   6. A modern minicomputer is as powerful as ENIAC.
   7. First-generation computers were large.
   8. Scientists are hopeful because of recent developments.

B. Write each sentence. Underline the verb. Write *LV* if it is a linking verb or *AV* if it is an action verb.

   9. The microchip appeared in the 1970s.
   10. Capabilities of computers grew because of microchips.
   11. Powerful minicomputers remain popular.
   12. Some machines look very complex.

C. Mixed Practice   Write each sentence. Underline the verb. Write *LV* if it is a linking verb or *AV* if it is an action verb.

   13. Computers became smaller with transistors.
   14. The need for computers grew with the space age.
   15. The memory of a computer is a storage center.
   16. Information in the memory remains available.
   17. The information appears on a screen.
   18. Some people feel uncertain about computers.
   19. Many users, however, have grown dependent on the machines.
   20. Computers have remained a vital part of technology.

Apply : Learning Log

In your learning log, write about the part of this lesson that you found most difficult. In your notes, you might suggest some ways to distinguish between action and linking verbs.

129

Main and Helping Verbs

A **verb phrase** is made up of a main verb plus one or more helping verbs. A **main verb** expresses the action or tells something about the subject. A **helping verb** works with the main verb to make the meaning more specific.

A. A helping verb comes before the main verb in a verb phrase.

Consuela and Kimiko were admiring the trees.

helping verb   main verb

Some common helping verbs are listed in this chart.

am	be	was	do	have	may	could	will
is	been	were	does	has	might	would	shall
are	being		did	had	must	should	can

The listed forms of the verbs *be, have,* and *do* can be used as either helping verbs or main verbs.

B. Some verb phrases can be interrupted by another word, such as *not*. Verb phrases can also be interrupted when the word order of a sentence is inverted, as in a question.

Will old sequoia trees survive for many more years?
Some people do not think so.

Strategy

Be sure to look for all the words in a verb phrase. Be on the alert for three-word verb phrases. These are made up of one main verb and two helping verbs.

Many sequoias have now been growing for centuries.

Check Your Understanding

A. Write the letter that identifies the underlined verb.
   1. Many huge sequoias are standing in California.
      a. main verb   **b.** helping verb   **c.** verb phrase
   2. These ancient trees might be our key to the past.
      a. main verb   **b.** helping verb   **c.** verb phrase

B. Write the letter of the verb phrase in each sentence.

    3. People have often called sequoias friendly giants.

      a. called   **b.** have often called   **c.** have called

    4. We should not have used these trees for lumber.

      a. should not have used   **b.** used

      c. should have used

Practice

A. Write each sentence. Underline each helping verb once and each main verb twice.

    5. Naturalists had worried about sequoias at one time.

    6. No new trees had appeared for many years.

    7. The species may become extinct.

    8. Some experts did predict exactly that.

B. Follow the instructions for Practice A.

    9. Sequoia seeds must usually have heat for growth.

    10. Most seeds could not flourish otherwise.

    11. A huge forest fire did finally occur.

    12. Would many seeds now sprout?

C. Mixed Practice Write each sentence. Underline each helping verb once and each main verb twice.

    13. These seeds will produce new trees.

    14. Will a new forest of sequoia trees grow?

    15. Sequoias may even be older than Egypt's pyramids.

    16. Have you ever visited Sequoia National Park?

    17. Nature has given the giant trees great strength.

    18. Sometimes a lightning bolt will shatter one.

    19. Many trees must undoubtedly have had very interesting histories.

    20. Some trees might have been living 5,000 years ago.

Apply: Work with a Partner

Write five sentences about trees or another topic of your choice, using at least one helping verb in each sentence. Then exchange papers with a classmate and rewrite the sentences by changing the helping verbs. How do the meanings of the sentences change? Discuss your findings in class.

Present, Past, and Future Tenses

A verb can show when the action or state of being in a sentence takes place. **Tense** is the time expressed by a verb.

A. The chart below tells about the present, past, and future tenses.

Tense	Use	Example
present	tells about something that is happening now	Skyscrapers <u>appear</u> majestic. Many <u>are standing</u> in New York City.
past	tells about something that happened in the past and is now over	Engineers <u>constructed</u> one in 1884. It <u>was standing</u> until 1931.
future	tells about something that will happen in the future	New skyscrapers <u>will be</u> even taller. Architects <u>will be designing</u> them.

B. Verbs have simple present, past, and future tenses. You can follow the rules shown below to form simple tenses.

Tense	Verb	Rule	Example
simple present	verb with singular noun subject; <u>he</u>, <u>she</u>, or <u>it</u>	verb + <u>s</u> or <u>es</u>	A skyscraper <u>towers</u> over a city.
	verb with plural noun subject; <u>I</u>, <u>you</u>, <u>we</u>, or <u>they</u>	verb	Some companies <u>own</u> skyscrapers. I <u>own</u> it. You <u>own</u> it.
simple past	most verbs	verb + <u>ed</u> or drop <u>e</u> and add <u>ed</u>	William Jenney <u>designed</u> the first. He <u>advanced</u> building design.
simple future	all verbs	<u>will</u> or <u>shall</u> + verb	Skyscrapers <u>will soar</u> to new heights. We <u>shall see</u> new plans for them.

Strategy

Do not use the present tense when talking about something that occurred in the past.

Incorrect: Yesterday Jane tells me about a new skyscraper.
Correct: Yesterday Jane told me about a new skyscraper.

132

Check Your Understanding

A. Write the letter that identifies the tense of the underlined verb in each sentence.

1. Skyscrapers <u>compete</u> for space on the skyline today.
   a. past tense   **b.** present tense   **c.** future tense
2. Skyscrapers <u>looked</u> futuristic years ago.
   a. past tense   **b.** present tense   **c.** future tense

B. Write the letter of the correct verb form.

3. Chicago now _____ the world's tallest skyscraper.
   a. boast   **b.** boasts   **c.** will boasts
4. New skyscrapers _____ greater heights.
   a. will reaches   **b.** will reach   **c.** will reached

Practice

A. Write each sentence. Underline the verb. Label its tense.

5. The Empire State Building stands in New York City.
6. For 40 years it remained the world's tallest building.
7. This year almost two million people will visit it.

B. Write each sentence. Write the correct tense of the verb.

8. The building still (look) very impressive. (present)
9. The first skyscraper (appear) in the 1880s. (past)
10. Perhaps all cities (have) skyscrapers some day. (future)

C. Mixed Practice   Write each sentence. Write the correct tense of the verb.

11. Chicago (claim) many huge skyscrapers. (present)
12. The tallest skyscraper now (stand) 1,454 feet. (present)
13. Architects (display) their talents in skyscrapers. (past)
14. They (change) the look of many American cities. (past)
15. Soon there (be) even grander skyscrapers. (future)
16. People in the future (live) in them. (Choose the correct tense.)
17. Soon they (design) new ones. (Choose the correct tense.)

Apply: Journal

In your journal write six sentences about a skyscraper you have seen or would like to visit. Use present, past, and future tense verbs in your sentences.

Perfect Tenses ◆

Read the following sentences. Discuss how the difference in verbs changes your sense of the time in each sentence.

Juana attended the meetings.
Juana has attended the meetings.
Juana had attended the meetings.

A. Verbs in the **perfect tenses** express past action in relation to another time.

Tense	Use	How to Form	Examples
present perfect	tells of an action that took place at an indefinite time in the past or that began in the past and is still going on	*have* or *has* + *ed* form of main verb	Thousands of visitors have viewed Stonehenge. Stonehenge has existed in England for centuries.

B. The **past perfect** tense can also be used to express past action.

Tense	Use	How to Form	Example
past perfect	tells of an action that took place in the past before another action or some specific time	*had* + *ed* form of main verb	Builders had erected Stonehenge before the dawn of history.

Strategy

To decide whether *have* is a main verb or a helping verb, look at the words that follow it. If one of them is also a verb, then *have* is probably a helping verb. If not, then *have* is the main verb.

Main verb: I have a book about Stonehenge.
Helping verb: I have read it many times.

Check Your Understanding

A. Write the letter of the words to complete each sentence.
    1. Stonehenge _____ a mystery to this day.
        a. has remains   **b.** has remain   **c.** has remained
    2. Scholars _____ about it for years.
        a. have talked   **b.** have talk   **c.** has talk

B. Write the letter of the words to complete each sentence.

3. Who _____ this giant ring of stones in England?

    a. had arranged   **b.** had arrange   **c.** has arrange

4. The builders of Stonehenge _____ the heavy stones from miles away.

    a. has dragged   **b.** had dragged   **c.** have drag

Practice

A. Write each sentence using the present perfect tense of the verb in parentheses.

5. By now, experts _____ the age of Stonehenge. (determine)

6. It _____ for over three thousand years. (survive)

7. People _____ for years about its builders. (wonder)

8. No one _____ its origins yet, however. (confirm)

B. Write each sentence using the past perfect tense of each verb in parentheses.

9. Workers _____ many years before its completion. (labor)

10. They _____ the stones many miles from the site. (carve)

11. They _____ it without modern tools. (construct)

12. Builders _____ a plan for construction. (develop)

C. Mixed Practice Write each sentence. Write the verb in parentheses. Use the perfect tense indicated.

13. Scholars (offer) many theories. (present perfect)

14. Perhaps it (serve) as an observatory. (past perfect)

15. Many tourists (visit) Stonehenge. (present perfect)

16. They (question) its original purpose. (present perfect)

17. No one (answer) these questions. (present perfect)

18. Now the government (erect) a fence. (present perfect)

19. Before that, people (deface) some stones. (Choose the correct tense.)

20. Stonehenge (amaze) people ever since its discovery. (Choose the correct tense.)

Apply: Work with a Partner

Imagine that it is the year 4000 and you are an archaeologist studying the twentieth century. Work in pairs to write ten sentences about your work. Use perfect tense verbs, and underline them.

Principal Parts of Regular Verbs

A. A verb has four forms, or **principal parts**.

Principal Part	Example	How to Form	Uses
present	look	Use basic present.	Present tense: I look.
present participle	looking	Add <u>ing</u> to present.	Used with forms of *be*: I am looking. You were looking.
past	looked	Add <u>ed</u> to present.	Simple past tense: I looked. She looked.
past participle	looked	Add <u>ed</u> to present.	Perfect tenses (with forms of *have*): I have looked. I had looked.

B. The spelling of some regular verbs changes from the present to the past, the past participle, or the present participle.

Type of Verb	Spelling Change	Examples
verbs ending in <u>e</u>	Drop final e; add <u>ed</u> or <u>ing</u>.	move → moved → moving revolve → revolved → revolving
verbs ending in consonant + <u>y</u>	Change <u>y</u> to <u>i</u> and add <u>ed</u>; or <u>ing</u>.	reply → replied → replying supply → supplied → supplying
regular verbs ending in consonant + vowel + consonant with accented final syllable	Double last consonant; add <u>ed</u> or <u>ing</u>.	scan → scanned → scanning omit → omitted → omitting occur → occurred → occurring

Strategy

If you are not sure about the spelling of a principal part of a verb, check your dictionary.

Check Your Understanding

A. Write the letter that identifies the principal part.
1. Books <u>tell</u> of the discovery of King Tut's tomb.
   a. present   **b.** present participle   **c.** past
2. The king's subjects had <u>constructed</u> a fabulous tomb.
   a. past participle   **b.** past   **c.** present

B. Write the letter of the verb form that completes each sentence.

    3. The people ____ many treasures for it.
       a. supplyed   **b.** supplyd   **c.** supplied
    4. At one time guards had ____ the tomb.
       a. patroled   **b.** patrolled   **c.** patrol

Practice

A. Write each sentence. Underline the principal part of the main verb and name it.

    5. Archaeologists are discovering many sites in Egypt.
    6. Egypt has shared its treasures with the world.
    7. Museums today owe Howard Carter a debt.
    8. In 1922 he unearthed King Tutankhamen's tomb.

B. Write each sentence. Use the indicated principal part of the verb in parentheses.

    9. Tut's subjects (bury) him with great ceremony. (past)
   10. The priests had (control) religious rituals. (past part.)
   11. An English nobleman was (supply) Carter with aid. (present part.)
   12. Today some archaeologists are (commit) much of their time to the search for other tombs. (present part.)

C. Mixed Practice Write each sentence. Use the correct form of the verb in parentheses. Write the name of the principal part you use.

   13. King Tut's treasures still ____ viewers. (amaze)
   14. Carter never had ____ his persistence. (regret)
   15. Tons of rubble were ____ his progress. (delay)
   16. Carter had ____ into the tomb. (crawl)
   17. His partner ____, "Can you see anything?" (call)
   18. Carter ____, "Yes, wonderful things." (answer)
   19. Researchers are still ____ treasures. (uncover)
   20. Many people have ____ and ____ Tut's treasures. (visit)(enjoy)

Apply: Learning Log

Write an entry in your learning log about the part of this lesson that you found most difficult. Then write some suggestions to help you understand it.

Principal Parts of Irregular Verbs

An **irregular verb** is a verb that does not form the past tense and past participle by adding *ed*.

A. The chart shows the past forms of some irregular verbs.

Verb	Past		Verb	Past
become	became		make	made
bring	brought		mean	meant
come	came		read	read
find	found		run	ran
keep	kept		spread	spread
let	let		tell	told

B. The past participles of the same irregular verbs are shown in this chart.

Verb	Past Participle			Verb	Past Participle	
become	(have, has, had)	become		make	(have, has, had)	made
bring	(have, has, had)	brought		mean	(have, has, had)	meant
come	(have, has, had)	come		read	(have, has, had)	read
find	(have, has, had)	found		run	(have, has, had)	run
keep	(have, has, had)	kept		spread	(have, has, had)	spread
let	(have, has, had)	let		tell	(have, has, had)	told

Strategy

There are no rules for forming the principal parts of irregular verbs. The best strategy is to remember the forms of each verb. If you are unsure how to spell an irregular verb, check your dictionary.

Check Your Understanding

A. Write the letter of the correct principal part that completes each sentence.

1. A forager bee ____ back from a flower bed.
   a. came **b.** come **c.** comed **d.** camed
2. News of a food source ____ through the hive.
   a. spreaded **b.** spread **c.** spreaden **d.** spreat

B. Write the letter of the correct principal part that completes each sentence.

   3. Somehow the forager bee had ____ the others.
     a. telled   **b.** tell   **c.** tells   **d.** told
   4. The bee had ____ a large food source.
     a. finds   **b.** find   **c.** found   **d.** founded

Practice

A. Write each sentence. Use the correct past form of the verb in parentheses.

   5. The other bees ____ it into the hive. (let)
   6. The forager bee ____ in a circle. (run)
   7. The "dance" ____ other bees the flower's location. (tell)
   8. The other bees ____ the dancer's movements. (read)

B. Write each sentence. Use the correct past participle of the verb in parentheses.

   9. The dance's shape and speed had ____ something. (mean)
   10. The hive had ____ very busy. (become)
   11. The others had ____ the food source. (find)
   12. They have now ____ nectar back to the hive. (bring)

C. Mixed Practice Write each sentence. Use the correct past or past participle form of the verb in parentheses.

   13. Karl von Frisch ____ many studies of honeybees. (make)
   14. He ____ records of the bees' movements. (keep)
   15. The bees ____ his life's work. (become)
   16. He had also ____ other studies of honeybees. (read)
   17. Von Frisch's work has ____ him fame. (bring)
   18. His ideas have ____ around the world. (spread)
   19. More than once his bees had ____ him. (sting)
   20. Von Frisch ____ a Nobel Prize for his work. (win)

Apply: Work with a Group

Look at the principal parts of the twelve verbs given in this lesson. What patterns can you see in how these parts are formed? As a group, find other verbs that fit these patterns. Compare your patterns and the verbs you found to those of other groups.

More Irregular Verbs

A. This chart shows some more irregular verbs. Notice that the past participles of these verbs end in *n* or *en*.

Verb	Past
be	was, were
choose	chose
eat	ate
give	gave
grow	grew
hide	hid
see	saw
speak	spoke
take	took
write	wrote

Verb	Past Participle	
be	(have, has, had)	been
choose	(have, has, had)	chosen
eat	(have, has, had)	eaten
give	(have, has, had)	given
grow	(have, has, had)	grown
hide	(have, has, had)	hidden
see	(have, has, had)	seen
speak	(have, has, had)	spoken
take	(have, has, had)	taken
write	(have, has, had)	written

B. Many people have trouble with three particular pairs of verbs: *lie* and *lay*, *rise* and *raise*, and *sit* and *set*. This chart shows the meanings and principal parts of these verbs:

Verb and Meaning	Past	Past Participle	
lie (to put oneself or to be in a lying position)	lay	(have, has, had)	lain
lay (to put or place something)	laid	(have, has, had)	laid
rise (to go up or to get up)	rose	(have, has, had)	risen
raise (to move something upward)	raised	(have, has, had)	raised
sit (to put oneself or to be in a sitting position)	sat	(have, has, had)	sat
set (to put or place something)	set	(have, has, had)	set

Strategy

Remember that many irregular verbs that end in *en* or *n* are past participles. They require a form of *have* as a helping verb.

Check Your Understanding

A. Write the letter of the correct past or past participle of the verb to complete each sentence.

    1. People have _____ many books about Egypt's pyramids.
        a. wrote **b.** writen **c.** written **d.** writtn

    2. The pyramids _____ tombs for Egyptian pharaohs.
        a. were **b.** be **c.** been **d.** is

B. Write the letter of the correct principal part of the verb that completes each sentence.

    3. The Egyptians ____ kings' treasures in the pyramids.
        a. sit   **b.** set   **c.** sat
    4. They had ____ these temples in the desert.
        a. rose   **b.** raised   **c.** risen

Practice

A. Write each sentence with the correct past or past participle form of the verb in parentheses.

    5. The Egyptians had ____ treasures in vaults. (hide)
    6. In their view, kings ____ food in the afterlife. (eat)
    7. Scribes ____ messages to the king's loved ones. (write)
    8. The first pyramid had ____ shape by 2500 B.C. (take)

B. Write each sentence. Choose the correct verb in parentheses.

    9. Many workers ____ giant stones into place. (sat, set)
   10. Machines ____ up the stones. (rose, raised)
   11. They had ____ the stones with much human toil. (lain, laid)
   12. Sand dunes have ____ around the tomb. (risen, raised)

C. Mixed Practice Write each sentence with the correct past or present participle of the verb in parentheses.

   13. Statues have ____ for centuries at Abu Simbel. (sat, set)
   14. Pharaohs have ____ in pyramids now empty. (lain, laid)
   15. Egypt's ancient name had ____ the word for *black*. (was, been)
   16. Egypt's crops ____ in black silt. (grew, grown)
   17. Every year the Nile ____ with the silt. (rose, raised)
   18. Planners ____ sites near the river. (chose, chosen)
   19. Egyptians have always ____ food made from crops grown near the Nile. (ate, eaten)
   20. The pyramids have, in a way, ____ from the Nile. (risen, raised)

Apply: Test a Partner

    Write a list of 10 irregular verbs not given in this lesson, and exchange papers with a classmate. List the principal parts of your classmate's verbs. Then exchange papers again, and use a dictionary to check your classmate's work.

141

Prefixes and Suffixes

A **base word** is a word to which other word parts are added. A **prefix** is a word part added to the beginning of a base word. A **suffix** is a word part added to the end of a base word.

A. Adding a prefix to a base word changes the word's meaning. The new word has the meaning of the two parts. For example, *pre-* means "before," and *precook* means "cook beforehand."

Prefix	Meaning	Examples
extra-	beyond; more than	extracurricular
im-, in-	not	impolite, incorrect
mis-	wrong; badly	misspell
non-, dis-	not; opposite of	nonfiction, dislike
over-	above; more than	overhead
pre-	before	prearrange

B. Adding a suffix also changes the meaning of a base word. For example, *loudness* is the "state of being loud."

Suffix	Meaning	Examples
-ness	state of being	hardness
-ment	act of	enjoyment
-ly	in a ____ way	loudly
-y, -ful	full of	sunny, hopeful
-able, -ible	able to be	readable, resistible
-less	without	careless

Strategy

You can use word parts to find the meaning of an unfamiliar word. Put together the meanings of the base word and the prefix or suffix to find the meaning of the new word.

Check Your Understanding

A. Write the letter of the word that has a prefix.
   1. Many early explorers used inaccurate maps.
      a. Many   **b.** used   **c.** inaccurate
   2. They had many extraordinary adventures.
      a. many   **b.** extraordinary   **c.** adventures

B. Write the letter of the word that has a suffix.

    3. They hastened the advancement of Western culture.

        a. They   **b.** advancement   **c.** culture

    4. The explorers saw many colorful sights.

        a. many   **b.** colorful   **c.** sights

Practice

A. Write each sentence. Underline the word that contains a prefix shown in the chart on page 142. Write the meaning of the word.

    5. Many explorers were discontented with Europe.

    6. Some explorers overreached their abilities.

    7. Many stories about the New World were nonsense.

    8. Settlers became impatient for new lands.

B. Write each sentence. Underline the word that contains a suffix shown in the chart on page 142. Write the meaning of the word.

    9. Explorers met fearless people in the New World.

    10. Many people rapidly settled along the rivers and coasts.

    11. Their toughness helped them build a new society.

    12. They survived hot summers and icy winters.

C. Mixed Practice Rewrite each sentence. Replace the words in parentheses with a word that has a prefix or suffix.

    13. Explorers' discoveries sped the (act of developing) of the New World.

    14. Their fears (opposite of appeared) in the new land.

    15. The new land had fossils from (before historic) times.

    16. Our (state of being fond) for this land remains.

    17. (Wrong understandings) caused disputes over territory.

    18. Settlers (in a quick way) grabbed the best farmland.

    19. Successful settlers lived (in a way full of care).

    20. The marvels of America were (not able to be described).

Apply: Work with a Partner

Choose a passage from a reading selection that contains words with prefixes or suffixes from this lesson. List these words, and exchange lists with a partner. Write the meaning of each word by breaking it into its base word and prefix or suffix. Use a dictionary if necessary.

Language in Action

Reading a Bus Schedule

Bus schedules are useful. They can be confusing because they contain a lot of information in a limited amount of space. Look at the example, and then read the explanation that follows.

Hansom	Carteret		Lessing		Thalia		Plattsburg
8:10	8:17	8:19	9:37	9:47	10:05	10:07	10:43
8:35	→		9:45	9:55	→		10:47
10:00	10:07	10:09	11:27	11:37	11:55	11:57	**12:33**
12:05	**12:12**	**12:14**	**1:32**	**1:42**	**2:00**	**2:02**	**2:38**
3:10	**3:17**	**3:19**	**4:37**	**4:47**	**5:05**	**5:08**	**5:52**
5:05	**5:12**	**5:14**	**6:32**	**6:42**	**7:00**	**7:02**	**7:39**
5:30	→		**6:40**	**6:50**	→		**7:35**
7:05	**7:12**	**7:14**	**8:32**	**8:42**	**9:00**	**9:02**	**9:38**
9:05	**9:12**	**9:14**	**10:32**	**10:42**	**11:00**	**11:02**	**11:38**
11:05	**11:12**	**11:14**	12:32	12:42	1:00	1:02	1:38

☐ means departure ☐ means arrival → denotes express Times in **dark type** are P.M.

- ◆ Each bus is listed separately in a row. The schedule should be read from left to right. Each entry in the first vertical row shows when the bus first departs. Then the schedule shows when the bus makes stops along the way. The last entry in each horizontal row shows when the bus arrives at its final destination. The names listed at the top of the columns are the places where the bus goes.
- ◆ Most schedules, like the example, list two times for each stop. The first time shows when the bus arrives. The second time shows when it leaves.
- ◆ Does the bus leave in the a.m. or p.m.? Most schedules indicate a.m. or p.m. in dark type or shading.
- ◆ Note the stops made by express buses. Express buses don't stop at every place. By skipping stops, they arrive at their final destination sooner than local buses.

Practice

On a separate sheet of paper, answer the following questions based on the bus schedule.

1. When does the first bus leave Hansom for Plattsburgh?
2. Does the 8:35 a.m. bus stop in Thalia?
3. If you leave Hansom at 8:35 a.m., when will you arrive in Plattsburg?
4. You live in Hansom and are going to meet your grandmother for lunch in Lessing. You have to be there by 11:45 a.m. What time does the last bus that you can take leave Hansom?
5. If you want to be in Thalia by 7:15 p.m., which bus should you take from Carteret?
6. If you leave Hansom on the 5:30 p.m. bus, when should you arrive in Plattsburg?
7. You are going to the movies in Lessing. You have to be home in Thalia by 9:30 p.m. When do you have to leave Lessing?
8. You just finished doing your homework with your friend Kim at her house in Hansom. It's 5:15 p.m. What is the time of the earliest bus you can take to Carteret?
9. When does the last bus leave Hansom for Plattsburgh?
10. You live in Thalia and need to get to Plattsburg. It is 7:20 p.m. What is the next bus you can take?
11. You are waiting in Lessing for friends who caught the 10:09 a.m. bus from Carteret. What time will you meet their bus?
12. You are traveling from Lessing to Thalia but cannot leave before 8:30 p.m. What is the earliest time you can arrive in Thalia?
13. Of all the buses that leave Hansom, which one arrives in Plattsburg in the shortest amount of time?
14. Which bus from Hansom takes the longest time to reach Plattsburg?

Apply

Make up a bus schedule. Include some of the towns in your area. Exchange bus schedules with a partner. Ask your partner questions about your bus route. Then answer questions about your partner's bus route.

Words from French

Everyone who speaks English speaks a little bit of French, too. Even before you went to school, you knew what a crayon was. Did you know that *crayon* (kre yä') was the French word for pencil?

Many other English words are, in fact, French words whose meanings have changed a little bit.

Reveiller (re ve ye') means *to wake up* in French. In English, *reveille* is the tune played by a bugler to awaken people in the morning. *Encore* (ä kôr') is the French word for *again*. In the United States, we shout *encore* after a concert when we want the performer to sing again. No one ever shouted "encore" after reveille.

Boise is the capital of Idaho. *Boisé* (bwa ze') means "wooded" in French. When French trappers first went there, they were impressed by all the trees.

Many cities in the United States end in the suffix *-ville*. There is Jacksonville, Greenville, Amityville, and others. *Ville* (vil) is the French word for city.

If you visit Jacksonville or Boise, you may bring back a souvenir. You may know that a souvenir is an object you keep to help you remember a place you visited. Did you know that *souvenir* (sùv nēr') means "to remember" in French?

Activity

Rewrite these sentences. Complete each one with a word from the box.

coupon	crochet	parachute	rouge

1. *Chuter* means "to fall" in French. A _____ is used to fall from the sky.
2. In English, _____ is red or pink makeup. In French, it simply means "red."
3. You cut a _____ out of a magazine or a newspaper. It comes from the French verb *couper*, which means "to cut."
4. The French word for *hook*—_____—is the English word for making woolen items by using a long, hooked needle.

UNIT REVIEW

Book Reports (page 107)

1. List at least three characteristics of a book report.

Finding a Book in the Library (pages 110–111)

Answer each question below by writing which card (*subject, title,* or *author*) you would look up to find the needed information.

2. Who wrote *A Tale of Two Cities*?

3. What books did Robert Louis Stevenson write?

4. What nonfiction books have been written about Mark Twain?

Supporting an Opinion with Facts (pages 114–115)

Write each of the following statements. Next to the statement, write whether it is an opinion or a fact.

5. The best adventure story I ever read was *Robinson Crusoe.*

6. *Robinson Crusoe* tells the adventures of a shipwrecked sailor.

7. *The Swiss Family Robinson* is another adventure you'll enjoy.

8. Johann David Wyss and his two sons wrote *The Swiss Family Robinson.*

Combining Sentences (pages 118–119)

Combine each pair of sentences. Make a single sentence of each pair by using the words *and, but,* or *or.*

9. Stuart and Sandra loved adventure. They never expected to be stranded on a magic island.

10. Stuart got lost in a giant mushroom grove. Sandra had to find him.

11. Will the twins be rescued? Will they live on the island forever?

Punctuating Titles (pages 120–121)

Write each sentence below, adding the correct capitalization and punctuation.

12. I read the magazine American Heritage regularly.

13. I enjoyed the article Citizen Ford very much.

14. A good book is Inventions that Made history by Daniel C. Cooke.

15. Have you ever read a short story called The Rocking-Horse Winner ?

16. I heard the song Happy Birthday sung in Japanese.

17. The only newspaper I read is the Joietteville Gazette.

18. The second chapter in this book is entitled Childhood Days.

Action Verbs (pages 126–127)

Write each sentence. Underline each action verb.

19. The forces of nature possess incredible power.

20. Earthquakes shake buildings apart.

21. Residents of some cities await the next quake.

22. Scientists observe patterns in the earth.

23. They predict future earthquakes for many areas.

Linking Verbs (pages 128–129)

Write each sentence. Underline each linking verb.

24. A thesaurus is a useful reference source.

25. Some words seem more appropriate than others at certain times.

26. The thesaurus remains the best source for synonyms and antonyms.

27. Some writers feel more confident with a thesaurus.

28. Thesauruses are dictionaries of synonyms.

Main and Helping Verbs (pages 130–131)

Write each sentence. Underline each helping verb once and each main verb twice.

29. The number of grizzly bears is dwindling.

30. There might be as few as 600 in the 48 continental states.

31. Grizzlies were living here long before Europeans.

32. The grizzly may someday become extinct.

33. Will we protect the grizzly's habitat?

Present, Past, and Future Tenses (pages 132–133)

Write each sentence using the tense of the verb indicated.

34. Almost 150 million people (live) in Brazil. (present)

35. Millions (settle) its western frontier. (past)

36. The region near Turiacu (produce) cotton. (present)

37. This nation (become) a world power. (future)

38. Native Americans once (inhabit) this area. (past)

Perfect Tenses (pages 134–135)

Write each sentence using the correct tense of the verb indicated.

39. Joyce (purchase) a new home recently. (present perfect)

40. Some of us (visit) her there already. (present perfect)

41. She (look) at many houses before today. (past perfect)

42. Many friends (help) her with her earlier decisions. (past perfect)

43. She (furnish) two of the rooms already. (present perfect)

Principal Parts of Regular Verbs (pages 136–137)

Write each sentence using the correct form of the verb in parentheses. Write the name of the principal part you use.

44. Robert Frost's poetry still (inspire) people.

45. Many students are (study) the rhythmic verses.

46. At one time, Frost had (live) as a simple Vermont farmer.

47. Universities (award) him honorary degrees.

48. His work (remain) dear to Americans.

Principal Parts of Irregular Verbs (pages 138–139)

Write each sentence using the correct past or past participle form of the verb in parentheses.

49. Railroads once (bring) many goods to market.

50. They (run) all across our vast country.

51. New methods of transportation have (become) more popular.

52. Big trucks (mean) less work for trains.

53. Grass and weeds have (spread) over many train tracks.

54. Goods have (find) new ways to markets.

55. New methods of transport have (make) trade easier.

More Irregular Verbs (pages 140–141)

Write each sentence using the correct past or past participle form of each verb in parentheses.

56. The Constitution has ____ us a strong government. (gave, given)

57. This document ____ the government in motion. (sat, set)

58. Many challenges to it have ____. (risen, raised)

59. But it ____ a good foundation for the nation. (lay, laid)

60. Our country has ____ under the Constitution. (grew, grown)

61. This document has ____ of untold value to our country. (was, been)

62. Other countries have ____ the American Constitution for their model. (took, taken)

Prefixes and Suffixes (pages 142–143)

Rewrite each sentence. Replace the words in parentheses with a word that has a prefix or a suffix.

63. Robert Peary was a (without fear) Arctic explorer.

64. He never (guided wrongly) the members of his crew.

65. Peary's expeditions involved (more than ordinary) preparation.

66. The (state of being cold) of the climate was a special concern.

67. His journeys (in a significant way) improved travel to the Arctic.

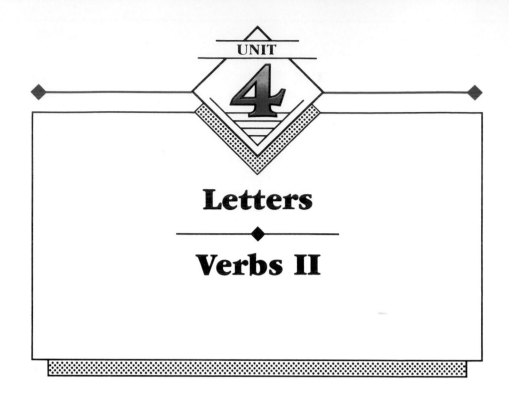

UNIT
4

Letters

◆

Verbs II

What Do You Know?

"I can't wait till the mail comes!"

How often have you thought that? Perhaps you were waiting for a special letter from a close friend. Friendly letters are a marvelous way for people to share good news with each other. You can make your letter as funny, cheerful, and creative as you wish.

Perhaps you have also received business letters in the mail. You may have gotten an offer to join a book club or to buy a new magazine. A business letter is also a way for you to request information, order merchandise, or make a complaint.

Thinking About Letters

What Is a Letter?

A **friendly letter** has these characteristics:

◆ It shares news with a friend or relative.
◆ It is written in casual language.
◆ It has a heading, greeting, body, closing, and signature.

You often write friendly letters just to say "hello." The letter might be a short paragraph or several pages. Either way, it tells your reader that you are thinking of him or her.

A **business letter** has these characteristics:

◆ It requests information, orders merchandise, or makes a complaint.
◆ It is written in formal language.
◆ It has a heading, inside address, greeting, body, closing, and signature.

Business letters are very different from friendly letters. They are brief and to the point. Your purpose is to conduct some official business, such as to order a book or to seek information about a new TV show.

Discussion

1. What special friendly letters have you received lately?
2. What interesting business letters have you written or received in the past?
3. What kinds of letters do you most look forward to getting in the mail?

Reading a Friendly Letter

In the following friendly letter, the composer Wolfgang Amadeus Mozart, age 14 at the time, shares good news with his sister. Note the casual language and friendly tone, beginning with the playful nickname Mozart gives his sister—"Nannerl."

This letter is from a biography of Mozart entitled *Letters to Horseface* by F. N. Monjo.

heading

December 27, 1770

greeting

Dear Old Nannerl—

Everyone applauded my opera!

We had the good luck we hoped we'd have. Papa says it's a success.

On the 26th, when the curtain fell, people shouted "Long live the little composer!" During the performance Signora Bernasconi had to repeat one of her arias— because so many cried out "*Fuora!*" —"Again!" This is something that almost *never* happens at an opening night in Milan.

body

How I wish that you and Mama could have been there to hear it all.

Tickets are selling well in advance, and Papa says we shall certainly have more than twenty performances. The copyist is smiling more broadly than ever.

Papa asked me what I would most like to have as my reward. I said, "Some liver dumplings and sauerkraut— just the way Mama fixes them!" So now Papa is trying to find someone here who knows just how to prepare them.

Tell Mama that I can hardly wait to get into the coach on our return journey to the Alps, and to Austria, and home! I long to see you both, and meanwhile, kisses (times 10,000) for you and Mama.

closing

Your homesick brother,

signature

Wolferl

P.S. Here is a riddle, Nannerl. What is the same on each end, and double in the middle? Answer: the year 1771. *That* is the year when Wolferl will be coming home, to Salzburg.

152

Understanding What You've Read

Answer these questions about Mozart's letter.

1. When was the letter written?
2. What nicknames did Mozart use to refer to himself and to his sister?
3. What good news did Mozart share in his letter?
4. Which parts of the letter sound friendliest and most casual?
5. Imagine Mozart had written to his music teacher instead of his sister. How do you think the contents of the letter might have been different?

Writing Assignment

As you can see, Mozart was a creative composer of music—and letters! Now it is your turn to be a creative composer. In this unit, you will compose two letters—one business letter and one friendly letter. You will start with the business letter.

In the **business letter**, your **audience** will be the company or official you are writing to. Your **purpose** will be to ask for information, to order an item, or to make a complaint.

In the **friendly letter,** your **audience** will be a friend or relative receiving your letter. Your **purpose** will be to share good news about yourself.

Choose Your Purpose

Make a list of five specific purposes you might have for writing a business letter, such as *to ask for information about traveling to another state*. Save your choices for the next lesson.

Planning a Business Letter

Read the following business letter. Notice how the parts differ from a friendly letter and how the language is more formal.

1. heading

2. inside address

3. greeting

4. body

5. closing
6. signature

297 Valley Road
Bronx, New York 17885
December 8, 1988

Lincoln Concert Hall
2188 Broadway
New York, New York 10016

Dear Sir or Madam:

    I would like two balcony seats for the Marvelous Mozart concert on December 28, 1988, at 8:00 p.m. Enclosed is a check for $18.00 for the tickets.
    If the December 28 performance is sold out, please send tickets for the performance either on December 29 or December 30.

Sincerely,

Timothy Berenson

Timothy Berenson

1. The **heading** shows the writer's address and the date of the letter.
2. The **inside address** is the name and address of the person or company receiving the letter.
3. The **greeting** contains either the person's name, the company's name, or *Dear Sir or Madam* followed by a colon.
4. The **body** gives all the necessary information briefly.
5. The **closing** says good-bye and ends with a comma.
6. The **signature** is the writer's full name, written and then printed or typed.

In a business letter, all information must be complete and correct. When ordering clothing, for example, give necessary details such as size, color, material, and catalog number.

You should write a business letter in **formal language.** Formal language is polite and does not include slang.

Practice

Read the business letter below. Then answer the questions that follow it.

---

33 Cherry Lane
August 8

Witmar Record Company
Detroit, Michigan 64456

Dear somebody in charge,

    I ordered a Mozart record from your store, but it arrived in the mail broken. So, what happens now?

Michael

---

1. What information is missing in the heading?
2. What information is missing in the inside address?
3. What is wrong with the wording and punctuation in the greeting?
4. What necessary information is missing in the body?
5. What is wrong with the closing?
6. What parts are missing in the signature?

> What information will the company need in order to meet my request?

Plan Your Business Letter

APPLY STEP BY STEP

    Look back at the list of purposes for a business letter. Choose a purpose that reflects a need of yours: to seek information, to order an item, or to make a complaint. Jot down the name and address of the company you will write to. Also make notes on the necessary information you will include in the body of your letter. Save your work for the next lesson.

Writing a First Draft

Read the first draft of the business letter below. The writer wasn't worried about making it perfect. It will be changed later.

---

79 Cornell Avenue
Ithaca New York 10876
March 20, 1989

Marvelous Music Shop
2500 Alameda Drive
Tucson, Arizona 32907

Dear Marvelous Music Shop,

   My music class would like to order ten of your T-shirts with the cartoon pictures of Mozart on the front. My class would like to order the purple ones. We would like the hand-painted ones. However, we are on a tight budgit. We would like to have them mailed cheaply. And we would like to have them mailed quickly.

   Please send us your order form. Also, send any other useful information that you have. And please send any necessary information, too.

                                        Sincerly:

                                        Virginia Holmes

                                        Virginia Holmes
                                        Class Tresurer

Write Your First Draft

   You may first discuss your ideas with your teacher or a classmate; or you may begin writing without a discussion. In your business letter, be sure to include all necessary information in the heading, inside address, greeting, body, closing, and signature. If you are ordering items, state details such as size, color, and price. If you are making a complaint, be specific about the action you would like to see taken. Save your draft for the next lesson.

Discussing a First Draft

After finishing your letter, look for ways to improve it. One way is to discuss the draft with a partner.

Discussion Strategy

When you are discussing your partner's work, put yourself in his or her shoes. Think of how you would want someone to comment on your work. Try to word your comments the way you would like to hear them.

Use the Content Checklist to discuss with your class the business letter on the previous page.

Content Checklist

✔ Does the letter request information, order merchandise, or make a complaint?

✔ Does the letter have a complete heading, inside address, greeting, closing, and signature?

✔ Does the body of the letter contain all information the receiver will need in order to respond?

✔ Is the letter written in formal language?

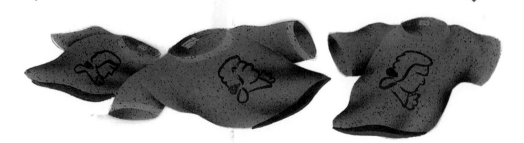

Revise Your First Draft for Content

To the Reader: Exchange letters with a classmate. Read your partner's letter. Imagine you are the person it is written to. Decide what further information, if any, you need in order to respond to the letter. Use the Content Checklist for help. Discuss ways to make the content clearer.

To the Writer: Listen to your partner's suggestions for improvement. Then revise your draft for content. Save your work.

Combining Sentences for Style

    In the letter below, some of the sentences are short and choppy. The writer could improve the draft by combining these sentences.

    One way to combine is to link words that describe the subject. Notice how commas are used to separate the descriptive words in the examples below.

    You can combine the sentences in several ways.

The orchestra is famous. The orchestra is skilled. It is a large orchestra.	The famous, skilled orchestra is large. The orchestra is large, famous, and skilled. The large orchestra is famous and skilled.

    Another way to combine sentences is to link words that describe action.

The audience entered quickly. They entered quietly. They entered respectfully.	The audience entered quickly, quietly, and respectfully.

    Some sentences can be combined by linking words that describe the subject and words that describe the action.

The musician performs. She performs well. The musician is distinguished. She is young.	The distinguished, young musician performs well. The young, distinguished musician performs well.

    This is how the writer combined sentences in the letter.

>   My music class would like to order ten of your *purple, hand-painted* T-shirts with the cartoon pictures of Mozart on the front. ~~My class would like to order the purple ones. We would like the hand-painted ones.~~ However, we are on a tight budgit. We would like to have them mailed cheaply *or* ~~And~~ we would like to have them mailed quickly.

Practice

Combine each set of sentences. Write your new sentence.

1. The music festival was long. It was exciting. The festival was superb.
2. The violinist plays skillfully. She plays melodically. She plays brilliantly.
3. The symphony is complex. It is lovely. It is graceful.
4. The music student practices. He practices faithfully. He is young. The student is serious.
5. The composer writes music. He writes quickly. He is well-known. The composer is busy.

Revising Checklist

✔ Have I included all of the characteristics of a business letter?
✔ Which sentences can be varied? (p. 72)
✔ Can I combine any sentences?

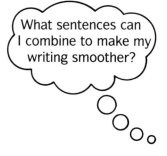

What sentences can I combine to make my writing smoother?

APPLY
STEP BY STEP

Revise Your First Draft for Style

Check for the items on the Revising Checklist. Combine sentences where you can. Make the changes on your draft. Keep your work for the next lesson.

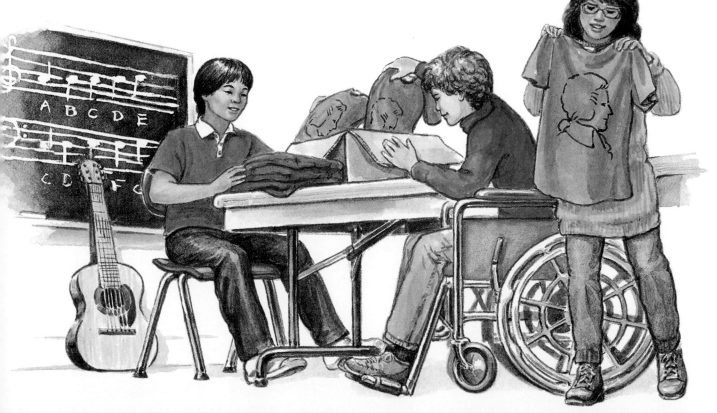

Punctuating a Letter

Here are the rules for capitalizing, punctuating, and abbreviating the different parts of a letter.

Rules	Examples
Capitalize names of companies, streets, cities, and states.	Worldwide Travel Agency 500 Oak Boulevard Cleveland, Ohio
Capitalize the name of the month. Use a comma between the day and the year.	January 6, 1988
Capitalize initials and the first letter of an abbreviation. Use a period after each.	Mr. Samuel L. Cohen 245 E. Broadway
Capitalize both letters of the official postal abbreviation for each state. Do not use a period at the end.	Tulsa OK Newark NJ
Capitalize the first word in the greeting and closing of a letter.	My dear friend Sue, Dear Mr. Lee: Yours truly,
Use a comma after the greeting in a friendly letter. In a business letter, use a colon.	Dear Tom, Dear Sir or Madam:
Use a comma after the closing in any letter.	Very sincerely, Your friend,
Use a comma between the name of a city and a state. Omit the comma when you use a postal abbreviation.	Selma, Alabama Selma AL

Follow this form for addressing an envelope. Use a zip code in each address.

return address —— Virginia Holmes
79 Cornell Ave.
Ithaca NY 10876

receiver's address —— Marvelous Music Shop
2500 Alameda Dr.
Tucson AZ 32907

Practice

Write each item below with correct punctuation and capitalization. Write your answers on a separate sheet of paper.

1. june 6 1988
dear Mary

2. Mister Richard R Kelly
Hampton corporation
711 McDonald avenue
Miami Florida 33127

Dear Mr Kelly

3.

Dr Roberta Wilson
15 W Ninth street 10003
New York, NY

Mister William Cruz
220 east Tremont Rd
New York NY 14230

Proofreading Checklist

✔ Did I indent the first word of each paragraph? (p. 36)
✔ Did I end my sentences with the correct punctuation? (p. 36)
✔ Did I punctuate the heading, inside address, greeting, and closing correctly?
✔ Have I used abbreviations correctly?
✔ Do the subjects and verbs agree?

Proofread Your Draft

Check your letter for correct punctuation and capitalization. Make sure that any abbreviations you used in your letter and on your envelope are correct. Use a dictionary if necessary. Use the Proofreading Checklist to help you correct your draft. Then address an envelope for your letter. Save your work for the next lesson.

State	Abbr.
Alabama	AL
Alaska	AK
Arizona	AZ
Arkansas	AR
California	CA
Colorado	CO
Connecticut	CT
Delaware	DE
District of Columbia	DC
Florida	FL
Georgia	GA
Hawaii	HI
Idaho	ID
Illinois	IL
Indiana	IN
Iowa	IA
Kansas	KS
Kentucky	KY
Louisiana	LA
Maine	ME
Maryland	MD
Massachusetts	MA
Michigan	MI
Minnesota	MN
Mississippi	MS
Missouri	MO
Montana	MT
Nebraska	NE
Nevada	NV
New Hampshire	NH
New Jersey	NJ
New Mexico	NM
New York	NY
North Carolina	NC
North Dakota	ND
Ohio	OH
Oklahoma	OK
Oregon	OR
Pennsylvania	PA
Rhode Island	RI
South Carolina	SC
South Dakota	SD
Tennessee	TN
Texas	TX
Utah	UT
Vermont	VT
Virginia	VA
Washington	WA
West Virginia	WV
Wisconsin	WI
Wyoming	WY

Checking Spelling/Writing a Final Copy ◆

Spelling Strategy

Sometimes a memory hint can help you spell a word. *Example:* Which spelling is correct, *separate* or *seperate?* Use this memory hint: There is *a rat* in sep*a*rate.

Select several words you have misspelled recently. Invent a memory hint to help you spell it correctly.

Here is part of the revised and proofread letter.

Proofreading Marks	
∧	add
⸜	delete
¶	indent
≡	capitalize
/	lowercase
⬭	check spelling
∼	transpose
⋏	comma
⸌⸍	quotation marks
⊙	period
⤻	move

Dear ~~Marvelous Music Shop,~~ *Sir or Madam* :

My music class would like to order ten of your *purple* ∧ *hand-painted* T-shirts with the cartoon pictures of Mozart on the front. ~~My class would like to order the purple ones. We would like the hand-painted ones.~~ However, we are on a tight bud̲git⃝ *budget*. We would like to have them mailed cheaply. ∧ And we would like to have them mailed quickly.

Please send us your order form. Also, send any other useful ∧ *and necessary* information that you have. ~~And please send any necessary information, too.~~

~~Sincerly:~~ *Sincerely* ⋏

Virginia Holmes

Virginia Holmes

Class ⟨Tresurer⟩ *Treasurer*

Check Your Spelling

Use the proofreading marks to correct errors in spelling. Add any misspelled words to your spelling log. Then write a neat, final copy of your letter. Keep your final copy.

Sharing Your Business Letter

Speaking/Listening Strategy

When you are reading aloud, pause for a moment at the end of a paragraph or section to signal to the listener that you will begin a new part. When you are listening to a classmate read, pay attention to those pauses. They can help you understand the material better.

Choosing a Way to Share

After writing a neat, final copy of your business letter, share it with others. You may do this in several ways.

Reading Aloud Read your business letter aloud to classmates. Make the tone of your voice match the purpose of the letter. For example, if you are making a complaint, be businesslike but firm.

Holding a Business Conference Imagine you are the president of the company receiving your business letter. Have a few of your classmates pretend to be your staff. Discuss the purpose of the letter and what you will write in response.

Making a Bulletin Board Display Display your business letter together with your classmates' letters on a bulletin board entitled *The Letterbox*. You may wish to answer some of the letters. Post your answers on the bulletin board as well.

Share Your Business Letter

Choose the way you prefer to share your business letter. Present it and discover your audience's reaction. You may wish to send your completed letter in the mail.

Add to Your Learning Log
- Am I happy with the final draft of my business letter?
- What was the most interesting part of writing my letter?
- In what ways can I improve my skills in writing a business letter?

Writing a Friendly Letter ◆

Read the following friendly letter a student wrote.

heading ——————

23 Harper Drive
Huntsville, Alabama 38385
March 26, 1988

greeting followed by a ——————
comma

Dear Cousin Maybelle,

body ——————

I just returned home from a Marvelous Mozart concert, and it was <u>fabulous</u>! I sat in the sixth row, so there was no problem hearing every note. The conductor was so intense! Every time she waved her baton, I could practically feel a breeze. And the musicians—well, they couldn't have been better. I can still hear the blaring of the trumpets and the sweet sounds of the violins.

I hope you can visit Huntsville soon so we can both go to another Marvelous Mozart concert together.

closing followed by a ——————
comma

Your cousin,

signature ——————

Suzi

Practice

Answer these questions about the letter above.

1. When was the letter written?
2. Who lives at 23 Harper Drive in Huntsville, Maybelle or Suzi?
3. How is the punctuation in the greeting different in this friendly letter than in a business letter?
4. What part of a business letter does not appear in a friendly letter?
5. Why do you think you must sign and then print (or type) your full name in a business letter, while in a friendly letter you sign only your first name?

Write Your Own Friendly Letter

Follow these steps to write your own friendly letter.

Planning
◆ Decide on a friend or relative with whom you would like to share some news. Jot down the person's name.
◆ Think of an amusing, interesting, or unusual experience you had recently. It might be something that happened at school, at home, or in another place.
◆ Make notes on the details that occurred.

Composing
◆ Begin your letter with a heading that includes your address and the date of your letter.
◆ In the greeting, write *Dear* and the name of the person receiving the letter.
◆ In the body of the letter, describe the experience you have chosen. Use casual language and a friendly tone.
◆ End with a closing and your signature.

Revising
◆ Use the Content Checklist to discuss and revise your letter for content.

Proofreading
◆ Check for errors in spelling, punctuation, and grammar.
◆ Write a neat, final copy of your friendly letter.

Presenting
◆ Send the letter to the person to whom it is written.

Content Checklist
✔ Does the letter share news with a friend or relative?
✔ Does it contain the five parts of a friendly letter?
✔ Is the language casual and the tone friendly?

The Literature Connection: Verbs ◆

Can you imagine a story in which nothing happens? It is difficult to try to picture a story of that sort because most good writing involves action. Action words, or **verbs,** are important. Different verbs help us picture different actions in a story.

Verbs do more than merely indicate the action in a story. The *tense* of a verb tells you when the action happens. *Mr. Johnson swam the English Channel* tells you an action has been completed; *Mr. Johnson will swim the English Channel* indicates that this accomplishment is still in the planning stage. A change in tense makes a big difference in meaning.

Verbs can also indicate differences between very similar actions. The poem below tells about different kinds of travel. Notice how the verbs help you picture each one clearly.

There Are So Many Ways of Going Places
by
Leslie Thompson

Big yellow trolley limbers along,
Long black subway sings an under song,
Airplanes swoop and flash in the sky,
Noisy old elevated goes rocketing by,
Boats across the river—back and forth they go,
Big boats and little boats, fast boats and slow.
Trains puff and thunder; their engines have a headlight;
They have a special kind of car where you can sleep all night.
Tall fat buses on the Avenue,
They will stop for anyone—even—just—you.
All kinds of autos rush down the street.
And then there are always—your own two feet.

Discussion

1. Which words describe actions that happen in the poem?
2. Which verbs sound like the noises the planes, trains, and cars make?
3. What other verbs might describe the actions of a bus, car, plane, and boat?

166

The Writing Connection: Verbs

In your own writing, your choice of verbs can be very important in creating images. Two verbs, even those that have similar meanings, can create different pictures in a reader's imagination. Read the following:

> I am a bicycle. I race and speed through the city.
> Sometimes I coast and ramble through the countryside.

Do you see the difference verbs can make in the meaning of a sentence? The verbs *race* and *speed* create an image that is different from the image created by *coast* and *ramble;* yet, all of these verbs refer to actions related to bicycling. In your own writing, use verbs in creative and original ways to create a desired image.

Activity

Imagine that you are one of the pairs of feet pictured above. Use a variety of verbs to describe how you would travel under different conditions. Examples are shown below:

> I am a pair of feet. I stroll along on a sunny day.
> Sometimes I scurry to the bus stop to catch the bus.

Imagine that you are other forms of transportation, such as a hot air balloon, a helicopter, and a truck. For each form of transportation you choose, write sentences describing different actions. Use the form below.

> I am a ____. I ____.
> Sometimes I ____.

Direct Objects

A **direct object** is a noun or a pronoun that follows an action verb in a sentence and receives the action of the verb. The direct object answers the question *whom?* or *what?* after the verb.

A. Here is a way to find the direct object of a sentence. First, find the action verb and the subject of the sentence. Then, ask this question: What does (the subject) (action verb)?

Sentence	Question to Ask	Direct Object
Some plants eat insects.	What do some plants eat?	insects
The leaves trap them.	What do the leaves trap?	them
Special juices dissolve the bugs.	What do special juices dissolve?	bugs
The pitcher plant drowns insects.	What does the pitcher plant drown?	insects

B. The word that is the direct object of a sentence may not be so easy to identify. There may be many words after the verb. The direct object is the one noun or pronoun that answers the question *whom?* or *what?*

Sentence	Question to Ask	Direct Object
Venus's-flytrap captures prey in its leaves.	What does the flytrap capture?	prey
The plant attracts it with a sweet scent.	What does the plant attract?	it

Strategy

An action verb does not always have a direct object. Try the test question: What (or Whom) does (subject) (action verb)? Remember that a direct object must be a noun or a pronoun.

The sundew plant sprouts sticky hairs. (*noun*—direct object)

The sundew plant sprouts quickly. (*adverb*—not a direct object)

Check Your Understanding

A. Write the letter of the direct object of each sentence.
   1. Some plants trap insects.
      a. plants   **b.** trap   **c.** insects
   2. Botanists study plants.
      a. Botanists   **b.** study   **c.** plants

B. Write the letter of the direct object of each sentence.

    3. These plants absorb important food from the insects.

       a. plants   **b.** food   **c.** insects

    4. Other plants produce nourishment on their own.

       a. produce   **b.** nourishment   **c.** own

Practice

A. Write each sentence, and underline the direct object. Write the question you would ask to find the direct object.

    5. Some of these plants produce an odor.

    6. The leaves contain triggers.

    7. Small insects touch them.

    8. The sticky leaves trap the insects.

B. Follow the directions for Practice A.

    9. These plants get necessary nitrogen from insects.

    10. They develop special organs for this activity.

    11. The plant lays a clever trap for prey.

    12. The trap captures an unwary insect.

C. Mixed Practice Write each sentence, and underline the direct object. Write the question you would ask to find the direct object.

    13. Venus's-flytrap grows leaves with hinges.

    14. Delicate hairs detect the touch of an insect on a leaf.

    15. The leaf captures it.

    16. The plant secretes certain digestive juices.

    17. The juices dissolve the insect.

    18. These plants absorb nitrogen from the insect.

    19. They use chemicals and minerals for growth.

    20. Other plants get nitrogen and oxygen from the environment.

Apply: Work with a Group

Write about your own marvelous imaginary plant by filling in the blanks below. Compare sentences with those of other groups.

Our (subject) eats (direct object) for dinner. It also (action verb) (direct object). It grows (direct object) on its leaves. These (subject) (action verb) (direct object). At night it quickly (action verb) little (direct object).

Indirect Objects

An **indirect object** is a noun or a pronoun that follows an action verb and tells *to whom* or *for whom* the action is done. An indirect object can appear only in a sentence that has a direct object.

A. To find the indirect object, follow two steps. First, find the direct object. Then, ask *to whom* or *for whom* the action is done. For example:

Sentence: John Roebling built New Yorkers the Brooklyn Bridge.

To Find:	Ask:	Answer:
direct object	What did (subject) (action verb)? Example: What did John Roebling build?	Brooklyn Bridge
indirect object	To whom or for whom (was the action done)? Example: For whom did he build the bridge?	New Yorkers

B. When trying to find direct and indirect objects, don't be confused by other words that describe them, such as adjectives and adverbs.

Roebling built grateful <u>New Yorkers</u> a beautiful <u>bridge</u>.
        indirect object   direct object

     Looking for indirect objects can be confusing. If the word that tells *to whom* or *for whom* already has *to* or *for* in front of it, the word is not an indirect object.

     Roebling built a bridge <u>for</u> <u>New Yorkers</u>.

New Yorkers is not an indirect object because *for* comes in front of it.

Strategy

     When looking for the indirect object of a sentence, remember to find the direct object first. The indirect object is always found between the action verb and the direct object.

Check Your Understanding

A. Write the letter of the indirect object of each sentence.
   1. Roebling showed the officials a plan.
     a. Roebling   **b.** officials   **c.** plan
   2. He told the committee his ideas.
     a. He   **b.** committee   **c.** ideas

B. Write the letter of the indirect object of each sentence.

    3. He offered the busy city a link between boroughs.

        a. city   **b.** link   **c.** no indirect object

    4. He gave a true masterpiece to the city.

        a. masterpiece   **b.** city   **c.** no indirect object

Practice

A. Write each sentence. Underline the direct object once and the indirect object twice.

    5. New York State awarded Roebling the contract.

    6. He built travelers a crossing.

    7. The bridge offered workers opportunities.

    8. Roebling left New Yorkers a landmark.

B. Write each sentence. Underline the direct object once and the indirect object twice. If there is no indirect object, write none.

    9. They gave the contract to his son after Roebling's death.

    10. Underwater work can give some divers a disease.

    11. This illness brought great pain to the young Roebling.

    12. It caused him painful backaches.

C. Mixed Practice Write each sentence. Underline the direct object once and the indirect object twice. If there is no indirect object, write none.

    13. Roebling then taught his wife the job of an engineer.

    14. Emily Roebling carried new instructions for the workers.

    15. The workers brought questions for her each day.

    16. At night she told Roebling the worst problems of the day.

    17. The workers gave Emily Roebling their support.

    18. She brought professionalism to her job.

    19. The completion of the bridge gave officials and commuters a cause for celebration.

    20. The bridge brought the Roeblings great praise and acclaim.

Apply: Learning Log

What part of this lesson was most difficult for you? Write a plan in your learning log that will help you understand and remember that part of the lesson.

Transitive and Intransitive Verbs ◆

A. Verbs can be classified as transitive or intransitive.

A **transitive verb** is a verb that is followed by a direct object.

> Researchers <u>study</u> magnificent blue whales.
> Movie crews <u>film</u> them.
> Whales <u>swallow</u> prey whole.

An **intransitive verb** is a verb that is not followed by a direct object.

> All whales <u>swim</u>.   Scientists of all types <u>experiment</u>.

Many verbs can be either transitive or intransitive.

> Transitive: Scientists <u>observe</u> whales in the oceans.
> Intransitive: Scientists <u>observe</u>.

B. When identifying a transitive verb, do not be confused by words other than the direct object that follow the verb.

> Whales swim gracefully.
> (*Gracefully* is not a noun or a pronoun, and so it is not a direct object. Therefore, *swim* is intransitive.)

> The boat followed behind the whale.
> (*Whale* is a noun, but it is not a direct object. It does not answer the question *whom*? or *what*? after the verb. Therefore, *followed* is intransitive.)

Strategy

Here is a way to remember the difference between transitive and intransitive verbs. The word part *trans-* means "across." Verbs that carry an action across to the direct object are transitive. The word part *in-* means "not." Verbs that do not carry an action to a direct object are intransitive.

Check Your Understanding

A. Write the letter of the term that identifies each verb.
  1. People in many parts of the world <u>hunted</u> whales.
    a. transitive verb   **b.** intransitive verb
  2. Young whales in the wild often <u>play</u>.
    a. transitive verb   **b.** intransitive verb

B. Write the letter of the term that identifies each verb.

   3. Scientists <u>observe</u> their playful behavior.
      a. transitive verb   **b.** intransitive verb

   4. Whales sometimes <u>swim</u> near the observers' boats.
      a. transitive verb   **b.** intransitive verb

Practice

A. Write each sentence. If there is a direct object, underline it. If there is no direct object, write none.

   5. All members of the whale species breathe air.
   6. The largest and smallest of whales dive.
   7. The enormous animals just disappear.
   8. A layer of blubber controls their temperature.

B. Write each sentence. Underline the verb, and write whether it is transitive or intransitive.

   9. Whales sleep near the water's surface.
   10. Huge whales eat tiny sea creatures.
   11. Special plates filter them from the seawater.
   12. Whales breathe at the surface of the ocean.

C. Mixed Practice Write each sentence. Underline the verb once, and write whether it is transitive or intransitive. If there is a direct object, underline it twice.

   13. Whales swim almost continuously.
   14. These friendly creatures travel widely.
   15. Many countries protect them.
   16. They produce strange sounds underwater.
   17. These sounds carry for many miles.
   18. Scientists record these sounds with sensitive equipment.
   19. They hear the songs and music of the whales.
   20. Whales sing for communication and socialization.

Apply: Journal

In your journal, write six sentences about whales or another animal that you are interested in. Write three sentences with transitive verbs and three sentences with intransitive verbs. Underline and label each of the six verbs.

173

Predicate Nouns and Adjectives

A linking verb joins the subject of a sentence with a predicate noun or a predicate adjective. Common linking verbs include:

Forms of *be*	Sense Verbs	Others
am, are, is, was, were verb phrases ending in *be, been, being*	look, feel, taste, smell, sound	seem, resemble, appear, become

A. A **predicate noun** is a noun that follows a linking verb in a sentence and identifies the subject of the sentence. To find a predicate noun, ask: *Who or what is (subject)?*

> Mount Rushmore Memorial is a sculpture by Gutzon Borglum.
>> (*Sculpture* identifies the subject, *Mount Rushmore Memorial.* Ask: Who or what is Mount Rushmore Memorial?→sculpture)

B. A **predicate adjective** is an adjective that follows a linking verb and describes the subject of the sentence. To find a predicate adjective, ask: *What is (subject) like?*

> Gutzon Borglum was persistent in his work.
>> (The adjective *persistent* describes the subject, *Borglum.* Ask: What was Gutzon Borglum like? → persistent)

Strategy

If you are not sure whether a noun that follows a linking verb is a predicate noun, insert it in the following sentence with the subject: (Subject) is a ____. If the sentence makes sense, the noun is a predicate noun.

Check Your Understanding

A. Write the letter of the question you would ask to find the predicate noun.
1. Gutzon Borglum (gut′sun bär′glum) was the son of Danish parents.
   a. Who or what was Borglum?
   b. What were Borglum's parents?
2. Rushmore Memorial is the world's largest sculpture.
   a. What is the largest sculpture?
   b. What is Rushmore?

B. Write the letter of the question you would ask to find the predicate adjective.
  3. The sight is impressive.
    a. What is the sight like?   **b.** What is the sight?
  4. The faces are enormous.
    a. What are enormous?   **b.** What are the faces like?

Practice

A. Write the question you would ask to find the predicate noun. Write each sentence, and underline the predicate noun.
  5. Mount Rushmore is a national memorial.
  6. It is a huge carving on a granite cliff.
  7. Borglum was a sculptor from Idaho.
  8. Presidents of the United States were his heroes.

B. Write each sentence. Underline the predicate adjective, and write the question you would ask to find it.
  9. The images of the presidents appear lifelike.
  10. Many viewers of Mount Rushmore feel patriotic.
  11. The four presidents look realistic.
  12. The expressions on their faces are proud.

C. Mixed Practice Write the question you would ask to find the predicate noun or predicate adjective. Write each sentence. Underline the predicate noun or adjective, and tell which it is.
  13. The sculpture is a memorial to four great Americans.
  14. One of them is George Washington.
  15. Another one is Thomas Jefferson.
  16. The figures look mysterious under nighttime illumination.
  17. The sculpture is part of the National Park System.
  18. The presidents' faces are very dignified.
  19. They look strong and proud of their heritage.
  20. Its most impressive features are its dignity and size.

Apply: Test a Partner

Write five sentences about a monument you know about. Use a predicate noun or a predicate adjective in each sentence. Exchange papers with a classmate. Underline the predicate nouns and adjectives in the sentences. Then exchange papers again, and correct your partner's work.

Word Roots

A **root** is a word part that can be combined with prefixes, suffixes, and other parts to form words.

A. A word root can appear at the beginning, the middle, or the end of a word. Many word roots take their meanings from Latin or Greek. Study the roots in the chart below.

Root	Meaning	Example
astro	star or space	astronomy
centi	one hundred or hundredth	centigrade
kilo	one thousand	kilowatt
logy	science or study of	geology
meter	instrument for measuring	speedometer
micro	small	microcomputer
multi	many	multivitamin
photo	light	photograph
port	carry	transport
psycho	of the mind	psychologist
scope	instrument for viewing	microscope

B. Knowing what a root means can help you understand the words that contain the root. For example, knowing the meaning of the word parts *psycho-* and *-logy* can help you understand the word *psychology*.

Strategy

The meanings of roots can help you figure out new words, but remember that some roots have more than one meaning. For example, look up the roots *-meter* and *micro-* in a dictionary, and find their meanings in the words *kilometer* and *microphone*.

Check Your Understanding

A. Write the letter of the word that contains a root from the chart.
1. Rainbows are multicolored displays of reflected light.
   a. Rainbows **b.** multicolored **c.** displays
2. Photographers take beautiful pictures of these marvels.
   a. Photographers **b.** beautiful **c.** pictures

B. Write the letter of the meaning of the underlined root.

    3. The tiny <u>centi</u>pede has numerous pairs of legs.

        a. one hundred   **b.** small   **c.** one thousand

    4. Each tiny leg looks almost <u>micro</u>scopic.

        a. many   **b.** light   **c.** small

Practice

A. Write each sentence. Underline the word that contains a root from the chart. Underline the root twice, and write its meaning.

    5. Galileo viewed the moon with a simple telescope.

    6. Modern astronomers use more advanced equipment.

    7. Much of this equipment is small and portable.

    8. The use of multipurpose equipment has advanced the science.

B. Write the answer to each question.

    9. If *trans-* means "across," what does *transport* mean?

    10. If *bio-* means "life," what does *biology* mean?

    11. If *ex-* means "out," what does *export* mean?

    12. If *path-* means "disease," what does *pathology* mean?

C. Mixed Practice Complete each definition with a word from the box.

astrology	photometer	microfilm	multinational
multistory	kilogram	micrometer	microscope

    13. A _____ building has many floors.

    14. A _____ equals one thousand grams.

    15. A _____ is an instrument for measuring small items.

    16. _____ was originally the study of stars and space.

    17. A _____ is an instrument for viewing small objects.

    18. A _____ is an instrument for measuring light.

    19. _____ is film on which the image is very small.

    20. A _____ company operates in many nations.

Apply: Exploring Language

    Choose four roots from the chart, and make a list of all the words you can think of that contain those roots. Then use a dictionary to check the spellings and definitions of your words. Compare your list with those of your classmates.

Language in Action

Filling Out Forms

Let's say that you want to receive the *Young World* newspaper at home. You ask your teacher how to subscribe to the newspaper. He hands you a piece of paper that is covered with lines, spaces, words, and boxes. You have to fill out this form and mail it to the newspaper. What do you do with it?

You have probably filled out some forms for your school. You will need to fill out many other forms during your lifetime to get a driver's license or a job, for example. Here are some guidelines for filling out forms.

- Remember that neatness is important. The person who will read your form probably has to read hundreds of others just like it. The easier your form is to read, the quicker it will be processed.
- Take as much time as you need. Forms can be confusing. Some entries, such as writing your name and address, will not be difficult. Others might require more thought. Fill in each line as you come to it. If you skip from one line to another, you may accidentally leave one blank.
- Fill in the entire form. If an item doesn't apply to you, cross out the line for the answer. If you make a mistake, cross it out neatly. If you make too many mistakes, ask for a new form. It's better to spend a little more time on it than to hand in a messy form that will be difficult to read.

Practice

Read the completed form on page 179. On a separate sheet of paper, list the four mistakes that the person made in completing the form. Number each mistake.

Apply

Make up a form. It may be a form to get a pet license, a library card, or something of your choice. Exchange papers with a partner, and complete your partner's form.

YOUNG WORLD
subscription

Dana Chin

Name

25 Elm Street   Norwalk

Address

Connecticut

City   **State**   **Zip**

751 - 3204   *11*

Phone   **Age**

George Washington   *6*

School   **Grade**

4 George Washington Avenue

Address

Norwalk   *Connecticut*

City   **State**   **Zip**

☐	I would like to receive 12 issues.
✓	I prefer to receive 6 issues for now.

Do you read:	yes	no
newspapers?	☐	✓
magazines?	✓	✓
books?	✓	☐

TEST TAKING

Following Test Directions

When you take a test, make sure you read the directions carefully.

Look at the different kinds of tests shown below. Notice how the sample shows how to follow the directions.

Directions: Write the word that best completes the sentence in the blank space provided.
Sample: France is in **Europe**.

Europe   Africa   Australia

Directions: Fill in the circle next to the correct answer.
Sample: $3 \times 15 =$ _____   ○ 3   ○ 5   ● 45

Directions: Circle the word that does not belong in the group.
Sample: hammer   screwdriver   bicycle   saw

Practice

Notice how a student answered the items on the test below. Then, answer the questions that follow.

Directions: Draw a line under the word in each group that is spelled incorrectly.
Sample: they're   there   thier
          1. recieve   accept   except
          2. television   telefone   radio
          3. mistake   simple   purfect

---

1. In what way did the student fail to follow the directions in question 1?
2. In what way did the student fail to follow the directions in question 2?
3. What did the student do wrong in question 3?

Apply: Learning Log

Decide which information from this lesson was the most helpful to you. Write the information in your learning log.

UNIT REVIEW

Business Letters (page 151)

1. List three characteristics of a business letter.

Planning a Business Letter (pages 154–155)

Identify the following parts of a letter. Write whether each would be used in a business letter, a friendly letter, or both.

2. 785 West End Avenue
New York, New York 10025
October 19, 1988

3. Dear Sarah,

4. Your pal,

5. Mr. George Applethwaite
311 Hollow Hill Lane
Branford, Connecticut 06405

6. Yours truly,

7. Dear Sir or Madam:

Combining Sentences (pages 158–159)

Combine each set of sentences.

8. Leonardo Da Vinci painted the *Mona Lisa*. He painted *The Last Supper*. He painted the *Battle of Anghiari*.

9. The *Mona Lisa* is mysterious. It is dramatic. It is beautiful.

10. The artist painted slowly. He painted gracefully. He was famous. He was Italian.

11. Today Da Vinci's paintings may be found in museums. They also can be found in art galleries. In addition, they are found in a few private collections.

12. The fine work that Da Vinci produced explains his reputation as a respected artist. He was a productive artist. Da Vinci was also a gifted artist.

Punctuating a Letter (pages 160–161)

Rewrite each item from a business letter with correct capitalization and punctuation.

13. dear mr. darcy

14. please send me information about your museum

15. my address is 12 hidden drive littlestown pennsylvania

16. very sincerely
elizabeth barret

Writing a Friendly Letter (pages 164–165)

17. List the characteristics of a friendly letter.

Direct Objects (pages 168–169)
Write each sentence, and underline the direct object. Write the question you would use to find the direct object.
18. The Appalachian Trail thrills hikers.
19. Millions of people have hiked the trail.
20. This scenic 2,100 mile-long trail attracts many people to the wilderness.
21. The route of the trail follows the Appalachian Mountains from Georgia to Maine.
22. The trail crosses fourteen states.
23. Benton MacKaye proposed the route in 1921.
24. Workers began construction the next year.
25. They completed their work in 1937.
26. Many hikers challenge their stamina on the trail.
27. Some hardy hikers complete the entire length of the Appalachian Trail each year.

Indirect Objects (pages 170–171)
Write each sentence. Underline the direct object once and the indirect object twice. If there is no indirect object, write *none.*
28. Glaciers gave Iceland its name.
29. Eruptions from volcanoes created Iceland.
30. Viking ships brought the island its first settlers.
31. These settlers carried their traditions to a new land.
32. Natural underground streams bring Iceland much energy.
33. These hot springs can supply many homes throughout the island with heat.
34. Volcanoes and glaciers gave the country its unusual landscape.
35. A volcanic explosion in 1965 formed a new island off Iceland's southern coast.
36. The glaciers bring the rivers a continuous supply of water.
37. The Gulf Stream brings the island warmer air from the south.
38. Schools offer the students in Iceland excellent education.
39. New explosions from the island's volcanoes mean new troubles for Icelanders.
40. The region of Gullfoss offers tourists an excellent view of a beautiful waterfall.
41. Today, Iceland gives the world much seafood.
42. The southern area of Iceland contains many farms.

Transitive and Intransitive Verbs (pages 172–173)

Write each sentence. Underline the verb, and write whether it is *transitive* or *intransitive*. If there is a direct object, underline it twice.

43. Tornadoes carry winds as fast as 230 miles per hour.

44. These winds destroy everything in their path.

45. Some tornadoes travel very rapidly.

46. Danger arises in a town or a city.

47. About 850 tornadoes strike this country each year.

48. Most tornadoes occur in the Midwest.

49. Meteorologists study the formation of tornadoes.

50. They make predictions from these studies.

51. Go to the center of the house in the event of a tornado.

52. Radio broadcasts help in such a situation.

Predicate Nouns and Predicate Adjectives (pages 174–175)

Write each sentence. Write the question you would ask to find the predicate noun or adjective. Underline the predicate noun or predicate adjective, and tell which it is.

53. Waterton-Glacier International Peace Park is beautiful.

54. Waterton Lakes National Park is a Canadian treasure.

55. Glacier National Park is a vast area.

56. The year of their joining was 1932.

57. The scenery in the park is spectacular.

58. The majestic mountains look unreal.

59. The crystal clear water tastes wonderful.

60. The grizzly bear and timber wolf are inhabitants.

61. The area seems peaceful.

62. The park remains a wonder to all its visitors.

Word Roots (pages 176–177)

Complete each definition with a word from the box.

imports	centiliter	kilovolt	psychotherapy	multilateral

63. A _____ is one hundredth of a liter.

64. _____ is treatment for a disease of the mind.

65. A shape that is _____ has many sides.

66. Products carried in from other countries are _____.

67. A _____ equals 1,000 volts.

MAKING ALL THE
CONNECTIONS

You and several classmates will write a letter to the editor. What you have learned about sharing opinions will help you.

You will do the following in your letter to the editor:

- Describe a problem and a suggested solution.
- Use both facts and opinions to support your solution.
- Include all the features of a business letter.

Reading a Letter to the Editor

Read this letter to the editor. The letter points out a problem concerning a marvelous natural resource. Notice that the sidenotes point out the letter's characteristics. After discussing the letter, work in a group to write your own letter to the editor.

All the features of a business letter are included.

431 Hill Street
Madison, Michigan 43122
November 18, 1988

Editor, The Madison News
Madison, Michigan 43122

Dear Sir or Madam:

The problem is clearly stated.

The Great Lakes, five of our most important natural marvels, are in grave danger. These lakes contain 95 percent of all the surface fresh water in the United States. But this water is being poisoned by chemicals and other pollutants. Insecticides are carried by winds into the lakes. Buried wastes leak into groundwater and seep into the lakes. Our lakes are dying.

Details of the problem are given.

A solution to the problem is suggested.

We need action now. A task force must be formed to address this issue. The group should include members from both the U.S. and Canada, the two nations

184

affected by the problem. Both governments should be required to follow the task force's recommendations. Let's act now! We can't waste any more time.

Facts and opinions support the suggestion.

Sincerely yours,

Marci Traub

Marci Traub

Speaking and Listening

Your teacher will assign you to a group. Choose a discussion leader. Discuss these questions:

1. What problem is stated in the letter?
2. What can you learn about the problem from the above map?
3. What solution is suggested?
4. Why does the writer believe that both nations should work toward a solution?
5. How do you think the writer feels about the problem?

Thinking

Brainstorming

Choose one person from your group to be a notetaker. Have that person take notes as all group members discuss the following questions. Save the notes from your discussion.

1. What are some problems faced by your school or your community? Try to think of problems that affect you. Choose one of these problems for your letter.
2. Think of solutions for the problem. Devise more than one solution if possible.
3. List facts and opinions to support each solution.

Organizing

Before you write a letter to the editor, it helps to organize your ideas. Study the chart below. It shows the ideas that were used in Marci Traub's letter.

As a group, organize your brainstorming notes into a chart like the one below. Have one group member fill in the chart from your discussion.

PROBLEM: The Great Lakes are in danger from pollution.		
SUGGESTED SOLUTION: A two-nation task force must be formed.		
Details of Problem	**Facts to Support Solution**	**Opinions to Support Solution**
◆ Insecticides are blown in by wind. ◆ Chemical wastes leak in through groundwater.	◆ Both the United States and Canada are affected by the problem.	◆ The Great Lakes are important. ◆ We cannot afford to waste more time.

Writing a Letter to the Editor ◆

Imagine that you are part of a group that feels very strongly about a particular issue. Your group wants to call other people's attention to the problem and to your solution. You and the other group members will write a problem-solving letter to the editor of your local paper. Use your chart to help you write the letter.

Planning

◆ Review the chart you made after the discussion. Add any new ideas that you think of.
◆ In the first paragraph of your letter, describe the problem. Include details that will help people understand the problem.
◆ In the second paragraph, describe your proposed solution(s). Include facts and opinions to support each solution.
◆ Organize your information into an outline. The first part will include information about the problem. The second will include information about the solution(s).

Composing

- Work with your group to write your problem-solving letter. Choose one member to write down the first draft as all group members suggest ideas.
- Be sure to follow the format of a business letter.
- Decide on a clear way to word the sentences in the first paragraph that state and describe the problem.
- Next, decide how to word the sentences in the second paragraph that state and support the solution.

Revising

- As a group, reread your letter sentence by sentence. Think of ways to improve its content.
- Check that your ideas are expressed clearly and in a logical order.

Proofreading

Now proofread your letter as a group. Choose one group member to make proofreading changes on the first draft. Answer these questions:

- Is each sentence complete and punctuated correctly?
- Are all verbs used correctly?
- Are both addresses written correctly?
- Are all words spelled correctly?

Presenting

- Choose one group member to write a neat, final copy of your letter.
- Organize a debate. Have one member read your group's letter aloud to the class. Have some class members present an opposing viewpoint. Take turns speaking on the topic. Each side should try to convince the other side to agree with its viewpoint.
- Take a poll. Have all class members vote on whether the procedures recommended in the letter should be followed.

CUMULATIVE REVIEW

A. Write the letter of the correct end punctuation for each sentence. *(pages 36–37)*

1. Whose dog is that
    a. .   **b.** ?   **c.** !

2. How cute he is
    a. .   **b.** ?   **c.** !

3. He is a poodle
    a. .   **b.** ?   **c.** !

4. Please walk him
    a. .   **b.** ?   **c.** !

B. Write the letter of the term that identifies each sentence or group of words. *(pages 42–43)*

5. Chekhov was a fine playwright.
    a. sentence   **b.** fragment

6. Produced many wonderful works.
    a. sentence   **b.** fragment

7. Have you ever seen *The Cherry Orchard?*
    a. declarative   **b.** interrogative   **c.** imperative   **d.** exclamatory

8. What a magnificent piece of work!
    a. declarative   **b.** interrogative   **c.** imperative   **d.** exclamatory

C. Write the letter that identifies the underlined part in each sentence. *(pages 44–47)*

9. Mt. Washington lies in the White Mountains of New Hampshire.
    a. simple subject   **b.** complete predicate   **c.** simple predicate

10. Its peak is one of the windiest places on Earth.
    a. complete subject   **b.** complete predicate   **c.** simple subject

11. Observers at its summit once recorded a 231-miles-per-hour gust.
    a. complete subject   **b.** simple predicate   **c.** simple subject

12. Many visitors have driven to the summit in good weather.
    a. simple subject   **b.** complete predicate   **c.** simple predicate

D. Write the letter of the subject in each sentence. *(pages 48–51)*

13. Where did she put them?
    a. Where   **b.** she   **c.** them

14. There is the empty case.
    a. There   **b.** case   **c.** is

15. Here are the glasses.
    a. Here   **b.** are   **c.** glasses

16. Bring them tomorrow.
    a. them   **b.** Bring   **c.** (You)

E. Write the letter of the proper noun that is *not* correctly capitalized. *(pages 80–81)*

17. a. Senator Chan   **b.** Po River   **c.** dr. Gonzalez
    d. Inn at the Sea

18. a. Atlantic Ocean   **b.** France   **c.** Iowa
     d. The Black hills
19. a. april   **b.** Carson City   **c.** Italy   **d.** Friday

F. Write the letter of the correct plural form of each singular noun.
(pages 82–83)

20. radio   **a.** radioes   **b.** radios   **c.** radio
21. series   **a.** series   **b.** serieses   **c.** serial
22. half   **a.** halfs   **b.** halfes   **c.** halves
23. man   **a.** men   **b.** mans   **c.** mens

G. Write the letter of the correct possessive form of each noun.
(pages 84–87)

24. Gus   **a.** Gus'   **b.** Gus's   **c.** Gus'es
25. women   **a.** women's   **b.** women'   **c.** womens'
26. brothers   **a.** brothers's   **b.** brother's   **c.** brothers'
27. Edna   **a.** Edna's   **b.** Edna'   **c.** Ednas'
28. hourglass   **a.** hourglasses   **b.** hourglass's   **c.** hourglass'
29. people   **a.** peoples'   **b.** peoples   **c.** people's

H. Write the letter of the correct abbreviation for each word. *(pages 88–89)*

30. Professor   **a.** Pr.   **b.** Prof.   **c.** Prof
31. United Nations   **a.** UN   **b.** un   **c.** Un
32. Avenue   **a.** Av   **b.** Ave.   **c.** Aven.
33. December   **a.** Dec.   **b.** De.   **c.** Decen.

I. Write the letter of the title that is *not* punctuated correctly.
(pages 120–121)

34. a. American Photographer (magazine)
     b. "Yes, We Have No Bananas" (song)
     c. Crossing the Bar (poem)
35. a. "Hedda Gabler" (play)
     b. "Raymond's Run" (short story)
     c. "Caring for Canaries" (article)
36. a. "Morning Snowfall" (poem)
     b. "David Copperfield" (book)
     c. "The Blue House" (short story)

J. Write the letter of the term that identifies the verb in each sentence.
(pages 126–129)

37. Gertrude Stein was a creative writer and a patron of the arts.
     a. action verb   **b.** linking verb

38. She encouraged Pablo Picasso and other painters.
    a. action verb   **b.** linking verb

39. Gertrude Stein lived in Paris, France.
    a. action verb   **b.** linking verb

K. Write the letter of the term that identifies the underlined verb. *(pages 130–131)*

40. Dentists are <u>using</u> highly sophisticated instruments nowadays.
    a. main verb   **b.** helping verb

41. Dentistry <u>may</u> be completely different in the future.
    a. main verb   **b.** helping verb

42. Dentists do <u>perform</u> difficult operations.
    a. main verb   **b.** helping verb

L. Write the letter of the term that identifies the tense of each verb. *(pages 132–133)*

43. Early cabinetmakers used a variety of different hand tools.
    a. present tense   **b.** past tense   **c.** future tense

44. Tomorrow's craftsworkers will rely more and more on power tools.
    a. present tense   **b.** past tense   **c.** future tense

M. Write the letter of the verb form that correctly completes each sentence. *(pages 134–135)*

45. Many researchers have _____ to tropical rain forests.
    a. journey   **b.** journeys   **c.** journeyed

46. These forests had _____ before the arrival of settlers.
    a. flourished   **b.** flourish   **c.** flourishes

N. Write the letter of the term that identifies the principal part of the underlined verb in each sentence. *(pages 136–139)*

47. Jodyne is <u>photographing</u> everyone at her family reunion.
    a. present   **b.** present participle   **c.** past   **d.** past participle

48. She has <u>recorded</u> the event for everyone's enjoyment.
    a. present   **b.** present participle   **c.** past   **d.** past participle

O. Write the letter of the verb form that correctly completes each sentence. *(pages 140–141)*

49. The level of civilization _____ after the invention of the alphabet.
    a. rose   **b.** rise   **c.** risen   **d.** raise

50. The need for the written word has _____ in the modern age.
    a. grow   **b.** grew   **c.** grown   **d.** growed

P. Write the letter of the part of a letter that is *not* punctuated correctly. *(pages 160–161)*

51. **a.** Dear Sir:
    b. 1076 Tresser Ave.
    c. Yours truly,
    d. Boston, MA

52. **a.** Ms. Jackie Wu
    b. 102 Ridgeley Ave
    c. Fairfield, Maine
    d. September 27, 1988

Q. Write the letter of the term that identifies the underlined word or words in each sentence. *(pages 168–175)*

53. The Supreme Court interprets laws for our nation.
    a. direct object **b.** indirect object

54. The Constitution gives the courts their power.
    a. direct object **b.** indirect object

55. Its nine justices can designate legislation as unconstitutional.
    a. direct object **b.** indirect object

56. Presidents nominate judges to the highest court in the land.
    a. direct object **b.** indirect object

57. The Senate gives nominees its recommendation.
    a. direct object **b.** indirect object

58. Architects design buildings and homes.
    a. transitive verb **b.** intransitive verb

59. Some architects work at large firms.
    a. transitive verb **b.** intransitive verb

60. Others perform services for their own clients.
    a. transitive verb **b.** intransitive verb

61. The career of an architect develops gradually.
    a. transitive verb **b.** intransitive verb

62. Interesting buildings have appeared in many cities.
    a. transitive verb **b.** intransitive verb

63. Judy Garland was a very successful singer.
    a. predicate noun **b.** predicate adjective

64. She was a hit as Dorothy in *The Wizard of Oz*.
    a. predicate noun **b.** predicate adjective

65. Garland seemed perfect in the role.
    a. predicate noun **b.** predicate adjective

66. "Somewhere Over the Rainbow" remains quite popular.
    a. predicate noun **b.** predicate adjective

67. Garland's daughters have also become performers.
    a. predicate noun **b.** predicate adjective

PART THREE

Turning Points

Two roads diverged in a wood, and I —
I took the one less traveled by,
And that has made all the difference.

from "The Road Not Taken"
by Robert Frost

◆

There are sometimes moments in life that stand out—
moments when everything changes. Such **turning points**
are often what people remember most when they look back
on their lives. Each turning point is a new beginning or a
path toward the future. In the coming units, consider the
turning points that have changed your life the most.

Descriptive Writing

◆

Pronouns

What Do You Know?

"I wish I had a picture of that!"

Have you ever been so impressed by something you've seen that you wanted to capture the image permanently? Photographers and painters capture vivid images of people, places, and things on film or canvas. Writers capture images in words.

You may have returned from a vacation to a special place and told your friends details that made the place very real to them. Perhaps, after a visit to the mountains, you told your friends about the fresh scent of the pine trees, the brisk sound of the wind, the coldness of the mountain stream, and the clearness of the sky. You used your own words to describe the things that you could sense most clearly.

Whenever you use words to give details that you can sense through your powers of sight, hearing, taste, smell, or touch, you are using descriptive language. When you use these details in your writing, you are using **descriptive writing**.

194

Thinking About Descriptive Writing

What Is Descriptive Writing?

Descriptive writing has these characteristics:

- It describes a particular person, place, or thing.
- It describes details that appeal to one or more of the five senses: sight, sound, touch, taste, and smell.
- It paints a vivid picture with precise and imaginative words.

Descriptive writing is an important part of stories, poems, magazine articles, and many other forms of written work. By using carefully chosen words, the writer helps us to see, hear, smell, taste, or touch the subject being described.

The appeal to our senses is so strong that we can almost *see* the weathered grayness of a deserted old barn, *hear* the rustle of wind-swept leaves, *smell* the honeyed fragrance of a magnolia tree in bloom, *taste* the juicy sweetness of a ripe pear, and *feel* the chilling wetness of an autumn rainstorm.

Discussion

1. Tell about a vivid description you have recently read.
2. What did the description make you see, hear, taste, smell, or feel?
3. What special place or thing would you like to describe? Explain why.

195

Reading Descriptive Writing

These descriptive paragraphs are from a true story of important events in the life of a young girl. Esther, the main character, and her family have been forced to work in a mine in Siberia during World War II. There is little joy in their lives. Each day is exactly like the one before. Ten-year-old Esther yearns for some excitement. In these paragraphs, she describes her first visit to a village fair, where crops and other items are traded. Her family has carefully selected the items Esther and her grandmother will trade. Her mother sends a beautiful slip, her father chooses a silk shirt, and her grandmother decides to trade her elegant silver-handled umbrella. Esther and her grandmother set out across the vast treeless plain, the endless steppe, and journey to the village of Rubtsovsk.

The Endless Steppe
by
Esther Hautzig

I thought Sunday would never come. When it did, Grandmother and I set off down the dusty road before anyone else. Along with our wares—the slip, the shirt, and the umbrella, after all—we had wrapped some bread in one of my father's handkerchiefs; the bread was to be our lunch.

It was shortly after six o'clock, the air was still cool and fresh, a hawk was soaring overhead, and feeling oddly disloyal, I thought that the steppe was just a tiny bit beautiful that morning.

I glanced back over my shoulder. No one was coming after us to order us to return to the mine, but I quickened my pace and urged Grandmother to hurry. "Nonsense!" she said. "We will drop dead if we walk too fast." But she too looked back over her shoulder.

When the mine was out of sight, when there was nothing but Grandmother and me and the steppe, nothing else, not even a hawk in the sky, I didn't shout—I wouldn't dare because of the way sound

Esther describes how early morning feels to her.

196

carried—I didn't sing very loud, but I sang, and my funny little voice sounded strange to me. And I felt light, as if I could do a giant leap over the steppe.

She describes the sound of her voice.

"Grandmother, do you know what?"

"What?"

"We are doing something we *want* to do. All by ourselves. We are fr-r-r-eeeee. . . ."

"Shh!" Grandmother looked around. "Not so loud."

She was dressed in her best dress, a rumpled blue silk that was also beginning to fade, and her little Garbo hat. In spite of her tininess, Grandmother had always been the *grande dame*; walking down the dusty road that day, she still was.

Esther gives a vivid picture of her grandmother.

We walked for about three hours across the uninhabited steppe without meeting one other person. Before long, I had tied my sweater around my waist— my pleated school skirt and blouse had become my uniform—and Grandmother had opened her umbrella.

We saw a bump in the distance. This turned out to be the first of the widely scattered huts, which meant that before too long, we would be in Rubtsovsk.[1]

Esther sees the village for the first time.

The village had appeared on the horizon like a mirage always receding from us, but we finally did reach it and it was real. Wonderfully real to my starved eyes.

Rubtsovsk, at that time, had an unused church with its onion top, a bank, a library, a pharmacy, a school—even a movie house and a park with a bandstand. But all I saw that day was the square alive with people and, only vaguely, a rather mean cluster of wooden buildings and huts.

We squeezed our way through the crowd—the men in peaked caps, here and there an old military cap, women in *babushkas*,[2] friendly faces sometimes scarred from frost-bite, friendly voices. And some Kazhaks;[3] Asia at last! Colorful costumes, the women with their long pigtails encased in cloth and leather pouches, and, sad to see, men, women, and children all with rotting teeth. But Kaz-haks!

The sounds and sights of the village fair are described.

[1] rüb tsôvsk'
[2] bə büsh' kəs
[3] kä' zäks

197

Trading was going on all around us. There were the stalls around the square with produce from the collective farm—and the small farmers too—and there were the buildings with signs proclaiming them to be state-operated stores where one made purchases only if one had been issued ration books, which we had not been. In one corner, sunflower seeds were being roasted over an open fire. The smell was ravishing. "Come on, Grandmother." I nudged her. "Let's begin to trade."

We made our way to the *baracholka*,* where wooden horses were set up all over the interior of the square and where piles of stuff were heaped onto blankets or onto the bare stones: old books, jackets, *babushkas*, books, pots, pans—anything and everything.

The descriptive paragraphs you have just read are part of a narrative. Descriptive details bring the story to life and help the reader become involved in the events. Other kinds of writing use descriptive details to create vivid images. The following poem, for example, creates a powerful picture of springtime. As you read the poem, look for particular words and phrases that describe how trees suddenly burst forth with green leaves and how the sudden change, or metamorphosis, catches people by surprise.

Metamorphosis

Always it happens when we are not there—
The tree leaps up alive into the air,
Small open parasols of Chinese green
Wave on each twig. But who has ever seen
The latch sprung, the bud as it burst?
Spring always manages to get there first.

Lovers of wind, who will have been aware
Of a faint stirring in the empty air,
Look up one day through a dissolving screen
To find no star, but this multiplied green,
Shadow on shadow, singing sweet and clear.
Listen, lovers of wind, the leaves are here!

—May Sarton

*bär ä' chôl kə

Understanding What You've Read

Write your answers on a separate sheet of paper.

1. In the story, which details describe the people at the fair?
2. Which details describe the items at the fair?
3. In the poem, what does the poet say that "lovers of wind" will have been aware of?
4. What details help you feel the emptiness of the land that Esther and her grandmother travel across?
5. What senses does the author of "Metamorphosis" use in her description of spring?
6. During their journey, Esther removes her sweater and her grandmother opens the umbrella. What details might you add to describe the increasing heat of the summer day?
7. If you were writing a poem, how might you describe the signs of spring?

Writing Assignment

In "The Endless Steppe," the author uses descriptive language to create a word picture of a village market crowded with people and things. Think about some special place you would like to describe for your classmates. In the lessons that follow, you will learn how to write a descriptive paragraph, step by step. You will learn how to select details and how to use vivid, interesting language. You will also learn how to write a poem using descriptive language.

Your **audience** will be your teacher and your classmates. Your **purpose** will be to describe your special place as clearly and colorfully as you can.

Choose a Place

Begin by choosing the special place that you will describe. You may select a place from this list, or you may choose some other place that interests you.

- a garden
- a quiet room
- a seashore or beach
- a sports field

Organizing Sensory Details

In "The Endless Steppe," the author describes the bustle and colorful excitement of a village fair. She chooses details that help us experience the sounds and smells as well as the sights of the marketplace. When you write a description, you want to include details that appeal to one or more of the five senses. Details that appeal to any of the five senses are **sensory details**.

How can you choose the details to include? One way is to close your eyes and imagine the place you want to describe. What can you see, smell, hear, taste, and touch? Think of sensory details. You can organize your details by using a **cluster map** like the one below.

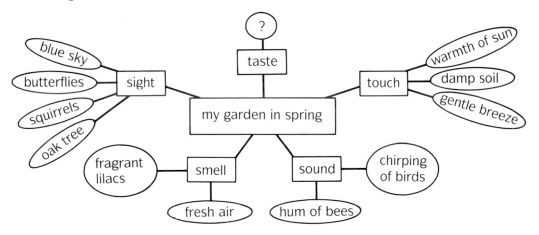

The subject appears in the center of the map. The five senses are grouped around the subject. Now you can jot down words or phrases to describe your sensory details. Sometimes you will not be able to include details for all five senses. For example, it is difficult to think of something you might taste in a spring garden. That is why there is a question mark next to that box.

Practice

A. Copy the cluster map below onto a sheet of paper. Then complete it with details relating to the senses that are shown.

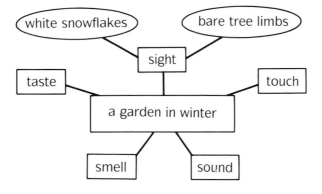

B. Think about your classroom. What do you see? What can you hear? How do your desk and seat feel? Make a cluster map with your classroom as the subject. Put "My Classroom" in the middle. Then arrange the five senses in boxes around the topic. For each sense, try to provide two details. Share your cluster map with your class. Discuss how the details on your maps are similar and how they are different.

Organize Your Details

Think about the place you chose to describe. Using all your senses, think of words and phrases to describe the sensory details of the place you chose. Make a cluster map to organize the words and phrases you think of. Save your work for the next lesson.

Using Precise Details

When you describe something, you want to present a sharp, clear image of your subject. You don't want your description to be vague and unclear. Therefore, you must think carefully about the exact details and words you will use to describe your subject. Try to choose specific words that will show how the object you are describing is different from other objects that may be similar to it.

Suppose you are describing garden tools. Look at the four pictures below.

How would you describe one of the tools so that readers would know exactly which one you were talking about? Consider the shape and size of each tool. Read this description: *long wooden handle, metal at one end.* These details are too vague. They could describe any of the tools. You need to include more precise details, such as these: long wooden handle, metal *teeth* at one end. This is more accurate, but it could still describe two of the tools. More exact details are needed. You can include distinguishing features: long wooden handle, *flexible* metal *teeth shaped like a fan* at one end.

At last! Only one of the tools has all of those features. This precise description tells how the broomlike leaf rake is different from the other tools pictured.

Practice

Look at each group of pictures. Pick one picture from each group and list details that describe the subject precisely. Include details that tell how the subject you chose is different from the other subjects pictured in the group.

1.

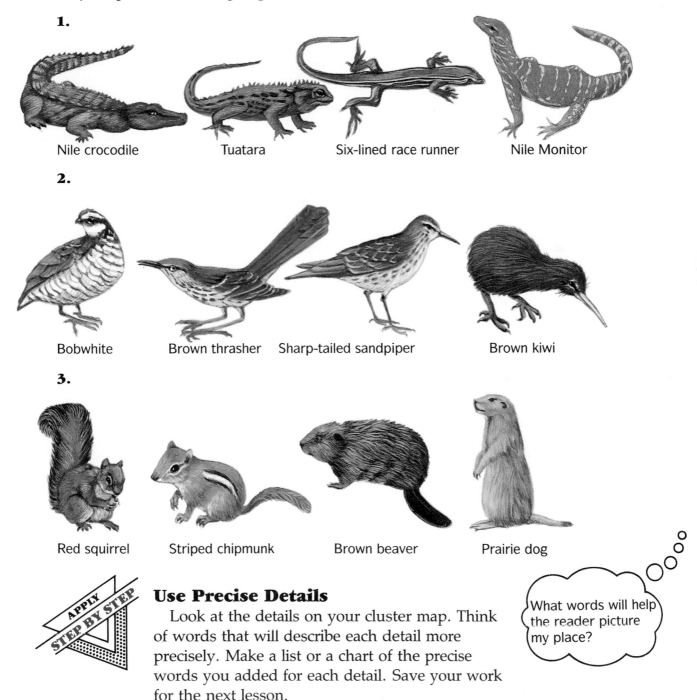

Nile crocodile   Tuatara   Six-lined race runner   Nile Monitor

2.

Bobwhite   Brown thrasher   Sharp-tailed sandpiper   Brown kiwi

3.

Red squirrel   Striped chipmunk   Brown beaver   Prairie dog

Use Precise Details

APPLY STEP BY STEP

Look at the details on your cluster map. Think of words that will describe each detail more precisely. Make a list or a chart of the precise words you added for each detail. Save your work for the next lesson.

What words will help the reader picture my place?

Using Figurative Language

Many writers use figurative language, or figures of speech, to make their writing more descriptive and colorful. **Figurative language** changes the usual meaning of words in order to create a dramatic effect. Notice the way in which sunlight is described in this sentence:

> Sunlight dappled through the trees onto the grass like spots on a leopard's coat.

The sunlight on the grass is compared to a leopard's spots. A comparison that shows how two very different things are in some way alike is one kind of figurative language.

Many writers also use the way a word sounds to create interesting effects. The repetition of words beginning with the letter *m* creates a smooth flow in the following sentence:

> The moon made a magnificent maze of light on the lake.

The charts below give examples of figurative language and sound devices.

Figures of Speech	Examples
A **simile** is a comparison that shows how two different things are alike. A simile always uses the word *like* or *as*.	The clouds were as white as snow. The tulips looked like a troop of tall, red-hatted soldiers.
A **metaphor** is a statement that compares two different things without using *like* or *as*.	The daffodils were trumpets of gold. The waterfall was a hushed symphony.
Personification gives human qualities to animals or objects.	The sparrows bragged about their winter adventures. The trees stretched their arms and waved a friendly greeting.

Sound Devices	Examples
Alliteration is the repetition of the same consonant sound at the beginnings of words.	The soft, sweet-scented breezes are signs of spring's approach.
Onomatopoeia is the use of words that imitate or suggest the sounds they make.	The birds' chirps were accompanied by the scratch and twang of my garden rake.

Practice

A. Write whether each sentence contains an example of a simile, a metaphor, personification, alliteration, or onomatopoeia.

1. Gardeners groom the ground for growing.
2. The fire crackled and sputtered in the hearth.
3. The stars were tiny diamonds in the coal-black sky.
4. Tender green grass will soon spill across the soft ground.
5. Birds glided across the sky like graceful skaters on a winter pond.
6. The sun was a warm golden sweater while I worked.
7. Two squirrels sat and gossiped on a nearby branch.
8. The night was silent except for the hiss of the wind and the rattle of the trees.
9. The moon stubbornly hid behind the clouds.
10. Spring had arrived as quietly as a cat.

B. Write each sentence. Add words to complete the sentence with the kind of language called for in parentheses.

1. The sun shone _____.(alliteration)
2. Puffy spring clouds _____. (metaphor)
3. The noisy owls _____. (onomatopoeia)
4. The cold wind _____. (personification)
5. The rain-soaked soil felt _____. (simile)
6. Bright blossoms _____. (alliteration)
7. The big bumblebees _____. (onomatopoeia)
8. Happy butterflies _____. (personification)
9. The flowers looked _____. (simile)

APPLY STEP BY STEP

Use Figurative Language

Look at the details on your cluster map. Find details that you could describe more vividly by using figurative language. Make a list or a chart of the phrases and words you think you might use. Save your work for the next lesson.

Writing a First Draft

Read the first draft of the descriptive paragraph below. The writer wasn't worried about making it perfect. It will be changed later.

> I love this quiet corner of the garden. Most of all, I love it in early spring. The earth is wakeing after a long sleep. The sun is a pale yellow jewel in the bright blue sky. Slowly, the golden glow warms the soft, damp earth, and tiny lilacs send a sweet perfume through the crisp, fresh air. In the gentle breeze butterflies move like tiny, colorful kites while the blossoms stand as straight as soldiers, The lazy humm of the bumblebees mingles with the cheerful chirping of the sparrows. High up in the old oak tree, two bushy-tailed squirrels move from limb to limb and play a game of hide-and-seak. Everywhere in the garden there is new growth and the promis of blossomming life.

APPLY STEP BY STEP

Write Your First Draft

Before you begin writing, you may wish to discuss your description with a classmate or your teacher. Using your cluster map and your lists of words and phrases, begin writing your description. Include precise details and figurative language to make your writing more interesting.

Write one paragraph about the place you chose. Don't worry about making mistakes in spelling or punctuation. Just write on every other line of your paper. You can go back and make corrections later. When you have finished, save your first draft for the next lesson.

Discussing a First Draft

After writing your first draft, look for ways to improve it. Discussing your draft with a partner may help you find ways to make your descriptions clearer and more vivid.

Discussion Strategy

Take turns speaking during your discussion. If only one of you talks almost all the time, the other will stop listening. Be careful not to interrupt your partner when he or she is speaking. You will have a chance to express your own ideas after your partner has finished.

Use this Content Checklist to discuss with your class the descriptive writing on the previous page.

Content Checklist
- ✔ Does the paragraph tell about one particular place?
- ✔ Does it include details that appeal to one or more of the five senses?
- ✔ Does it paint a vivid picture with precise and imaginative words?

APPLY STEP BY STEP

Revise Your First Draft for Content

To the Reader: Exchange papers with a classmate. As you read your partner's paper, try to imagine the place being described. See if you can picture the place in your mind. If the picture is unclear, discuss ways to improve the first draft. Use the Content Checklist for help.

To the Writer: Listen to your partner's suggestions. Use them to help you revise your draft for content. Save your work for the next lesson.

In the draft about the garden, the writer included these details:

Butterflies move like tiny, colorful kites.
Two bushy-tailed squirrels move from limb to limb.

Notice that the word *move* appears in both sentences. Repeating the same word can make your writing seem dull. Think of synonyms for *move*. Make a word map of synonyms like the one shown below.

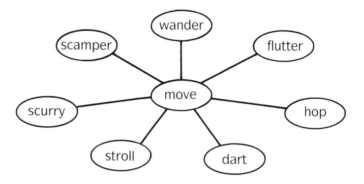

The writer wanted to say that the butterflies moved in a light, gentle way. After studying the map, the writer chose a more precise word.

Butterflies <u>flutter</u> like tiny, colorful kites.

In the second sentence, the writer wanted to show how quickly and playfully the squirrels moved. The writer chose a more precise word and rewrote the sentence.

Two bushy-tailed squirrels <u>scamper</u> from limb to limb.

You may wish to use a thesaurus to help you find synonyms and create a word map.

Practice

A. Make a word map for the underlined word in each sentence. Then rewrite the sentences using the best word from your map to replace the original word.

    1. The sunlight was <u>bright</u>.
    2. The green stems <u>grew</u> out of the ground.
    3. A <u>number</u> of fish swam in the fountain.
    4. The <u>small</u> buds developed slowly.
    5. The flowers <u>moved</u> in the breeze.

B. Rewrite each sentence below, replacing the underlined word with a more precise, vivid word.

    6. I took a <u>quiet</u> stroll in the garden.
    7. The <u>rough</u> grass made me itch.
    8. There was a <u>nice</u> breeze.
    9. The pond was a <u>bright</u> blue.
   10. The <u>hot</u> sun dried the grass.

Revising Checklist

✔ Does my first draft contain all the characteristics of a descriptive paragraph?
✔ Where can I combine sentences? (pp. 34, 118, and 158)
✔ What sentences can I change to vary the word order? (p. 72)
✔ Where can I replace words to avoid repetition?

Revise Your First Draft for Style

Reread the first draft of your descriptive paragraph. If you find a word you used too often, prepare a word map for it. Then replace some of the repetitions with more precise or colorful synonyms from the word map. Use the Revising Checklist to make other changes that will help improve your draft. Save your work for the next lesson.

209

PROOFREADING
Using Commas and Semicolons

In Unit 2, you learned some rules for using commas. Here are some additional uses for commas, as well as two rules for using semicolons.

Rule	Example
Use a comma after introductory expressions such as *yes*, *no*, *oh*, and *well*.	Yes, we will plant a garden. No, we will not plant vegetables. Oh, what a great idea! Well, what flowers should we choose?
Use commas to separate a person's name from the rest of the sentence when the person is spoken to directly.	Donna, is this your garden? I think, Sam, that the roses are beautiful. I agree with you completely, Mother.
Use commas to separate the word *too* when it means "also."	I want a garden, too. He, too, grows roses.
Use commas to separate words like *however*, *therefore*, and *though* from the rest of the sentence when these words are used to connect ideas.	I planted seeds. Not all of them bloomed, though. Kiyoko, however, planted bulbs. Therefore, she started her gardening early.
A semicolon may replace a comma and the word *and*, *but*, or *or* in a compound sentence.	The breeze is gentle, and the ocean is calm. The breeze is gentle; the ocean is calm. Friday it rained, but today it is sunny. Friday it rained; today it is sunny.

Practice

Write the sentences below on a separate sheet of paper. Add commas and semicolons where they are needed.

1. Tomatoes are an important food source they are eaten around the world.
2. For centuries however tomatoes were only grown in Mexico and Peru.
3. Spanish explorers took seeds to Europe the plant was grown for ornamental use there.
4. Europeans considered the tomato poisonous however.
5. Ms. Grey how did the tomato become a popular food item?
6. Well the tomato was first introduced early in our nation's agricultural history.
7. Therefore many farmers were willing to experiment with new plants such as the tomato.
8. Today however the tomato is more than a successful experiment it is our nation's third largest vegetable crop.
9. Scientists categorize the tomato as a fruit most people call it a vegetable though.
10. Yes even the United States Supreme Court has referred to the tomato as a vegetable.
11. Leila why is this fruit often called a vegetable?
12. Well many people think produce must be sweet and have pits in order to be called fruit.

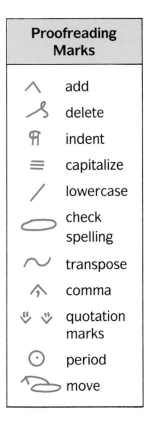

Proofreading Marks	
∧	add
ℒ	delete
¶	indent
≡	capitalize
/	lowercase
◯	check spelling
∼	transpose
∧	comma
⧗ ⧗	quotation marks
⊙	period
◠	move

Proofreading Checklist
- ✔ Is every sentence punctuated and capitalized correctly? (p. 36)
- ✔ Are commas and semicolons used correctly? (p. 74)
- ✔ Did I use any irregular verbs incorrectly?

APPLY STEP BY STEP

Proofread Your Draft

Reread your descriptive paragraph. Check for correct capitalization, punctuation, and grammar. Use the Proofreading Checklist as a guide. Be sure to add commas where they belong. You may wish to combine some sentences with semicolons. Mark the changes on your draft. Save your work for the next lesson.

Checking Spelling/Writing a Final Copy

◆

Spelling Strategy

Many words belong to the same word family. Recognizing word families can help you spell.

> **Example:** Which spelling is correct, *strategy* or *stratigy*? This word belongs to the same word family as *strategic*; you can hear the long *e* sound (strat*e*gic). This can help you remember that *strategy* is the correct spelling.

Here is the revised, proofread paragraph about the garden.

I love this quiet corner of the garden. Most of all, I love it in early spring. The

waking

earth is ~~wakeing~~ after a long sleep. The sun is a pale yellow jewel in the bright blue

sky. Slowly, the golden glow warms the soft, damp earth, and tiny lilacs send a

flutter

sweet perfume through the crisp, fresh air. In the gentle breeze, butterflies move

like tiny, colorful kites while the blossoms stand as straight as soldiers. The lazy

hum

~~humm~~ of the bumblebees mingles with the cheerful chirping of the sparrows. High

scamper

up in the old oak tree, two bushy-tailed squirrels ~~move~~ from limb to limb and play

seek

a game of hide-and-~~seak~~. Everywhere in the garden there is new growth and the

promise   *blossoming*

~~promis~~ of ~~blossomming~~ life.

Check Your Spelling

Check your descriptive paragraph for spelling mistakes. Use the proofreading marks to correct the errors. Apply the Spelling Strategy. Add any misspelled words to your spelling log.

Write a Final Copy

Write a neat, final copy of your descriptive paragraph. Include all the corrections you made on your first draft. Keep the final copy.

Learning About Poetry

Descriptive writing is a way of painting pictures with words. Both a descriptive paragraph and a poem can contain images that appeal to the senses. In a paragraph, images are described in detail with many words and complete sentences. In a poem, however, images are usually created with fewer words. Each word in a poem is carefully chosen and is full of meaning.

Read the descriptive paragraph and the poem. Look for images created by the different words in each piece of writing.

The sky looked as if someone had thrown a mass of sparks into the night. Suddenly a burst of light broke away from a cluster of stars and began to fall from the sky in a huge, arching loop. It fell slowly at first, as if almost reluctant to move. Then, in the huge wall of darkness, the falling star gathered speed and fell faster and faster. At last, it was only a streaking blur of light that finally disappeared in the darkest part of the sky— just above the horizon.

The Falling Star

I saw a star slide down the sky,
Blinding the north as it went by,
Too burning and too quick to hold,
Too lovely to be bought or sold,
Good only to make wishes on
And then forever to be gone.
—Sara Teasdale

Rhyme

One way in which poetry differs from other writing is its use of words that **rhyme**. Words that rhyme end in the same sound, such as the words *amble* and *ramble* or the words pina*fore* and meta*phor*. The rhyming words are often arranged at the end of the lines of poetry in a regular pattern. Read the poems (at the top of the next page) and notice how the words that rhyme are arranged.

Waiting for Spring

I wait for Spring to shake off sleep
Through crocus eyelids, she will peep,
And donning apple blossom frills,
She'll gossip with the daffodils.

—M. Batchelder

Winter Seems Forever

Winter stays and seems forever,
March winds shove and then grow bolder,
Just when I think Spring is never,
Her laughing breezes tap my shoulder.

—M. Batchelder

In "Waiting for Spring," the last words in each pair of lines rhyme. In "Winter Seems Forever," the last words in every other line rhyme. The first rhyme pattern is called *aabb*. The second rhyme pattern is called *abab*.

Rhythm

The words in a poem are often arranged to form a regular pattern of accented sounds. The pattern, or **rhythm,** creates a musical effect. In the poem below, notice how the two-syllable words have been arranged to take advantage of their natural accents.

Escape from the City

I seek a quiet country life
Without the city's bustling strife.
I seek the sight of trees ablaze
Instead of streets that form a maze.

—Barbara Klinger

Free Verse

A poem that does not use rhyme or have a regular rhythm is called **free verse**. Like rhyming poems, free verse makes use of figurative language and sound devices. Look for examples of personification and alliteration in the poem on the next page.

214

Autumn Evening

As I walked out one Autumn evening,
The tangled wheat stalks shivered in the wind,
And the sun streamed ragged through the flint-grey
　　clouds.
A thrush in the orchard's burdened trees
Sang to the silence, to the weather's cutting chill.
No echo brought that song back from the hills that
　　held it,
Yet it lingered in my mind, that last clear voice
Not choked by the grip of winter's warning
But lightly, swiftly working, turning, lacing
Threads of melody around the darkening day.
　　　　　　　　　　　　　—M. Daniel Hoff

The phrase "wheat stalks shivered" is an example of personification. Examples of alliteration are "Sang to the silence" and "hills that held." The idea of a song lacing threads of melody is a metaphor. Other poems may use similes and onomatopoeia as well. You may wish to review these terms on page 204.

Practice

Use these poems to answer the questions that follow them.

An April Kite

The clownish kite upon its string,
Will dance on April's sunny sky.
My gaudy hunter has its fling
And startles sparrows as they fly.

The Summer Storm

The rush and rage of summer storm,
The scowling, growling, rumbling clouds,
The first, fast flash of lightning's snap,
And those who cannot flee must bow.

1. Which poem has a rhyme pattern? What is the rhyme pattern of that poem?
2. What are some examples of figurative language in the poems?
3. What are some examples of alliteration in each poem?
4. Which poem has examples of onomatopoeia?

Tanka and Acrostic Poems

Free verse can be written in many different ways. In some instances, the poem has a definite form or structure. One ancient Japanese form of poetry is called a **tanka**. A tanka has five lines. The first and third lines each have five syllables. The other lines each have seven syllables. The two poems below are both examples of tanka.

City

I can't remember
the hills on fire in autumn,
the scent of wide fields.
The only beauty I trust,
is the broad face of the
  moon.

Traveling Home

The train tracks are wet.
Trees resemble upturned
  brooms.
When I think of you,
the pound of wheels is the
  surf
on a distant shore we knew.

Another form of free verse is an **acrostic poem**. In an acrostic poem, each line begins with a certain letter in order to spell out vertically the subject of the poem. Sometimes each line contains only one word. In other acrostic poems, the number of words used in each line varies. Here are examples of both types. If you write the first letter of each line, it spells *springtime*.

Springtime

Sweet
Promise
Rises
In
New
Growth
That
I
May
Enjoy

Springtime

Sometimes I
Pretend that
Roses bloom
In winter.
Nature
Gently
Tells me that my
Imaginings
Must wait until the
Early spring.
—D. Heath

Practice

A. Write the beginning of each tanka below. Complete the tanka by providing the missing line. Remember to write the correct number of syllables.

1. Hungry seagulls float,
   wings outstretched to grasp the wind.
   Their calls sound hollow,
   as they sweep and ride the wind,

   _____

2. The blossom floats like
   a fragment of a spring cloud
   and parachutes down.
   I watch for the flags of Spring

   _____

B. Write each acrostic poem on a separate sheet of paper. Complete each poem by providing the missing line.

Garden

Growing
Always
Rare
Delights
Entrancing
N_____

Garden

Grampa says
A seed needs
Rainfall to grow into a
D_____
Every day I watered it, and
Now it blooms in the sun.

Choose the Subject for Your Poem

Look at your descriptive paragraph. Find some aspect of the description you could write about in a poem. You may want to describe one object, or you may want to describe the feeling you have when you read your description. When you have selected your subject, make a list of words and phrases that best express your ideas. Save your work for the next lesson.

Writing a Poem

Read the first draft of a student's tanka about a garden.

Spring Garden

I watch my garden's
red fence, green grass, and wet soil.
Why don't sleepers wake,
shake snow and ice from my thoughts,
and bring a message of Spring?

Use the Content Checklist to discuss the student's tanka with your classmates.

Content Checklist

✔ If the poem is a tanka, does it have the correct number of syllables in each line?

✔ If the poem is an acrostic, do the first letters of each line spell out its subject?

APPLY STEP BY STEP

Write Your Poem

Decide whether you will write a tanka or an acrostic poem to describe the subject you selected. Use the list of words and phrases you made in the last lesson and put them into the form you think is best.

Revise Your Poem

Exchange poems with a classmate. Discuss each other's poems according to the Content Checklist. Use the suggestions to revise your work. Make a neat, final copy of your poem. Save it for the next lesson.

Sharing Your Descriptive Writing

Speaking/Listening Strategy

Be aware of the movements you make with your hands as you speak. Use gestures to illustrate your points and make your speech seem natural to your audience. Avoid gestures or movements that will be distracting to your audience.

Choosing a Way to Share

Here are some ways to share your paragraph and poem.

Read Aloud   Read your descriptive paragraph and your poem aloud to the class. Use as much expression as possible in your voice to help convey your feelings about the place you are describing. Be aware of rhythm and other poetic devices as you read your poem. Practice reading it so that your presentation is smooth.

Create a "Picture This" Bulletin Board   After you have read your paragraph and poem aloud, challenge your listeners to draw a picture of the special place you have described. Select the drawing that you think comes closest in appearance and mood to the place you've described and place it next to your paragraph and poem in a bulletin-board display.

Share Your Descriptive Writing

Choose the way you prefer to share your paragraph and poem. Encourage your listeners to share their reactions.

Add to Your Learning Log

- Which do I like better—my poem or my paragraph?
- Which step in the descriptive writing was the most interesting for me?
- After presenting my work, what part of my poem or paragraph would I like to change?

The Literature Connection: Pronouns

Good writing is concerned with form as well as meaning. Even the liveliest subject can seem dull when it is written in a dry, repetitive style. Pronouns can make your writing less repetitive. **Pronouns** are words that are used to replace nouns in sentences.

The poem below shows how language itself can be fun. Pronouns are an important part of this fun. They set up word play and double meanings in the poem.

As you read, try to identify who or what each pronoun in the poem refers to. However, be alert! You may become very confused!

The White Rabbit's Verses
by Lewis Carroll

They told me you had been
to her,
And mentioned me to him:
She gave me a good
character,
But said I could not swim.

He sent them word I had not
gone
(We know it to be true):
If she should push the
matter on,
What would become of you?

I gave her one, they gave
him two,
You gave us three or more;
They all returned from him
to you,
Though they were mine
before.

If I or she should chance to
be
Involved in this affair,
He trusts to you to set them
free,
Exactly as we were.

My notion was that you had
been
(Before she had this fit)
An obstacle that came
between
Him, and ourselves, and it.

Don't let him know she liked
them best,
For this must ever be
A secret, kept from all the
rest,
Between yourself and me.

Discussion

1. How many different pronouns are in the above poem? List them.
2. About how many people do the pronouns in the poem refer to?
3. Would you like this poem more or less if proper nouns, rather than pronouns, had been used? Explain your answer.

The Writing Connection: Pronouns

You can use pronouns to make your writing smoother and more interesting.

Suppose Alice had written about her adventures in Wonderland, but she forgot how to use pronouns. Here is what her story might have sounded like.

> The Hare gave a tea party in the Hare's home. The Hare invited the Dormouse and the Mad Hatter to the party. Alice also came to the party.

Alice's story would have sounded much better if she had used some pronouns insteads of nouns.

> The Hare gave a tea party in *his* home. *He* invited the Dormouse and the Mad Hatter to *his* party. Alice also came to *it*.

Activity

Below are sentences that tell about the tea party (shown above). Rewrite each sentence so that a pronoun replaces a noun that is repeated.

- Alice spilled milk on Alice's dress.
- The Mad Hatter played chess, but the Mad Hatter lost.
- The guests said the guests admired the tea table.
- A strange girl came to the party, and everyone looked at the girl.
- Alice thanked the Hare, and the Mad Hatter thanked the Hare, too.

Subject Pronouns

◆

A **pronoun** is a word that takes the place of a noun or nouns in a sentence. A **subject pronoun** is a pronoun that is used as the subject of a sentence.

A. Study the subject pronouns in the following chart

subject	singular:	I, you, he, she, it
pronouns	plural:	we, you, they

A pronoun replaces one or more nouns in these examples.

Chiang visited Philadephia. She visited Philadelphia.
Eva and Kiyo saw the city. They saw the city.

B. A subject pronoun is also used to replace a noun that follows a linking verb. A **predicate nominative** is a noun or pronoun that follows a linking verb and identifies the subject.

The author of the document was Thomas Jefferson.

predicate nominatives

The author of the document was he.

In formal writing, you must use a subject pronoun as a predicate nominative. In informal writing and speaking, you may use an object pronoun if it sounds less awkward.

Formal: The writer was she. Informal: The writer was her.

Strategy

To test whether you've used the right pronoun when replacing a predicate noun, rearrange the sentence.

Incorrect: That person was me. (Me was that person.)
Correct: That person was I. (I was that person.)

Check Your Understanding

A. Write the letter of the subject pronoun that correctly replaces the underlined subject of each sentence.

  1. Ramona memorized part of the Declaration of Independence.
    a. They **b.** Her **c.** She **d.** It

  2. Samuel and John Adams were two famous leaders.
    a. Them **b.** They **c.** We **d.** It

B. Write the letter of the subject pronoun that replaces the underlined predicate nominative in each sentence.

    3. The publisher of *Common Sense* was <u>Thomas Paine</u>.
        a. it   **b.** he   **c.** they   **d.** she

    4. The writer of the report on Thomas Paine was <u>Elise</u>.
        a. they   **b.** her   **c.** them   **d.** she

Practice

A. Write each sentence. Replace the underlined subject with the correct subject pronoun.

    5. <u>John Hancock</u> led the Continental Congress.
    6. <u>The delegates and he</u> signed the Declaration.
    7. <u>Kim and I</u> read a book about John Hancock's life.
    8. <u>The book</u> told of his term as Massachusetts's governor.

B. Write each sentence. Replace the underlined predicate nominative with a subject pronoun.

    9. The victors at Saratoga were <u>the Americans</u>.
   10. The British general was <u>John Burgoyne</u>.
   11. The victorious general was <u>Horatio Gates</u>.
   12. One critic of the British was <u>Mercy Warren</u>.

C. Mixed Practice Write each sentence. Replace the underlined word or words with a subject pronoun. Label it either *subject* or *predicate nominative*.

   13. <u>You and Polly</u> traveled to the battle site.
   14. The British loyalists in the colonies were <u>the Tories</u>.
   15. <u>The Declaration of Independence</u> stated important ideas.
   16. One of the revolution's heroes was <u>George Washington</u>.
   17. <u>A treaty</u> officially ended the Revolutionary War in 1783.
   18. <u>Celia and I</u> read a copy of the treaty.
   19. <u>My brother and sister</u> studied the revolution last year.
   20. The leaders of the revolution were <u>Washington and the Congress</u>.

Apply: Work with a Partner

With your partner, write six sentences of *informal* dialogue between members of a class committee. Include at least four pronouns as predicate nominatives. Then rewrite the dialogue as *formal* sentences. How have you changed the predicate nominative pronouns?

Object Pronouns

An **object pronoun** takes the place of a noun or nouns used as a direct object or an indirect object.

object	singular:	me, you, him, her, it
pronouns	plural:	us, you, them

A. A **direct object** is a noun or pronoun that follows an action verb and receives the action of the verb.

> American voters elected Herbert Hoover in 1928.
> American voters elected him in 1928.

> Hard times affected Americans and Europeans in 1929.
> Hard times affected them in 1929.

B. An **indirect object** is a noun or pronoun that follows an action verb and tells *to whom* or *for whom* the action is done.

> Fumiko lent Kurt a book about the Great Depression.
> Fumiko lent him a book about the Great Depression.

> Magdelena showed friends the book.
> Magdalena showed them the book.

Strategy

If you are unsure whether a noun following a verb should be replaced by a subject pronoun or an object pronoun, look at the verb itself. Action verbs are followed by object pronouns. Linking verbs are followed by subject pronouns.

Check Your Understanding

A. Write the letter of the pronoun that correctly replaces the underlined words in each sentence.

   1. The voters elected Franklin D. Roosevelt in 1932.
   a. him   **b.** he   **c.** them   **d.** they

   2. Roosevelt proposed laws and policies for economic relief.
   a. it   **b.** them   **c.** him   **d.** they

B. Write the letter of the pronoun that correctly replaces the underlined word in each sentence.

    3. Roosevelt's New Deal program brought <u>people</u> relief.
        a. them   **b.** it   **c.** they   **d.** him

    4. The policies won <u>Roosevelt</u> new supporters.
        a. them   **b.** him   **c.** they   **d.** he

Practice

A. Write each sentence. Replace the underlined word with an object pronoun.

    5. Bankruptcy left <u>men and women</u> without jobs.
    6. One-fourth of those with jobs lost <u>the jobs</u>.
    7. The bankrupt firm fired <u>the woman</u>.
    8. People with money lost <u>money</u>.

B. Write each sentence. Replace the underlined words with an object pronoun.

    9. No one would offer <u>the man</u> a job.
   10. People owed <u>bill collectors</u> debts.
   11. Relief agencies brought <u>families</u> food.
   12. They would give <u>a mother</u> bread and milk.

C. Mixed Practice Write each sentence. Replace the underlined word or words with an object pronoun.

   13. The National Recovery Administration helped <u>businesses</u>.
   14. The Tennessee Valley Authority employed <u>Grandpa</u>.
   15. Yolanda read <u>Grandma and me</u> a report about the Great Depression.
   16. The reporter gave <u>readers</u> details of the depression.
   17. Grandpa read the <u>report</u> also.
   18. Roosevelt's policies aided <u>the needy and unfortunate</u>.
   19. The depression troubled <u>Franklin Roosevelt and his wife, Eleanor</u>.
   20. It brought <u>Franklin and Eleanor</u> many problems.

Apply: Test a Partner

Write six sentences about a historical topic. Try to include a direct and an indirect object in each sentence. Then exchange papers with a partner. Replace one object in each sentence with a pronoun. Check your partner's paper.

Using Pronouns Correctly

A. Subject and object pronouns are used in different ways in sentences. A pronoun's use tells you what form it takes.

Type of Pronoun	Forms	Uses	Examples
subject pronoun	I, you, he, she, it, we, they	subject of sentence predicate nominative	We read the article. The author is she.
object pronoun	me, you, him, her, it, us, them	direct object indirect object	Rosa brought them. Todd gave her a pen.

B. A subject, predicate nominative, direct object, or indirect object may consist of two or more pronouns. Be sure to use the correct form of each pronoun.

Subject: He and I study together.
Predicate nominative: The best athletes are she and I.
Direct object: Jimmy invited them and us.
Indirect object: Shirley told him and her a story.

Strategy

Most problems with choosing subject or object pronouns occur when the subject or object has two parts. To help you choose the correct pronoun, use each in a separate sentence.

Her courage amazed (he, him) and (I, me).
Her courage amazed him. Her courage amazed me.
Her courage amazed him and me.

Check Your Understanding

A. Write the letter of the correct pronoun to replace the underlined word or words.
  1. Wilma read an autobiography of Helen Keller.
     a. Her   **b.** She   **c.** He   **d.** They
  2. Helen Keller overcame her problems.
     a. it   **b.** she   **c.** them   **d.** they

226

B. Write the letter of the correct pronouns to replace the underlined words.

3. Juan and Sarah read the book also.
   a. He and she   b. Him and her
   c. He and her   d. He and them
4. Keller's inner strength inspired Sarah and Juan.
   a. she and he   b. her and he
   c. her and they d. her and him

Practice

A. Write each sentence. Replace the underlined word or words with the correct form of the pronoun.

5. Helen Keller lost her sight and hearing as a baby.
6. Such a loss must have frightened Helen greatly.
7. Helen's strongest supporters were her parents.
8. They gave the girl the best of everything.

B. Write each sentence. Replace each underlined word with the correct pronoun.

9. Mike and Sue read about Anne Sullivan, Helen's teacher.
10. The story of Anne's work impressed Mike and Sue.
11. Anne gave Helen and her parents a chance.
12. The readers of the story were Mike and Sue.

C. Mixed Practice Write each sentence. Replace each underlined word with the correct form of the pronoun.

13. Anne was only 19 years old at their first meeting.
14. Helen resisted Anne at first.
15. Anne gave Helen an opportunity for change.
16. Abdul and Louisa studied Helen Keller's life.
17. Our teacher told Abdul and Louisa about Keller.
18. The best student in the class was Abdul.
19. Abdul, Louisa, and the class learned sign language.
20. These signs represent those words.

Apply: Work with a Group

Working as a group, write four sentences about a person you admire. In each sentence, use one of the following types of pronouns: *subject*, *predicate nominative*, *direct object*, or *indirect object*. Then check the pronouns in your sentences.

Pronouns and Antecedents ◆

Pronouns take the place of nouns. The noun to which a pronoun refers is called its **antecedent**.

A. A pronoun must agree with its antecedent.

> Japanese airplanes bombed Pearl Harbor. They sank 18 ships. (plural)
> Franklin D. Roosevelt was President. He led the United States during World War II. (singular, male)
> The congresswoman heard about the attack. The news shocked her. (singular, female)

B. When writing, be sure a pronoun's antecedent is clear. If it is not, the sentence may be confusing.

> Denise told her sister the news. She was very anxious. (*Who* was anxious, Denise or her sister?)

If either of two nouns could be the antecedent, it would be better to repeat the correct noun than to use a pronoun.

> Denise told her sister the news. Her sister was very anxious.

Strategy

Sometimes a pronoun's antecedent is not found in the previous sentence. The antecedent must still be clear, however.

> World War II affected many people. Most people's lives changed forever. It also transformed the map of Europe.

Check Your Understanding

A. Write the letter of the correct pronoun.
   1. The damage was serious. Few ships survived ____.
      a. it   **b.** they   **c.** him   **d.** them
   2. Dad was at Pearl Harbor in 1941. ____ saw the attack.
      a. They   **b.** Him   **c.** She   **d.** He

B. Write *a* if the antecedent of the underlined pronoun is clear. Write *b* if it is not clear.

   a. The antecedent is clear.   **b.** The antecedent is not clear.

   3. Many ships sank. The navy repaired most of them.
   4. Gail lent Eve a history book. She brought it to school.

Practice

A. Write the paragraph. Underline each pronoun once and its antecedent twice.

(5) Britain had several leaders during World War II. They led the war effort. (6) The first was Neville Chamberlain. Winston Churchill succeeded him in 1940. (7) The people of Britain loved Churchill. He was a great statesman. (8) Clement Attlee replaced him in 1945.

B. Write each pair of sentences. Underline the pronoun. Underline the antecedent twice if it is clear. If the antecedent is not clear, write *not clear*.

9. Roosevelt took action. He signed a declaration of war.

10. World War II began in 1939. It ended in 1945.

11. Churchill, Roosevelt, and Stalin led the allied powers. He was the leader of the Soviet Union.

12. Roosevelt died in 1945. Harry Truman succeeded him.

C. Mixed Practice Write each pair of sentences. Fill in the blank with one of the choices in parentheses. Choose a pronoun only if its antecedent is clear.

13. The attack on Pearl Harbor occurred in 1941. _____ stunned the nation. (The attack, It)

14. Enemy planes damaged many vessels. _____ were at the center of the attack. (The vessels, They)

15. Janet and Aisha studied the war in school. _____ learned about its effects. (Janet and Aisha, They)

16. Janet helped Aisha. _____ was a good student. (Janet, she)

17. Mary's grandmother wrote a book about the war. _____ was very proud. (Mary, she)

18. The war lasted six years. _____ caused much grief. (It, The war)

19. Fifteen million Americans served in the war effort. Some of _____ were only teenagers. (the Americans, them)

20. Several prime ministers led the people of Britain. One of _____ was Winston Churchill. (them, the prime ministers)

Apply: Journal

In your journal, write five sentences about a historical event. Use at least four pronouns.

Possessive Forms of Pronouns

Possessive forms of pronouns show ownership or possession.

A. You can add 's to a noun to show possession. You can also use a pronoun to show possession. Possessive forms of pronouns may appear before a noun or may stand alone.

Used Before Nouns		
singular:	my, your, his, her, its	Her car is expensive. Your car shines like glass.
plural:	our, your, their	Our car is green.
Used Alone		
singular:	mine, yours, his, hers, its	That sports car is mine.
plural:	ours, yours, theirs	The car with the dent is theirs.

B. Some possessive forms and contractions sound alike. A **contraction** is a shortened form of two words using an apostrophe in place of one or more letters. Do not confuse these possessive forms and contractions.

Possessive Forms	Contractions
Your motor is noisy.	You're in need of a new car.
Its tire went flat.	It's an old tire.
Their car has power brakes.	They're brand new cars.
Theirs is an imported car.	There's an imported car.

Remember: Contractions *always* contain an apostrophe.
Possessive forms of pronouns *never* do.

This doesn't make sense. I should use a possessive.

Strategy

If you are not sure whether to use a possessive pronoun or a contraction, say both words of the contraction aloud.

Incorrect: You're car drives well.　　You are car drives well.
Correct: Your car drives well.

Check Your Understanding

A. Write the letter of the word that correctly completes each sentence.
   1. The invention of the automobile changed ____ lives.
      a. our   **b.** ours   **c.** theirs   **d.** mine
   2. This book about the history of the automobile is ____.
      a. my   **b.** mine   **c.** your   **d.** their

B. Follow the directions for Check Your Understanding A.
   3. ____ the story of the automobile's invention.
      a. It's   **b.** Its
   4. Various inventors contributed ____ creative ideas.
      a. they're   **b.** their

Practice

A. Write each sentence using the correct possessive form.
   5. Inventors introduced (their, theirs) first cars in 1896.
   6. Henry Ford introduced (his, its) in that year.
   7. The antique car is (her, hers).
   8. Her car is older than (your, yours).

B. Write each sentence. Fill in the correct word.
   9. (Your, You're) the owner of that new car.
   10. (Its, It's) an unusual automobile.
   11. (Your, You're) history book shows Nicolas Cugnot's 1770 steam vehicle.
   12. (They're, Their) car always looks (its, it's) best.

C. Mixed Practice Write each sentence. Fill in the correct word.
   13. (Theirs, There's) one problem with the electric car.
   14. (Its, It's) a very slow car.
   15. (My, Mine) car travels much faster.
   16. Americans have always loved (their, they're) cars.
   17. (Their, They're) necessary transportation for people.
   18. The Duryea brothers are famous for (theirs, their).
   19. (Their, Theirs, They're) car made (its, it's) first successful ride in 1894.
   20. (Your, You're) car is faster than (my, mine) or (her, hers).

Apply: Learning Log

Which part of this lesson did you find most difficult? Write two suggestions that will help make that part easier for you.

Homophones and Homographs

A. When you write, you may be confused by words that sound alike.

Homophones are words that sound the same but have different spellings and meanings.

The underlined words in these sentences are homophones.

Here is the site of the Civil War memorial.
We will hear more about this impressive sight.

To decide which homophone is correct, think of how the word is used in the sentence.

B. When you read, you may be confused by words that are spelled alike.

Homographs are words that are spelled alike but have different meanings.

Homographs may be pronounced the same or differently. The underlined words in each sentence below are homographs.

Soldiers pitch their tents close to here.
They close tears in their tents with pitch from pine trees.

What does the word *close* mean in the first sentence? In the second sentence? What does *pitch* mean in each sentence?

Strategy

Don't let two words that sound or look alike confuse you. Read sentences carefully to determine each word's correct meaning. Sometimes reading a sentence aloud will help. When in doubt, consult a dictionary.

Check Your Understanding

A. Write the letter of the homophone for the underlined word.
1. An army captain leads troops forward into battle.
   a. forehead   **b.** ahead   **c.** foreword   **d.** backward
2. The captain will receive orders from the colonel.
   a. general   **b.** kernel   **c.** colony   **d.** colonial

B. Write the letter of the homograph in each sentence.

   3. The captain gave stern orders from the ship's stern.

     a. gave   **b.** stern   **c.** orders   **d.** ship's

   4. Soldiers in the desert must never desert their posts.

     a. trained   **b.** desert   **c.** never   **d.** post

Practice

A. Write each sentence, using the correct homophone.

   5. The country had much at (stake, steak) in the Civil War.

   6. The war was a turning point for (hour, our) nation.

   7. Soldiers brought supplies (threw, through) the blockade.

   8. (Their, There) were many close battles.

B. Write each sentence. Underline each homograph, and write its meaning. Consult a dictionary for help.

   9. Greater resources would tip the scales in the Union's favor. Fights in Congress were the tip of the iceberg.

  10. A major might lead troops into battle. Factories made rifle bullets from lead.

  11. We feel the war's effects even to the present day. Historians must present a clear picture of such events.

  12. The cavalry charged across the open plain. Their ragged uniforms were plain and unadorned.

C. Mixed Practice Write each sentence using a word from the box. (You'll use some words twice.) Use a dictionary to help you write each word's meaning in each sentence.

ground	rein
wound	rite
reign	write
right	

  13. The soldier received a _____ in his left arm.

  14. The cavalry commander pulled the _____ of his horse.

  15. Mills _____ grain for the soldiers' bread.

  16. War brought an end to the _____ of that tyrant.

  17. The line of soldiers _____ through the hills.

  18. A life of peace is the most basic human _____.

  19. The soldiers _____ their boot heels into the _____.

  20. Authors _____ stories of battle as a _____ of passage.

Apply: Work with a Group

With your group, write five funny sentences using homophones, like this one: *"I'm a little hoarse today," he whinnied.* Share the best ones with your class.

Language in Action

Giving Directions

Imagine this situation: You are on your way home from school. Someone walks up to you and says, "Excuse me. How can I get to the post office from here?" You want to help the person by giving accurate directions. You don't want to confuse the person. You don't want the person to get lost. What do you say?

Giving directions is something that everyone has to do from time to time. Sometimes you will have time to write the directions. Often, however, you will have to give directions orally. In either case, you will have to make some choices. Which route should you choose? How much detail should you include? Here are some guidelines for giving directions.

- Before you say anything, picture clearly in your mind as many direct routes as you can. Then choose the route that is the easiest to describe. You might know a shortcut. But if the person gets lost by following it, your shortcut wasn't helpful.
- Break down the route into decision points. A **decision point** is a place where someone must turn right or left.
  "Keep going until you reach the park. Then turn left."
- Give your directions in the order in which they should be followed.
- Always tell the person which way to turn.
  "At the library, turn onto High Street." (incorrect)
  "At the library, turn left onto High Street." (correct)
- Give the person an idea of the distance between decision points, especially if it is very long or very short.
  "Turn left and then immediately right."
  "Go for about a mile until you come to the mall. Then turn right."
- If there is a prominent landmark on the way, mention it.
  "Turn right, and continue for three blocks. You'll pass a huge grain elevator. When you get to the firehouse, turn right again."

234

Practice

Study the map below. Then, on a separate sheet of paper, write directions for getting from the train station to the Gates Motel. Describe and number each step of the route.

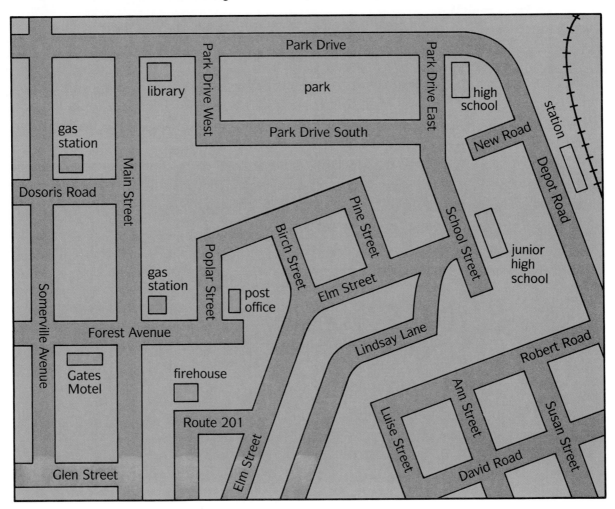

Apply

Work in pairs for this activity. Pick a store or other location in your community. Give your partner directions from the school to that place. See if your partner can name the store or location by listening to your directions. Then listen to your partner's directions, and try to figure out the exact location.

HISTORY OF LANGUAGE

Words from Place Names

Lloyd's mother is going to run in the Boston marathon. A marathon is a 26-mile, 385-yard foot race. The name *marathon* comes from the Greek city of Marathon. In 490 B.C., a battle took place there. After the battle, a messenger ran all the way from Marathon to Athens to announce the victory. The distance was 26 miles, 385 yards. Runners still run this exact distance in honor of that famous messenger.

Lloyd's sister knows other words that came from a place in Greece. *Magnesia* is a region where naturally magnetic stones are found. *Magnet* and *magnetic* come from the name of the region of Magnesia.

Then Lloyd remembered a word that he learned in school. A geyser is a stream that shoots out hot water, steam, or mud. The word *geyser* comes from Geysir in Iceland. Geysir is where geysers were first discovered. Lloyd decided to find out more about words that come from place names. Here is a game he made up using the words he found.

Activity

Rewrite each sentence completing it with a word from the box.

attic	cheddar	cologne	hallmark	palace

1. The word _____ comes from the German city of Cologne, which is famous for its perfumes.
2. In Attica, a Greek province, people lived in two- and three-story houses. This was unusual for the time, and gave us the word _____.
3. A _____ was stamped on gold and silver pieces that passed certain quality tests in Goldsmiths' Hall in London.
4. The Palatine Hill in Rome was where Roman emperors had large, fancy homes. This hill gave us the word _____.
5. The English town of Cheddar was where the hard cheese _____ was first made.

UNIT REVIEW

Descriptive Writing (page 195)
1. List at least two characteristics of descriptive writing.

Using Figurative Language (pages 204–205)
Write whether each sentence contains an example of a *simile*, a *metaphor*, *personification*, *alliteration*, or *onomatopoeia*.
2. The unexpected storm had its joke, laughed, and moved on.
3. Traffic inched its way along like a caterpillar.
4. Several pigs oinked and grunted while they chomped their food.
5. In the sky, slender seagulls soared and swooped.
6. The beavers were a busy corps of engineers.

Using Commas and Semicolons (pages 210–211)
Write the sentences below. Add commas and semicolons where they are needed.
7. Safety pins are commonplace items however few people know about the inventor.
8. Well the safety pin was invented by Walter Hunt in 1849.
9. Hunt invented an ice plow and a sewing machine too.
10. Hunt however never patented his sewing machine Elias Howe is usually credited with that invention.
11. Actually Hunt developed the first pin and Howe refined the item later.
12. So what other questions do you have about Walter Hunt?
13. Hunt did not invent the paper clip another inventor did that.
14. No I do not recall the inventor's name at the moment.

Poetry (pages 213–217)
Read the following three poems. Then, answer the questions below.

An eagle floating high	Do you remember	Eagle
Glides without sound,	when the sky was dark and gray	Aloft,
Unaware that I	and the rain tumbled	Gliding,
Observe from the ground.	until the clouds grew weary?	Looking
	I knew there'd be a rainbow.	Everywhere.

15. What is the rhyme pattern of the first poem?
16. Which lines have the same number of syllables in the second poem?
17. What is the subject of the third poem?

Subject Pronouns (pages 222–223)
Write each sentence. Replace the underlined words with a subject pronoun. Label the pronoun either *subject* or *predicate nominative*.
18. The victors in the tennis match were Joan and Frank.
19. Lucinda won the singles tournament.
20. Phillipe and Jean finished second in the doubles.
21. The challenger in the finals was Yvonne.
22. Boris won the tournament last year.

Object Pronouns (pages 224–225)
Write each sentence. Replace the underlined word or words with an object pronoun.
23. Stradivari made violins of excellent quality for musicians.
24. He sold the masterpieces to grateful musicians.
25. Stradivari produced violins and violas in his workshop in Italy around 1700.
26. Many violinists throughout the world still seek the Stradivarius violin.
27. Stradivari's violins have given Stradivari an important place in music history.
28. Their sound gives other listeners and me great joy.
29. The sound of a Stradivarius impressed Ali and me.
30. Stradivarius violins bring a unique sound to music.
31. Today's violinmakers cannot match Stradivari.
32. None give violinists and audiences the same gift.

Using Pronouns Correctly (pages 226–227)
Write each sentence. Replace each underlined word with the correct form of the pronoun.
33. Myron and Bernice are geology majors.
34. Their best friends are Jane and Ralph.
35. Bernice gave Myron a party.
36. Myron had completed the semester with honors.
37. Jane brought Bernice and Myron a bouquet of flowers in a beautiful basket.
38. Ralph brought Al and Phoebe to the party.
39. Myron was quite surprised by the party.
40. Bernice and her friends had not told him about it.
41. Professor Burns and her husband are chairpersons of the geology department.
42. The guest of honor was Professor Burns.

Pronouns and Antecedents (pages 228–229)

Write each pair of sentences. Use one of the choices in parentheses to complete the second sentence. Choose a pronoun only if its antecedent is clear.

43. The seven continents were once all one area of land. _____ formed a supercontinent. (The seven continents, They)

44. Scientists gave the supercontinent a name. They called _____ Pangaea. (the supercontinent, it)

45. Pangaea has spread all over the earth. The seven continents float around on _____. (the earth, it)

46. These continental movements cause earthquakes. _____ occur at the edge of continental plates. (They, Earthquakes)

47. California slides over the Pacific Ocean floor. _____ is the site of many earthquakes. (It, California)

Possessive Forms of Pronouns (pages 230–231)

Write each sentence with the correct word in parentheses.

48. (Your, You're) new home is beautiful.

49. The green ranch on the corner is (my, mine).

50. (Their, They're) house was the first one here.

51. (Their, They're) new to the neighborhood.

52. (Our, Ours) home has solar heating.

53. (Its, It's) boiler never worked properly.

54. The house with two chimneys is (theirs, there's).

55. This house seems larger than (our, ours).

56. (Your, You're) welcome here anytime.

57. (My, Mine) door is always open.

Homophones and Homographs (pages 232–233)

Write each sentence, completing it with a homophone or a homograph of the underlined word. Write whether it is a homophone or homograph. Choose from the words in the box.

content	batter	bored	sale	sight

58. The sailor bought a new sail at the annual sports _____.

59. The students were _____ with the content of the lesson.

60. The batter on the Little-League team mixed the _____ for the team's baking contest.

61. Tom nailed the last board on his treehouse and then became very _____.

62. At the building site, we saw a spectacular _____.

6

Research Report

◆

Adjectives

What Do You Know?

"Why don't you look it up?"

When you want to know what shows are on television or what movies are playing nearby, you can look up the information in a newspaper. When you want to spell a word correctly, you can look it up in a dictionary. To learn the recipe for a favorite dessert, you can look in a cookbook.

Though you may not think of it as research, these are all ways of finding information. Research is just that—a way of gathering information. When you write a research report, you go through a similar process, but in a more detailed, organized way. The finished report presents your research in written form, for others to learn from.

Thinking About Research Reports

What Is a Research Report?

A **research report** has these characteristics:

- It gives information on a particular topic.
- The topic may be divided into several main ideas.
- Each main idea is supported by facts or details.
- All information in the report is true and based on research.

You probably associate research reports with school. However, research reports appear in many places, including books and magazines. Research reports may be on topics in many subjects, such as social studies, history, literature, and science. You might research an ancient culture, a distant planet, or a species of insect life; perhaps you want to investigate something you have talked about with friends.

Research reports are interesting to read as well as to write. In this unit, you will learn how to find, organize, and present information on a topic that interests you.

Discussion

1. What topic has interested you the most recently?
2. What questions would you like to have answered about this topic?
3. Where do you think you might find the information to answer your questions?

241

Reading a Research Report

Read the following research report about Pompeii. Notice how the main idea in each paragraph is supported with facts.

The End of Pompeii

title
introduction

Two thousand years ago, Pompeii was a small but thriving Roman city. Then, one day in A.D. 79, Pompeii suddenly disappeared. This lost city eventually became one of the most important archaeological finds ever made.

The first paragraph of the body covers one main idea.

During the first century A.D., Pompeii was a prosperous trading city near the Bay of Naples. The city stood under the shadow of Mt. Vesuvius, a volcano that was thought to be extinct. Then, on August 24 of A.D. 79, Mt. Vesuvius erupted suddenly and violently. Pompeii was taken by surprise. Most people escaped quickly with a few possessions, but thousands did not. By the next morning, the whole city was buried under tons of volcanic ash. Only the tops of the tallest buildings could be seen, and soon they too had disappeared. The city was completely gone.

All information is true and based on research.

Pompeii lay almost forgotten for over a thousand years. Then, in 1709, workers digging a well discovered a nearby city that had been buried at the same time as Pompeii. Later, in 1748, a Spanish engineer discovered Pompeii itself when he dug through the hardened ash and uncovered a temple.

Pompeii is unique among ancient ruins because, unlike other ancient cities, it was left almost intact. The ash that covered the city preserved its contents. Besides the artfully decorated buildings themselves, many everyday tools and untensils have been found. The houses, the shops, and the household items reveal much about how Pompeii's inhabitants worked and lived so long ago.

conclusion

Much of Pompeii remains to be excavated, and new discoveries will continue to tell scientists about the past. Because Roman civilization laid the foundation for much of our culture, Pompeii provides us with a unique view of our own past.

Understanding What You've Read

Write the answers to these questions:

1. When did Pompeii disappear?
2. What kinds of things were found in the ruins?
3. What do the findings tell us about the people who lived there?
4. Why do you think Pompeii was not rediscovered earlier than it was?
5. What are some of the ways in which scientists help us understand the past?

Writing Assignment

Everyone enjoys reading magazines. Now you and your classmates will have a chance to put together a brand-new magazine called *Research World*. Each student will write a research report on a topic he or she finds interesting. Each report will be five paragraphs long. All of the research reports will be included in the magazine.

Your **audience** will be your teacher and your classmates. Your **purpose** will be to write a research report that is both accurate and interesting to others.

Choose a Topic

Make a list of five general topics that interest you, such as uses of natural resources, trade between nations, and life in modern China. Choose one of the topics and narrow it down as you learned in Unit 1. Save your topic for the next lesson.

Organizing a Research Report

A research report has three basic parts: the introduction, the body, and the conclusion.

The **introduction** begins the report. It states the main ideas the report will focus on. The introduction should interest a reader and tell him or her what the report will be about.

The **body** is the main part of a research report. It gives detailed information about the main ideas in the report. The body may contain one or more paragraphs. Each paragraph develops an idea and presents supporting facts and details.

The **conclusion** sums up and ties together the main ideas in the report, usually in one paragraph. Following the conclusion is a **bibliography**, which is an alphabetical list of all the information sources you used.

Once you choose a topic, you will have to narrow it down and decide what main ideas to cover in the body of your report. A topic wheel can help you. A topic wheel shows many questions around a general topic. Later, you choose the specific questions you will discuss in your report.

Look at the topic wheel below. It covers the general topic of the Roman Empire.

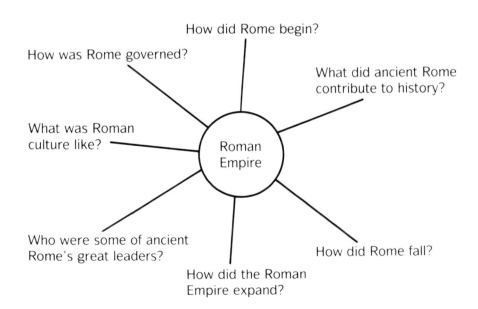

Practice

A. Make a topic wheel for each general topic below. Write at least three questions that you could ask about each topic.

1. written language
2. skyscrapers
3. Yellowstone National Park
4. the Nile River
5. photography
6. rain
7. immigration to the United States
8. American literature
9. gold
10. holidays

B. Choose two of the topic wheels you made in Exercise A. Under each question, write down all the information you already know about the answer. Then write where you might look to find more information for each answer.

Make a Topic Wheel

Using the topic that you narrowed in the previous lesson, make a topic wheel that lists at least six questions you have about that topic. Under each question, write any information you already know about the answer. Choose three of the questions for your research report. Then write where you might look to find more information to answer these questions. Save your work for the next lesson.

Using Reference Materials

The reference section of the library has many sources of information for a research report. Some are explained below.

An **encyclopedia** contains informative articles on many different subjects. The articles are arranged alphabetically by subject. Most encyclopedias are divided into many volumes. Each volume is labeled alphabetically and numerically. To locate a particular article, go to the volume with the same first letter as your subject. A person is listed under the first letter of his or her last name. For other subjects, look up the **key word**, or most important word, in a title or phrase. For example, to research a report on the history of Rome, the key word would be *Rome*.

The *Readers' Guide to Periodical Literature* can help you find magazine articles on your subject. Each volume covers a period of one year. Articles are indexed by both subject and author. To find out if any new discoveries of Roman ruins have been made, look in recent volumes of the *Readers' Guide* under *R* for *Rome* or *A* for *archaeology*. If you find a relevant article listed, copy the information and try to get the periodical you need. The most current periodicals can also be found in the reference section of the library.

Other useful sources of information in the reference section include almanacs and atlases.

An **almanac** is an annual book that lists current facts, figures, charts, and records about different subjects. For example, in an almanac you can find out what book has sold the most copies in the previous year or what the grain imports were in a given year.

An **atlas** is a collection of maps and charts in book form. An atlas contains indexes of place names and facts of interest about places in the world. In an atlas, you can find information about the population, geology, or climate of a particular place.

Practice

Read the topics listed below. For each topic, write the key word or words and the source in which you would find information.

1. the history of space exploration
2. the causes of the Revolutionary War
3. the invention of the printing press
4. recent developments in computers
5. political changes in Africa since 1950
6. the names of the five seas that border Italy
7. the discovery of penicillin
8. the current population of the United States
9. the Brooklyn Bridge: 100 years of history
10. how sound changed motion pictures
11. the election of Grover Cleveland

Find Your Topic in Reference Books

Use an encyclopedia, the *Readers' Guide*, or another reference source to find more information to answer your three questions. Look in each volume that might contain helpful articles. Jot down the name, volume number, and page numbers for each source you plan to use. Save your work.

Understanding the Parts of a Book

When writing a report, you may need more detailed information than you can find in the library's reference section. For example, to write a report on Rome you might want to know: *How did the Roman Empire begin?* and *How did the government work?* There are many books about Rome. How can you know which ones will answer your questions without reading them all? The main parts of each book will tell you more about its contents.

A History of Rome
   by Robert A. Lovecraft
Arkham University Press
   Arkham, Massachusetts

The **title page** is in the front of a book. It names the book's title, author, publishing company, and the company's location. On the back of the title page, the copyright date tells when the book was published.

Table of Contents

Introduction   3
1. Early History   5
2. The Republic 20
3. Roman Influence 48
4. Roman Culture 73

The **table of contents** follows the title page. It lists the chapter or unit titles in the order they appear. It shows the beginning page number for each chapter.

Index

Remus, 6
Roman
   gods, 3, 75–77
   laws, 35, 52
   republic, 23
Romulus, 6
Sculpture, 68, 81
Senate, 17–18, 51

The **index** is in the back of the book. It alphabetically lists all the main topics discussed in the book. Some topics may have more specific subtopics listed under them. The index shows the page or pages on which each topic and subtopic is found.

Practice

Use the title page, table of contents, and index on the previous page to answer these questions.

1. Who is the author of *A History of Rome*?
2. Which company published the book?
3. What is the first chapter of the book about?
4. On what page does chapter 3 begin?
5. Would you find information about the founding of Rome before page 50 or after page 50?
6. On what page can you find information about Remus and Romulus?
7. Is there more information about Roman gods or about Roman sculpture?
8. What pages would you look on to find information about the Senate?
9. What chapter would you look in to find out whether modern governments have used the Roman government as a model?
10. Why do you think someone doing a research report would be interested in the date that a book was published?

Find Books on Your Topic

- Find books on the topic you chose for your research report. Use textbooks or library books.
- Check the title page, table of contents, and index of each book to learn more about each book's contents.
- List the titles of the books that would be most helpful in answering your questions about the topic.
- List the page numbers in each book you've chosen that contain information about your topic.
- Save your work.

Taking Notes in Your Own Words

After finding the books and encyclopedia articles to use for your report, you are ready to take notes on the materials.

Taking notes means writing down only the most important information that you find. Your notes can be in the form of phrases or complete sentences. Write down in your own words the information you will want to include in your report.

Below is one article used for a report on ancient Rome and the notes that were taken on it.

According to legend, the founder of Rome was Romulus, one of two sons of Mars, the Roman god of war. The two sons were said to have been raised by wolves. Romulus supposedly founded the city near the Tiber River in 753 B.C.

Archaeologists believe that Rome was in fact founded in the mid-700s B.C. Later, a people called the Etruscans settled there and made Rome part of their kingdom. In 509 B.C., the people of Rome rebelled against the Etruscans and formed a republic.

Until Rome fell, it ruled a large part of the world. Rome was defeated in the fifth century after a series of many wars.

In Naples, paintings, pottery, and other objects have been found in Etruscan tombs. These show that the Etruscans had a civilization and a culture that combined parts of Southwest Asian and Greek cultures. They had a written language and were fine builders.

How did Rome begin?
- legend says by Romulus, in 753 B.C.
- founded mid-700s B.C.
- ruled by Etruscans until 509 B.C.
- became a republic in 509 B.C.

How did Rome fall?
- defeated in a series of wars
- fell in fifth century.

Look at the notes. At the top of each note card, the student wrote one of the questions to be answered in the report. This helped the student decide which details to include in the notes. The student did not take notes on the last paragraph in the article because it did not relate to the questions on the note cards.

The article does not give all the information needed for the report. The writer needed to check other sources.

Practice

A. Imagine you are writing a research report on the Etruscans. Take notes from the article on the previous page. At the top of your paper, write the question that you want to answer. Take notes only on details about the topic of Etruscans. Put the notes in your own words.

B. Read the following article. Take notes that could be used to answer the question of how Rome was governed.

After the Romans drove out the Etruscans, they started a republic. A republic is a form of representative government in which citizens elect the officials they wish to govern them. A republic can be an oligarchy or a democracy, depending upon the number of people who rule. In Rome, 300 noblemen, or patricians, made up the Senate and created Roman law.

The common people, or plebians, were represented in the government by elected officials called tribunes. The job of a tribune was to protect the people's rights.

Most Romans were plain, hard-working farmers. Parents taught their children loyalty and courage. The Romans' sense of duty strengthened the republic.

Take Notes for Your Report

Review the three questions that you listed about your topic. Write each of these questions at the top of a piece of paper or a note card. Then take notes from the books and encyclopedias you chose. Put each detail under the question it helps to answer. Write down only the most important information or main ideas. Put the notes in your own words. Save your work.

List the Sources for Your Report

List information about each source you use. For each book, include the title, the author's name, the publisher, the place and date of publication. For each encyclopedia article, include the title and volume number of the encyclopedia, the title of the article, and the page numbers of the information. Save your work.

Making an Outline

After taking all the notes for your report, you are ready to organize them into an outline.

An outline helps you put your information into a logical order. It organizes the information into main ideas and supporting details. Each main idea appears next to a Roman numeral. The facts and details supporting that main idea are listed next to capital letters under the Roman numeral. Later, when you write your report, you will include each main idea and its supporting details in a paragraph.

Here are some notes and the outline for the report on Rome.

How did Rome begin?
- Founding of small city approx. 753 B.C.
- Details unknown. Legend say by Romulus.
- Romans revolted to start a republic
- Etrucans ruled until 509 B.C.

I. Rome was founded about 753 B.C.
  A. Legend says Romulus founded Rome.
  B. Etruscans ruled until 509 B.C.
  C. The Roman Republic began after the revolt.

How was Rome governed?
- A republic gives citizens voice in government.
- 300 senators made laws.
- Romans protected in senate by veto.

II. Rome was a republic with elected officials.
  A. In a republic, citizens elect those who govern.
  B. Romans elected officials.
  C. Laws were made in the Senate.
  D. The veto protected citizens' rights.

How did Rome fall?
- Republic expanded to become an empire.
- People fought to control the government.
- This brought about confusion
- Greed and conquest scattered Roman armies.
- In A.D. 476, enemies invaded Rome and won.

III. Greed and conflict caused the fall of Roman Empire.
  A. The Republic grew into a powerful empire.
  B. A power struggle arose in government.
  C. Confusion developed.
  D. Roman Army was weakened by greed.
  E. Rome was invaded and conquered in A.D. 476.

Practice

A. Answer these questions about the outline on page 252.
1. What are the three main ideas in the outline?
2. How many details support the first main idea?
3. What is the first detail that supports the second main idea?
4. Based on this outline, how many paragraphs would the body of this report be?

B. Read the two main ideas below and the details that follow. Make an outline by listing each main idea and the details that belong under it.

I. Greece is the birthplace of much of our culture.
II. Two reasons for the rise of Greece were its mild climate and its location on the sea.

1. Sailors could easily exchange goods with people in other lands.
2. Medicine was first practiced scientifically in Greece.
3. All written knowledge was collected and stored in libraries.
4. It was located between the main cities of Africa and Asia.
5. Greeks created the first plays and realistic art.
6. The Greeks produced skillful sailors and a strong navy.
7. Greeks raised important questions about art, science, and the meaning of life.
8. The clear, warm weather allowed for outdoor discussion, which promoted widespread education among the Greeks.

Make an Outline

Look at the notes you took in the last lesson. Use these notes to make an outline. Write your main ideas next to roman numerals. List the supporting details next to capital letters under each main idea. Save your outline for the next lesson.

Read this part of a first draft of a research report. The writer wasn't worried about making it perfect. It will be changed later.

The Ancient Romans

The ancient Romans played a major role in history. For over five hundred years, they ruled a large portion of the Western World. During that time, they developed political ideas that are still in use by governments today.

Roman civilization began with the founding of a small city on the coast of Italy. Legend says that the city was founded in 753 B.C. by Romulus, the son of the war god, Mars. Although the details of Rome's founding are not known, archaeologists believe that the date is correct. Until 509 B.C., Rome was ruled by the kings of its powerful neighbors, the Etruscans. In that year, however, the Romans drove out the Etruscans and started the Roman Republic.

A republic is a system of government in which the citizens elect people to govern them. Laws were made by officials in a group of 300 people called the Senate. Any Senate decision could be stoped by a veto from representitives of the common people. A veto is used today when our President decides against a proposed law.

The Roman Republic expanded until it controled all of Italy and much of the land beyond. The city of Rome then became the center of a worldwide empire. The empire later fell. Among the reasons for the fall was that people fought each other for political power.

Write Your First Draft

You may discuss your report with your teacher or classmates, or start work by yourself. Follow your outline. Begin the first paragraph of the body with your first main idea. Then write the details that tell more about it. Do the same for the second and third paragraphs of the body. Afterward, use your main ideas to write your introduction and conclusion. Save your work.

REVISING
Discussing a First Draft

The writer of the research report finished the first draft. To improve it, the writer discussed the report with a classmate.

Discussion Strategy

Never say to your partner, "You're wrong." If you do, your partner will probably stop listening to your suggestions. Even if you think that you are right, remember that there is often more than one "correct" way to write something.

Use this Content Checklist to discuss with your classmates the research report that you have read.

Content Checklist

✔ Does the research report give information on a particular topic?
✔ Is the topic divided into several main ideas?
✔ Is each main idea supported by facts and details?
✔ Is all information in the report based on research, not on the writer's opinions?

APPLY STEP BY STEP

Revise Your First Draft for Content

To the Reader: Trade papers with a classmate. Read your partner's report. Try to identify the main idea in each paragraph. If anything is unclear, discuss ways to improve the report. Use the Content Checklist and Discussion Strategy for help.

To the Writer: Listen to the suggestions your partner gives you. Then revise your draft for content. Save your work.

DETAILS

FACTS

MAIN IDEA

REVISING
Using Transition Words

In a research report, it is important for your readers to follow your sequence of thoughts. Sometimes transitions between sentences or paragraphs can be unclear, leaving the reader confused. Transition words or phrases help make clear relationships between sentences. These words often appear at the beginning of a sentence. Like other introductory words, they are followed by a comma.

The following words express relationships of <u>time</u>: *afterward, some time later, then, before that.*

> Example: For a long time, the Romans ruled over a large world empire. Centuries later many modern governments use the Romans' political ideas.

These words express relationships of <u>cause and effect</u>: *as a result, because of this, therefore.*

> Example: Many people fought for power. As a result, confusion developed.

Here are words that express relationships of <u>contrast</u>: *however, on the other hand, in contrast, nevertheless.*

> Example: Rome lost its role as the world's greatest power. However, its influence lives on.

These words express relationships of <u>similarity</u>: *in addition, also, besides, similarly, in the same way.*

> Example: Any Senate decision could be stopped by a veto from the representatives of the common people. Similarly, a veto is used today when our President decides against a proposed law.

Transitions can also be made between paragraphs. One method is to begin a paragraph with a word, phrase, or idea from the previous paragraph. This repetition indicates a connection between the ideas.

> Example: ...Roman land was invaded by enemies, and Rome itself was conquered in A.D. 476.
> After this defeat, Rome lost its role as the world's greatest power.

Practice

Make the relationships between the following pairs of sentences clearer by using transition words. Use transition words that express the relationships shown in parentheses.

1. Rome was a republic for almost five hundred years. Not all people enjoyed the same rights. (contrast)
2. Rome was a republic from 509 B.C. until 27 B.C. It became an empire. (time)
3. Rome conquered Carthage. It conquered Athens. (similarity)
4. The Roman Empire grew too large for one government. It was split into two parts. (cause and effect)
5. In 27 B.C., Octavian changed his name to Augustus and declared himself emperor. The Roman Republic became the Roman Empire. (cause and effect)
6. The Roman Empire governed in peace from 27 B.C. until A.D. 180. It became entangled in wars for a century. (time)
7. The Western Roman Empire was weakened by the splitting up of the empire. It was weakened by attacks from European invaders. (similarity)
8. The Western Empire was defeated in A.D. 476. Its Eastern counterpart survived until 1453. (contrast)

Revising Checklist
- ✔ Have I included all the characteristics of a research report?
- ✔ Where can I combine sentences? (pp. 34, 118, 158)
- ✔ Where can I revise sentences for variety? (p. 72)
- ✔ Where can I link sentences with transition words?

Revise Your First Draft for Style
Check for the items on the Revising Checklist. Where possible, include transition words to connect sentences and paragraphs. Mark your changes on the draft. Save your work.

Punctuating a Bibliography

A research report ends with an alphabetical list of sources called a **bibliography**. Its purpose is to document all the sources of your information. There is a special form for entries in a bibliography.

Each book in a bibliography should include the author, title, city of publication, publisher, and publication date.

> Ogden, Sara L. The Story of Rome. Chicago: Harris, Cross & Co., 1988.

Magazine articles are listed by the author's last name. Include the volume number and date of the issue the article appeared in.

> Tanaka, Michael. "Ancient Rome Rules the World." History Monthly, vol. 15, August 1987, pp. 27-35.

Most encyclopedia articles have no listed author. Put the title of the article in alphabetical order, and list the volume and page numbers of the article.

> "Pompeii." Encyclopedia of History, vol. 13, 1983 ed., pp. 187-194.

The chart below shows how to punctuate entries in a bibliography.

Rule	Example
Indent the second line of each entry. Use a period after each entry.	Emery, Mabel. Rome and its Legacy. Detroit: Tiger Press, 1988.
Write each author's last name first. Use a period after the author's name(s).	Ruiz, Roberto. "Ancient Findings." Archives, vol. 4, October 1989, pp. 78–84.
In books, use a colon after the city of publication. Use a period after book titles. Use a comma after magazine and encyclopedia titles, publisher's names, and volume and edition numbers and dates.	Lee, Alan. The Gods of Rome. Chicago: McDay Press, 1987. "Rome." Modern Age Encyclopedia, vol. 6, 1985 ed., pp. 219–227.

Practice

This list shows the books, encyclopedias, and articles used by one student. On a separate sheet of paper, rewrite the list as a bibliography. Remember to alphabetize the list and to punctuate correctly.

1. "The Roman Republic," written by Carlos Torres and printed on pages 13-21 of History magazine, volume 3 in February 1988
2. Louis Chun's book, *The Stones of Rome*, published in 1986 by Silverado Publishers in Denver
3. an article from the 1983 edition of *National Encyclopedia*, volume 9, called "Roman Empire" and appearing on pages 12-32
4. a magazine article called "A New Look at Rome" by David Kiley, printed on pages 21-27 in Volume 4 of Topics in April of 1987
5. A book by Margaret Ailey published by Dolphin Press of Miami in 1986 and titled *Rome: Republic to Empire*.

Proofreading Checklist
✔ Did I indent the first word of each paragraph? (p. 36)
✔ Did I capitalize names correctly? (p. 36)
✔ Did I end each sentence with the correct punctuation? (p. 36)
✔ Did I use commas and semicolons correctly? (pp. 74, 210)
✔ Did I capitalize and punctuate titles of books, magazines, and articles correctly? (p. 120)
✔ Did I punctuate the bibliography correctly?
✔ Does each pronoun have an antecedent?

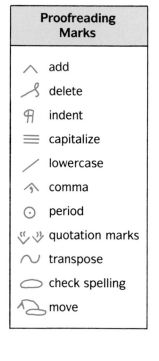

Proofreading Marks	
∧	add
⌀	delete
¶	indent
=	capitalize
/	lowercase
⌃	comma
⊙	period
⌄⌄	quotation marks
∼	transpose
⌯	check spelling
⌐	move

Write a Bibliography
Check your list of sources and order them alphabetically. Use index cards or a separate piece of paper for each entry. Then make a final copy of your bibliography to include with your research report.

Proofread Your Research Report
Check for correct capitalization, punctuation, and grammar in your research report. Use the Proofreading Checklist. Make corrections on your draft. Save your work for the next lesson.

Checking Spelling/Writing a Final Copy ◆

Spelling Strategy

Sometimes remembering a rule can help you spell a word.

<u>Example:</u> Which spelling is correct, *beleive* or *believe*? Use this rule: *i* before *e* except after *c* (bel*ie*ve).

Now read this part of the revised and proofread report.

A republic is a system of government in which the citizens elect people to govern them. Laws were made by officials in a group of 300 people called the Senate. Any Senate decision could be *stopped* ~~stoped~~ by a veto from *representatives* ~~representitives~~ of the common people. *Similarly,* A veto is used today when our President decides against a proposed law.

The Roman Republic expanded until it *controlled* ~~controled~~ all of Italy and much of the land beyond. The city of Rome then became the center of a worldwide empire. *However,* The empire later fell. Among the reasons for the fall was that people fought each other for political power. *As a result,* Confusion developed in the government. *In addition,* Greed for wealth and conquest weakened the army. Roman land was invaded by enemies, and Rome itself was *conquered* ~~conquered~~ in A.D. 476. *After this defeat,* Rome lost its role as the world's greatest power. *However,* Its influence lives on. Many modern ideas of law and government had their beginnings in early Rome.

Check Your Spelling

Use the proofreading marks to correct spelling mistakes. Add any misspelled words to your spelling log. Then, write a neat, final copy of your research report.

PRESENTING
Sharing Your Research Report

Speaking/Listening Strategy

Practice reading your work aloud when you are alone. You will then be more familiar with what you have written and will do a better job of reading to others. As you practice, pay special attention to the parts that may be more difficult to read.

Choosing a Way to Share

Here are several ways to share your report with others.

Reading Aloud Collect or draw pictures to illustrate your report. Mount them on colored construction paper. Be sure they are large enough to be seen by your audience. As you read your report to your classmates, place the pictures on an easel or the chalk tray. When you are finished, answer any questions your audience may have.

Presenting a Show Choose some aspect of your report that will have a connection to the lives of your audience. For example, you might illustrate daily events in a Roman home. Work out a short skit with a classmate. After the skit, you might discuss the ideas and events you presented.

Create a Magazine Use the class's research reports to create a magazine. Work in small groups to make a table of contents. Design a cover for the magazine. You may choose to include pictures and diagrams to illustrate the reports. Display the magazine in your classroom.

Share Your Research Report
Choose the way you prefer to share your report. Practice so that your presentation is smooth and easy to understand.

Add to Your Learning Log

♦ What pleases me most about my report?
♦ What part of my research was most interesting?
♦ If I were to write another research report, what different choices would I make?

The Literature Connection: Adjectives

Good writing can tell us how people feel during important moments, or turning points, in their lives. It records sounds and sights. It also gives us a picture of the way things are.

Adjectives can help paint these pictures. They describe the look, color, and texture of things. Writers use adjectives to help us see and feel things for ourselves.

Consider this sentence: *Sandy got a dog.* You can hardly form a very colorful picture in your mind from this group of words. However, now consider this sentence: *Sandy got a tall, white, furry, noisy dog.* What a difference the string of adjectives makes! Writing is always much more vivid with well-chosen adjectives to describe people, animals, and things.

The selection below describes a scene from the book *The Wind in the Willows*. Notice the crisp, colorful adjectives that the author uses to describe the scene.

from **The Wind in the Willows**
by
Kenneth Grahame

It was a cold still afternoon with a hard steely sky overhead, when he [Mole] slipped out of the warm parlour into the open air. The country lay bare and entirely leafless around him, and he thought that he had never seen so far and so intimately into the insides of things as on that winter day when Nature was deep in her annual slumber and seemed to have kicked the clothes off.

Discussion

1. What adjectives does the author use to describe how things looked?
2. What adjectives does the author use to describe how things felt?
3. Does the mood of the scene seem friendly or scary to you? Explain.

The Writing Connection:
Adjectives

In your own writing, adjectives can give you the power to describe. You can change the meaning of an entire sentence by changing the adjective. For instance, the mood of the paragraph from *The Wind in the Willows* would change if the scene took place in warm weather. Read the first sentence in *The Wind in the Willows* in which the adjectives have been changed.

It was a warm, breezy afternoon with a soft, blue sky. . . .

Activity

Rewrite the paragraph from *The Wind in the Willows* as though the scene had taken place in the summer. Change as many of the adjectives as you can. When you have finished, read your paragraph, noting how the adjectives you have used have completely changed the description of the scene.

Adjectives ◆

An **adjective** is a word that tells about a noun or pronoun.

A. An adjective gives a picture of a noun by answering *what kind*, *how many*, or *which one*.

What Kind?	How Many?	Which One?
famous, young black, musical	three, one several, many	this, these that, those

The Supremes were a <u>black</u> <u>musical</u> trio.
The <u>three</u> women recorded <u>several</u> hits.
<u>This</u> group sang <u>those</u> songs.

B. Articles are special kinds of adjectives. The **definite article,** *the*, identifies a specific person, place, or thing. The **indefinite articles,** *a* and *an*, identify any one person, place, or thing in a group. Use *an* before words beginning with a vowel sound.

The Supremes lived in <u>the</u> city of Detroit.
They prepared <u>an</u> act for <u>a</u> contest at school.

Strategy

Remember that a sentence can contain many adjectives. Watch for nouns that are described by more than one adjective.

The <u>bright</u> and <u>able</u> <u>young</u> women rose to <u>great</u> fame.

Check Your Understanding

A. Write the letter that lists all the adjectives, not including articles.

1. The young women entered that contest as a vocal group.
   a. women, contest, group   **b.** young, that, vocal
   c. women, as, vocal   **d.** young, entered, group

2. These three friends won first prize.
   a. These, three, first   **b.** friends, won, prize
   c. These, friends, prize   **d.** three, won, first

264

B. Write the letter of the correct indefinite article.

    3. Motown Records gave them _____ contract.

        a. the   **b.** a   **c.** an

    4. They recorded _____ album together in 1961.

        a. the   **b.** a   **c.** an

Practice

A. Write each sentence and underline the adjectives. Do not underline articles.

    5. Few black groups had achieved success before 1960.

    6. The Supremes made several gold albums for Motown.

    7. They were the top female group for many years.

    8. This group led the vocal charts 11 times.

B. Write each sentence, using the form of the article shown in parentheses.

    9. Berry Gordy was _____ young songwriter. (indefinite)

    10. Gordy founded _____ legendary record company. (indefinite)

    11. He had worked in _____ auto factory in Detroit. (indefinite)

    12. He named _____ company Motown after that city. (definite)

C. Mixed Practice Write each sentence. Underline all the adjectives, including the articles. Write *definite* or *indefinite* above each article.

    13. Gordy supported popular black music.

    14. He guided the Supremes to a brilliant career.

    15. They were the first group with five top hits in a row.

    16. Berry Gordy helped them with the early records.

    17. The Supremes toured several foreign countries.

    18. They became a hot act in the music business.

    19. They were the biggest Motown group of the decade.

    20. The Supremes and Motown Records paved the way for today's popular black music.

Apply: Work with a Partner

Choose a song that both you and your partner know. Each of you should write five sentences describing the song. Then exchange papers, and discuss how the adjectives describe certain features of the song.

Proper Adjectives

Proper adjectives are adjectives formed from proper nouns. Like proper nouns, proper adjectives are capitalized.

A. Many proper adjectives are formed by changing the spelling of proper nouns. Here are some proper adjectives.

Noun	Adjective	Noun	Adjective	Noun	Adjective
Mexico	Mexican	Japan	Japanese	England	English
Cuba	Cuban	China	Chinese	Israel	Israeli
Italy	Italian	Portugal	Portuguese	Europe	European
Canada	Canadian	Spain	Spanish	France	French

B. Some proper adjectives take the same form as proper nouns. This is usually the case with the names of states and cities. A person's name is sometimes used as a proper adjective.

> The ship anchored off the <u>Florida</u> coastline.
> The <u>Columbus</u> crew was a brave one.

Strategy

Sometimes a possessive can be used instead of a proper adjective. Either one is correct. Notice that the possessive of a proper noun is usually not used with a definite or an indefinite article.

the Indian trade routes   Mexican rivers
India's trade routes   Mexico's rivers

Check Your Understanding

A. Write the letter of the correct proper adjective.
   1. Christopher Columbus was _____ by birth. (Italy)
      a. Italy   **b.** Italy's   **c.** Italan   **d.** Italian
   2. He learned _____ methods of navigation. (Portugal)
      a. Portuguese   **b.** Portugal   **c.** Portugalian
      d. Portugish

B. Write the letter of the correct proper adjective.

    3. The _____ coast was a site of exploration. (Florida)

        a. Florida   **b.** Floridahian   **c.** Florida's

    4. Columbus is the subject of a _____ painting. (Picasso)

        a. Picasso's   **b.** Picassan   **c.** Picasso

Practice

A. Write the sentence using the proper adjective.

    5. _____ explorers made risky sea voyages. (Europe)

    6. The _____ queen Isabella supported Columbus. (Spain)

    7. Columbus explored the _____ coast. (America)

    8. He was searching for _____ riches. (India)

B. Write each sentence. Underline and capitalize the proper adjective.

    9. The first florida city was St. Augustine.

    10. De Soto's army crossed the mississippi wilderness.

    11. A new york river bears Henry Hudson's name.

    12. No one had yet discovered the texas coast.

C. Mixed Practice Write the sentence using the proper adjective.

    13. Hernando Cortez was a famous _____ explorer. (Spain)

    14. He founded the _____ city of Veracruz. (Mexico)

    15. Cortez fought the _____ chief Montezuma. (India)

    16. _____ explorers also visited the New World. (Portugal)

    17. England won control of much _____ territory. (China)

    18. Cortez had the _____ governor's support. (Cuba)

    19. Cortez conquered the _____ Empire. (Aztec)

    20. The _____ and _____ empires flourished in the sixteenth century. (Spain, England)

Apply: Test a Partner

Write a list of the names of 10 countries. Exchange your list with a partner, and change each other's proper nouns to proper adjectives. Then exchange lists once again, and correct your partner's papers. Use your dictionary to check answers.

Predicate Adjectives

Adjectives do not always precede the nouns or pronouns they describe. Adjectives can also follow linking verbs.

A. As you learned in Unit 3, a linking verb is a verb that links the subject of a sentence to a word or words that describe or identify it. The most common linking verbs are forms of the verb *be*: *am, is, are, was, were,* and verb phrases ending in *be, been,* or *being.*

> Dance is a grand art.
> Dance has been popular throughout history.

These "sense verbs" are often linking verbs: *look, smell, taste, feel,* and *sound.* Other linking verbs are *remain, become, grow,* and *seem.*

> Some forms of dance look natural.
> Modern dance has become popular in this century.

B. A **predicate adjective** is an adjective that follows a linking verb and describes the subject of the sentence.

> Modern dance is young.   Ballet has remained elegant.

A predicate adjective can also describe a pronoun that is the subject of a sentence.

> She is lovely.   They sound beautiful.

Strategy

Not all adjectives that follow linking verbs are predicate adjectives. Adjectives can describe nouns that follow verb.

> Ballet is classical dance. (Classical describes dance.)

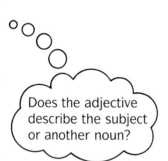

Does the adjective describe the subject or another noun?

Check Your Understanding

A. Write the letter of the linking verb or verb phrase.
1. Isadora Duncan was a pioneer of modern dance.
   a. was   **b.** pioneer   **c.** modern   **d.** dance
2. Duncan had become unhappy with ballet.
   a. Duncan   **b.** had become   **c.** unhappy   **d.** ballet

B. Write the letter of the predicate adjective.

    3. Classical dance felt tiresome to her.

        a. Classical   **b.** dance   **c.** felt   **d.** tiresome

    4. She was eager for a new kind of dance.

        a. was   **b.** eager   **c.** new   **d.** kind

Practice

A. Write the sentence. Underline the linking verb or verb phrase.

    5. Ballet had been prominent since the fifteenth century.

    6. Isadora Duncan's dance was different.

    7. The stage was empty except for her.

    8. Her feet were bare throughout her dance.

B. Write the sentence, underline the predicate adjective, and draw an arrow to the noun or pronoun it describes.

    9. Duncan's new style seemed natural.

   10. Her costumes were untraditional.

   11. Her movements were smooth, unlike ballet steps.

   12. Isadora Duncan became famous throughout the world.

C. Mixed Practice Write the sentence. Underline the linking verb once, and underline the predicate adjective twice.

   13. Martha Graham also is legendary.

   14. Graham's contributions were revolutionary.

   15. Personal expression was important to her.

   16. She was emotional in her dance pieces.

   17. Not all of her dances looked pretty.

   18. Sometimes these emotions seemed painful.

   19. Duncan and Graham were courageous and influential.

   20. Modern dance has remained inspirational to dancers and magical for audiences.

Apply: Learning Log

What was the hardest part of this lesson for you? Write an entry in your learning log to help you understand it better.

Comparisons with Adjectives

Use the **comparative** form of an adjective to compare two people, places, or things. Use the **superlative** form of an adjective to compare three or more people, places, or things.

A. Add *er* to most one-syllable adjectives and to some two-syllable adjectives to form the comparative. Add *est* to these adjectives to form the superlative. You must change the spelling of some adjectives to add *er* or *est*.

Type of Adjective	Spelling Rule	Example of Adjective	Comparative	Superlative
most adjectives	no change	dark	darker	darkest
word ending in e	Drop final e.	wise	wiser	wisest
word ending in consonant + y	Change y to i.	healthy	healthier	healthiest
one-syllable word ending in one vowel + one consonant	Double final consonant.	hot	hotter	hottest

B. Use *more* to form the comparative of most adjectives of two or more syllables, including those ending in suffixes like *-ful, -less, -ous,* and *-able.* Use *most* to form the superlative of these adjectives.

Adjective	Comparative	Superlative
cheerful	more cheerful	most cheerful
famous	more famous	most famous
reliable	more reliable	most reliable

Strategy

Do not use both *er* and *more* or *est* and *most* in one comparison. For example, it is incorrect to say *more older* or *most finest*.

Check Your Understanding

A. Write the letter of the correct adjective.
1. Antibiotics kill the ____ infections of all.
    a. deadly   **b.** deadliest   **c.** more deadly
2. People are ____ now than in the past.
    a. most healthy   **b.** healthiest   **c.** healthier

B. Write the letter of the correct adjective.

    3. Doctors treat the _____ diseases of all with antibiotics.
        a. harmfuller   **b.** harmfullest   **c.** most harmful

    4. Infections were _____ in the past than today.
        a. more dangerous   **b.** most dangerous
        c. dangerouser

Practice

A. Write each sentence with the correct form of the adjective given in parentheses.

    5. Today's antibiotics are (quick) than early ones.
    6. Alexander Fleming was one of the (wise) scientists of his time.
    7. He did the (early) experiments of all with penicillin.
    8. It has seen (wide) use than any other antibiotic.

B. Follow the directions for Practice A.

    9. Antibiotics are (helpful) than other treatments.
    10. They are the (effective) cure in all of medicine.
    11. New production methods are (complex) than old ones.
    12. Penicillin is one of the (impressive) drugs of our time.

C. Mixed Practice Write each sentence with the correct form of the adjective given in parentheses.

    13. Antibiotics are among the (safe) drugs of all.
    14. Some of the (new) antibiotics of today are synthetic.
    15. One of the (bright) researchers of all was Selman Waksman.
    16. His discovery of streptomycin is his (famous) discovery of all.
    17. Streptomycin is (potent) than many antibiotics.
    18. Antibiotics have made situations (hopeful) than ever.
    19. They are the (dependable) remedy of all for the (ugly) diseases of yesterday.
    20. The hope for cures is (real) than ever before.

Apply: Work with a Group

With your group, choose a paragraph from one of your reading selections. List 15 of the adjectives in the selection. Then write the comparative and superlative forms next to each of them. Compare your list with those of other groups in the class.

Irregular Comparisons

Some adjectives have special comparative and superlative forms.

A. The adjectives *good* and *bad* use the following forms for making comparisons.

Adjective	Comparative (compares two)	Superlative (compares three or more)
good	better	best
bad	worse	worst

The goal of Socrates was a good life.
For Socrates, knowledge was better than ignorance.
Socrates was the best teacher of all the philosophers in ancient Greece.

B. The adjectives *much*, *many*, and *little* also have special comparative and superlative forms.

Adjective	Comparative	Superlative
much, many	more	most
little	less	least

Did Socrates possess more wisdom than Plato?
Socrates's work brought him the most fame of any philosopher in the Western world.

Strategy

Use only the forms of comparison shown above for the adjectives *good* and *bad*. There is no such word as *badder, worser, baddest,* or *goodest* in correct written English.

Check Your Understanding

A. Write the letter of the correct adjective.
1. Falsehood is _____ than truth.
   a. worst   **b.** worser   **c.** worse   **d.** worstest
2. The _____ virtue of all is the quest for knowledge.
   a. best   **b.** bestest   **c.** better   **d.** goodest

B. Write the letter of the correct adjective.

3. Socrates had _____ patience than other teachers.
   a. more **b.** most **c.** much **d.** least

4. Some students paid _____ attention than others.
   a. less **b.** least **c.** little **d.** leastest

Practice

A. Write each sentence with the proper form of the adjective given in parentheses.

5. Some of his students were (good) than others.
6. His (good) student of all was Plato.
7. Ignorance is (bad) than laziness in many opinions.
8. Peace is (good) than war.

B. Follow the directions for Practice A.

9. Socrates had (much) courage than many philosophers.
10. He showed the (little) fear of all of them.
11. His attackers displayed (little) honesty than he.
12. He had the (much) confidence of all in the power of truth.

C. Mixed Practice Write each sentence with the proper form of the adjective given in parentheses.

13. His teachings receive (much) attention than anyone else's.
14. Discussions were (good) than lectures for his students.
15. Jealous opponents were his (bad) critics of all.
16. He had (much) courage than most people.
17. He was the (good) professor in all of Athens.
18. Yet some Athenians had (little) interest in justice than in the false charges against Socrates.
19. Socrates was the (much) influential philosopher of his time.
20. Was Athens (good) or (bad) off without him?

Apply: Journal

In your journal, write five sentences about the qualities you value most in a person. Use a form of *good, bad, much, many,* or *little* in each sentence.

Prepositions and Adjective Phrases

You have learned that one or more adjectives can describe a noun. Another way to describe a noun is to use a group of words with a preposition.

A. A **preposition** relates a noun to another word in the sentence. Some common prepositions are *in*, *with*, *on*, *at*, *to*, *about*, *of*, *for*, and *around*. The noun or pronoun that follows a preposition is called the **object of the preposition**.

Jane Addams

> One winner of the Nobel Peace Prize was Jane Addams.
>
> preposition   object of preposition
>
> Hull House in Chicago was her project.

B. A **prepositional phrase** contains the preposition, its object, and all the words that describe the object of the preposition.

> Hull House was a home to Chicago's needy people.

A prepositional phrase can act as an adjective by describing a noun. It answers questions such as *"which one?"* or *"what kind?"*

> She helped many new immigrants in Chicago.
>
> Hull House was a shelter for the city's poor.

Strategy

When you write, vary your sentence patterns by making some adjectives into prepositional phrases and some prepositional phrases into adjectives.

> She aided Chicago's people.
> She aided the people of Chicago.

Check Your Understanding

A. Write the letter of the preposition.
   1. Sarah Winnemucca sought peace for all peoples.
      a. peace **b.** for **c.** all **d.** peoples
   2. She pleaded the cause of Native Americans' rights.
      a. the **b.** cause **c.** of **d.** rights

B. Write the letter of the word each prepositional phrase describes.

   3. The government broke its agreements with her.
   a. government   **b.** broke   **c.** its   **d.** agreements

   4. Concern about Native American claims is still strong.
   a. Concern   **b.** claims   **c.** still   **d.** strong

Practice

A. Write each sentence. Underline each preposition once. Underline the object of the preposition twice.

   5. Mary McLeod Bethune founded a college for blacks.
   6. She improved the educational opportunities of blacks.
   7. She was the minority affairs adviser to Roosevelt.
   8. Those around her always admired her commitment.

B. Write each sentence. Underline the prepositional phrase once. Draw two lines under the noun it describes.

   9. Dolores Huerta helps Americans of Mexican heritage.
   10. Her devotion to this cause is strong.
   11. She has been an organizer for the United Farm Workers.
   12. Members at her meetings find her inspirational.

C. Mixed Practice Write each sentence. Underline the prepositional phrase once. Underline the preposition twice. Write the word the prepositional phrase describes.

   13. Fans of opera know opera's first lady, Leontyne Price.
   14. Price overcame many obstacles in her way.
   15. She was the first black star of the Metropolitan Opera.
   16. Her debut with the company was spectacular.
   17. Every major stage in the world has hosted Price.
   18. She possesses a voice of "liquid gold."
   19. The operas of Verdi display her voice at its best.
   20. Her best role is in an opera about love in ancient Egypt.

Apply: Exploring Language

Write five sentences about a famous woman you admire. Use an adjective in each sentence. Then rewrite them, replacing adjectives with prepositional phrases where you can.

Leontyne Price

275

Synonyms and Antonyms

◆

A. Read the sentences below.

> Immigrants have brought tasty foods to America.
> Immigrants have brought delicious foods to America.

The words *tasty* and *delicious* are synonyms.

Synonyms are words that are the same or similar in meaning.

Often one synonym is more specific than another.

> This fig is great. The fig is scrumptious.

Describing the fig as *great* doesn't tell much about it. It just means that the writer likes it. Describing the fig as *scrumptious* means it tastes good. *Scrumptious* is more specific than *great*.

B. Read the sentences below.

> Maeda ate quickly. Isabel ate slowly.

The words *quickly* and *slowly* are *antonyms*.

Antonyms are words that are opposite in meaning.

Use antonyms in your writing to show clear contrasts.

> The soup was cheap, but the main course was expensive.

Strategy

Make your writing more interesting by using vivid, precise synonyms. You can find lists of synonyms in a thesaurus. Remember that most synonyms do not mean *exactly* the same thing.

Check Your Understanding

A. Write the letter of the synonym that best replaces the underlined word.
1. Immigrants have introduced new foods to our country.
   a. newborn   **b.** unfamiliar   **c.** recent
2. These have helped change the way Americans eat.
   a. transform   **b.** money   **c.** reverse

B. Write the letter of the antonym for each underlined word.

    3. Many <u>unusual</u> foods are now _____ American dishes.

        a. strange   **b.** common   **c.** delicious

    4. Our foods come from <u>distant</u> lands and _____ farms.

        a. faraway   **b.** large   **c.** nearby

Practice

A. Write each sentence. Write the synonym shown in the box that best replaces the word *cook*.

barbecue	boil	bake

    5. Asians <u>cook</u> soybeans in water to make tofu.

    6. Many Europeans <u>cook</u> bread made from rye.

    7. On an outdoor grill, you can <u>cook</u> chopped meat to make a dish named for the German city of Hamburg.

B. Write each sentence with an antonym of the underlined word.

    8. <u>Cold</u> Swedish fruit soup is good on a _____ day.

    9. You can <u>begin</u> a meal with a Mexican avocado and _____ it with an Asian fig.

    10. Some Italian noodles are <u>wide</u>, and others are _____.

C. Mixed Practice Write each sentence. Choose the word that best completes the sentence. Tell whether the word is a synonym or an antonym of the underlined word.

    11. I can <u>make</u> pancakes or (build, prepare) French crepes.

    12. Rice can be served <u>with</u> or (in, without) meat.

    13. Hamburgers are <u>easy</u> to make, but Hungarian goulash is more (difficult, carefree).

    14. Tacos are <u>good</u>, and burritos are also (tasty, kind).

    15. You cook <u>well</u> and prepare dishes (expertly, badly), but I cook (expertly, badly) and often eat out.

    16. Eggs cook <u>quickly</u>, while stew cooks (immediately, slowly). If you must eat (immediately, slowly), make eggs.

Apply: Work with a Group

Have each member of your group write a sentence about food, using a general word such as *good*. Pass the work around the group. Have each student rewrite the sentences, using specific synonyms. Discuss the meaning of each synonym.

Language in Action

Giving an Oral Report

Imagine this situation: Your teacher gives you an assignment. You have to do an oral science report. You've written research reports before, and so you know how to begin. You go to the library and do research. You read books and articles on the science topic that you've chosen. You take notes and outline the report. Now what do you do?

An **oral report** is similar to a written research report. The main difference is that the information in an oral report is presented aloud. All of the background work is the same. Here are some tips for giving an oral report.

♦ Find a topic, do the research, and organize your report just as you would if you were writing it.

♦ Make notes on a sheet of paper or on index cards. These notes will serve to remind you of the points that you wish to make and the order in which you want to make them. Only you can decide how much information to include in your notes. Maybe you can remember everything you want to say about Gregor Mendel, for example. If so, the word *Mendel,* written on an index card, will be enough. If not, you will want to write more information.

♦ Use visual aids. Often, the audience can understand your information more easily if it is accompanied by a chart, graph, map, or diagram. You may also use an object such as a telephone or a model car as part of a demonstration. As you speak, point to the visual aid when it helps to illustrate your explanation. Use a pointer or your hand to direct the audience's attention.

♦ Practice. Rehearse your report. You might practice presenting the report to your family. Rehearse until you have learned the material and can make an effective presentation to the class and answer any questions the students might have.

♦ Speak loudly and clearly. Speaking to your class is not like talking to a friend on the phone. When you give an oral report, you want everyone to hear and to understand you.

Practice

A. Below are some of the steps involved in giving an oral report. On a separate sheet of paper, write the steps in the correct order.

1. Practice the report.
2. Find a topic.
3. Speak loudly and clearly.
4. Make reminder notes for yourself.
5. Outline the report.
6. Do the research.

B. Answer the following questions on a separate sheet of paper.

7. How is the research for an oral report different from the research for a written report?
8. Why should you rehearse your report before you present it to the class?
9. How complete should your reminder notes be?
10. How should the way you speak when you give the report be different from the way you normally speak?
11. What is the aim of speaking this way?
12. How many times should you practice your report?

Apply

Give an oral report to your class. You may use the same topic you used for your written research report, or you may pick another topic. Talk to your teacher about it. Once you have chosen your subject, research the topic thoroughly. Take notes on index cards and then organize them in the order in which you will use them. Think of creative visual aids that will help hold the audience's attention and help explain the ideas in your report. Practice your report several times, in front of friends or family or in front of a mirror. Make your hand motions seem as natural as possible. Also practice the tone of voice you will use for the audience. When you feel completely confident and familiar with your material, present your oral report.

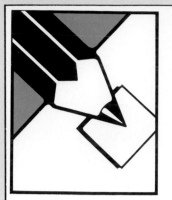

TEST TAKING

Planning Your Time

When you take a test, you want to receive full credit for everything you know. To do this, you need to answer as many questions on the test as possible.

Here are some steps that will help you make better use of your time while taking a test.

- ◆ Read every question on the test once. As you do, answer the questions that you know. If there is a question that you don't know the answer to, skip it, and move on to the next question.
- ◆ After you've read the test, go back to the beginning. This time, work on the questions that you didn't know the first time you read the test. If there are still questions that you can't answer, skip them and go on.
- ◆ After you have read the test the second time, go back and work on any questions that you haven't answered.
- ◆ If you have answered all of the questions and there is still time left, check your answers.

Practice

Write sentences that tell how each of the students could have made better use of the test-taking time.

1. Caroline answered all but five questions on the test. She spent the remaining time daydreaming.
2. Sylvia decided the best way to answer the questions that she wasn't sure of was to pick every other answer.
3. While working through the test the second time, Gary got stuck on the fourth problem. He worked on it until the teacher said to stop.

Apply: Learning Log

Decide which information from this lesson was the most helpful to you. Write the information in your learning log.

UNIT REVIEW

Research Reports (page 241)

  1. List at least three characteristics of a research report.

Using Reference Materials (pages 246–247)

For each topic below, write the key word and the reference source in which you would look to find information (encyclopedia, *Readers' Guide to Periodical Literature,* atlas, or almanac).

  2. the history of the guitar
  3. the amount of silver produced worldwide in 1980
  4. the path of the Hudson River through New York state
  5. the results of current research on whales

Making an Outline (pages 252–253)

Read the two main ideas listed below and the details that follow. Make an outline by writing each detail under the main idea to which it belongs.

 I. Yellowstone National Park is the nation's oldest and largest.
 II. Yellowstone offers visitors a range of natural wonders.

  6. Was part of Louisiana Purchase in 1803
  7. Includes rugged mountains, deep canyons, evergreen forests, and beautiful fields
  8. Was set aside as park by Congress in 1872
  9. Has hotsprings, geysers, and waterfalls
  10. Is wildlife preserve for bears, elks, buffaloes
  11. Covers more than 2,200,000 acres

Using Transition Words (pages 256–257)

Rewrite the following pairs of sentences, and improve them by using transition words to make the relationships between ideas clearer.

  12. The platypus swims in the water and lays eggs. It is a mammal.
  13. This mammal has webbed feet and a ducklike bill. It is sometimes called a duckbill.
  14. All platypuses have claws. The males have spurs on their hind feet.
  15. Platypuses seem like interesting creatures. I would not want one for a pet.
  16. The platypus and duck have several similarities. People occasionally confuse the two.

Adjectives (pages 264–265)

Write each sentence. Underline all the adjectives, including the articles.

17. Luxembourg is a tiny nation.
18. It lies in central Europe.
19. The small, independent country borders Belgium, West Germany, and France.
20. Luxembourg is a country of exquisite, natural beauty and colorful cities and towns.
21. The Ardennes Mountains run through a region in northern Luxembourg.
22. The mines in the southern region of the country produce valuable resources.
23. A parliament rules this prosperous country.
24. Luxembourg started as a military fortress.
25. The ancient Romans built it for necessary protection.
26. Many old castles reveal the interesting history of this picturesque nation.

Proper Adjectives (pages 266–267)

Write each sentence using a proper adjective from the proper noun in parentheses.

27. (Mexico) food is often very spicy.
28. *Sushi* is a traditional (Japan) meal.
29. Many different (Europe) dishes are quite popular in the United States.
30. Pasta is perhaps the most famous (Italy) food throughout several continents.
31. (New York City) restaurants are famous for their excellent foreign cuisine.

Predicate Adjectives (pages 268–269)

Write each sentence. Underline the linking verb once and the predicate adjective twice.

32. Willa Cather's writings are powerful.
33. Cather became famous for her stories about life in the American West.
34. These stories seem real to us today.
35. Cather's work is remarkable for its treatment of life in midwestern America.
36. Her impressive novels remain popular among many American readers today.

Comparisons with Adjectives (pages 270–271)

Write each sentence with the correct form of the adjective given in parentheses.

37. Marble is one of the (hard) stones of all.

38. It has (wide) use in building than in works of art.

39. Its (important) use of all is in sculpture, however.

40. Michelangelo sculpted his (large) works of all in marble.

41. Marble from the hills near Carrara, Italy, is generally the (desirable) of all types of marble.

Irregular Comparisons (pages 272–273)

Write each sentence with the proper form of the adjective given in parentheses.

42. Alaska has (much) land than any other state.

43. But there is (little) publicity about the state of Alaska than about the state of Texas.

44. This state has some of the (good) scenery in the world.

45. It also experiences some of the world's (bad) weather.

46. It has the (more) tourism of all during the summer.

Prepositions and Adjective Phrases (pages 274–275)

Write each sentence. Underline the prepositional phrase once. Draw a second line under the preposition. Write the word the prepositional phrase describes.

47. People have called silk "the queen of textiles."

48. Tiny silkworms in large numbers produce this fiber.

49. Small spinners around the worms' mouths spin the silk.

50. Silk from China has long been world famous.

51. China is the country with the largest silk industry.

Synonyms and Antonyms (pages 276–277)

Write each sentence. Use the word in parentheses that best completes the sentence. Write whether this word is a synonym or an antonym of the underlined word.

52. Sprinters are very <u>fast</u> and can run (quickly, widely).

53. The winner had the <u>best</u> time, but the last runner had the (better, worst) time.

54. Emilio's <u>leap</u> broke a record in the long (run, jump).

55. The hurdles may look <u>easy</u>, but in reality the technique is quite (difficult, swell) for beginners.

56. Johnson got off to a quick <u>start</u> but was beaten at the (finish, opening).

MAKING ALL THE
CONNECTIONS

You and several classmates will now write a historical play together as a group. What you have learned about describing people and places will help you in your writing.

You will do the following in your historical play:

- Include characters, a setting, a plot, and stage directions.
- Base the play on a true historical event, but add fictional details, if you wish.
- Use imaginary as well as real characters, if you wish.

Reading a Historical Play

Read the following scene from a historical play. A father is telling his children of his experiences as a delegate to the Constitutional Convention of 1787, a turning point in U.S. history. Notice the sidenotes that point out the characteristics of the play. After discussing the play, you and your classmates will have a chance to write a play of your own.

Imaginary characters and setting may be included.

The play is based on a true event.

Stage directions tell how the actors should speak or move.

Real characters are introduced.

CHARACTERS: Father, his children Sally and Charles
SETTING: *a farmhouse kitchen in winter, 1800*
SALLY: Papa, if all the delegates disagreed so much, how did they ever agree to sign the Constitution?
FATHER: Well, everyone tried to resolve the differences. After months of hard work, we developed compromises that were acceptable to most of the delegates.
CHARLES: And so everyone voted for it, right, Papa?
FATHER: *(laughing softly)* No, my boy. Several men refused to sign at all. Others signed unwillingly.
CHARLES: How did you feel when you signed?
FATHER: I was a bit worried about how people back home would react. Benjamin Franklin's words

helped, though.

SALLY: What did he say, Papa?

FATHER: He said, "I have stared at the carving on George Washington's chair for weeks. It could show a rising or a setting sun. Now, as we sign the Constitution, I see that it is the rising sun of a proud new nation."

Speaking and Listening

Your teacher will assign you to a group. Choose a discussion leader. Talk about these questions:

1. What historical characters are named in the play?
2. How did the playwright use the children's questions to introduce historical information?
3. What can you learn from the picture?
4. What historical event is described in the play? What do you learn about this event?

Thinking

Brainstorming

Choose one person in your group to take notes as you discuss the following questions. Save your notes.

1. What historical event might make a good play? What real characters were involved in that event? Where and when did it take place?
2. What imaginary characters could play roles in the play?
3. How do the characters feel about the events? How might they show these feelings?

Organizing

Before you begin to write, you must organize your ideas and notes. Look at the chart below. It was used to organize ideas for the play about the Constitution. Notice that the real details and the imaginary details appear in separate columns.

SETTING: A farmhouse in winter, 1800			
PLOT: A father tells his children of his experiences as a delegate to the Constitutional Convention.			
Real Characters	**Imaginary Characters**	**Real Details**	**Imaginary Details**
Benjamin Franklin	Father	the delegates' compromises	Father's feelings
George Washington	Sally	the signing of the Constitution	children's questions
	Charles	Franklin's speech	

With your group, make a chart for your play. Use your brainstorming notes to organize your ideas. Have one group member fill in the chart.

Writing

Imagine that you and your group have been asked to write a play about a historical event for an American heritage fair. The audience for your play will be students your own age. You must write a scene that will show the main points of the event. Use the chart as you write.

Planning

- ◆ Review your chart. Add new ideas that occur to you.
- ◆ Begin with the setting of the play. Decide how you will describe the setting. Make a list of characters. Some will be real; others will be imaginary.
- ◆ Organize your plot into an outline. Use the outline as a guide when you begin to write your play.

Composing

- Work with your group to write your historical play. Choose one member to write down the first draft of your play as your group works.
- Decide on the main point of the scene you will write.
- Decide on the wording of each line. Also discuss how each character might feel or move while speaking.

Revising

- Reread your play with the group. Think of ways to improve its content and wording.
- Be sure your plot is set out clearly and that historical details are correct. Add stage directions where appropriate.

Proofreading

Work with the group to proofread your play. Have one group member make the proofreading changes on the first draft. Answer these questions:

- Does each sentence have the correct end punctuation?
- Are all pronouns used correctly?
- Does each pronoun have a clear antecedent?
- Are commas used correctly?
- Are all words spelled correctly?

Presenting

- Choose one member of the group to write a clean, final copy of your play. You may want to make this copy on a duplicating master so that each member of your group can have a copy.
- Rehearse your play. Decide who will be the actors in your play. Then, have two or three rehearsals so the actors can practice how they are going to say each of their lines. Decide what props and costumes you need. The actors may wish to memorize their lines.
- Present the play to your classmates. Use costumes and props. Follow the stage directions in your performance.

CUMULATIVE REVIEW

A. Write the letter of the term that identifies each sentence. *(pages 42–43)*

   1. Mark Twain wrote that?

      a. declarative **b.** interrogative **c.** imperative **d.** exclamatory

   2. Read this book, please.

      a. declarative **b.** interrogative **c.** imperative **d.** exclamatory

B. Write the letter of the term that identifies the underlined word or words. *(pages 44–47)*

   3. Mark Twain captured the American spirit in his books.

      a. complete subject   **c.** complete predicate

      b. simple subject   **d.** simple predicate

   4. His love of freedom and adventure inspires us.

      a. complete subject   **c.** complete predicate

      b. simple subject   **d.** simple predicate

   5. His easy, cheerful humor delights readers to this day.

      a. complete subject   **c.** complete predicate

      b. simple subject   **d.** simple predicate

   6. Most of his books were popular during his lifetime.

      a. complete subject   **c.** complete predicate

      b. simple subject   **d.** simple predicate

C. Write the letter of the correct plural form of each singular noun. *(pages 82–83)*

   7. video **a.** videos **b.** videoes **c.** videose

   8. crisis **a.** crisis **b.** crises **c.** crisises

D. Write the letter of the correct possessive form of each noun. *(pages 84–87)*

   9. children **a.** children's **b.** children' **c.** childrens'

  10. Russ **a.** Russ' **b.** Russ'es **c.** Russ's

  11. officers **a.** officer's **b.** officers's **c.** officers'

  12. son **a.** son's **b.** sons' **c.** son'

E. Write the letter of the term that identifies each underlined verb. *(pages 126–129)*

  13. Simon and Garfunkel were a successful musical team.

      a. action verb **b.** linking verb

  14. Paul Simon composed many beautiful songs for the duo.

      a. action verb **b.** linking verb

F. Write the letter of the term that identifies the tense of each underlined verb. *(pages 132–133)*

15. Art Garfunkel's melodious voice <u>enchanted</u> the ear.
   a. past tense   **b.** present tense   **c.** future tense
16. Perhaps the pair <u>will sing</u> together again someday.
   a. past tense   **b.** present tense   **c.** future tense

G. Write the letter of the word that correctly completes each sentence. *(pages 136–141)*

17. Many other performers have _____ their songs.
   a. record   **b.** records   **c.** recorded
18. Even before their stardom, they had _____ loyal fans.
   a. gained   **b.** gains   **c.** gain
19. Their music _____ the style for popular folk songs.
   a. sat   **b.** sit   **c.** set
20. They have _____ us a wonderful musical legacy.
   a. give   **b.** gave   **c.** given

H. Write the letter of the term that identifies each underlined word. *(pages 168–175)*

21. The Internal Revenue Service sends <u>taxpayers</u> their tax forms through the mail.
   a. direct object   **b.** indirect object   **c.** predicate adjective
22. This agency collects <u>taxes</u> from citizens.
   a. direct object   **b.** predicate noun   **c.** indirect object
23. The Internal Revenue Service employs many <u>accountants</u> around the country.
   a. predicate noun   **b.** indirect object   **c.** direct object
24. April 15 is the <u>deadline</u> for tax payments.
   a. predicate noun   **b.** predicate adjective   **c.** indirect object
25. The IRS is quite <u>busy</u> at this time of year.
   a. predicate noun   **b.** predicate adjective   **c.** direct object
26. This deadline seems too <u>early</u> for many taxpayers.
   a. indirect object   **b.** predicate adjective   **c.** direct object

I. Write the letter of the sentence that is punctuated correctly. *(pages 210–211)*

27. **a.** Yes, a picnic is a wonderful idea.
   b. Will you come with us too Will?
28. **a.** We'll all go; and we'll have a great time.
   b. Teri will not be able to come, however.

J. Write the letter of the term that identifies the underlined pronoun. *(pages 222–223)*

   29. She is a professional illustrator.
   a. subject   **b.** predicate nominative

   30. The painter of that picture is he.
   a. subject   **b.** predicate nominative

   31. After that, we framed the drawings.
   a. subject   **b.** predicate nominative

K. Write the letter of the pronoun that correctly completes each sentence. *(pages 222–229)*

   32. Marta entered _____ in the competition.
   a. they   **b.** them

   33. The winners of the competition were _____.
   a. they   **b.** them

   34. The judges awarded Ted and _____ the first prize.
   a. I   **b.** me

   35. Carla wrote a wonderful essay. _____ entered it in the contest.
   a. Her   **b.** Them   **c.** She   **d.** Me

   36. Juan wrote an essay also. The judges gave _____ second prize.
   a. him   **b.** he   **c.** they   **d.** I

   37. Jill and I wrote a play. Chuck helped _____.
   a. we   **b.** I   **c.** she   **d.** us

   38. Ed and Lucy read the entries. Careful judges were _____.
   a. they   **b.** we   **c.** me   **d.** them

L. Write the letter of the word that correctly completes each sentence. *(pages 230–231)*

   39. _____ story is very imaginative.
   a. Your   **b.** You're   **c.** Yours   **d.** Mine

   40. The one-act play is _____.
   a. ours   **b.** our's   **c.** my   **d.** our

   41. _____ quite a dramatic work.
   a. Its   **b.** Their   **c.** It's   **d.** It

   42. The best work is _____ full-length play.
   a. theirs   **b.** their   **c.** they're   **d.** there

M. Write the letter of the answer to each question. *(pages 258–259)*

   43. Which punctuation marks are used in writing a bibliography?
   a. period   **b.** colon   **c.** comma   **d.** a, b, and c

44. Which part of an author's name appears first in a bibliography?
   a. first name   **b.** last name   **c.** middle name

N. Write the letter of the item that includes all the adjectives in each sentence. *(pages 264–265)*
   45. The first automobiles were noisy and slow.
      a. The, first, noisy, slow   **b.** first, noisy, slow   **c.** The
   46. A horse could outrun those early vehicles.
      a. those, early   **b.** A, those, early   **c.** A, early

O. Write the letter of the word that completes each sentence. *(pages 266–267)*
   47. _____ inventors were actually the first carmakers.
      a. France   **b.** Francean   **c.** French
   48. The Ford Model A was an early _____ car.
      a. American   **b.** Americen   **c.** America
   49. _____ companies soon began construction of cars.
      a. Europe   **b.** European   **c.** Europese

P. Write the letter of each predicate adjective. *(pages 268–269)*
   50. Ford's Model T was tough under harsh conditions.
      a. under   **b.** tough   **c.** harsh
   51. Automobiles became necessary to the American way of life.
      a. necessary   **b.** the   **c.** American

Q. Write the letter of the word or words that complete each sentence. *(pages 270–273)*
   52. Some cars are _____ than other cars.
      a. expensiver   **b.** more expensive   **c.** expensivest   **d.** expensive
   53. Large cars often get _____ gas mileage than small cars.
      a. least   **b.** littler   **c.** less   **d.** lesser
   54. Carmakers are _____ of all at the start of the model year.
      a. most busy   **b.** most busiest   **c.** busierest   **d.** busiest

R. Write the letter of the word that each underlined prepositional phrase describes. *(pages 274–275)*
   55. Manufacturers from many countries produce many different cars.
      a. Manufacturers   **b.** from   **c.** world   **d.** cars
   56. The twentieth century has been the age of the automobile.
      a. century   **b.** the   **c.** age   **d.** automobile

PART FOUR

Aspirations

We never know how high we are
Till we are asked to rise
And then if we are true to plan
Our statures touch the skies—

Emily Dickinson

◆

You will never know what you are really capable of unless you try your very best in everything you do. Most people have **aspirations** and goals they would like to achieve. In these units, think about your own personal aspirations and how you might go about doing your best to realize them.

UNIT 7

Persuasive Essay

◆

Adverbs

What Do You Know?

"Buy now and save!" "We're the best!" "Shop smart!"

You hear advertising messages like these on radio and television and read them in newspapers and magazines all the time. They urge people to buy a certain product or shop in a certain store. You also hear messages that are aimed at convincing people to support some organization, cause, or idea. These messages may not all sound like ads, but their goal is the same—to persuade people to act or think in a certain way.

Sometimes you may want to convince someone to act or think in a certain way through your writing. This is not an easy task. Your ideas and opinions must be clear. You must present strong, reasonable arguments that your audience can accept. One form of writing in which you present your opinion and offer reasons to support it is called a **persuasive essay**.

Thinking About Persuasive Essays

What Is a Persuasive Essay?

A **persuasive essay** has these characteristics:

- It states an opinion about a particular topic.
- It aims to persuade readers to accept that opinion.
- A statement of the opinion appears at the beginning of the essay, and a restatement appears at the end.
- The opinion is supported by facts or examples.

You will find examples of persuasive essays in many areas of communication. A newspaper or a magazine usually has an editorial page that prints the opinions of the editor or publisher. Letters from readers express agreement or disagreement with those views. Columnists also write persuasive essays, giving their views on a variety of controversial topics.

Politicians often deliver speeches that are really persuasive essays in spoken form. Many of those speeches are broadcast to a nationwide audience, while others are addressed to a particular audience. If a speech is noteworthy, it may be recorded in print for future generations to read. The inaugural addresses of Presidents Lincoln and Kennedy are examples of such speeches.

Discussion

1. What examples of persuasive essays have you read or heard lately?
2. How did these persuasive essays affect your point of view or opinion?
3. What issues do you think would make good topics for persuasive essays?

Reading a Persuasive Speech

This persuasive essay was presented in the form of a speech. In it, a famous American leader expresses his hopes for the nation's future. The time was 1963. The place was Washington, D.C. More than 200,000 people had gathered with the aim of influencing Congress to pass laws that would truly grant full equality to all Americans. The following is part of what Dr. Martin Luther King, Jr., said. As you read the speech, notice how Dr. King uses examples to support the opinion he expresses in the first paragraph. Also notice how the language creates an inspirational mood and supports the purpose of the speech.

"I Have a Dream"
by
Dr. Martin Luthur King, Jr.

The writer's opinion is stated at the beginning.

I say to you today, my friends, even though we face the difficulties of today and tomorrow, I still have a dream. It is a dream deeply rooted in the American Dream. It is a dream that one day this nation will rise up and live out the true meaning of its creed: "We hold these truths to be self-evident, that all men are created equal."

The introduction includes a quotation from the Declaration of Independence.

I have a dream that one day on the red hills of Georgia the sons of former slaves and the sons of former slave-owners will be able to sit down together at the table of brotherhood.

I have a dream that one day even the state of Mississippi, a state sweltering with the heat of injustice and oppression, will be transformed into an oasis of freedom and justice.

The opinion is supported by examples throughout the speech.

I have a dream that my four little children will one day live in a nation where they will not be judged by the color of their skin but by the content of their character.

I have a dream today.

I have a dream that one day down in Alabama . . . little black boys and little black girls will be able to join hands with little white boys and little white girls as sisters and brothers.

I have a dream today.

I have a dream that one day every valley shall be exalted, every hill and mountain shall be made low. The rough places shall be made plain and the crooked places will be made straight. . . .

This is my hope and this is the faith with which I go back to the South. With this faith we will be able to hew out of the mountain of despair a stone of hope. . . . With this faith we will be able to work together, to pray together, to struggle together . . . to stand up for freedom together knowing that we will be free one day.

This will be a day when all of God's children will be able to sing with new meaning . . ."let freedom ring." Let freedom ring from the hilltops of New Hampshire. Let freedom ring from the mighty mountains of New York. Let freedom ring from the snow-capped Rockies of Colorado. But not only that, let freedom ring from Stone Mountain of Georgia and Lookout Mountain of Tennessee—from every hill and molehill and from every mountainside.

When we allow freedom to ring—when we let it ring from every village and every hamlet, from every state and every city, we will be able to speed up that day when all of God's children, black men and white men, Jews and Gentiles, Protestants and Catholics, will be able to join hands and sing in the words of the Negro spiritual, "Free at last, Free at last, Thank God Almighty, we are free at last."

Civil rights march from Selma to Montgomery, Alabama   March 1965

Understanding What You've Read

Write the answers to these questions on a sheet of paper.

1. What belief about the nation is expressed in the first paragraph?
2. What are some examples of equality Dr. King hoped to see?
3. In the first part of the speech, Dr. King repeats the phrase "I have a dream. . . ." What phrase does he repeat in the second part?
4. Why does Dr. King repeat certain words and phrases?
5. How does Dr. King's examples help to persuade the listener to share his beliefs?
6. Do you think that in his speech Dr. King did a good job of persuading people to agree with his opinion? Explain your answer.

Writing Assignment

Imagine that your school is putting up a bulletin board called "Sound Off!" You will write a four-paragraph persuasive essay on a subject that you have a strong feeling about. The topic may concern your school, your town, or even the nation or the world.

The **audience** for your essay will be your classmates and the teachers who read it. Your **purpose** will be to write a persuasive essay that convinces readers to share your opinion.

Choose Topics and Write Opinions

Think of several topics that really interest you. Be sure you have a strong opinion on each topic. For each topic, write a sentence stating your opinion. Here are some examples:

What topic *really* interests me?

> Community clean-up: We need a day to pick up litter in the playground.
> Recreational Programs: Our town should have an Activities Center.
> Problems with advertising: There should be no advertising on television.

Jot down as many topics and statements of opinion as you can. Save your work for the next lesson.

Supporting an Opinion

◆

You know that a persuasive essay expresses the writer's opinion. An **opinion** is a personal feeling that cannot be proved true or false. Here are some opinions:

> Tomato soup is best for lunch.
> Our state needs a new state song.
> There should be more national parks.

These statements are neither right nor wrong. They simply express the writer's personal feelings. The purpose of a persuasive essay, however, is to convince readers to *share* an opinion. To do this, the writer gives reasons that explain *why* he or she holds this opinion. For example, tomato soup might be preferred either *because it is nutritious* or *because it is easy to prepare.*

The writer must also back up each reason with facts and examples. A **fact** is a statement that can be proved true. You read about the use of facts to support an opinion in Unit 3.

An **example** is an illustration of a broader or more general statement. An example gives a specific situation or instance that helps to prove the truth of the general statement. Compared with a fact, an example is less likely to contain statistics.

> **Opinion:** Americans should use the metric system.
> **Reason:** Using the metric system will help our country conduct business with other nations.
> **Fact:** The United States is now the only major country that is not using the metric system exclusively.
> **Example:** England, which formerly used its own measurement system, now uses the metric system.

When writing a persuasive essay, be sure to include only facts and examples that help support your opinion. Do not use statements that are irrelevant or statements that could support the opposing view. Read the following statements.

> The metric system was first used in France in 1795.
> It would cost millions to convert to the metric system.

The first statement is irrelevant; it doesn't really support the opinion. The second statement could be an argument *against* having people learn the metric system.

Practice

A. Below are two opposing opinions on one subject. Write these opinions on a sheet of paper. Then write each detail from the list under the opinion it supports.

> Opinion I: Our town should have a large new park.
> Opinion II: Our town cannot afford a new park.

1. Our parks are crowded and need repairs.
2. Some parts of town are miles from a park.
3. A new park would cost millions of dollars.
4. A park has to be maintained and supervised.
5. The town needs more playing fields and tennis courts.
6. The town's recreation budget was cut by the Town Council.
7. People want to rest in the shade of trees in summer.
8. Land in our town is very expensive.
9. Taxes cannot be raised to pay for a new park.
10. A large park could be used for concerts and meetings.

B. Choose one of the opinions below. Think of two reasons to support the opinion you choose. Then think of three examples to support each reason. Write the opinion, your reasons, and your examples on another sheet of paper.
1. Our school playground needs improvement.
2. A cat is a perfect pet.
3. Everyone should read a newspaper every day.
4. Our state should have a state insect.
5. Cars should not be built to go faster than 70 miles per hour.

List Your Reasons and Examples

Choose one of the opinions you wrote in Lesson 1. Then write two reasons to support your opinion. For each reason, list at least three examples. Be sure your examples are specific and support your opinion. Save your work for the next lesson.

Structuring a Persuasive Essay

A persuasive essay has three main parts: an introduction, a body, and a conclusion. Each part serves a different but important purpose.

Introduction

The first paragraph of the essay is the **introduction.** In this paragraph, the writer states the opinion he or she wants readers to share. The first sentence should capture the reader's attention. The second sentence should summarize the main ideas of the essay. This summary sentence is called the **thesis statement.** It tells the reader the main point of the essay.

Body

The **body** is the middle part of the essay. This part contains the reasons that support the writer's opinion. These reasons expand on the thesis statement. Each paragraph states one reason for the opinion and contains the facts and examples that support that reason.

For example, one writer thought there was a need for a program to bring students together with the residents of senior citizen homes. The writer wrote the following thesis statement: *We need a program to bring senior citizens and students together.* The following two reasons were listed to support the opinion:

Senior citizens would benefit from student visitors.
Students would learn much from the experience.

Each of these sentences became the main idea for a paragraph.

Conclusion

The final part of the essay is the **conclusion.** This section restates the thesis, or central idea, and reemphasizes the most important points of the essay. The final sentence often makes a strong, emotional appeal to convince readers to share the writer's viewpoint.

Practice

A. Read each group of sentences. Write whether the sentence should appear in the *introduction*, the *body*, or the *conclusion* of a persuasive essay.

1. Choosing a new state bird
   a. The new bird would be familiar to everyone and would remind people of our great state.
   b. Let's choose the new, familiar bird soon.
   c. We should select a new state bird that is more representative of our state.
   d. Our current state bird is seen in only a few areas.

2. Having a town history parade
   a. It will instill pride in our town.
   b. Our town should hold an annual history parade.
   c. Let's start planning our history parade soon.
   d. It will attract business and tourism.

3. A holiday for August
   a. August should have its own national holiday.
   b. Let's choose a holiday for August soon.
   c. It is a hot month, and people need a rest.
   d. Every other month has an important holiday.

4. The danger of skateboarding
   a. Write a letter insisting that skateboards be made safer.
   b. A few design changes and safety equipment would help.
   c. Many people are injured on skateboards each year.
   d. Skateboards are now dangerous and should be made safer to use.

Structure Your Essay

Organize the reasons and the examples you have listed for your persuasive essay. First, review the reasons that support your opinion. State each reason in the form of a topic sentence. Next, write a thesis statement, a sentence that expresses both of your reasons. Finally, write a sentence that suggests a specific action to be taken. Save your work for the next lesson.

Writing a First Draft

Read this persuasive essay. Identify its introduction, body, and conclusion. The writer wasn't worried about making the first draft perfect. It will be changed later.

> Our towns missing something! We need a program to bring senior citizens and students together. This program would benefit both the residents of senior citizen homes and the students who would visit them weekly.
>
> The senior citizens would benefit in many ways. They would have new people to talk to and to listen to. They could enjoy concerts and parties prisented by the students. They would be sure of visitors on a regular basis. The seniors would feel more a part of the community and would feel better about themselves. They could get the help they need for errands or short walks.
>
> The students would benefit as well. They would feel more important if they knew somone depended on them. They would learn responsability and the importance of keeping to a schedule. They would gain self confidence by helping others. They could learn about earlier times from their new friends.
>
> This program shouldnt wait. So many people would benefit from it. We need a planning meeting as soon as possible!

Write Your First Draft

Begin your persuasive essay with an interesting one-paragraph introduction that includes your thesis statement.

You may wish to write the body of your essay first and then write the introduction and conclusion. It's your choice.

The body of your essay should be two paragraphs, each giving one reason that supports your opinion. Include facts and examples in each paragraph. End your essay with a conclusion that restates your opinion and summarizes your main points. Try to suggest some action for your readers to take.

Discussing a First Draft

After you write your first draft, look for ways to make it better. Discuss your persuasive essay with a classmate.

Discussion Strategy

When making suggestions to your partner, you may find it helpful to tell about a time when you had a similar problem and how you solved it. Your partner may then be more open to your suggestions.

Use this Content Checklist to discuss with your class the draft on the previous page.

Content Checklist
- ✔ Does the introduction contain a good opening and a strong thesis statement, telling the writer's opinion?
- ✔ Does the conclusion restate the main ideas and urge readers to take some action?
- ✔ Does each paragraph in the body give a reason that supports the thesis statement?
- ✔ Does each paragraph in the body contain facts and examples to support the reason?

Revise Your First Draft for Content

To the Reader: Read your partner's persuasive essay. Identify the thesis statement. Read each topic sentence in the body, and be sure that it gives a reason to support that opinion. Be sure the detail sentences in each paragraph back up the topic sentence. Then talk about ways the essay could be made stronger or clearer. Use the Discussion Strategy and the Content Checklist for help.

To the Writer: Listen to your partner's suggestions. Then revise your draft for content. Save your work for the next lesson.

Revising for Order of Presentation

Persuasive writing is more effective when the most important ideas come first. After rereading the first draft of the persuasive essay, the student decided it could be improved by reordering the examples in the second paragraph.

Here is a simple way to put the ideas in your paragraphs in order. Make a list of your facts and examples for the paragraph. Decide which is the most important fact or example. Write *1.* next to this. Then number each of the other facts or examples in their order of importance. When you write your paragraph, just put the sentences in the order of the numbers.

This is how the student reordered the ideas in the second paragraph.

Benefits for senior citizens
4. *new people to talk to and listen to*
5. *concerts and parties presented by students*
1. *visitors on a regular basis*
3. *feel more in touch with outside; better about selves*
2. *help for errands or short walks*

Here is the new paragraph:

> The senior citizens would benefit in many ways. They would be sure of visitors on a regular basis. They could get the help they need for errands or short walks. The seniors would feel more a part of the community and would feel better about themselves. They would have new people to talk to and to listen to. They could enjoy concerts and parties presented by the students.

The new paragraph is more powerful. It catches the reader's attention with the most important example and then presents the other examples. The examples are now in the order that will most effectively convince readers of the student's point of view.

Practice

A. Write each thesis statement and the supporting reasons on another sheet of paper. Number the reasons in the order of importance that you think will work the best.

1. A monument to Franklin Roosevelt should be built.
   a. He guided our country through a depression and a war.
   b. He served longer than any other president.
   c. He backed many important pieces of legislation.
2. We should stay on daylight saving time all year.
   a. Daylight isn't as important in the early morning.
   b. It causes confusion to switch from daylight saving to standard time.
   c. It would make daylight last longer in the afternoon, when more people are outside.
3. Television has a strong influence on society.
   a. It reaches millions of people every day.
   b. The average person watches more than 30 hours each week.
   c. Many people get most of their information from TV.
4. School should be held year-round.
   a. Much of what is learned is forgotten during summer vacation.
   b. Students could learn much more in a longer school year.
   c. Time is wasted reviewing the last year's work at the start of each new year.

Revising Checklist
- ✔ Have I included the characteristics of a persuasive essay?
- ✔ Where can I combine sentences? (pp. 34, 118, 158)
- ✔ Where can I vary the word order or avoid repetition? (pp. 72, 208)
- ✔ Where can I add transitions between sentences and paragraphs? (p. 256)
- ✔ Where can I revise to present information in a better order?

Revise Your First Draft for Style
Check for items on the Revising Checklist. Be sure the detail sentences in each paragraph are listed in order of importance. Mark the changes on your draft. Save your work.

Using Apostrophes and Hyphens

You may need to use apostrophes and hyphens in your essay. Follow these rules for using apostrophes and hyphens.

Rule	Example
Use an apostrophe to show where letters are missing in a contraction.	is not = isn't it is = it's of the clock = o'clock
Use an apostrophe to make numbers and letters plural.	Mind your *p*'s and *q*'s. Two *3*'s make 6.
Use an apostrophe and *s* to make singular nouns possessive.	student → student's James → James's
Use only an apostrophe to make plural nouns possessive when the noun ends in *s*.	girls → girls' cars → cars'
For plurals that do not end in *s*, add an apostrophe and *s*.	women → women's children → children's
Use a hyphen at the end of a syllable when you need to divide a word at the end of a line. Divide words between syllables. Do not divide a word of one syllable.	Always make the division between syllables of a word.
Some compound nouns contain hyphens. Use a dictionary to check for such words.	mother-in-law twenty-one to ninety-nine
Use a hyphen to separate certain prefixes from their root words.	self-respect, self-taught ex-president, ex-athlete
Use a hyphen to form a compound adjective.	tear-filled, six-story ink-stained, high-level

Practice

A. Write each of the following sentences correctly. Use apostrophes and hyphens where necessary.

1. Didnt you read about both candidates aspirations?
2. I found the meaning of *candidate* among the *c*s in the dictionary.
3. *Candidatus* is Latin for "white robe," the clothing worn by self nominated seekers of political office in ancient Rome.
4. Isnt it strange that many common phrases have action packed historical origins?
5. "Getting the ball rolling" comes from one of our countrys famous political campaigns.
6. William Henry Harrisons clever thinking supporters actually rolled a large ball from town to town.
7. Theodore Roosevelt was forty two years old when he succeeded ex President McKinley.
8. Roosevelts childrens names were Kermit, Ethel Carow, Archibald Bulloch, Quentin, and Theodore, Jr.

B. Copy each word below on a separate sheet of paper. Use a hyphen to show where you would divide each word into syllables. Check a dictionary if you need to.

1. absence
2. aspiration
3. candidate
4. evaporate
5. management

Proofreading Checklist
✔ Does each sentence have the correct capitalization and end punctuation? (p. 36)
✔ Have commas and semicolons been used correctly? (pp. 74, 210)
✔ Have apostrophes and hyphens been used correctly?
✔ Have all adjectives been used correctly?

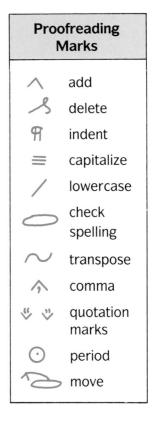

Proofreading Marks	
∧	add
⨍	delete
¶	indent
≡	capitalize
/	lowercase
⬭	check spelling
∼	transpose
⋏	comma
⩗ ⩗	quotation marks
⊙	period
⤸	move

Proofread Your Draft

Check for correct capitalization, punctuation, and grammar in your sentences. Use the Proofreading Checklist as a guide. Mark the changes on your draft. Save your work for the next lesson.

Checking Spelling/Writing a Final Copy

Spelling Strategy

You may have trouble remembering whether a word ends in *-el*, *-al*, or *-il*. If so, try saying the word with stress on the syllable that gives you difficulty.

> camel (say "cam EL")
> medal (say "med AL")
> pupil (say "pu PIL")

Read how the essay on student volunteers has been revised and improved.

Our town's missing something! We need a program to bring senior citizens and students together. This program would benefit both the residents of senior citizen homes and the students who would visit them weekly.

The senior citizens would benefit in many ways. They would be sure of visitors on a regular basis. They could get the help they need for errands or short walks. The seniors would feel more a part of the community and would feel better about themselves. They would have new people to talk to and to listen to. They could enjoy concerts and parties presented by the students.

The students would benefit as well. They would feel more important if they knew someone depended on them. They would learn responsability and the importance of keeping to a schedule. They would gain self-confidence by helping others. They could learn about earlier times from their new friends.

This program shouldn't wait. So many people would benefit from it. We need a planning meeting as soon as possible!

Check Your Spelling

Use the proofreading marks to correct any spelling errors. Apply the spelling strategy. Add any words you misspelled to your spelling log. Then, write a neat, final copy of your persuasive essay. Remember to proofread your work.

PRESENTING
Sharing Your Persuasive Essay

Speaking/Listening Strategy

When you are speaking aloud, you should be aware of your audience at all times. Be sure to look directly at people as you speak. This eye contact will help keep your audience interested in what you are saying. It will also help you adjust your presentation to the reactions and needs of your listeners.

Choosing a Way to Share

Here are some ways to share your persuasive essay.

Read Your Essay Aloud
Present your essay aloud as a speech to the class. Your goal is to convince your listeners to share your opinion. Practice your speech beforehand to perfect the expression and emphasis you will use. You may also wish to prepare charts or other visual aids to help you present the material. Refer to these as you speak.

Lead a Class Discussion
Imagine that you are a candidate for an elected office. Use your essay as part of a short campaign speech. Then encourage questions from the audience about your views.

Make a Bulletin Board
Put your persuasive essay up on the "Sound Off" bulletin board for your class. You may wish to add charts, lists, or pictures to the display to further illustrate your points.

Share Your Persuasive Essay
Choose the way you wish to share your persuasive essay with your class.

Add to Your Learning Log

- Which part of my persuasive essay is the most convincing? Why?
- What did I like best about writing my essay?
- The next time I write a persuasive essay, what might I do differently?

311

The Literature Connection: Adverbs ◆

In your writing, it is not enough to attempt to tell what happened. Readers need more than the bare facts to form vivid pictures in their minds. For this reason, writers often use **adverbs** to make actions more vivid. Adverbs are words that tell more about verbs. They tell whether things are being done quickly or slowly, carefully or carelessly, boldly or bashfully. Writers use adverbs in stories and poems to make actions seem vivid and real.

Think about the picture you form in your mind from this sentence: Gina swam. The picture may not be very clear because no adverbs tell you how Gina swam. Now consider these sentences.

Gina swam <u>awkwardly</u>.   Gina swam <u>gracefully</u>.
Gina swam <u>far</u>.   Gina swam <u>slowly</u>.

Each underlined adverb helps you form a clearer picture of how Gina swam.

In the poem below, adverbs are used to help create a colorful picture of the busy wasp.

The Wasp
by
William Sharp

When the ripe pears droop heavily,
   The yellow wasp hums loud and long
   His hot and drowsy autumn song:
A yellow flame he seems to be,
   When darting suddenly from high
   He lights where fallen peaches lie.

Yellow and black—this tiny thing's
A tiger-soul on elfin wings.

Discussion

1. Which adverb in the poem tells how the ripe pears droop?
2. Which adverbs tell how the wasp hums?
3. Imagine that you are observing a wasp near a fruit tree. What adverbs can you use to describe the activity you see?

The Writing Connection: Adverbs

In your own writing, adverbs help you shape colorful, detailed images for your readers. The adverbs in "The Wasp" give a clear picture of the wasp's movements near the pears and peaches. You can describe the actions of other insects by using adverbs and the words that go with them. Read these examples.

The caterpillar crawls steadily along the limb.

An ant carries a crumb of bread carefully from the table to its hole.

Always remember to use adverbs that accurately describe the actions taking place in your sentences.

Activity

Imagine you are watching the insects on an apple tree. You have studied their motions and want to describe the scene vividly. Write sentences that tell about the activity. Complete each sentence below so that it tells about the insects' movements. To describe the verbs, use vivid adverbs and words that go with them.

A butterfly near the apple ____.

A lazy worm ____.

Two busy ants ____.

A lone spider ____.

Adverbs

An **adverb** is a word that describes a verb, an adjective, or another adverb.

A. An adverb can answer *how? when?* or *where?* about an action.

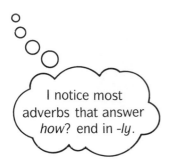

I notice most adverbs that answer *how?* end in *-ly*.

> The boy watched <u>carefully</u>. (*How* did the boy watch?)
> He <u>often</u> studied <u>plants</u>. (*When* did he study plants?)
> Peanuts grow <u>there</u>. (*Where* do peanuts grow?)

Here are some adverbs that answer these questions.

How?	quickly, badly, loudly, brightly, slowly, loosely
When?	now, then, tomorrow, often, sometimes, again, once
Where?	here, there, around, outside, nearby, everywhere, somewhere

B. An adverb can also describe an adjective or another adverb. Here are some adverbs often used in this way.

very	quite	rather	nearly	extremely	fully	enormously
too	totally	slightly	almost	completely	barely	so

One way to find an adverb that describes an adjective or another adverb is to ask a question with the word *how* right before the adjective or adverb.

> She was <u>very</u> bright. (How bright? *very* bright; modifies adjective)
> He learned <u>quite</u> quickly. (How quickly? *quite* quickly; modifies adverb)

Strategy

When an adverb describes an adjective or another adverb, it is usually next to that word. An adverb that describes a verb can appear in other places in the sentence.

Check Your Understanding

A. Write the letter of the adverb in each sentence.
1. George Washington Carver always had a dream.
   a. always **b.** had **c.** dream
2. He would somehow help his people.
   a. would **b.** somehow **c.** help

B. Write the letter of the word that the underlined adverb describes.

   3. He found a <u>very</u> unusual method.
      a. found   **b.** unusual   **c.** method

   4. He devoted his time <u>almost</u> entirely to plants.
      a. devoted   **b.** his   **c.** entirely

Practice

A. Write the sentence. Underline the adverb, and write which question it answers about the verb: *how, when,* or *where.*

   5. Carver sometimes observed plants as a child.
   6. Various plants grew nearby.
   7. Carver quickly learned their names and traits.
   8. People often called him the plant doctor.

B. Write the sentence. Draw an arrow from the underlined adverb to the word it describes. Then tell whether that word is an adjective or an adverb.

   9. Carver experienced poverty <u>too</u> closely in his lifetime.
   10. A college education was <u>almost</u> impossible for him.
   11. He was <u>exceptionally</u> ambitious.
   12. He was <u>also</u> an <u>extremely</u> patient scholar.

C. Mixed Practice Write each sentence. Underline each adverb, and draw an arrow to the word it describes.

   13. Carver eventually earned a professorship.
   14. He quietly studied agriculture in the South.
   15. Carver's work changed agriculture dramatically.
   16. His research made him extremely famous.
   17. He consistently observed plants' effects on the soil.
   18. One of his discoveries was quite extraordinary.
   19. Peanut plants improved the soil very quickly.
   20. Here emerged a completely new opportunity for agriculture.

Apply: Journal

Write several sentences in your journal about a goal that you would like to achieve. Use adverbs to tell where, when, and how you will achieve your goal.

Comparisons with Adverbs

Adverbs, like adjectives, can be used to show comparisons. The **comparative** form compares the actions of two people, things, or groups. The **superlative** form compares the actions of three or more people, things, or groups.

A. Add -er or -est to adverbs of one syllable and to *early*. Use *more* or *most* before most adverbs that end in -ly and other two-syllable adverbs such as *often*.

Adverb	Comparative Form	Superlative Form
soon	sooner	soonest
early	earlier	earliest
often	more often	most often
gracefully	more gracefully	most gracefully

Lisa arrived <u>sooner</u> than Raoul.
She threw the ball <u>most gracefully</u> of all the jugglers.

B. The adverbs *well* and *badly* have special comparative and superlative forms.

Adverb	Comparative Form	Superlative Form
well	better	best
badly	worse	worst

Laura juggles <u>better</u> than her sister.
Pasqual juggles <u>worst</u> of the three of us.

Strategy

As with adjectives, such forms as *more faster* or *most oftenest* are incorrect. Use either *more* or -er or *most* or -est to compare.

Check Your Understanding

A. Write the letter of the correct form of the adverb.
   1. The juggler threw the torch _____ than ever before.
      a. highest   **b.** more high   **c.** higher
   2. She caught the torches _____ of all the performers.
      a. more skillfully   **b.** most skillfully   **c.** skillfuller

B. Write the letter of the correct form of the adverb.

    3. Sun Lee juggles _____ of the five performers.
        a. badly   **b.** worst   **c.** worse

    4. Pak performs _____ than Sun Lee.
        a. well   **b.** best   **c.** better

Practice

A. Write each sentence. Write the correct form of the adverb in parentheses.

    5. The juggler concentrated (hard) than the clown.
    6. She juggled the oranges (precisely) than he.
    7. Silk scarves come down (slowly) of all.
    8. Dinah practices (frequently) of all of us.

B. Follow the instructions for Practice A.

    9. The jugglers entertained us (well) of all.
    10. Joan juggles (well) than her brother.
    11. They performed (badly) yesterday than today.
    12. Tuesday's show went (badly) of all.

C. Mixed Practice Write each sentence. Write the correct form of the adverb in parentheses.

    13. She juggled the hoops (well) than the plates.
    14. Egyptians juggled (early) of all ancient peoples.
    15. Jugglers entertained royalty (often) of all audiences.
    16. Juggling reduces stress (effectively) than some other activities.
    17. Adults often juggle (badly) than children.
    18. Children may learn (fast) than adults.
    19. Beginners can juggle bean-bags (well) and (skillfully) of all items.
    20. They can catch hoops (easy) and (readily) than plates.

Apply: Work with a Partner

  With a partner, compare three or more people that are involved in one sport or field of entertainment. Tell which player or performer you prefer. Be sure to focus on what your subjects *do*. Include adverbs that compare in all your sentences.

Adverb or Adjective?

An **adjective** describes a noun or a pronoun. An **adverb** describes a verb, an adjective, or another adverb.

A. Use an adverb to describe a verb and an adjective to describe a noun.

> The wise pupil studied. (adjective—describes *pupil*)
>
> The pupil studied wisely. (adverb—describes *studied*)

Adverbs often come after verbs, but not every descriptive word after an action verb is an adverb.

> She read medical books. (adjective—describes *books*)

B. Adjectives are most often confused with adverbs when they come after linking verbs. An adjective is often used after a linking verb to describe the subject. Adverbs are usually used with action verbs.

> Elizabeth was patient. (adjective—describes *Elizabeth*)
>
> Elizabeth waited patiently. (adverb—describes *waited*)

When the word *well* means "in good health," it is an adjective. Otherwise, *well* is an adverb. The word *good* is always an adjective.

> The child was well. (adjective—describes *child*)
>
> The doctor advised us well. (adverb—describes *advised*)

Strategy

Remember that *good* is always an adjective. *Well* is an adjective only when it is used to describe someone's health. Otherwise, *well* is an adverb used with an action verb.

Check Your Understanding

A. Write the letter of the adverb in each sentence.
1. Medical schools rarely accepted women students.
   a. Medical **b.** rarely **c.** women
2. But Elizabeth Blackwell eventually earned her medical degree.
   a. eventually **b.** earned **c.** medical

318

B. Write the letter of the word that the underlined word describes.

    3. Blackwell <u>eagerly</u> established her medical practice.
        a. Blackwell   **b.** established   **c.** practice

    4. Patients became <u>well</u> because of her care.
        a. Patients   **b.** became   **c.** care

Practice

A. Write each sentence. Underline the adverb.

    5. People often criticized Blackwell for her aspirations.

    6. Blackwell methodically pursued her goal.

    7. Elizabeth Blackwell stubbornly applied to many medical schools.

    8. Geneva Medical College in New York then accepted her application.

B. Write each sentence. Write *adjective* or *adverb* to identify the underlined word. Write the word it describes.

    9. Twenty-nine medical schools <u>routinely</u> denied her.

    10. Medical school was not <u>easy</u> for Elizabeth.

    11. Her fellow students <u>sometimes</u> teased her.

    12. Elizabeth was a <u>good</u> student, however.

C. Mixed Practice Write each sentence. Underline the adjective once and the adverb twice. Don't underline articles.

    13. Blackwell performed well in spite of strong opposition.

    14. The young doctor next traveled to England.

    15. She worked there in several hospitals.

    16. She then began a medical practice in New York.

    17. Elizabeth often encountered open prejudice.

    18. She was patiently tolerant of it.

    19. Americans should be very grateful to Blackwell.

    20. She worked well with the skillful people in the clinic.

Apply: Learning Log

What was the most difficult part of this lesson for you? In your learning log, write some hints that could help you tell the difference between adjectives and adverbs.

Adverb Phrases

An **adverb phrase** is a prepositional phrase that works like an adverb to describe a verb.

A. An adverb phrase can answer the question *how?*, *where?*, or *when?* about a verb.

> Gandhi fought without violence. (*How* did he fight?)
> He studied law in London. (*Where* did he study law?)
> He died after World War II. (*When* did he die?)

B. An adverb phrase often appears right after the verb it describes. But it can also appear in other places in the sentence.

> Until 1947, Great Britain ruled modern India.
> Many Indians struggled against British tyranny.
> Gandhi continued the struggle throughout his life.

Strategy

When you write, add variety to your sentences by putting adverb phrases in different places in your sentences. For example, don't write three or four sentences in a row that begin with an adverb phrase.

Check Your Understanding

A. The adverb phrase in each sentence is underlined. Write the letter of the question the adverb phrase answers.
   1. Mohandas K. Gandhi was born in 1869.
      a. how?   **b.** where?   **c.** when?
   2. He lived in Porbandar, India.
      a. how?   **b.** where?   **c.** when?

B. The adverb phrase in each sentence is underlined. Write the letter of the word the adverb phrase describes.
   3. At school Gandhi studied law.
      a. At   **b.** Gandhi   **c.** studied
   4. He practiced law in South Africa.
      a. practiced   **b.** law   **c.** South Africa

Practice

A. Write each sentence. Underline each adverb phrase. Tell whether it answers the question *how?*, *where?*, or *when?*

5. The British ruled South Africa in those days.
6. White South Africans discriminated against Indians.
7. Gandhi campaigned across the country.
8. He wanted government reform at once.

B. Write each sentence. Underline each adverb phrase once. Underline twice the word or words it describes.

9. Gandhi won concessions during his campaign.
10. His greatest struggle still lay before him.
11. In 1915, Gandhi returned home.
12. Within five years, he was leading the Indian nationalist movement.

C. Mixed Practice Write each sentence. Underline each adverb phrase once. Underline twice the word or words it describes. Tell whether the phrase answers the question *how?*, *where?*, or *when?*.

13. India suffered during British rule.
14. Gandhi fought with unusual methods.
15. Indians protested without violence.
16. Across India, Gandhi taught peaceful disobedience.
17. Around the nation, people disobeyed unjust laws.
18. However, people avoided violence during the protests.
19. Independence finally came to India in 1947.
20. During his life, people called Gandhi *Mahatma*, or "Great Soul."

Apply: Test a Partner

Write five sentences about someone you know of who made the world a better place. Use an adverb phrase in each of your sentences. Exchange papers with a partner. Underline the verbs that the adverb phrases describe. Tell whether the adverb phrases answer the question *how?*, *where?*, or *when?* Then correct your partner's work.

Avoiding Double Negatives

A **negative** word expresses the idea of "no" in a sentence.

A. The adverbs *not* and *never* are negatives. Other common negatives are *no, none, nobody, no one, nothing, nowhere, neither,* and *nor.*

> Jackie Robinson would <u>not</u> quit.
> He <u>never</u> abandoned his dreams.

Contractions formed from *not* and a verb are also negatives.

> He <u>wasn't</u> a quitter. (was <u>not</u>)

B. One negative word makes a sentence negative. It is incorrect to use two negative words in a sentence when only one is needed. This error is called a **double negative.**

> Incorrect: Jackie Robinson <u>wasn't</u> <u>no</u> ordinary player.
> Correct: Jackie Robinson <u>wasn't</u> an ordinary player.

To avoid a double negative, remove one of the negative words or replace one with a related affirmative word.

negative	no	no one	none	never	nothing	nowhere	nobody
affirmative	any, a	anyone	any	ever	anything	anywhere	anybody

Strategy

Words such as *barely, hardly,* and *scarcely* are also negative words. Avoid using other negative words in sentences that contain these words.

Check Your Understanding

A. Write the letter of the negative sentence.
1. **a.** Robinson joined the Brooklyn Dodgers in 1947.
   b. Baseball hadn't been Robinson's best sport.
   c. He had been a football star in college.
2. **a.** Jackie Robinson was a native of Georgia.
   b. He played baseball for 10 seasons.
   c. None of his opponents could speak badly of him.

B. Write the letter of the word that correctly completes the sentence.

   3. There weren't _____ major league teams with black players then.

   a. no **b.** any **c.** none

   4. There hadn't _____ been a black athlete like Robinson.

   a. not **b.** never **c.** ever

Practice

A. Write each sentence. Underline the negative word.

   5. Major league baseball had no black players in 1946.

   6. The big leagues did not welcome black players.

   7. Black players had never played on major league teams.

   8. The baseball commissioner didn't tolerate prejudice, however.

B. Each sentence contains a double negative. Rewrite the sentence, replacing one negative with an affirmative word.

   9. The first black player couldn't be no ordinary man.

   10. The commissioner didn't want no one weak.

   11. He couldn't find nobody better than Jackie Robinson.

   12. There had not been a finer college athlete nowhere.

C. Mixed Practice Write each sentence. Choose the word or words to form a correct negative sentence.

   13. Robinson (ever, never) lost his temper under pressure.

   14. The commissioner didn't have (no, any) doubts about him.

   15. (Nobody, Anybody) worked harder in the field.

   16. No one could say (nothing, anything) against him.

   17. His first game was (nothing, anything) special.

   18. Even so, he wasn't (never, ever) discouraged.

   19. He (could, couldn't) scarcely contain his enthusiasm.

   20. Hardly (anyone, no one) was a better player.

Apply: Work with a Group

With your group, write 10 sentences stating your opinions about your favorite sports. Exchange papers with another group. Make each sentence negative by adding a negative word. In how many different ways can you make each sentence negative?

323

Context Clues

The words and sentences that surround a certain word make up that word's **context. Context clues** are words that help you figure out the meaning of an unfamiliar word.

A. Context clues can be synonyms, antonyms, or explanatory phrases that appear in the same sentence as the unfamiliar word.

> Many nations aim to improve their economies through international commerce, or trade.

> Tariffs, or taxes on imports, can limit trade by making products costly rather than cheap.

Which word in the first sentence is a synonym for *commerce*? In the second sentence, which phrase explains what *tariffs* are? Which word is an antonym for *costly*?

B. Context clues can also appear before or after the sentence in which an unfamiliar word appears.

> Trade agreements require careful negotiation. Nations must discuss and settle trade problems on fair terms.

What does *negotiation* mean? What clues help you figure out the meaning?

Strategy

In your reading, you may come across an unfamiliar usage of a word you already know. Try to figure out the new meaning through context clues. If you're still not sure, check a dictionary.

Check Your Understanding

A. Write the letter of the underlined word's meaning.
  1. Cotton and wheat are two commodities, or products, that nations trade.
  a. products   **b.** nations   **c.** money
  2. Nations trade agricultural, or farming, products.
  a. popular   **b.** farming   **c.** expensive

B. Write the letter of the underlined word's meaning.
  3. Nations trade manufactured goods, such as cars and clothing. These industrial items can be costly.
  a. foreign   **b.** from farms   **c.** manufactured

4. Certain trade items are more <u>profitable</u> than others. They can make a great amount of money for the seller.
  a. making money   **b.** costing money
  c. causing losses

Practice

A. Use context clues to figure out the correct meaning of the underlined word. Write the meaning.
  5. Many nations become <u>prosperous</u>, not poor, through trade.
  6. In trade discussions, officials must <u>compromise</u>, or give up a part of their demands.
  7. But sometimes officials are <u>obstinate</u>, stubbornly insisting on getting terms favorable to their nations.

B. Follow the directions for Practice A.
  8. Some nations try to become <u>self-sufficient</u>. They attempt to produce everything they need.
  9. Nations depend on one another for different products. This <u>interdependence</u> is the basis of world trade.
  10. <u>Financial</u> conditions affect trade. Matters related to money are an essential part of trade.

C. Mixed Practice Use context clues to write the meaning of each underlined word.
  11. Trade does not harm but rather <u>benefits</u> most nations.
  12. Trade is important to a nation's <u>welfare</u>, or well-being.
  13. Advanced nations carry on the greatest <u>volume</u>, or amount, of trade.
  14. Nations <u>promote</u> rather than discourage trade.
  15. When a nation <u>imports</u> more than it exports, it spends more than it earns. The result is a <u>deficit</u>.
  16. Nations try to increase their <u>productivity</u> and <u>efficiency</u>. Not wasting energy increases the ability to produce.

Apply: Work with a Partner

Write five sentences about world trade that have difficult words. Use context clues to explain the meaning of the words. Exchange papers with a partner and define the difficult words.

Language in Action

Recognizing Propaganda

Believe it or not, you encounter propaganda every day of your life. Propaganda is an attempt to convince people to believe something or to do something. Political speeches, advertisements, and fund-raising appeals are all forms of propaganda. Here are some commonly used propaganda techniques.

- **Name Calling** This kind of propaganda is usually easy to spot. This technique is based on saying unfavorable things about the competition.

    Our hopelessly misguided mayor has done it again.

- **Glittering Generality** This technique associates the propagandist's view with something that is desirable.

    For healthy, white teeth, use Scrubodent.

- **Transfer** This technique associates the propagandist's view with a person or group that is highly respected.

    Four out of five doctors recommend Jonas Vitamins.

- **Celebrity Endorsement** This technique depends on using the name of a famous person to support the propagandist's view.

    Hi. This is Cameron Beatty urging you to vote "yes" on the newspaper-recycling proposition.

- **Plain Folks** This is the opposite of the celebrity endorsement, but it is just as effective because it appeals to a broad audience.

    I'm not an actor. I'm just an ordinary guy who likes Heath's Whole Wheat Muffins.

- **Bandwagon** This technique relies on the idea that people are likely to do something when they think that everyone else is doing it.

    Twenty thousand people drive Zephyrs. Shouldn't you?

- **Loaded Words** Word choice is very important in propaganda. Choosing one word instead of another can make a big difference in the impact of a speech.

    This new Can-O-Matic is *electric*. (fact)
    This new Can-O-Matic is *sensational*. (propaganda)

Practice

Read each item of propaganda. On a separate sheet of paper, write the propaganda technique(s) used in each one.

1. a hidden-camera interview in which shoppers tell why they like a certain brand of tea
2. "UnEsCorp is the largest company in this country. When they need a messenger service, they call us."
3. "Harding paper towels are strong. The other leading brand is weak and flimsy."
4. "Vote for a richer, freer America. Vote for Felice Hernandez."
5. "Here is Perry Westinghouse, Heismann Trophy winner, to speak to you about Lemur sneakers."
6. "Two million people bought Stirling luggage last year. Did you?"
7. Do you want something plain or something glamorous?
8. Television star Kelly O'Day says, "I always shop at Avery's."
9. "All across America, people are rushing to Harker's."
10. ". . . Emily Dent, medical secretary and allergy sufferer."
11. Don't settle for a cheap, poorly-built Econocar when you can buy the solidly-made Standard instead.
12. Everybody who's anybody is wearing Flying Sneaks this year. So don't be left out. Get your pair today.
13. For beautiful, new-looking shoes, buy Gleam-o Shoe Polish.
14. Sandy Brilliant, last year's spelling bee champion, uses Grapho-Pencils, and you should, too.
15. Take the advice of nine doctors out of ten. Take Pain-Away for muscle aches.

Apply

Try writing propaganda. First, choose a cause or a product. It can be real or imaginary. Write a speech endorsing that cause or product. Direct your speech to newspaper, magazine, or billboard readers or to a radio or a television audience. Convince people to support your cause or to buy your product. Be sure to use one or more of the techniques mentioned in this lesson.

HISTORY OF LANGUAGE

Animal Words

Julie *craned* her neck to get a better view. Do you know the expression *to crane your neck*? It means "to stretch your neck, usually to see something." A *crane* is a large wading bird that has a long neck. *To crane your neck* also means "to make it long, like a crane's."

There are many verbs that come from animal names. Some, like *to crane,* come from an animal's physical features. Others refer to the animal's behavior. Have you ever tried to open a live clam shell? It is very hard to do because the clam is tightly closed. That's why we say people *clam up* when they keep their mouths shut tight.

Monkeys are famous for swinging from trees. They seem to play all day long. *To monkey around* means "to play or to have a lot of fun."

Have you ever seen squirrels gather and save acorns for the winter? They hide them in holes in trees and other places. Someone who puts things into hiding places is said *to squirrel them away*.

Activity

Write the sentences. Complete each one with the correct form of the verb from the box.

outfox	parrot	bug	duck	hound

1. The girl _____ under the archway.
2. Jack _____ everything his brother said.
3. She really _____ me when she pulls my hair.
4. Carmen is so smart that she _____ her mother in checkers.
5. Sam's dad keeps _____ him to clean his room.

UNIT REVIEW

Persuasive Essay (page 295)
1. List at least three characteristics of a persuasive essay.

Supporting an Opinion (pages 300–301)
Below are two opposing opinions on the same subject. Choose one opinion. Support that opinion with appropriate details from the list shown here.

Opinion I: Animated cartoons are harmful to young viewers.
Opinion II: Animated cartoons are not harmful to young viewers.

2. Cartoons show people and animals in a humorous light.
3. Many cartoons show people and animals acting in a cruel way toward each other.
4. Many cartoons are beautifully drawn and tell classic stories.
5. Most youngsters can tell the difference between cartoon behavior and real life.
6. Young viewers think cartoons show life accurately.
7. Youngsters who don't realize a character's behavior is exaggerated may be tempted to imitate such behavior.

Structuring a Persuasive Essay (pages 302–303)
Write whether the following statements would appear in the introduction, the body, or the conclusion of a persuasive essay.
8. America has some of the world's finest examples of architecture.
9. Let's find ways immediately to restore our old buildings and keep our heritage alive.
10. If we let these buildings be destroyed, we can never replace them.
11. America's architectural heritage must be preserved.

Using Apostrophes and Hyphens (pages 308–309)
Write each of the following sentences correctly. Use apostrophes and hyphens where they are needed.
12. I cant imagine a more fun filled day than our trip to the carnival last summer.
13. The childrens favorite ride was the colorful merry go round.
14. Gladyss mount was a pearl colored elephant.
15. By the days end, we had all ridden the hand painted animals.

Adverbs (pages 314–315)

Write each sentence. Underline each adverb, and draw an arrow to the word it describes.

16. People have constantly hunted whales throughout history.

17. Whales became almost extinct as a result.

18. Whales became a very rare sight for sailors.

19. Hunters have always wanted whales for meat and blubber.

20. Some people still hunt these intelligent creatures.

21. Whales are quite gentle animals.

22. Many nations now protect whales.

23. Whale populations have increased considerably.

24. Oceangoers can quite readily view whales these days.

25. The whale protection campaign has been extremely successful.

Comparisons with Adverbs (pages 316–317)

Write each sentence. Write the correct form of the adverb given in parentheses.

26. Wanda drives (quickly) than Inez.

27. Her car runs (well) of the three.

28. He arrived (soon) than you.

29. Bo's truck performed (badly) than mine.

30. Last night, Flo left (early) of all the guests.

31. That truck drives (smoothly) than Bo's truck.

32. It rides (badly) of all our trucks.

33. The truck turns (well) to the left than to the right.

34. Bo drives (often) than I do.

35. Kim drives (skillfully) of all my friends.

Adverb or Adjective? (pages 318–319)

Write each sentence. Underline the adjective once and the adverb twice.

36. The waves of light in lasers are perfectly straight.

37. Complete alignment greatly concentrates the light.

38. The waves are exactly identical in color.

39. Early lasers precisely measured the distance to the moon.

40. A powerful beam actually bounced off the moon.

41. Scientists simply timed the swift return of the beam.

42. Other lasers are now used in surgery.

43. Surgeons can make precise cuts accurately with lasers.

44. They can perform delicate operations safely.

45. Lasers can vastly improve modern telecommunications.

Adverb Phrases (pages 320–321)

Write each sentence. Underline each adverb phrase once. Underline twice the word or words it describes. Tell whether the phrase answers the question *how?*, *where?*, or *when?*

46. Researchers search for new energy sources.

47. Their work continues around the clock.

48. World energy use has risen during this century.

49. Windmills bring power to many areas.

50. Solar energy succeeds in sunny places.

51. Nuclear energy has caused controversy over the years.

52. Waves can provide energy near the seashore.

53. Fusion research has advanced science at a rapid rate.

54. Alternative energy sources will help us to a great extent.

55. We must develop these resources without delay.

Avoiding Double Negatives (pages 322–323)

Choose the word or words that form a sentence with only one negative.

56. The quality of Shakespeare's plays and poems will (ever, never) fade.

57. No one has (ever, never) surpassed him.

58. There was no finer writer (anywhere, nowhere) in England.

59. No other writer of English has a reputation (anything, nothing) like Shakespeare's.

60. None of the ideas for his plays (are, aren't) original, however.

61. He wrote (no, any) plays about his own times.

62. There are (any, no) plays about Queen Elizabeth, for example.

63. Scarcely (anything, nothing) is known about Shakespeare's own life.

64. None of his contemporaries (ever, never) wrote about him.

65. The journals of his time give (any, no) clues to the mystery of Shakespeare's life outside the theater.

Context Clues (pages 324–325)

Use context clues to write the meaning of each underlined word.

66. The Constitution's requirements of a presidential candidate are simple. It makes only three demands.

67. The candidate must be 35 years old and must have resided, or lived, in the United States for at least 14 years.

68. Only natural-born United States citizens are eligible. Those who become citizens after birth are not qualified.

69. The Constitution now stipulates, or specifies, that a president cannot run for reelection after two full terms.

UNIT

8

Story

◆

Sentences II

What Do You Know?

"You should really read this!"

What was the best story you read recently? What did you especially like about it? Maybe there was a character you found interesting or heroic. Perhaps the story took place in an exotic setting that you would like to visit. Perhaps the events in the story were so exciting that you couldn't wait to find out what was going to happen next.

Character, plot, and setting are important elements of every story. They work together to draw us into the story and help us feel that we are experiencing the action. Well-written stories make us care about the characters and make us want to read more. They let us picture faraway places, visit the past, or see what the future might be like. They can even help us to learn something about ourselves. A good story can be an enriching as well as an entertaining experience.

332

Thinking About Stories

What Is a Story?

A story has these characteristics:

- It has a plot, or a series of events that occur.
- It has characters, or people and animals that take part in the events.
- It has a setting, or the time and place of the events.
- The introduction describes the characters and setting.
- The problem tells what difficulties a character faces.
- The solution attempts are the ways the characters try to solve the problem.
- The outcome tells how the problem is solved.

A good story sparks our imaginations. It enables us to picture the people, places, and events described by the writer. We face the hardships that the characters face, and we follow their attempts to find solutions. The characters and plot are often so intriguing that we don't want to leave the world created by the writer. Finishing a truly excellent story makes us eager to begin reading another story that we'll enjoy just as much.

Discussion

1. What is your favorite story?
2. What was the best story you read recently?
3. What do you look for when you choose a story to read?

Reading a Story

The following is a contemporary story that takes place in New York City. It describes how a young girl feels about her brother and about some of her classmates who do not treat him with respect. The narrator of the story is 13-year-old Hazel Porter, who is nicknamed Squeaky. Her main rival is 13-year-old Gretchen. As you read the story, think about the problems Squeaky faces and how she solves them.

"Raymond's Run"
by
Toni Cade Bambara

The main characters are introduced.

I don't have much work to do around the house like some girls. My mother does that. And I don't have to earn my pocket money by hustling; George runs errands for the big boys and sells Christmas cards. And anything else that's got to get done, my father does. All I have to do in life is mind my brother Raymond, which is enough.

Sometimes I slip and say my little brother Raymond. But as any fool can see, he's much bigger and he's older too. But a lot of people call him my little brother cause he needs looking after cause he's not quite right. And a lot of smart mouths got lots to say about that too, especially when George was minding him. But now, if anybody had anything to say to Raymond, anything to say about his big head, they have to come by me. And I don't play the dozens or believe in standing around with somebody in my face doing a lot of talking. I much rather just knock you down and take my chances even if I am a little girl with skinny arms and a squeaky voice, which is how I got the name Squeaky. And if things get too rough, I run. And as anybody can tell you, I'm the fastest thing on two feet.

There is no track meet that I don't win the first-place medal. I used to win the twenty-yard dash when I was a little kid in kindergarten. Nowadays, it's the fifty-yard dash. And tomorrow I'm subject to run the quarter-meter relay all by myself and come in first, second, and third. The big kids call me Mercury cause I'm the swiftest thing in the neighborhood. Everybody knows that—except two people who know better, my father and me. He can beat me to Amsterdam Avenue with me having a two fire-hydrant headstart and him running with his hands in his pockets and whistling. But that's private information. Cause can you imagine some thirty-five-year-old man stuffing himself into PAL shorts to race little kids? So far as everyone's concerned, I'm the fastest and that goes for Gretchen, too, who has put out the tale that she is going to win the first-place medal this year. Ridiculous. In the second place, she's got short legs. In the third place, she's got freckles. In the first place, no one can beat me and that's all there is to it.

335

I'm standing on the corner admiring the weather and about to take a stroll down Broadway so I can practice my breathing exercises, and I've got Raymond walking on the inside close to the buildings, cause he's subject to fits of fantasy and starts thinking he's a circus performer and that the curb is a tightrope strung high in the air. And sometimes after a rain he likes to step down off his tightrope right into the gutter and slosh around getting his shoes and cuffs wet. Then I get hit when I get home. Or sometimes if you don't watch him he'll dash across traffic to the island in the middle of Broadway and give the pigeons a fit. Then I have to go behind him apologizing to all the old people sitting around trying to get some sun and getting all upset with the pigeons fluttering around them, scattering their newspapers and upsetting the waxpaper lunches in their laps. So I keep Raymond on the inside of me, and he plays like he's driving a stagecoach, which is O.K. by me so long as he doesn't run me over or interrupt my breathing exercises, which I have to do on account of I'm serious about my running, and I don't care who knows it.

Now some people like to act like things come easy to them, won't let on that they practice. Not me. I'll high-prance down 34th Street like a rodeo pony to keep my knees strong even if it does get my mother uptight so that she walks like she's not with me, don't know me, is all by herself on a shopping trip, and I am somebody else's crazy child. Now you take Cynthia Procter for instance. She's just the opposite. If there's a test tomorrow, she'll say something like, "Oh, I guess I'll play handball this afternoon and watch television tonight," just to let you know she ain't thinking about the test. Or like last week when she won the spelling bee for the millionth time, "A good thing you got 'receive,' Squeaky, cause I would have got it wrong. I completely forgot about the spelling bee." And she'll clutch the lace on her blouse like it was a narrow escape. Oh, brother. But of course when I pass her house on my early morning trots around the block, she is practicing the scales on the piano over and over and over and over. Then in music class she always lets herself get bumped around so she falls accidentally on purpose onto the piano stool and is so surprised to find herself sitting there that she decides just for fun to try out the ole keys. And what do you know—Chopin's waltzes just spring out of her fingertips and she's the most surprised thing in the world. A regular prodigy. I could kill people like that. I stay up all night studying the words for the spelling bee. And you can see me any time of day practicing running. I never walk if I can trot, and shame on Raymond if he can't keep up. But of course he does, cause if he hangs back, someone's liable to walk up to him and get smart or take his allowance from him, or ask him where he got that great big pumpkin head. People are so stupid sometimes.

Another character is introduced.

The problem begins to take shape.

So I'm strolling down Broadway, breathing out and breathing in on counts of seven, which is my lucky number, and here comes Gretchen and her sidekicks: Mary Louise, who used to be a friend of mine when she first moved to Harlem from Baltimore and got beat up by everybody till I took up for her on account of her mother and my mother used to sing in the same choir when they were young girls, but people ain't grateful, so now she hangs out with the new girl Gretchen and talks about me like a dog; and Rosie, who is as fat as I am skinny and has a big mouth where Raymond is concerned and is too stupid to know that there is not a big deal of difference between herself and Raymond and that she can't afford to throw stones. So they are steady coming up Broadway and I see right away that it's going to be one of those Dodge City scenes cause the street ain't that big and they're close to the buildings just as we are. First I think I'll step into the candy store and look over the new comics and let them pass. But that's chicken and I've got a reputation to consider. So then I think I'll just walk straight on through them or even over them if necessary. But as they get to me, they slow down. I'm ready to fight, cause, like I said I don't feature a whole lot of chit-chat, I much prefer to just knock you down right from the jump and save everybody a lotta precious time.

The character considers solutions to a problem.

338

"You signing up for the May Day races?" smiles Mary Louise, only it's not a smile at all. A dumb question like that doesn't deserve an answer. Besides, there's just me and Gretchen standing there really, so no use wasting my breath talking to shadows.

"I don't think you're going to win this time," says Rosie, trying to signify with her hands on her hips all salty.

"I always win cause I'm the best," I say straight at Gretchen who is, as far as I'm concerned, the only one talking in this ventriloquist-dummy routine. Gretchen smiles, but it's not a smile, and I'm thinking that girls never really smile at each other because they don't know how and don't want to know how and there's probably no one to teach us how, cause grown-up girls don't know either. Then they all look at Raymond who had just brought his mule team to a standstill. And they're about to see what trouble they can get into through him.

"What grade you in now, Raymond?"

"You got anything to say to my brother, you say it to me, Mary Louise Williams of Raggedy Town, Baltimore."

"What are you, his mother?" sasses Rosie.

"That's right. And the next word out of anybody and I'll be *their* mother too." So they just stand there and Gretchen shifts from one leg to the other and so do they. Then Gretchen puts her hands on her hips and is about to say something with her freckle-face self but doesn't. Then she walks around me looking me up and down but keeps walking up Broadway, and her sidekicks follow her. So me and Raymond smile at each other and he says, "Gidyap" to his team and I continue with my breathing exercises, strolling down Broadway toward the ice man on 145th with not a care in the world cause I am Miss Quicksilver herself.

I take my time getting to the park on May Day because the track meet is the last thing on the program. The biggest thing on the program is the May Pole dancing, which I can do without, thank you, even if my mother thinks it's a shame I don't take part and act like a girl for a change. You'd think my mother'd be grateful not to have to make me a white organdy dress with a big satin sash and buy me new white baby-doll shoes that can't be taken out of the box till the big day. You'd think she'd be glad her daughter ain't out there prancing around a May Pole getting the new clothes all dirty and sweaty and trying to act like a fairy or a flower or whatever you're supposed to be when you should be trying to be yourself, whatever that is, which is, as far as I am concerned, a poor Black girl who really can't afford to buy shoes and a new dress you only wear once a lifetime cause it won't fit next year.

A new setting is described.

MAY DAY

I was once a strawberry in a Hansel and Gretel pageant when I was in nursery school and didn't have no better sense than to dance on tiptoe with my arms in a circle over my head doing umbrella steps and being a perfect fool just so my mother and father could come dressed up and clap. You'd think they'd know better than to encourage that kind of nonsense. I am not a strawberry. I do not dance on my toes. I run. That is what I am all about. So I always come late to the May Day program, just in time to get my number pinned on and lay in the grass till they announce the fifty-yard dash.

I put Raymond in the little swings, which is a tight squeeze this year and will be impossible next year. Then I look around for Mr. Pearson, who pins the numbers on. I'm really looking for Gretchen if you want to know the truth, but she's not around. The park is jam-packed. Parents in hats and corsages and breast-pocket handkerchiefs peeking up. Kids in white dresses and light-blue suits. The parkees unfolding chairs and chasing the rowdy kids from Lenox as if they had no right to be there. The big guys with their caps on backwards, leaning against the fence swirling the basketballs on the tips of their fingers, waiting for all these crazy people to clear out the park so they can play. Most of the kids in my class are carrying bass drums and glockenspiels and flutes. You'd think they'd put in a few bongos or something for real like that.

The character prepares to solve the problem.

341

Then here comes Mr. Pearson with his clipboard and his cards and pencils and whistles and safety pins and fifty million other things he's always dropping all over the place with his clumsy self. He sticks out in a crowd because he's on stilts. We used to call him Jack and the Beanstalk to get him mad. But I'm the only one that can outrun him and get away, and I'm too grown for that silliness now.

"Well, Squeaky," he says, checking my name off the list and handing me number seven and two pins. And I'm thinking he's got no right to call me Squeaky, if I can't call him Beanstalk.

"Hazel Elizabeth Deborah Parker," I correct him and tell him to write it down on his board.

"Well, Hazel Elizabeth Deborah Parker, going to give someone else a break this year?" I squint at him real hard to see if he is seriously thinking I should lose the race on purpose just to give someone else a break. "Only six girls running this time," he continues, shaking his head sadly like it's my fault all of New York didn't turn out in sneakers. "That new girl should give you a run for your money." He looks around the park for Gretchen like a periscope in a submarine movie. "Wouldn't it be a nice gesture if you were . . . to ahhh . . ."

The character reacts to the problem.

I give him such a look he couldn't finish putting that idea into words. Grown-ups got a lot of nerve sometimes. I pin number seven to myself and stomp away, I'm so burnt. And I go straight for the track and stretch out on the grass while the band winds up with "Oh, the Monkey Wrapped His Tail Around the Flag Pole," which my teacher calls by some other name. The man on the loudspeaker is calling everyone over to the track and I'm on my back looking at the sky, trying to pretend I'm in the country, but I can't, because even grass in the city feels hard as sidewalk, and there's just no pretending you are anywhere but in a "concrete jungle" as my grandfather says.

The twenty-yard dash takes all of two minutes cause most of the little kids don't know no better than to run off the track or run the wrong way or run smack into the fence and fall down and cry. One little kid, though, has got the good sense to run straight for the white ribbon up ahead so he wins. Then the second-graders line up for the thirty-yard dash and I don't even bother to turn my head to watch cause Raphael Perez always wins. He wins before he even begins by psyching the runners, telling them they're going to trip on their shoelaces and fall on their faces or lose their shorts or something, which he doesn't really have to do since he is very fast, almost as fast as I am. After that is the forty-yard dash which I use to run when I was in first grade. Raymond is hollering from the swings cause he knows I'm about to do my thing cause the man on the loudspeaker has just announced the fifty-yard dash, although he might just as well be giving a recipe for angel food cake cause you can hardly make out what he's sayin for the static. I get up and slip off my sweat pants and then I see Gretchen standing at the starting line, kicking her legs out like a pro. Then as I get into place I see that ole Raymond is on line on the other side of the fence, bending down with his fingers on the ground just like he knew what he was doing. I was going to yell at him but then I didn't. It burns up your energy to holler.

Every time, just before I take off in a race, I always feel like I'm in a dream, the kind of dream you have when you're sick with fever and feel all hot and weightless. I dream I'm flying over a sandy beach in the early morning sun, kissing the leaves of the trees as I fly by. And there's always the smell of apples, just like in the country when I was little and used to think I was a choo-choo train, running through the fields of corn and chugging up the hill to the orchard. And all the time I'm dreaming this, I get lighter and lighter until I'm flying over the beach again, getting blown through the sky like a feather that weighs nothing at all. But once I spread my fingers in the dirt and crouch over the Get on Your Mark, the dream goes, and I am solid again and am telling myself, Squeaky, you must win, you must win, you are the fastest thing in the world, you can even beat your father up Amsterdam if you really try. And then I feel my weight coming back just behind my knees then down to my feet then into the earth and the pistol shot explodes in my blood and I am off and weightless again, flying past the other runners, my arms pumping up and down and the whole world is quiet except for the crunch as I zoom over the gravel in the track. I glance to my left and there is no one. To the right, a blurred Gretchen, who's got her chin jutting out as if it would win the race all by itself. And on the other side of the fence is Raymond with his arms down to his side and the palms tucked up behind him, running in his very own style, and it's the first time I ever saw that and I almost stop to watch my brother Raymond on his first run. But the white ribbon is bouncing toward me and I tear past it, racing into the distance till my feet with a mind of their own start digging up footfuls of dirt and brake me short. Then all the kids standing on the side pile on me, banging me on the back and slapping my head with their May Day programs, for I have won again and everybody on 151st Street can walk tall for another year.

"In first place . . ." the man on the loudspeaker is clear as a bell now. But then he pauses and the

loudspeaker starts to whine. Then static. And I lean
down to catch my breath and here comes Gretchen
walking back, for she's overshot the finishing line too,
huffing and puffing with her hands on her hips taking
it slow, breathing in steady time like a real pro and
I sort of like her a little for the first time. "In first
place . . ." and then three or four voices get all mixed
up on the loudspeaker and I dig my sneaker into the
grass and stare at Gretchen who's staring back, we both
wondering just who did win. I can hear old Beanstalk
arguing with the man on the loudspeaker and then a
few others running their mouths about what the
stopwatches say. Then I hear Raymond yanking at the
fence to call me and I wave to shush him, but he keeps
rattling the fence like a gorilla in a cage like in them
gorilla movies, but then like a dancer or something he
starts climbing up nice and easy but very fast. And it
occurs to me, watching how smoothly he climbs hand
over hand and remembering how he looked running
with his arms down to his side and with the wind
pulling his mouth back and his teeth showing and all, it

occurred to me that Raymond would make a very fine runner. Doesn't he always keep up with me on my trots? And he surely knows how to breathe in counts of seven cause he's always doing it at the dinner table, which drives my brother George up the wall. And I'm smiling to beat the band cause if I've lost this race, or if me and Gretchen tied, or even if I've won, I can always retire as a runner and begin a whole new career as a coach with Raymond as my champion. After all, with a little more study I can beat Cynthia and her phony self at the spelling bee. And if I bugged my mother, I could get piano lessons and become a star. And I have a big rep as the baddest thing around. And I've got a roomful of ribbons and medals and awards. But what has Raymond got to call his own?

So I stand there with my new plans, laughing out loud by this time as Raymond jumps down from the fence and runs over with his teeth showing and his arms down to the side, which no one before him has quite mastered as a running style. And by the time he comes over I'm jumping up and down so glad to see him—my brother Raymond, a great runner in the family tradition. But of course everyone thinks I'm jumping up and down because the men on the loudspeaker have finally gotten themselves together and compared notes and are announcing "In first place— Miss Hazel Elizabeth Deborah Parker." (Dig that.) "In second place—Miss Gretchen P. Lewis." And I look over at Gretchen wondering what the "P" stands for. And I smile. Cause she's good, no doubt about it. Maybe she'd like to help me coach Raymond; she obviously is serious about running, as any fool can see. And she nods to congratulate me and then she smiles. And I smile. We stand there with this big smile of respect between us. It's about as real a smile as girls can do for each other, considering we don't practice real smiling every day, you know, cause maybe we're too busy being flowers or fairies or strawberries instead of something honest and worthy of respect . . . you know . . . like being people.

The outcome is described.

346

Understanding What You've Read

Write the answers to these questions on a sheet of paper.

1. Is Raymond older or younger than his sister Squeaky?
2. Who is the only person who can outrun Squeaky?
3. In what ways does Squeaky act differently from other girls she talks about?
4. What does the chance meeting on Broadway show about Squeaky's character?
5. How does Squeaky feel about Gretchen after the race is over?
6. Why is Raymond's skill at running more important to Squeaky than whether or not she has won the race?
7. How do you think Squeaky's pride in Raymond might influence her future behavior?

Writing Assignment

Imagine that you have entered a nationwide story-writing contest. A prize will be awarded to the best-written and most memorable story. In addition, the prize-winning stories will be published in a magazine read by students all over the country. In order to enter the contest, you must write a story that your classmates and teachers can recommend to the contest directors.

Your **audience** for the story will be the teachers and students in your school. Your **purpose** in writing the story will be to create the best story you can.

Choose an Incident

Think of an incident that might make an interesting story. It may be a real experience that you or a friend have had, or it may be imaginary, involving people from another time and place. The incident you choose should include some sort of problem for your characters to overcome. It may be a dangerous situation, such as being lost in the woods, or it may be a more everyday personal challenge, such as making a friend or caring for a sick pet. Make some notes about the incident you choose. Save your notes for the next lesson.

Creating Characters

Characters are the people who make events happen or who have events happen to them. Some characters are people like you. Others are imaginary people or historical figures who lived in another time or place. Some stories have animals as characters. Often these animals are portrayed as having human abilities, such as thought and speech.

Creating a character takes careful planning. Before you begin your story, think about what each character will be doing. Use these questions to plan your characters.

- What is the character's name?
- Is the character male or female?
- How old is the character?
- What does the character do?

In addition, each character has qualities that make him or her unique. Is the character kind or thoughtless? Is he or she a happy person or a sad one? Is the character confident or shy? Your characters begin to become real as they take shape in your mind. When they seem real to you, they will be easier to write about and will seem real to your readers. If you create your characters carefully before you begin, you will find it easier to write about them later.

One way to define a character is by preparing a **character sketch,** or a list of notes that describe the character. Here is a character sketch one student wrote for a story.

> — a girl named Tae Lee
> — thirteen years old
> — a talented violinist
> — wants to win music competition
> — naturally timid, but willing to work hard
> — comes from loving, supportive family
> — is able to learn from disappointments

Practice

A. Answer these questions about the character sketch on the previous page. Write your answers on a sheet of paper.

1. What is the name of the character?
2. What kind of family does this character have?
3. How old is the character?
4. What reasons do you think the character might have for wanting to win a contest?
5. How do you think the character would react to not winning the contest?
6. What other details would you add to the character sketch to make the character come alive in your mind?

B. The notes below are for an imaginary character. Copy the notes onto your paper. Fill in the blanks to complete the character sketch. Try to make the character as interesting as possible.

— a boy named _____
— _____ years old
— likes to play _____
— is very good at _____
— when he loses, he _____
— _____ when he wins
— very fond of _____
— his ambition is to _____
— has decided to try _____

Write a Character Sketch

Think about some characters you might create for your story. Decide which characters will be the most important ones. Prepare a character sketch for each of these important people. Include details that describe the person and tell what kind of a person he or she is. Save your character sketches for the next lesson.

What will my main character be like?

The Parts of a Story

The characters are one important aspect of a story. Two other important aspects are the setting and the plot.

The **setting** is the time and place of the story. You have to decide when and where your story will take place. You may use the same setting throughout the story, or you may move from one setting to another as the story unfolds. Your setting may be realistic or imaginary. It could be a modern school, a medieval castle, or a futuristic space station. It is important, however, that the characters and events be believable in any setting you choose.

The **plot** is the series of events that make up a story. A plot can be viewed as having four parts.

- The **introduction** sets up the events by introducing the main characters and the setting of the story.
- As the story progresses, a **problem** arises for one or more of the characters.
- The **solution attempts** are the ways the characters try to solve the problem.
- Finally, the story ending, or **outcome,** tells how the problem is solved and how the story ends.

To plan the parts of your story, you might make a chart like the one below. Notice how the plot is divided into four parts.

CHARACTERS: Tae Lee, other violinists, her family, judges			
SETTING: large and crowded concert hall, in the present			
PLOT: Introduction	Problem	Solution Attempts	Outcome
Tae Lee is waiting to play in a music contest.	Tae is shy and nervous. The other violinists seem more confident.	Tae tries to calm herself by thinking of her ambitions and of her family.	She plays well enough to win second prize. She plans to practice harder and win first prize next year.

Practice

A. Answer these questions about the chart on the previous page. Write your answers on a sheet of paper.
1. What is the setting of the story?
2. Who are the main characters?
3. Why is shyness a problem for Tae Lee?
4. How do you think her thoughts about her family could calm her down?
5. What other outcome might have been a good one for the story?

B. The chart below is for an imaginary story. Copy the chart onto a sheet of paper. Fill in the missing parts with details that will complete the story and make it more interesting.

CHARACTERS: Joey Mirales, a _____
SETTING: a small town on the coast of _____

PLOT:			
Introduction	**Problem**	**Solution Attempts**	**Outcome**
Joey and his mother come to the town for _____.	Joey wants to sail, but he is afraid of _____.	Joey and his mother take the ferry to _____. Joey _____ the ride.	Joey conquers his fear of _____ and learns to ____.

Plan the Parts of Your Story

Decide on the setting and plot for your story. Make a story chart that lists the characters, the setting, and the plot. Include the introduction, the problem, the solution attempts, and the outcome of the plot. Save your chart for the next lesson.

What will happen in my story? Where will it take place?

Writing a First Draft

◆

Read part of the first draft of a story that a student wrote. The writer wasn't worried about making it perfect. It will be changed later.

> The concert hall was crowded with people. They had come to hear the violinists. Tae Lee waited for her turn to go onstage. She listened to the melodious sounds of the other violinests who were playing for the judges. She flipped through her sheet music nervously.
>
> The other competitors all seemed so poised and so confident of winning the contest. At 13, Tae Lee was painfully shy. She wanted to run from the hall and hide. She wondered why she had entered the contest to begin with. Then she remembered how much she enjoyed playing the violin and how she wanted to become a violinist.
>
> Tae waited uncertainly. She tried to think calming thoughts. She thought about her family. Papa always called her Special One and praised her; and Mother always encouraged her to test the limits of her skill. Tae knew that whatever happened today, she would still have they're love. Then she tryed to imagine how it would feel to win. She imagined herself smiling. She was deep in thought. She jumped when her name was called. She could bearly breathe.

Write Your First Draft

Discuss your story ideas with your teacher or a partner, or begin work by yourself. Use your character sketches and your story chart as you write. Your story can be five or six paragraphs. Be sure to start with an introduction. In the next paragraph, describe the problem. Then, write one or more paragraphs explaining the solution attempts. Finally, write a paragraph that tells the outcome. Save your work.

Discussing a First Draft

After finishing your first draft, look for ways to improve it. You may discuss your story with a classmate.

Discussion Strategy

Read your partner's writing carefully before the discussion. Write down any questions or comments you think of while you are reading it, so that you won't forget them. Then think about how you will discuss these points. Your discussion will go more smoothly if it is well planned.

Use this Content Checklist to discuss with your classmates the story on the previous page.

Content Checklist
- ✔ Does the story have interesting characters?
- ✔ Is the setting stated in the story?
- ✔ Does the plot have an introduction, a problem, solution attempts, and an outcome?

APPLY STEP BY STEP

Revise Your First Draft for Content

To the Reader: Exchange stories with a partner. Read your partner's story. Try to identify the characters and the setting. Also identify the parts of the plot. Discuss ways to make the characters more interesting or realistic and ways to make the plot more exciting or believable. Use the Content Checklist and Discussion Strategy as you work.

To the Writer: Listen to the suggestions your partner makes. Then revise your draft for content. Save your work.

Combining Sentences for Style ◆

In the short story about Tae Lee, some of the sentences can be combined to make the story flow more smoothly.

Some sentences may be combined with a word that shows **time order**. Such words include *when, as, while, before, after,* and *until*. Notice that a comma separates the ideas if the word showing time comes first in the sentence.

> She was frightened. She waited to play.
>
>> She was frightened as she waited to play.
>> As she waited to play, she was frightened.

> She thought about her family. She became calmer.
>
>> When she thought about her family, she became calmer.
>> She became calmer when she thought about her family.

Another way to combine sentences is to connect them with a word that shows **cause and effect**, or tells *why*. These words include *because, since,* and *so that*.

> She practiced hard. She wanted to be a violinist.
>
>> She practiced hard because she wanted to be a violinist.

> She wanted to win. Her parents would be proud of her.
>
>> She wanted to win so that her parents would be proud of her.

If two sentences have the same subject, you can combine the sentences by replacing one of the subjects. *Who* is used only for people. *That* is used for animals and things.

> The people waited for her to play. They were in the concert hall.
>
>> The people who were in the concert hall waited for her to play.

> Fear threatened her success. The fear slowly disappeared.
>
>> The fear that threatened her success slowly disappeared.

Practice

Combine the sentences below by using the words shown in parentheses. Write your sentences on a sheet of paper.

1. Franz Schubert was a composer. He lived in the nineteenth century. (*who*)

2. Schubert met the composer Beethoven only once. Beethoven died in 1827. (*before*)

3. Schubert began music school at the age of 11. He studied musical composition. (*when*)

4. He attended music school in Vienna. Schubert wrote his first symphony in 1813. (*after*)

5. He was sitting in a restaurant. He wrote one song on the back of a menu. (*while*)

6. He wrote many lovely ballads. The ballads are popular even today. (*that*)

7. Schubert died at the age of 31. He was buried in a Vienna cemetery, near Beethoven. (*when*)

8. Schubert was a musical genius. He produced over 600 musical pieces in his short life. (*who*)

◆————————————————————————————◆

Revising Checklist

✔ Have I included all the characteristics of a short story?

✔ Where can I combine sentences with subjects, predicates, or descriptive words? (pp. 34, 158)

✔ Where can I combine sentences by using the words *and*, *but*, or *or*? (p. 118)

✔ What sentences can I change to vary the word order or to avoid repetition? (pp. 72, 208)

✔ Where can I add transitions between sentences and paragraphs? (p. 256)

✔ Where can I combine sentences by using words like *when*, *while*, *before*, *because*, *who*, and *that*?

◆————————————————————————————◆

Revise Your First Draft for Style

Check the items on the Revising Checklist. Look for sentences that you can combine to make your writing smoother. Use different ways to combine your sentences. Make the changes on your draft. Keep your work for the next lesson.

Punctuating Conversation

You may wish to add conversation to your story to make it more realistic. This chart tells how to punctuate conversation.

Rule	Example
Use quotation marks around the exact words of a speaker. Always capitalize the first word of the quotation. Use a comma to separate the speaker's words from the rest of the sentence. End the sentence with a period.	"I want to go sailing," said Joey. "That would be fun," his mother said. Joey said, "My friends will be surprised."
If a quotation is a question or an exclamation, use a question mark or an exclamation point to end the quotation.	"Are you frightened?" his mother asked. "I certainly am!" he replied with feeling. His mother asked, "How can I help?"
Sometimes a quotation is divided. If the divided quotation is one sentence, use commas to separate the quotation from interrupting words in the sentence.	"I'd like to go," Joey said, "but I'm a little nervous." "Well," said his mother, "you needn't be."
If a divided quotation is two sentences, use the appropriate punctuation mark for the first part of the quote and a period after the interrupting words. Begin the next sentence of the quote with a capital letter.	"I will go sailing with you," she said. "You will be safe." "Will you?" he asked. "I am so happy!"

Notice that a comma or a period always goes before the quotation marks at the end of the speaker's words. A question mark or an exclamation point goes before the closing quotation mark when the quotation itself is a question or an exclamation. Also notice that a new paragraph is used to show a change of speaker.

Practice

Write each sentence below, adding the correct capitalization and punctuation.

1. are the waves always so big Joey asked
2. no his mother replied it's very windy today
3. sailing is a great hobby said Mr. Ellis it's not as easy as it seems, though
4. let's take a ride on the ferry Joey's mother suggested
5. is it a long trip Joey asked
6. the whole ride Mr. Ellis replied is only an hour long
7. this is a fun trip Joey said I'm not scared at all
8. are you ready to go sailing now Joey's mother asked
9. I sure am Joey replied enthusiastically when can we go
10. he will make a fine sailor said Mr. Ellis

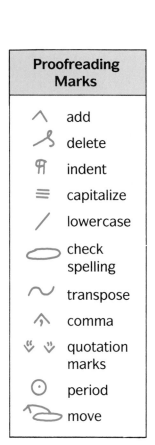

Proofreading Marks	
∧	add
⅄	delete
¶	indent
≡	capitalize
/	lowercase
⬭	check spelling
∼	transpose
∧	comma
⌄ ⌄	quotation marks
⊙	period
↝	move

Proofreading Checklist

✔ Does every sentence have the correct capitalization and end punctuation mark? (p. 36)

✔ Have commas and semicolons been used correctly? (pp. 74, 210)

✔ Are titles capitalized and punctuated correctly? (p. 120)

✔ Are apostrophes and hyphens used correctly? (p. 308)

✔ Is conversation punctuated and capitalized correctly?

✔ Have adverbs been used correctly?

APPLY STEP BY STEP

Proofread Your Draft

Check your work to be sure you have used correct capitalization, punctuation, and grammar. Use the Proofreading Checklist as a guide. You may find that adding conversation will make your story more realistic and interesting. Be sure you punctuate and capitalize the conversation correctly. Save your work.

Checking Spelling/Writing a Final Copy ◆

Spelling Strategy

Try to avoid a common mistake when you spell words that begin with a prefix. When the prefix ends with the same letter that the word begins with, do not leave out a letter; for example, immortal, innumerable, misstep, unnatural.

Here is the final part of the revised and proofread story.

Tae walked onto the stage and began to play. The soft notes and gentle harmonies *carried* ~~carryed~~ her along. Her bow danced across the violin strings. *after* She finished. She walked off the stage quietly and waited for the judges' decision. The decision came quickly.

Tae Lee had won second place. *As* She stepped forward to accept the prize. She was smiling just as she had imagined she would. *When* Papa later asked her if she minded not winning first prize. Tae smiled again. She planned to practice harder. ¶ "Next year," she said, "I will win first prize!" ¶ "I know you will," said Papa.

Check Your Spelling

Use the proofreading marks to correct errors in your spelling. Apply the Spelling Strategy. Add any misspelled words to your spelling log.

Write a Final Copy

Write a neat, final copy of your story. Remember to proofread your work. Keep your final copy.

Sharing Your Story

Speaking/Listening Strategy

Before you read aloud to your classmates, read the work aloud to yourself several times. This practice will help you decide which parts you want to read with emphasis. When you listen to a classmate read aloud, listen for the emphasized parts.

Choosing a Way to Share

The best part of writing a story is sharing it with your friends. Here are several ways to share your story.

Reading Aloud Have a Storyteller's Day in your classroom. You and your classmates will read your stories aloud. After each story is read, discuss the story with your classmates.

Presenting a Play Have classmates help you present and perform the play. Remember that in a play, you will have to tell most of the story in dialogue. You can use your classroom or the school auditorium. Use props and costumes to help tell the story.

Making a Book Make a class story book. Assemble all the stories in a book. Make a title page and a table of contents listing story titles and authors' names.

Share Your Story

Choose the way you prefer to share your story. Be sure you have prepared carefully so that your presentation will be fun and interesting.

Add to Your Learning Log

- What do I like best about my story?
- Which part of the story was the most fun to write?
- If I had to write another story, how would it be different from this story?

The Literature Connection: Sentences

You have learned much about the power of words. When words are combined in sentences, they can communicate to others just about any idea imaginable. Sometimes it is hard to find the right words to express a thought, but it can usually be done. Sometimes a thought may not become clear in your mind until the words you use to express it give it shape. In this way, words almost have the power to create ideas themselves.

Can you imagine one sentence that would describe everything in the entire world? It is impossible to write such a sentence! No single sentence could ever contain that much information. However, you can write sentences about any topic in the world. You can even write about things that do not exist at all.

Here is a verse about a character who wants to discuss everything. Notice how real and imaginary things are mixed in the poem.

from The Walrus and the Carpenter
by
Lewis Carroll

"The time has come," the Walrus said,
"To talk of many things:
Of shoes—and ships—and sealing-wax—
Of cabbages—and kings—
And why the sea is boiling hot—
And whether pigs have wings."

Discussion

1. Which things in the poem are purely imaginary?
2. Which things in the poem seem like serious subjects to you? Which seem humorous?
3. Imagine that you are having a conversation with the Walrus. What imaginary topic would you like to discuss?

The Writing Connection: Sentences

In your own writing, you can try to write about as many ideas as the poet did in "The Walrus and the Carpenter." When you write about your ideas, you can be realistic or fanciful. Whichever style you choose, your sentences will express the idea for you. Here is how one student expressed an idea about a science class.

> In science class, I like to study dolphins.

Here is another idea that the student expressed.

> In science class, I developed a wish that I could become a dolphin and live underwater.

Notice how the sentences express real and fanciful ideas about the same topic—science class.

Activity

Everyone has a secret wish. Some of us wish for something that is possible, whereas others develop fantastic wishes. Complete each sentence below. In the first sentence, write something that could happen. In the second, write a fanciful wish.

> In history class, I would like to _____.
> In history class, I developed a wish that I could _____.
> In math class, I would like to _____.
> In math class, I developed a wish that I could _____.
> In art class, I would like to _____.
> In art class, I developed a wish that I could _____.

Prepositional Phrases

A **preposition** is a word that shows a relationship between a noun or a pronoun and other words in a sentence. A **prepositional phrase** is a group of words that begins with a preposition and ends with the object of the preposition.

A. Prepositions can show location or direction.

He tucked the violin under his chin.

Here is a list of common prepositions.

about	along	below	down	inside	off	through	up
above	around	beneath	during	into	on	to	upon
across	at	between	for	like	outside	toward	with
after	before	beyond	from	near	over	under	within
against	behind	by	in	of	past	until	without

B. A preposition is usually followed by a noun or a pronoun called the **object of the preposition.** The preposition and its object together form a prepositional phrase.

preposition   object of the preposition

He played a violin concerto on it.

prepositional phrase

A prepositional phrase may also contain words that describe the object of the preposition.

He walked into the enormous auditorium.

Strategy

Try to remember the prepositions shown in the list above. Also remember that prepositions show relationships such as direction, location, and ownership.

Check Your Understanding

A. Write the letter of the preposition.
   1. Itzhak Perlman was born in Israel.
      a. was   **b.** born   **c.** in   **d.** Israel
   2. He heard a violin on the radio.
      a. He   **b.** a   **c.** on   **d.** the

B. The preposition in each sentence is underlined. Write the letter of its object.

    3. Itzhak wanted a violin from that moment.

        a. a   **b.** violin   **c.** that   **d.** moment

    4. He got his first violin after his third birthday.

        a. He   **b.** his   **c.** third   **d.** birthday

Practice

A. Write each sentence. Underline the preposition.

    5. Itzhak became ill with polio.

    6. The disease affected the muscles in his legs.

    7. He could no longer run around the house.

    8. He could walk only with crutches.

B. Write each sentence. The preposition is shown in heavy type. Underline the prepositional phrase. Put two lines under the object of the preposition.

    9. He poured his energy **into** his precious violin.

    10. The 13-year-old played **like** a true professional.

    11. A television producer was traveling **around** the world.

    12. Ed Sullivan was seeking performers **for** his show.

C. Mixed Practice Write each sentence. Underline the prepositional phrase. Write the preposition. Put another line under the object of the preposition.

    13. Young Itzhak played for Sullivan.

    14. Sullivan invited the boy to this country.

    15. Itzhak Perlman now gives concerts around the world.

    16. He has played with every great orchestra.

    17. Critics praise him for his enormous skill.

    18. He teaches violin students between his many concerts.

    19. He has worked for disabled people during his career.

    20. He moves through his busy schedule with energy and humor.

Apply: Exploring Language

Choose several paragraphs from one of your reading selections. Identify all the prepositional phrases in your selection, and make a list of all the prepositions. What relationships do the prepositional phrases show in the reading selection?

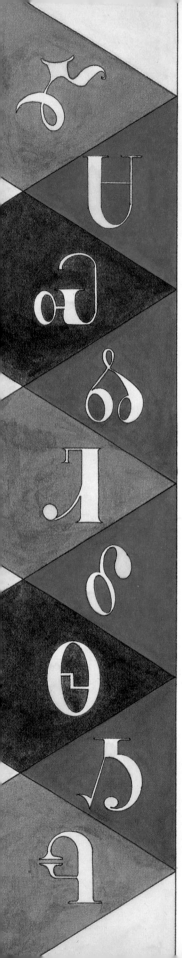

Conjunctions and Interjections

A **conjunction** is a word that joins other words or groups of words in a sentence. The most common conjunctions are *and*, *but*, and *or*. An **interjection** is a word or expression that is used to convey feeling. It has no close connection with the rest of the sentence.

A. Conjunctions can join similar words; for example, two nouns, two verbs, or two adjectives.

> Father and daughter worked together.
> Would they succeed or fail?

Conjunctions can also join similar groups of words.

> She heard the sentences and wrote them down.

B. An interjection is used to convey feeling.

> Aha! That will show them.

Here are some common interjections.

ah	aha	alas	goodness	hey	hurray	my
oh	oh no	oops	ouch	well	wow	yippee

An interjection that expresses a strong feeling is followed by an exclamation mark and stands alone. An interjection can also express mild feeling. When it does, it is followed by a comma and is part of a sentence.

> Wow! It really works!
> Well, he achieved his goal.

Strategy

Be careful not to overuse interjections when you write. If you do, they will lose their effect and make your writing dull.

Check Your Understanding

A. Write the letter of the conjunction in each sentence.
  1. No one read or wrote in the Cherokee language.
      a. No one   **b.** or   **c.** in   **d.** the
  2. Sequoyah and his daughter created the written form of Cherokee.
      a. and   **b.** his   **c.** made   **d.** it

B. Write the letter of the interjection in each sentence.

    3. My, that was a difficult task.

        a. My   **b.** that   **c.** was   **d.** a

    4. Hurray! It's finally done.

        a. Hurray   **b.** It's   **c.** finally   **d.** done

Practice

A. Write each sentence. Underline each conjunction.

    5. Sequoyah had an English father and a Cherokee mother.

    6. He was born and lived in Tennessee in the 1700's.

    7. English books were rare but precious in Tennessee.

    8. Sequoyah could not read or write English.

B. Write each numbered item. Underline each interjection. Write whether it expresses strong or mild feeling.

    9. Alas, the Cherokees had no written language.

  10. Well, Sequoyah would create one.

  11. Goodness! What an enormous job!

  12. Wow! The job took 12 years.

C. Mixed Practice Write each sentence. Underline each conjunction once and each interjection twice. Write whether the interjections express strong or mild feeling.

  13. Most people misunderstood or doubted Sequoyah.

  14. They considered his work foolish but harmless.

  15. Only Sequoyah and his daughter, Akoya, had faith in it.

  16. Aha! They demonstrated their alphabet.

  17. Sequoyah and Akoya stayed at opposite ends of town.

  18. Runners carried messages to one or the other.

  19. Bravo! Akoya could read and understand Sequoyah's words.

  20. Oh, what a wonderful and historic demonstration that was!

Apply: Journal

Write several sentences in your journal about a time when you or someone you know kept trying to do something until a goal was reached. Use interjections to show your feelings about it. Underline any conjunction you use.

Compound Subjects

The complete subject of a sentence may contain more than one simple subject. A **compound subject** is made up of two or more simple subjects that share the same predicate.

A. When two simple subjects form a compound subject, they are joined by the word *and*.

Orville and Wilbur Wright were inventors.

Wilbur and he enjoyed mechanical work.

When three or more simple subjects form a compound subject, they are separated from one another by commas. The word *and* must appear before the last simple subject.

Bicycles, gliders, and airplanes interested them.

B. Sometimes the complete subject contains words besides *and* and the simple subjects.

Orville and his older brother designed an airplane.

Strategy

When you use a compound subject, be sure to use a verb that agrees with a plural subject. To make sure that you do, substitute the word *they* for the complete subject. If *they* fits, use a verb that agrees with a plural subject.

Orville and Wilbur (was, were) mechanics.
They were mechanics. Orville and Wilbur were mechanics.

I can say *they* instead of *Orville and Wilbur*.

Check Your Understanding

A. Write the letter of the words that form the compound subject.
1. Orville and Wilbur Wright were brothers.
   a. Orville and Wilbur Wright **b.** Wilbur Wright
   c. brothers
2. Bicycles, machines, and gliders fascinated them.
   a. bicycles, machines, and gliders **b.** fascinated them
   c. gliders

B. Write the letter of the simple subjects in each sentence.

    3. The capable mechanic and his brother never finished school.
        a. capable, mechanic   **b.** mechanic, brother
        c. his, brother

    4. Careful work and mechanical genius brought success.
        a. Careful, work   **b.** mechanical, genius
        c. work, genius

Practice

A. Write each sentence. The complete subject is underlined. Underline each simple subject in the compound subject.

    5. Wilbur and Orville Wright built the first airplane.
    6. Bicycles, gliders, and kites came first.
    7. Orville and Wilbur practiced with gliders.
    8. Wilbur and he tossed a coin for the first flight.

B. Write each sentence. Underline each simple subject in the compound subject.

    9. Their close friends, family, and others had laughed.
    10. A small newspaper and a store were early businesses.
    11. Wilbur and his younger brother researched planes.
    12. Their hard work and careful research were worthwhile.

C. Mixed Practice Write each sentence. Underline each simple subject in the compound subject.

    13. Kites and gliders had helped the brothers understand flight.
    14. Bad storms, mechanical defects, and several other problems delayed the first flight.
    15. Wilbur, his friends, and several helpers watched Orville's flight.
    16. The first flight and the second took place the same day.
    17. Magazines and newspapers mentioned the event.
    18. Wilbur and his brother tested their planes many times.
    19. England, France, Germany, Italy, and other countries wanted airplanes from the Wrights.
    20. The first airplane and other airships and spacecraft are now in the National Air and Space Museum.

Apply: Learning Log

Write an entry in your learning log that will help you to find the simple subjects in compound subjects.

Compound Predicates

The complete predicate of a sentence may have more than one simple predicate. A **compound predicate** is made up of two or more verbs that share the same subject.

A. A compound predicate may contain two verbs, joined by the word *and*.

> Margaret listened and understood.

A compound predicate may have three or more verbs. Commas separate the verbs from one another. The word *and* must appear before the last verb in the compound predicate.

> The photographer stood, waited, and watched.

B. A complete predicate may include words besides *and* and the simple predicates.

> Margaret cleaned the camera and repaired it.
>
> She examined, judged, and criticized her own work.
>
> The flash popped and sizzled noisily.
>
> She checked the lens, attached it, and took the photo.

Strategy

Don't confuse a compound predicate with a simple predicate that includes several helping verbs.

> Compound Predicate: Photographs surprise and delight us.
> Simple Predicate: She had been viewing the slides.

Check Your Understanding

A. Write the letter of the simple predicates in each sentence.
  1. Margaret Bourke-White waited and observed.
  a. waited, and   **b.** and, observed   **c.** waited, observed
  2. The bright sun darkened and set.
  a. bright, sun   **b.** darkened, and   **c.** darkened, set

B. Write the letter of the simple predicates in each sentence.

    3. She lifted her camera and pressed the shutter.

        a. lifted, camera   **b.** lifted, pressed   **c.** and, pressed

    4. She captured and preserved the scene on film.

        a. captured, preserved   **b.** preserved, scene

        c. scene, film

Practice

A. Write each sentence. Underline each simple predicate in the compound predicate.

    5. Margaret aimed, focused, and shot.

    6. The camera clicked and whirred.

    7. She practiced and experimented.

    8. Margaret studied, learned, and improved.

B. Follow the directions for Practice A.

    9. Margaret chose industrial scenes and made them her specialty.

    10. She visited factories and photographed steel mills.

    11. She developed, enlarged, and printed her own work.

    12. Magazines hired her or bought her pictures.

C. Mixed Practice Write each sentence. Underline each simple predicate in the compound predicate.

    13. She traveled to London and photographed wartime scenes.

    14. In Syria, she took pictures and rode a camel.

    15. She traveled to Egypt, saw the pyramids, and made portraits of leaders.

    16. At home, she worked, wrote, and gave lectures.

    17. Her photography inspired, pleased, and instructed.

    18. She lugged cameras all over, and took beautiful pictures.

    19. During World War II, she was often working as the first woman war correspondent and was traveling overseas.

    20. Did people around the world buy and appreciate her photographs?

Apply: Test a Partner

Write five sentences with compound predicates about a career you might like. Then exchange papers with a partner. Underline the simple predicates in your partner's sentences. Check your papers. Did each of you find all the simple predicates?

Compound Sentences

◆

A **compound sentence** is a sentence that contains two simple sentences joined by one of the conjunctions *and, but,* or *or*.

A. A simple sentence has a subject and a predicate and expresses one idea. Two simple sentences that express related ideas can be joined to form a compound sentence by adding a comma and one of the conjunctions *and, but,* or *or*.

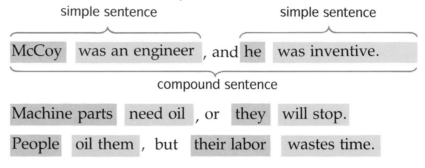

simple sentence   simple sentence

McCoy | was an engineer , and he | was inventive.

compound sentence

Machine parts | need oil , or | they | will stop.

People | oil them , but | their labor | wastes time.

B. Remember that a simple sentence may have a compound subject or a compound predicate. A compound sentence always contains two complete simple sentences.

Machines and engines | need lubrication.

(simple sentence with compound subject)

McCoy | designed and improved lubrication systems.

(simple sentence with compound predicate)

McCoy's system | worked , and | mechanics | used it.

(compound sentence)

Strategy

If you are not sure whether a sentence is a compound sentence, break it in two. Remove the *and, but,* or *or*. If each part is a complete sentence, the whole is a compound sentence.

Check Your Understanding

A. Write the letter that identifies each sentence.
　1. McCoy invented a lubrication cup for machines.
　　a. simple sentence　**b.** compound sentence
　2. It oils machines, and they run properly.
　　a. simple sentence　**b.** compound sentence

370

B. Write the letter that identifies each sentence.

    3. Elijah's mother and father escaped from slavery.

        a. simple sentence   **b.** compound sentence

    4. The invention worked, and Elijah was joyful.

        a. simple sentence   **b.** compound sentence

Practice

A. Write each sentence. Write *simple* or *compound* to identify it.

    5. Elijah McCoy was born in Ontario, Canada.

    6. His parents had been slaves, but Elijah was free.

    7. He wanted a career as an engineer, and they helped him.

    8. Few colleges of that time accepted black students.

B. Follow the instructions for Practice A.

    9. Elijah studied in Scotland and returned home.

   10. Jobs for black engineers were rare, but McCoy found work.

   11. He worked on the railroad and soon noticed something.

   12. Machinery needed oil, or it would overheat.

C. Mixed Practice Write each sentence. Write *simple* or *compound* to identify it.

   13. Mechanics oiled the machines, but this took too much time.

   14. McCoy designed a simple mechanical device.

   15. It oiled machines and kept them from wear.

   16. The device worked, and McCoy set up a business.

   17. Mechanics bought his devices, or they bought nothing.

   18. They asked for "the real McCoy," and they got it.

   19. Elijah McCoy and his device improved machinery and gave us a familiar expression.

   20. People get "the real McCoy" and are happy, or they get an inferior imitation and regret it.

Apply: Work with a Group

With a group, write 12 sentences about how something works. Take turns supplying simple sentences to explain the process. After you write your sentences, see how many you can combine into compound sentences. Share your sentences with other groups.

Avoiding Run-on Sentences

A **run-on sentence** is two or more sentences that are not separated by correct punctuation or conjunctions.

A. A run-on sentence occurs when one thought "runs on" into another without being separated by punctuation.

> The telescope brought the stars close Maria loved it.

This is a run-on sentence because it expresses two thoughts without separating them. To correct it, form two separate sentences or a compound sentence with a comma and a conjunction.

> The telescope magnified the stars. Maria loved it.
> The telescope magnified the stars, and Maria loved it.

B. A run-on sentence also occurs when two thoughts in a sentence are separated incorrectly.

> She was an amateur astronomer, she found a comet.

A comma is not enough to separate these two ideas. To write them correctly, make two sentences or add a conjunction.

> She was an amateur astronomer. She found a comet.
> She was an amateur astronomer, but she found a comet.

Strategy

When you divide a run-on sentence, be sure to split it where one thought ends and the next thought begins.

Check Your Understanding

A. Write the letter that identifies each sentence.
  1. Maria went to Europe and met many scientists.
    a. simple   **b.** compound   **c.** run-on
  2. They encouraged her she worked even harder.
    a. simple   **b.** compound   **c.** run-on

B. Write the letter that identifies each sentence.
  3. Maria Mitchell was a great teacher, but she was unusual.
    a. simple   **b.** compound   **c.** run-on
  4. She did not grade papers, she rewarded curiosity.
    a. simple   **b.** compound   **c.** run-on

372

Practice

A. Read each sentence. If it is a run-on sentence, correct it by writing two sentences or by adding a comma and a conjunction. If it is correct, write correct.

5. Maria didn't attend school her father taught her.
6. Maria lived in Nantucket she loved the nighttime sky.
7. Her father had a telescope, and he let her use it.
8. Maria enjoyed astronomy she studied the sky.

B. Follow the directions for Practice A.

9. She worked in a library, but astronomy was her love.
10. She sighted a comet astronomers named it after her.
11. For her discovery, the king of Denmark gave her a medal.
12. Maria studied solar flares they are spots on the sun.

C. Mixed Practice Correct each run-on sentence by writing simple sentences or by writing a compound sentence.

13. Mitchell became famous for her studies of sunspots she was most famous for her discovery of a comet.
14. She was a pioneer in science she was a pioneer for women.
15. Matthew Vassar founded a college he needed an astronomer.
16. Mitchell had many tasks as a professor she continued her research.
17. She was the first woman member of the American Academy of Arts and Sciences she later became a society fellow.
18. She entered the Academy's Hall of Fame in 1905 that was a great honor.
19. Mitchell was a great scientist she was also a great teacher her students loved her.
20. Mitchell had never gone to school she learned a lot she still has a place in the history of astronomy.

Apply: Learning Log

Write an entry in your learning log that will help you to remember what a run-on sentence is and how to fix it.

Denotation and Connotation

Denotation is the dictionary definition of a word. **Connotation** is the shade of meaning a word suggests in addition to its dictionary meaning, or denotation.

A. A dictionary definition expresses the exact, specific meaning of a word without additional associations.

> Mr. Chan bought an <u>old</u> bookcase.

The denotation of *old* in this sentence is "in existence for a long time." The denotation of this word does not create either a favorable or an unfavorable impression of the bookcase.

B. In addition to its denotation, a word may have one or more connotations. Connotations are meanings or associations that have arisen from usage or experience.

> Mr. Chan bought an <u>antique</u> bookcase.

> Mr. Chan bought a <u>worn-out</u> bookcase.

In these sentences, *antique* and *worn-out* both denote "old," but *antique* has a positive connotation, whereas *worn-out* has a negative connotation. Words such as these carry strong connotations, but some words—such as *old* in the sentence above—generally have only denotations.

Strategy

Pay close attention to the connotations of words by studying their contexts and using a dictionary. Knowing word connotations will enable you to use words precisely and to understand the impressions that a writer conveys.

Check Your Understanding

A. Write the letter of the denotation of each underlined word.
1. Most young people want a successful <u>career</u>.
   a. house   **b.** life work   **c.** car
2. A career in music requires great <u>discipline</u>.
   a. controlled training   **b.** strength   **c.** luck

B. Write the letter that describes the connotation of each underlined word.

   3. Some rock bands make a noisy racket.
   a. positive   **b.** negative
   4. Some band members are excellent musicians.
   a. positive   **b.** negative

Practice

A. Write the denotation of the underlined word in each sentence. Use a dictionary if necessary.

   5. Langston Hughes wrote many popular poems.
   6. The writer tells people to cling to their hopes.
   7. The poet encourages people's aspirations.
   8. People have interpreted the poem in different ways.

B. Write the sentences. Write whether the connotation of each underlined word is positive or negative.

   9. Some people have noble goals for living their lives.
   10. Irresponsible behavior might ruin a fine career.
   11. What you might think weird I might think intriguing.
   12. Some people are firm, yet others call them stubborn.

C. Mixed Practice   Write whether each underlined word has primarily only a *denotation* or whether it has a strong *connotation*. Write whether each connotation is *positive* or *negative*.

   13. The desire for fame may be a childish dream.
   14. Gifted performers often have confidence in their talents.
   15. Critics may rave about a performer's skills.
   16. A knowledgeable fan enjoys a good performance.
   17. Fame sometimes brings dubious rewards.
   18. Rash actions can damage a promising career.
   19. Some performers are known for their generosity.
   20. A renowned star can give a shallow performance.

Apply: Exploring Language

Write five sentences about a well-known performer or hero. Use words with both positive and negative connotations in your sentences. Label the connotations either positive or negative, and share your sentences with the class. Find out if your classmates agree with your labels.

Language in Action

Giving a Speech

Imagine that you are the vice president of a book club. Next week is the end-of-year banquet, and you are supposed to give a speech. What do you do?

Most people do not make speeches very often. Nonetheless, it is useful to know how to do so. The skills used in speaking to a group can be put to many other uses. Here are some tips on giving a speech.

* Remember who your audience is. If you were speaking at the book-club banquet, you might talk about the club's sales record during the previous year. The audience would probably include the members and employees of the club. You could talk about some of the reasons the club selected certain books.

* Write your speech. Write every word so that you can make sure that all the parts flow together. Be sure to include an *introduction*. Don't jump right into your topic. Also, include a closing.

* Good speakers usually begin with an **audience grabber,** a funny story or a question. The purpose of an audience grabber is to capture your audience's attention.

* Make notes. Don't read your speech word for word. That often sounds dull. Your notes should include key words and phrases that will remind you of what you want to say. You might also include notes to yourself. If, for example, a pause would add to the humor of a joke, write *(pause here)*. (Just be sure that you actually pause instead of saying "pause here.") Write your notes on a sheet of paper or on index cards. If you use index cards, be sure to number them in case you get them out of order.

* Practice your speech. Present it to your family. Practicing in front of a mirror can be helpful. Be sure to practice using your notes. Keep practicing your speech until you are comfortable saying it.

* Speak loudly, clearly, and distinctly. You are speaking to a group of people. You want them to hear and understand every word you say. Look directly at your audience.

Practice

On a separate sheet of paper, answer the following questions.

1. What is the first thing you should keep in mind when planning a speech?
2. What should you do to make sure that all the parts of your speech flow together?
3. What is an *audience grabber?*
4. What should your speech include?
5. When you give your speech, why should you not read from the written version?
6. If you write notes on index cards, how can you make sure that they can be put in the right order?
7. What two things should your notes include?
8. How should you speak when you give your speech?
9. What is the purpose in speaking that way?
10. Why do you think that you should look directly at your audience?
11. Why is it important to consider who your listeners are when you give a speech?
12. Why would it be a poor idea to give a speech without preparing your information beforehand?
13. Why is it important to begin your speech with an interesting story or a joke?
14. Why do you think it is helpful to practice a speech in front of other people?
15. Why is it important for the audience to hear everything you say?

Apply

Imagine that it is the last day of school. Your class is having a party. You have been asked to make a speech. In the speech, you will talk about what happened in the class during the school year. You may wish to make a humorous speech or a serious speech. Your topic should be interesting to your teacher and classmates. Plan your speech so that it will be three or four minutes long. Remember that writing a speech is like writing a composition. You may have to edit or revise the speech after you write it. Plan, practice, and present your speech.

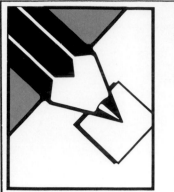

Answering Essay Questions

In some tests, you will be asked to answer the questions by writing a few sentences or a paragraph. Such questions are called essay questions. Here are the steps to follow to help answer essay questions.

◆ **Write a Topic Sentence:** You should begin your answer with a topic sentence. One way to write a topic sentence is to rewrite the question as a statement. For example: *Question:* In what ways is oxygen important for life? *Topic Sentence:* Oxygen is very important for life on this planet.

◆ **Plan Your Answer:** Using your topic sentence as a guide, make notes about the main ideas and details that you want to include in your answer.

◆ **Keep to the Subject:** Think about the question as you write your essay. Use sentences. Don't include any information that is not needed for your answer.

Practice

Write sentences that tell how each student could have improved the way he or she answered the essay question.

1. Karen is thinking about an answer to a question, but she doesn't know how to begin.
2. After reading the question, Sammy wrote the first thing that came into his head.
3. Patty wrote a series of phrases that outlined her answer and handed in her test.

Apply: Learning Log

Decide which information from the lesson was most helpful to you. Write the information in your learning log.

UNIT REVIEW

Short Story (page 333)

1. List four of the characteristics of a short story.

Parts of a Story (pages 350–351)

Write the part of the plot—*introduction, problem, solution attempts,* or *outcome*—that is described by each of the following items.

2. Max Goldman lives with his uncle Joseph and their dog Sasha in a cramped but orderly apartment.

3. Joseph is moved by a story Max has written about their life together, and at last, Joseph begins to encourage Max in his ambition.

4. Max dreams of becoming a writer, but his uncle disapproves and wants him to pursue another career.

5. Max secretly sends his stories to magazines. He hopes that one will be published and that his uncle will change his mind.

Combining Sentences (pages 354–355)

Combine each sentence pair by using the word shown in parentheses.

6. Charles Dickens was a great English novelist. He lived in the nineteenth century. (who)

7. Dickens worked in a factory at the age of 12. He pasted labels on bottles of shoe polish. (when)

8. Dickens wrote *The Pickwick Papers*. He became famous at the age of 24. (after)

9. Dickens's childhood was spent in poverty. Many of his books are about the lives of the poor. (because)

Punctuating Conversation (pages 356–357)

Write each sentence. Add the correct capitalization and punctuation.

10. uncle Joseph exclaimed Max I didn't know you were in here

11. I've been reading this story Max said Joseph

12. are you angry with me asked Max

13. how could I be angry with such a talented writer asked Joseph

14. I am aware Max said that you did not want me to become a writer

15. Joseph answered That was long ago, Max. Now I see you have a real talent with the pen

16. Don't forget my imagination, too! Max added.

Prepositional Phrases (pages 362–363)

Write each sentence. Underline the prepositional phrase. Write the preposition. Put a second line under the object of the preposition.

17. Ants have fascinated people through the ages.

18. They have developed successful methods for survival.

19. An ant colony works together like a large factory.

20. Each ant within the colony performs a specific function.

21. The efficiency of the operation is incredible.

Conjunctions and Interjections (pages 364–365)

Write each sentence. Underline each conjunction once and each interjection twice. Write whether the interjections express strong or mild feeling.

22. Wow! What a wonderful play!

23. The playwright and the director work well together.

24. The piece never dragged or bogged down.

25. The last scene was very moving but not too sentimental.

26. Alas, most theater is not as enjoyable.

Compound Subjects (pages 366–367)

Write each sentence. Underline each simple subject in the compound subject.

27. Satellites, radar, and computers aid today's meteorologists in the prediction of storms.

28. Airports and cities often have their own weather stations.

29. Storms and hurricanes appear in satellite photos.

30. Thunderstorms, hail, and tornadoes can wreak havoc on people's homes and property.

31. Meteorologists and researchers can now predict these storms earlier than in the past.

Compound Predicates (pages 368–369)

Write each sentence. Underline each simple predicate in the compound predicate.

32. Writers must discipline themselves and work every day toward their goals.

33. Editors read, criticize, and correct a writer's work.

34. Publishers print the books and promote them.

35. A writer must secure an agent and find a publisher.

36. A writer then waits, wonders, and hopes for acceptance of a book by the general public.

Compound Sentences (pages 370–371)

Write each sentence. Write *simple* or *compound* to identify it.

37. Mohandas Gandhi treasured freedom greatly, but he hated violence at the same time.

38. Britain controlled India and would not give Indians a voice in government.

39. Most Indians opposed British rule, and many of them protested against it.

40. Gandhi also opposed the British, but he pleaded for nonviolent revolution.

41. His nonviolent protest brought an end to British domination and made India an independent nation once again.

42. Many people had doubted the practicality of Gandhi's ideas, but his methods were ultimately successful.

43. Have you ever read any biographies of Gandhi or seen the film about his life?

Avoiding Run-on Sentences (pages 372–373)

Correct each run-on sentence by writing simple sentences or by writing a compound sentence.

44. Cities isolate us from nature, a city's environment is often unhealthy as well.

45. Modern conveniences are wonderful they are not absolutely essential.

46. Our ancestors lived without electricity and telephones, they flourished nonetheless.

47. Backwoods camping brings people closer to the earth, it gives them a better appreciation of the intricate workings of nature.

48. We are all a small part of a vast environment we should plan our actions with this in mind.

49. Our natural resources are important, we must protect them against pollution.

Denotation and Connotation (pages 374–375)

Write the underlined word in each sentence that has a strong connotation. Tell whether it is a positive or negative connotation.

50. The large paintings looked good in the monstrous room.

51. Each piece of work was a masterpiece.

52. The museum staff cherished the works the museum owned.

53. The guards watched as visitors gawked at the art.

MAKING ALL THE
CONNECTIONS

You and several classmates will now write an advertisement together as a group. What you have learned about persuasive writing will help you.

You will do the following in your advertisement:

- Aim to persuade your readers to buy something.
- Begin in a way that immediately attracts the readers' attention.
- Use vivid language to describe the item or product being sold.
- Describe vividly how readers will benefit by buying the item or product.
- Be brief and to the point.

Reading an Advertisement

Read the advertisement below. Notice that the sidenotes point out the characteristics of an advertisement. After discussing this advertisement, you and your classmates will work in small groups to write an advertisement of your own for a product that someone might aspire to sell.

OWN A HANDY, HAPPY HOUSEHOLD HELPER!

The beginning attracts the reader's attention.

The product and the benefits are described with vivid language.

The advertisement is brief and to the point.

Never again will you wash dishes or iron! If you're tired of dusting, vacuuming, cleaning, and other household chores, your troubles are at an end. The Handy, Happy Household Helper cleans, polishes, tidies, buffs, bustles, hustles, and even makes the bed! It costs just pennies a day to run this handy household robot. And, once it's programmed, you'll never need to touch it again. The remote control knobs help you guide it through its household chores. Take it home on approval and try it for just one week. If you like it, keep it and pay just $999.95, or pay four easy installments of $259.99. You'll never open the cleaning-closet door again. Grab this deal of a lifetime!

The ending emphasizes the benefits.

Speaking and Listening

Your teacher will assign you to a small group. Choose a discussion leader for your group. Then talk about these questions:

1. What is the purpose of this advertisement?
2. What examples of vivid language does the advertisement contain?
3. What does a Household Helper look like?
4. Why would people want to buy a Handy Household Helper?
5. How did the advertisement make you feel about buying a Household Helper for your home?
6. Which method of buying the Helper is cheaper; making one payment in full or paying four installments?

Thinking

Brainstorming

Choose one person from your group to take notes as you discuss the questions below. Save the notes. You will need them later.

1. What invention might be useful to people your own age?
2. What are some ways the invention would benefit those who used it?
3. What vivid words should be included to increase a buyer's interest in your invention?
4. What attention-grabbing appeals can you make?

Organizing

When you are gathering ideas for an effective advertisement, it helps to list your ideas in a chart. This helps you organize your thinking and also makes it easier to include all your ideas. Look at the chart below. It was used to create the advertisement for the Household Helper.

With your group, look back at your brainstorming notes. Make a chart like the one below. Have one group member fill in the chart with details from the notes.

Product	Benefits	Vivid Words	Attention-Grabbers
Household Helper	does all the cleaning is easy to use valuable product bargain price	hustles bustles deal of a lifetime costs pennies a day	tired of chores troubles at an end take home on approval never wash dishes or iron again

Writing an Advertisement ◆

Imagine that you work in an advertising agency. You and other members of your group have been asked to write an advertisement for the invention from your brainstorming session. Use the chart you made to organize your ideas.

Planning

◆ Review your chart. Add any new ideas or vivid words that occur to you.
◆ Decide what the main benefit of your invention is.
◆ Think of ways to persuade your readers that they will benefit by buying your invention. Choose attention-grabbers that appeal to the reader's needs.
◆ Think of a price for your product. Remember it should be a realistic price, or no one will be interested in buying the item.
◆ Organize your ideas in a brief outline. First list the attention-getting appeals you will make at the beginning of the advertisement. Then list the main features of the product and how they will benefit the buyer. Tell people how they can buy the item and tell its price. End with an additional appeal that emphasizes the benefits to the buyer.

Composing

- Work with your group to write your advertisement. Choose one person to write down the first draft as all of the group's members suggest ideas. Tell the writer to skip lines in the first draft so that the group can make corrections later.
- Decide on the exact wording of your opening sentence. Think of wording that will immediately capture a reader's interest and persuade the person to buy your product. Then think of the wording for each additional sentence.

Revising

- As a group, reread the first draft of the advertisement. Think of ways to improve the content.
- Try to replace general words with more vivid ones.
- Reword sentences to make sure that readers will want to buy your product.
- Be sure that your advertisement is short and clearly written.

Proofreading

Now your group is ready to proofread the advertisement. Choose one group member to mark the proofreading changes on the first draft. Answer these questions.

- Are all sentences complete?
- Are all sentences punctuated correctly?
- Are there any double negatives?
- Are sentences with interjections or conjunctions punctuated correctly?
- Are all words spelled correctly?

Presenting

- Have one member of your group use the revising and proofreading corrections to write a clean, final copy of the advertisement. Be sure it is correct.
- Pretend you are making a commercial for television. Have one member of the group read the advertisement aloud with emphasis and expression while the other group members demonstrate the benefits of the product.

385

CUMULATIVE REVIEW

◆━━━━━━━━━━◆━━━━━━━━━━◆

A. Write the letter of the term that identifies each sentence. *(pages 42–43)*

    1. What a storm that was!

        a. declarative   **b.** interrogative   **c.** imperative   **d.** exclamatory

    2. Check the backyard.

        a. declarative   **b.** interrogative   **c.** imperative   **d.** exclamatory

B. Write the letter of the term that identifies each underlined word or group of words. *(pages 44–47)*

    3. The breadbasket of America is the Midwest.

        a. complete subject   **c.** complete predicate

        b. simple subject   **d.** simple predicate

    4. Most of America's farms operate there.

        a. complete subject   **c.** complete predicate

        b. simple subject   **d.** simple predicate

    5. Many different crops grow in abundance.

        a. complete subject   **c.** complete predicate

        b. simple subject   **d.** simple predicate

    6. This fertile region grows more food than any other area on Earth.

        a. complete subject   **c.** complete predicate

        b. simple subject   **d.** simple predicate

    7. Midwestern farmers raise wheat, corn, and alfalfa.

        a. complete subject   **c.** complete predicate

        b. simple subject   **d.** simple predicate

    8. In the spring, Midwestern farmers plow the rich earth.

        a. complete subject   **c.** complete predicate

        b. simple subject   **d.** simple predicate

C. Write the letter of the correct plural form of each singular noun. *(pages 82–83)*

    9. leaf   **a.** leafs   **b.** leaves   **c.** leavs

    10. patio   **a.** patioes   **b.** patio   **c.** patios

    11. soprano   **a.** sopranoes   **b.** sopranos   **c.** soprani

    12. offspring   **a.** offspring   **b.** offsprings   **c.** offspringes

D. Write the letter of the correct possessive form of each noun. *(pages 84–87)*

    13. president   **a.** president's   **b.** president'   **c.** presidents'

    14. oxen   **a.** oxen'   **b.** oxen's   **c.** oxens'

15. youths   **a.** youths'   **b.** youths's   **c.** youth's

16. James   **a.** James'   **b.** James's   **c.** Jame's

E. Write the letter of the term that identifies each underlined verb. *(pages 126–129)*

  17. Vincent van Gogh <u>was</u> one of Europe's greatest painters.

     a. action verb   **b.** linking verb

  18. His paintings <u>dance</u> with color and life.

     a. action verb   **b.** linking verb

F. Write the letter of the term that identifies the tense of each underlined verb. *(pages 132–133)*

  19. Van Gogh <u>developed</u> into the most visionary artist of his age.

     a. past tense   **b.** present tense   **c.** future tense

  20. His life <u>matches</u> our romantic image of the artist.

     a. past tense   **b.** present tense   **c.** future tense

  21. Admirers <u>will value</u> his work long into the future.

     a. past tense   **b.** present tense   **c.** future tense

G. Write the letter of the verb tense that correctly completes each sentence. *(pages 134–139)*

  22. Van Gogh ____ other materials besides paints.

     a. had tried   **b.** had try   **c.** have tried

  23. Scholars ____ much about his life through his letters.

     a. have learn   **b.** had learn   **c.** have learned

  24. In his letters, he ____ his brother his most personal thoughts.

     a. tell   **b.** telled   **c.** told

  25. Ironically, his work ____ him little fame during his life.

     a. brought   **b.** bring   **c.** bringed

H. Write the letter of the term that identifies each underlined word or group of words. *(pages 168–175)*

  26. The word *geology* means "<u>the study of the earth.</u>"

     a. direct object   **b.** indirect object

  27. Geologists explore the <u>nature</u> of the earth itself.

     a. direct object   **b.** indirect object

  28. They give <u>people</u> information about earthquakes.

     a. direct object   **b.** indirect object

  29. They also explain our <u>world</u> to us.

     a. direct object   **b.** indirect object

  30. Geologists <u>work</u> in many different environments.

     a. transitive verb   **b.** intransitive verb

31. Many geologists <u>collect</u> minerals and crystals.
   a. transitive verb   **b.** intransitive verb
32. These beautiful crystals have become quite <u>popular</u> these days.
   a. predicate noun   **b.** predicate adjective
33. Exploration for oil is another <u>area</u> of geological interest.
   a. predicate noun   **b.** predicate adjective
34. Oil and natural gas remain important <u>resources</u>.
   a. predicate noun   **b.** predicate adjective
35. Geologists are <u>hopeful</u> about the search for new reserves.
   a. predicate noun   **b.** predicate adjective

I. Write the letter of the pronoun that completes each sentence.
   (pages 222–229)
   36. Beth and I fished on Loon Lake. ____ caught four fish.
      a. Us   **b.** Her   **c.** We
   37. The fish were small. We fried ____ for breakfast.
      a. them   **b.** they   **c.** it
   38. I sprinkled lemon juice on the fish. Beth gave ____ the pan.
      a. I   **b.** we   **c.** me
   39. Beth finished cooking the fish. ____ is the better cook.
      a. She   **b.** Us   **c.** Her

J. Write the letter of the word that correctly completes each sentence.
   (pages 230–231)
   40. ____ home is in New York City.
      a. Mine   **b.** My   **c.** Ours
   41. The apartment with the spiral staircase is ____.
      a. there's   **b.** their   **c.** theirs
   42. Is that ____ address on the envelope?
      a. yours   **b.** you're   **c.** your
   43. ____ a wonderful neighborhood!
      a. It's   **b.** It   **c.** Its

K. Write the letter of the item that lists all the adjectives in each sentence.
   (pages 264–267)
   44. The Soviet Union has the largest area of any country.
      a. largest, any   **b.** The, the, largest   **c.** The, the, largest, any
   45. The nation also encompasses fourteen smaller republics.
      a. fourteen, smaller   **b.** The, fourteen, smaller   **c.** The, fourteen
   46. The Russian language is rich and expressive.
      a. The, rich, expressive   **b.** rich, expressive
      c. The, Russian, rich, expressive

388

L. Write the letter of the adjective that best completes each sentence. *(pages 268–273)*

47. Russia is the ____ republic in the Soviet Union. (large)
   a. most large   **b.** largest   **c.** more larger

48. The Russian Republic is ____ than the other Soviet republics. (influential)
   a. more influential   **b.** influentialler   **c.** most influential

49. Other Soviet republics, such as Latvia, have ____ power than Russia. (little)
   a. littler   **b.** least   **c.** less

50. The Ukrainian Republic has the ____ farmland in the Soviet Union. (good)
   a. best   **b.** most good   **c.** goodest

M. Write the letter of the word that the prepositional phrase describes. *(pages 274–275)*

51. The people in the Uzbek Republic speak a Turkish language.
   a. people   **b.** republic   **c.** Turkish   **d.** language

52. The citizens of Estonia also speak their own language.
   a. citizens   **b.** Estonia   **c.** speak   **d.** their

53. The Soviet Union is a country with a diverse population.
   a. Soviet Union   **b.** country   **c.** with   **d.** population

N. Write the letter of the possessive or compound noun that is written incorrectly. *(pages 308–309)*

54. a. oxen's   **b.** exsinger   **c.** editor in chief   **d.** limousine's

55. a. Jess' book paper   **b.** bride-to-be   **c.** eleven o'clock
   d. blue-tinted paper

O. Write the letter of the adverb in each sentence. *(pages 314–315)*

56. The large supermarket has slowly replaced the small grocery.
   a. large   **b.** has   **c.** slowly   **d.** small

57. In suburban areas, this change is almost complete.
   a. suburban   **b.** this   **c.** almost   **d.** complete

P. Write the letter of the comparative adverb that correctly completes each sentence. *(pages 316–317)*

58. People visit supermarkets ____ than neighborhood grocery stores. (often)
   a. oftener   **b.** most often   **c.** more often

59. Neighborhood stores serve people ____ than supermarkets. (good)
   a. better   **b.** more good   **c.** gooder

Q. Write the letter of the term that identifies each underlined word. *(pages 318–319)*

    60. Many people must travel <u>far</u> to reach their supermarkets.
        a. adverb   **b.** adjective

    61. They can be <u>very</u> convenient.
        a. adverb   **b.** adjective

R. Write the letter of the verb that each adverb phrase describes. *(pages 320–321)*

    62. Grocery store employees work in many different capacities.
        a. store   **b.** employees   **c.** work   **d.** capacities

    63. The store's owner usually greets me with a smile.
        a. owner   **b.** usually   **c.** greets   **d.** me

S. Write the letter of the word that completes each negative sentence. *(pages 322–323)*

    64. There ____ nothing wrong with supermarkets.
        a. isn't   **b.** is

    65. No supermarket can ____ replace the corner grocery, however.
        a. ever   **b.** never

T. Write the letter of the sentence that is *not* punctuated correctly. *(pages 356–357)*

    66. a. Rita said, "we got a new dog!
        b. "I'll introduce you," she added. "You'll like him."

    67. a. "I never asked," she said, "whether you like dogs."
        b. "Are you kidding? came the response. "Of course I like dogs!"

U. Write the letter of the term that identifies each underlined word. *(pages 362–365)*

    68. <u>Oh</u>, what a beautiful Irish setter!
        a. preposition   **b.** conjunction   **c.** interjection

    69. I have a golden retriever <u>and</u> a cocker spaniel.
        a. preposition   **b.** conjunction   **c.** interjection

    70. I walk them <u>before</u> work every morning.
        a. preposition   **b.** conjunction   **c.** interjection

V. Write the letter of each prepositional phrase. *(pages 362–363)*

    71. Ancient peoples kept dogs before recorded history.
        a. dogs before   **b.** recorded history
        c. before recorded history

    72. Dogs of every description exist today.
        a. of every description   **b.** of every   **c.** exist today

W. Write the letter of the term that identifies the underlined words. *(pages 366–369)*

73. Retrievers and pointers are good hunters.
    a. compound subject   **b.** compound predicate
    c. simple predicate

74. Retrievers find game and bring it back.
    a. compound subject   **b.** compound predicate
    c. simple subject

75. Pointers freeze and point at game.
    a. compound subject   **b.** compound predicate
    c. simple subject

X. Write the letter of the term that identifies each sentence. *(pages 370–373)*

76. Setters and spaniels hunt well, and they also make good pets.
    a. compound sentence   **b.** run-on sentence

77. Dogs with pedigrees are beautiful, but many of them are nervous.
    a. compound sentence   **b.** run-on sentence

78. Mixed breeds often have better tempers they are happier dogs.
    a. compound sentence   **b.** run-on sentence

Resources
Table of Contents

	page
Thesaurus	393

Writing Handbook

Types of Writing
Personal Narrative	417
Biographical Sketch	418
Book Report	419
Business and Friendly Letters	420
Descriptive Writing	422
Research Report	423
Persuasive Essay	425
Short Story	427
Steps of Writing: When Time Matters	429
Steps of Writing: When You Use a Computer	431
Letter Forms	432
Spelling Strategies	434
Commonly Misspelled Words	435
Handwriting Model	436

Grammar and Mechanics Handbook

Grammar Definitions and Practice
Sentences I	437
Nouns	441
Verbs I	445
Verbs II	450
Pronouns	454
Adjectives	458
Adverbs	463
Sentences II	467

Mechanics Rules and Practice
Capitalization and End Punctuation	472
Commas	474
Other Punctuation	476
Punctuating Conversation	478
Diagraming	480
Troublesome Words	484

A thesaurus, like a dictionary, lists words in alphabetical order. Instead of defining words, however, a thesaurus provides synonyms for them; it may also list antonyms. There is an entry for each main word. Each entry contains the following parts:

part of speech   example sentence

entry word—**scare** *v.* Loud noises scare away the birds.
     Synonyms: frighten, terrify, startle, make ——— synonyms
     afraid, alarm, intimidate. *Antonyms*: **comfort,**
antonyms ——— embolden, soothe, reassure.

entry word

Notice that the different kinds of print identify each part of the entry. Entry words are printed in heavy, boldface type. Synonyms are in regular type, and antonyms are in colored type. A synonym or antonym that is in boldface is also an entry word.

When you are writing, a thesaurus can help you find the word you are looking for. You may have only a vague idea of what you want to say. Look up the word in the thesaurus and see if the entry suggests a more precise word to express your meaning. The thesaurus can also help you avoid repeating the same word over and over. If you select a word from the thesaurus, make sure you know what it means. If you aren't sure, look up the word in a dictionary.

Thesaurus

A a

abandon *v.* The captain is the last person to abandon a sinking ship. *Synonyms*: **leave**, desert, evacuate, yield, surrender. *Antonyms*: **cling** to, **stay** with, stand beside, abide, continue.

above *prep.* She stood on the cliff above the sea. *Synonyms*: over, on top of, upward. *Antonyms*: **below**, beneath, underneath.

absorb *v.* A sponge will absorb spilled water. *Synonyms*: **soak** up, digest, take in, consume, swallow, incorporate. *Antonyms*: leak, ooze, seep.

accident *n.* Knocking the glass off the table was an accident. *Synonyms*: chance, **mistake**, fluke, mishap. *Antonyms*: **plan**, purpose, design, intention.

act *n.* The baby's first act was to open its eyes. *Synonyms*: action, deed, feat, step, performance, exploit.

adjust *v.* It may take a long time to adjust to a new school. *Synonyms*: **change**, adapt, accept, accommodate, make the best of. *Antonyms*: reject, let alone, leave be, allow to remain.

adventure *n.* Life for the pioneers was full of adventure. *Synonyms*: **event**, experience, happening, incident, occurrence. *Antonyms*: schedule, routine, habit.

advice *n.* The visiting author gave us advice on how to write better. *Synonyms*: tip, counsel, suggestion, guidance, **warning**, recommendation.

afraid *adj.* I don't go swimming because I am afraid of the water.

agree *v.* The three friends agree to take turns riding the new bicycle. *Synonyms*: accept, acknowledge, side with, consent, conform, approve, concede. *Antonyms*: disagree, differ, oppose, deny, contradict, protest.

aim *v.* The player will aim for the center of the basket. *Synonyms*: point, intend, focus, strive.

394

aimlessly *adv.* The leaf drifted aimlessly downstream. *Synonyms*: at random, by chance, frivolously, unpredictably, pointlessly, erratically.

alike *adj.* The twins were exactly alike. *Synonyms*: equal, uniform, identical, equivalent, same, synonymous.

alive *adj.* The apple tree is still alive after the frost. *Synonyms*: existing, surviving, conscious, lively, energetic, living, vivacious. *Antonyms*: **dead**, expired, deceased, extinct, lifeless.

always *adv.* She always looked both ways before crossing the street. *Synonyms*: every time, regularly, invariably, inevitably, forever. *Antonyms*: never, infrequently.

angry *adj.* She was angry when she missed her bus. *Synonyms*: cross, upset, grumpy, raging, gruff, disgusted, furious, irritated, snarling, **sulky**, annoyed, fuming, outraged, indignant, grouchy, rebellious, wrathful, vexed, enraged, exasperated. *Antonyms*: pleased, **cheerful**, **calm**, **happy**, glad.

answer *v.* Answer these questions after you read the book. *Synonyms*: reply, respond, retort. *Antonym*: **question**, **ask**.

argue *v.* The ballplayer and the umpire began to argue during the ballgame. *Synonyms*: dispute, disagree, quarrel, bicker, debate. *Antonyms*: **agree**, concur, consent.

artistic *adj.* An artistic person can make every corner of a house look beautiful. *Synonyms*: tasteful, creative. *Antonyms*: tasteless, uncreative.

ashamed *adj.* He felt ashamed after teasing his sister. *Synonyms*: sheepish, embarrassed, humiliated, disgraced, red-faced. *Antonyms*: **proud**, dignified, arrogant.

ask *v.* The hikers ask the guide for directions. *Synonyms*: beg, plead, **question**, request, challenge, inquire, invite, appeal, beseech, invite. *Antonyms*: reply, **answer**, respond.

asleep *adj.* When the baby is asleep, the house is much quieter. *Synonyms*: sleeping, unaware, napping, unready, unconscious, dormant. *Antonyms*: awake, alert, aware, conscious.

attractive *adj*. The bright, yellow flowers were attractive to the bees. *Synonyms*: appealing, pleasing, alluring, irresistible. *Antonyms*: offensive, revolting, unappealing.

awful *adj*. Thunder made an awful roar. *Synonyms*: bad, terrible, dreadful, horrible, ghastly, appalling. *Antonyms*: **nice**, **wonderful**, pleasant, **good**.

B b

bad *adj*. The chemicals in the lab had a bad odor. *Synonyms*: evil, nasty, fake, wicked, naughty, **awful**, terrible, harmful, nightmarish, unfit, villainous, treacherous, sinister, roguish, faulty, defective, appalling, abominable. *Antonyms*: **good**, **heroic**, lovable, kind, excellent.

balance *n*. A tightrope walker must have good balance. *Synonyms*: steadiness, stability, symmetry. *Antonyms*: uncertainty, imbalance, fluctuation.

beach *n*. The white, sandy beach stretched to the blue ocean. *Synonyms*: coast, shore, seashore, waterfront.

beat-up *adj*. The old, beat-up car had dents on its hood. *Synonyms*: battered, mauled, dilapidated. *Antonyms*: untouched, unscathed, repaired, refurbished.

beginning *n*. The sun rises at the beginning of every day. *Synonyms*: opening, debut. *Antonyms*: **end**, termination, finish.

believe *v*. I believe all people try to do their best. *Synonyms*: **trust**, accept, have faith in, be convinced, rely on, be sure of. *Antonyms*: **doubt**, deny, be skeptical about, have reservations about, question, mistrust.

below *prep*. Far below the bridge, the river rushed over the boulders. *Synonyms*: beneath, under, underneath. *Antonym*: **above**.

bend *v*. When you bow, you bend at the waist. *Synonyms*: flex, curve, twist, fold, bow, crouch. *Antonyms*: straighten, smooth.

best *adj*. The best runner will finish first in the race. *Synonyms*: supreme, utmost, ultimate, foremost. *Antonyms*: worst, least, inferior.

better *adj*. A breakfast of orange juice, eggs, and toast is better than eating sugary cereal. *Synonyms*: superior, improved, upgraded. *Antonym*: worse.

big *adj*. Jupiter is a big planet. *Synonyms*: gigantic, **thick**, large, enormous, mighty, husky, sizable, colossal, huge, important, adult. *Antonyms*: **little**, **small**.

bigger *adj*. A walrus is bigger than a seal. *Synonyms*: magnified, multiplied, expanded, increased, amplified, enlarged. *Antonyms*: **smaller**, waning, decreasing.

bit *n*. There was a bit of meat left on the plate. *Synonyms*: crumb, pinch, speck, flake, sliver, thimbleful. *Antonyms*: lots, **plenty**, abundance.

bite *v*. I wanted to bite into the shiny apple. *Synonyms*: nip, chew, nibble, gnaw.

black *adj*. The black bear stood out against the white snow. *Synonyms*: inky, jet, ebony, raven, dark.

blue *adj*. The blue sky was reflected in the water of the lake. *Synonyms*: sapphire, turquoise, cobalt, indigo, aqua.

boring *adj*. I fell asleep during the boring movie. *Synonyms*: humdrum, drab, dull, uninteresting, monotonous. *Antonyms*: exciting, stimulating, **colorful**.

bother *v*. Don't bother the students who are quietly reading. *Synonyms*: annoy, pester, fret, nag, upset, disturb, vex, encumber. *Antonyms*: **help**, aid, assist.

brag *v*. It is impolite to constantly brag about your abilities. *Synonyms*: boast, bluster, swagger.

brave *adj*. Brave people are not afraid of danger. *Synonyms*: courageous, daring, plucky, bold, fearless, **heroic**, unafraid, intrepid, spunky, steadfast, valiant, brazen. *Antonyms*: **afraid**, **cautious**, timid, cowardly, **fearful**.

break *v*. Break two eggs into the hot frying pan. *Synonyms*: collapse, **snap**, shatter, smash, wreck. *Antonyms*: **fix**, heal, mend, repair.

395

breathe *v.* I like to breathe the fresh ocean air. *Synonyms*: inhale, pant, puff, gasp, snort, sniff, wheeze. *Antonyms*: choke, smother.

bright *adj.* The bright comet lit up the night sky. *Synonyms*: **flashy**, glittering, fiery, sparkling, radiant, twinkling, dazzling, brilliant, luminous, iridescent. *Antonyms*: dull, faded, pale.

bring *v.* Bring a towel to the swimming pool. *Synonyms*: fetch, carry, **gather**, transfer, import.

brown *adj.* The brown earth was full of broken twigs and stones. *Synonyms*: beige, tan, caramel, mahogany, tawny, khaki.

bulky *adj.* The bulky jacket kept her warm in the snow. *Synonyms*: massive, mammoth, monumental, **vast**, immense, clumsy. *Antonyms*: small, compact, sleek.

burn *v.* If you burn the dinner, the house will be full of smoke. *Synonyms*: blaze, smolder, kindle, char, scorch, ignite.

C c

call *v.* The birds call to each other from the trees. *Synonyms*: cry, **shout**, summon, beckon.

calm *adj.* The calm lake was as smooth as a mirror. *Synonyms*: tame, **polite**, **peaceful**, serene, **quiet**, poised, restful, smooth, placid. *Antonyms*: fierce, **wild**, uncontrolled, violent, **excited**, disturbed, stormy, aggressive.

carefree *adj.* The carefree children played all day long. *Synonyms*: untroubled, happy, lighthearted, breezy. *Antonyms*: careworn, downhearted, **sad**, weary.

careful *adj.* A careful person does not take chances. *Synonyms*: **cautious**, guarded, methodical, conscientious. *Antonyms*: reckless, rash.

carry *v.* Please carry the groceries into the house. *Synonyms*: lug, haul, convey, transport, tote.

catch *v.* Brown bears catch fish with their paws. *Synonyms*: capture, snag, snare, trap. *Antonyms*: set free, release, relinquish.

cautious *adj.* The cautious swimmer stayed near shore. *Synonyms*: wary, alert, **careful**. *Antonyms*: daring, brash.

change *v.* The weather will change when winter comes. *Synonyms*: alter, vary, transform, adapt, substitute, **adjust**, evolve, distort, vary. *Antonyms*: stay the same, remain fixed.

check *v.* Check the tire to see if it has enough air. *Synonyms*: observe, monitor, inspect, canvass, scrutinize, explore, verify, reconnoiter.

cheerful *adj.* The cheerful campers sang all the way home. *Synonyms*: **happy**, smiling, joyful. *Antonyms*: **sulky**, **sad**, frowning, miserable.

choice *n.* The choice of vegetable is peas or carrots. *Synonyms*: option, decision, vote, dilemma, alternative, selection.

choose *v.* Choose which outfit you want to wear today. *Synonyms*: pick, pick out, elect, select, opt. *Antonyms*: waver, reject.

circle *n.* The dancers joined hands and formed a circle. *Synonyms*: ring, circuit, orbit, loop, sphere. *Antonyms*: square, triangle.

clean *v.* Clean your hands with soap and water. *Synonyms*: bathe, scrub, wash, scour, straighten up, rinse out.

clear *adj.* The water was so clear that you could see the fish swimming. *Synonyms*: **pure**, **clean**, visible, transparent, cloudless. *Antonyms*: **dirty**, **murky**, clouded.

clever *adj.* The clever chimpanzee discovered a way to get out of its cage. *Synonyms*: witty, quick-witted, **bright**, cunning, skillful. *Antonyms*: **boring**, **dull**, bumbling, **stupid**, dim-witted.

climb *v.* It will take two days to climb to the top of that mountain. *Synonyms*: ascend, rise, go up, mount. *Antonym*: descend.

cling *v.* The ivy vines cling to the side of the old house. *Synonyms*: hold fast, grasp, **grab**, clutch, adhere. *Antonyms*: release, forsake, discard, **abandon**.

cloth *n.* The cloth for this quilt came from old dresses and shirts. *Synonyms*: material, stuff, fabric.

clothes *n.* He wore his new clothes to the party. *Synonyms*: garments, outfit, dress, garb, uniform, costume.

clumsy *adj.* The clumsy clowns with the big shoes made the audience laugh. *Synonyms*: awkward, fumbling, graceless, inept. *Antonyms*: deft, nimble, lithe, acrobatic, skilled, practiced, graceful, adroit.

cold *adj.* The ice was so cold that it made the glass frosty. *Synonyms*: cool, chilly, icy, frozen, wintry, clammy, numbing, unthawed. *Antonyms*: **hot**, steaming, warm, tropical, equatorial.

color *n.* The color of the sky is blue. *Synonyms*: dye, tint, hue, shade, tinge, pigment.

colorful *adj.* The colorful bird had feathers of red, green, orange, and blue. *Synonyms*: vivid, brilliant, vibrant, **bright, flashy**. *Antonyms*: faded, **dull**, dreary, lifeless, monochrome, **colorless**.

colorless *adj.* The colorless liquid looked like water but smelled of mint. *Synonyms*: **clear**, transparent, faded, bland. *Antonyms*: painted, dyed, stained, tinted, colorful.

come together *v.* Everyone in the house comes together at dinnertime. *Synonyms*: meet, unite, **join**, combine, **gather**, merge, blend. *Antonyms*: escape, flee, separate.

comfort *v.* Comfort a crying baby by holding it, rocking it, and singing softly. *Synonyms*: care, ease, cheer, console, soothe. *Antonyms*: **hurt**, distress, bother.

common *adj.* The dandelion is a common weed. *Synonyms*: usual, **ordinary**, familiar, natural, shared, regular, traditional. *Antonyms*: **special**, unusual, **rare**, unique.

complain *v.* People often complain about bad weather. *Synonyms*: grumble, whine, find fault, criticize.

compliment *v.* Let me compliment you on your good work. *Synonyms*: congratulate, appreciate, applaud, flatter. *Antonyms*: insult, criticize, condemn.

confused *adj.* We gave directions to a confused traveler. *Synonyms*: dazed, dizzy, bewildered, baffled, flustered, muddled, disoriented. *Antonyms*: logical, clear-headed, clear-thinking, organized.

connect *v.* The switch will connect these two wires to make the train run. *Synonyms*: **join**, fasten, unite, splice, tie, hinge, wed. *Antonyms*: **cut**, **break**, disconnect, separate.

container *n.* The food must be kept in a sealed container. *Synonyms*: box, can, jar, vessel, receptacle.

contents *n.* She unpacked the contents of the suitcase. *Synonyms*: **parts**, elements, ingredients.

control *v.* A valve will control the flow of water. *Synonyms*: direct, govern, regulate, manage, restrain. *Antonyms*: set free, release, vent.

cook *v.* We cook corn in a pot of hot water. *Synonyms*: bake, boil, fry, steam, stew, barbecue, broil, prepare.

copy *v.* The students copy what is written on the chalkboard. *Synonyms*: duplicate, imitate, reproduce, replicate, repeat.

cost *n.* The cost of the radio was more than I could pay. *Synonyms*: price, expense, value, worth.

count *v.* I will count all the pennies in the jar. *Synonyms*: estimate, take a census of, enumerate.

crash *v.* That heavy rock could crash through the ice. *Synonyms*: bump, collide, smash, shatter, collapse. *Antonyms*: dodge, avoid.

crease *v.* It is easier to tear paper after you crease it. *Synonyms*: fold, wrinkle, crumple, crimp. *Antonyms*: smooth, flatten, iron.

cry *v.* I always cry when I slice onions. *Synonyms*: sob, weep, whimper, whine, bawl, sniffle, wail, blubber, lament, groan, moan.

Thesaurus

curious *adj.* The curious woodpecker stuck its beak into the hole to look for bugs. *Synonyms:* inquisitive, probing, prying, **interested**. *Antonyms:* uninterested, complacent, indifferent.

curve *n.* We could not see around the curve in the road. *Synonyms:* arc, curl, loop, **circle**. *Antonyms:* angle, straight line.

cut *v.* We used scissors to cut the paper into four parts. *Synonyms:* carve, chip, chop, clip, crop, shred, slit, snip, split, slice, trim, whittle, shave, shear, nick, notch, prune, mince. *Antonyms:* glue, nail, screw, bolt, clamp together.

cute *adj.* The cute baby smiled when I played with him. *Synonyms:* appealing, charming, pretty, adorable. *Antonyms:* plain, **ugly**, homely.

D d

dangerous *adj.* Everyone fled the dangerous storm. *Synonyms:* perilous, risky, ominous, unsafe, threatening. *Antonyms:* safe, secure.

dare *v.* The climbers dare to scale the highest peak. *Synonyms:* risk, defy, challenge, chance. *Antonyms:* be careful, be cautious, heed.

dark *adj.* It is very dark when the lights are off. *Synonyms:* dim, **dull**, gray, shadowy, shady. *Antonyms:* light, **bright**, glaring.

daze *v.* A shock like that would daze anyone. *Synonyms:* befuddle, muddle, confuse, stun, stagger, stupify, bewilder, startle, flabbergast.

dead *adj.* The dead batteries made the radio powerless. *Synonyms:* deceased, lifeless, inert, inactive, extinct. *Antonyms:* **alive**, lively, animated.

decorate *v.* We will decorate the room with balloons and streamers. *Synonyms:* adorn, beautify, ornament, embellish. *Antonyms:* strip, simplify.

delicate *adj.* We packed the delicate glassware carefully for the move. *Synonyms:* fragile, dainty, sensitive, gentle. *Antonyms:* sturdy, **solid**, tough, durable.

demand *v.* The president will demand an explanation. *Synonyms:* command, require, insist, **order**. *Antonyms:* beg, plead.

deserve *v.* I deserve to get paid for my work. *Synonyms:* earn, merit, be entitled to, be due.

determined *adj.* The determined snail made its way up the wall and into the garden. *Synonyms:* resolved, strong-willed, resolute, relentless, ambitious, persistent. *Antonyms:* aimless, drifting, defeated.

different *adj.* Each person chose a different path. *Synonyms:* **odd**, distinguishable, distinctive. *Antonyms:* similar, identical, equivalent.

dig *v.* If you wish to dig a hole the big shovel is the best tool. *Synonyms:* burrow, plow, trench, unearth, excavate.

dirty *adj.* I could not see through the dirty windows. *Synonyms:* dusty, soiled, sandy, **muddy**, grimy, dingy, grubby, unclean, filthy, tacky, foul, hazy. *Antonyms:* neat, sparkling, spotless, antiseptic, stainless.

disappointed *adj.* The disappointed athlete lost the race. *Synonyms:* crestfallen, **sad**, frustrated, disheartened. *Antonyms:* satisfied, content.

discuss *v.* They discuss ideas for the project before they take action. *Synonyms:* negotiate, debate, talk over, confer.

disease *n.* Measles used to be a common childhood disease. *Synonyms:* illness, ailment, malady, sickness. *Antonyms:* health, wellness, well-being.

divide *v.* The waters of the Ohio River divide Ohio from Kentucky. *Synonyms:* split, distribute, separate, bisect, dissect. *Antonyms:* unite, wed, add to, multiply.

do *v.* Can you do all of this work in one day? *Synonyms:* perform, conduct, accomplish, achieve, fulfill.

doubt *v.* I doubt that I can finish that huge task today. *Synonyms:* be skeptical, be uncertain, disbelieve, distrust. *Antonyms:* **trust**, rely, **believe**, have confidence that.

draw *v.* I will draw a picture of that building with pen and ink. *Synonyms*: illustrate, depict, represent, diagram, sketch, delineate. *Antonyms*: erase, eradicate.

dream *n.* My greatest dream is to travel around the world. *Synonyms*: hope, ambition, **goal**, fantasy, illusion. *Antonyms*: reality, actuality, accomplishment.

drink *v.* If you drink enough water, you will not be thirsty. *Synonyms*: sip, gulp, guzzle.

drip *v.* The water will drip out of the hose until you turn it off. *Synonyms*: trickle, leak, dribble. *Antonyms*: gush, **flow**, flood, stream.

drop *v.* The dishes will break if you drop them. *Synonyms*: dump, fumble, release, discard, dispose of.

dry *adj.* The dry leaves crackled underfoot. *Synonyms*: waterproof, parched, arid. *Antonyms*: sopping, soaked.

dull *adj.* The dull lecture was of interest to no one. *Synonyms*: **boring**, **stupid**, uninteresting. *Antonyms*: lively, alert, engaging.

duty *n.* It is your duty to clean up after yourself. *Synonyms*: responsibility, obligation, task.

E e

eager *adj.* The eager children opened their gifts at the birthday party. *Synonyms*: enthusiastic, avid, fervent, industrious, dynamic, keen. *Antonyms*: reluctant, unwilling, indifferent.

early *adj.* They met for an early breakfast before work. *Synonyms*: premature, ahead of time, first, initial. *Antonyms*: late, tardy, belated.

earn *v.* Could we earn some money by mowing your lawn? *Synonyms*: **deserve**, merit, receive, be entitled to.

earthquake *n.* The earthquake shook buildings to the ground. *Synonyms*: tremor, cave-in, landslide, avalanche.

easy *adj.* Studying hard made the test seem easy. *Synonyms*: simple, uncomplicated, effortless. *Antonyms*: **hard** (2), difficult, strict, unconquerable.

eat *v.* Horses eat oats and hay. *Synonyms*: dine, feast on, lick, munch, swallow, gobble, graze, chew, munch, nibble, devour.

echo *n.* When sound bounces off a mountainside, an echo is produced. *Synonyms*: reverberation, repetition, reproduction, imitation.

edge *n.* We built a fence along the edge of our yard. *Synonyms*: boundary, border, margin, rim, threshold, brink, outskirts. *Antonyms*: insides, innards, interior, center.

effect *n.* The biggest effect of the snowstorm was that we left school early. *Synonyms*: result, upshot, outcome, consequence, aftermath, impact, influence.

elastic *adj.* The elastic waistband would not stretch any further. *Synonyms*: flexible, stretchable, rubbery, supple. *Antonyms*: stiff, rigid, **solid**.

emergency *n.* After the flood, the governor declared a state of emergency. *Synonyms*: disaster, danger, crisis, calamity, catastrophe, trial. *Antonyms*: normalcy.

empty *adj.* The lunch box was empty after she ate her meal. *Synonyms*: hollow, vacant, deserted, barren, void. *Antonyms*: **full**, filled, stuffed, overflowing.

end *n.* When the sun goes down, it is the end of the day. *Synonyms*: climax, deadline, conclusion, finish, termination. *Antonyms*: **beginning**, commencement, initiation.

energy *n.* Animals get energy from the food they eat. *Synonyms*: power, vitality, liveliness, strength, vigor. *Antonyms*: weakness, fatigue, sluggishness.

enter *v.* Enter the movie theater through the front door. *Synonyms*: proceed into, go in, trespass on, intrude, barge into. *Antonyms*: depart, exit, retreat from.

episode *n.* Beating the champions was the most exciting episode in the football season. *Synonyms*: incident, occasion, event, happening, affair, occurrence, chapter.

even *adj.* Use sandpaper to make both pieces even. *Synonyms*: equal, **smooth**, level, flat, uniform. *Antonyms*: uneven, crooked, awry, rough, unbalanced.

event *n.* The first event of the track meet was a footrace. *Synonyms*: celebration, ceremony, **holiday**, program, project, performance, **episode**, spectacle, **meeting**.

excited *adj.* The excited fans cheered the rock star. *Synonyms*: **eager**, frantic, enthusiastic, thrilled, frenzied, stimulated, roused, agitated. *Antonyms*: bored, **calm**, indifferent.

expect *v.* We expect many people to join our club. *Synonyms*: anticipate, predict, plan on, suppose, foresee.

extra *adj.* The airline charged the passenger for extra luggage. *Synonyms*: added, additional, surplus, excess, supplemental, auxiliary, unnecessary. *Antonyms*: insufficient, inadequate.

F f

fair *adj.* It was a fair contest because both sides were evenly matched. *Synonyms*: just, evenhanded, impartial, honest, accurate. *Antonyms*: cheating, unjust, **wrong**, questionable, marginal.

fake *adj.* Only an expert could tell the fake diamond from the real one. *Synonyms*: phony, mock, sham, forged, counterfeit, imitation, false, substitute. *Antonyms*: genuine, honest, original.

fall *v.* Drops of rain fall from the sky. *Synonyms*: **trip**, tumble, stumble, topple, drop, plunge, descend, collapse, lurch. *Antonyms*: rise, float, ascend.

family *n.* All the people who live in my house are part of my family. *Synonyms*: relatives, relations, kin. *Antonyms*: strangers, outsiders.

famous *adj.* The famous rock star is known all over the world. *Synonyms*: well-known, legendary, noted, renowned. *Antonyms*: unknown, obscure.

far *adj.* The barn stood on the far side of the field. *Synonyms*: distant, remote, yonder, far away. *Antonyms*: **near**, close, nearby.

fast *adj.* The fast jet broke all the old speed records. *Synonyms*: **quick**, speedy, swift, rapid, rushing, hasty, prompt, abrupt, staccato. *Antonyms*: **slow**, sluggish.

fault *n.* It was your fault that the work did not get done. *Synonyms*: failing, responsibility, shortcoming, error, slip.

fear *v.* Many people fear thunderstorms. *Synonyms*: dread, distrust, be afraid of. *Antonyms*: welcome, delight in.

fearful *adj.* Big dogs frightened the fearful child. *Synonyms*: frightened, nervous, apprehensive. *Antonyms*: **calm**, relaxed, fearless, confident.

feelings *n.* My feelings get hurt when you yell at me. *Synonyms*: mood, spirit, emotions, sensitivity, sentiment.

fight *v.* The winning teams fight for first place. *Synonyms*: attack, battle, struggle with, make war on, resist, quarrel, wrestle, combat, scuffle, spar, argue, dispute. *Antonyms*: surrender, **ignore**, make peace.

figure *v.* We must look at a map to figure how far it is between the cities. *Synonyms*: calculate, compute, add up.

find *v.* Can you find the secret entrance to the castle? *Synonyms*: discover, come upon, locate, recover, unearth, detect. *Antonyms*: lose, misplace, mislay.

finding *n.* The discovery of radiation was an important finding. *Synonyms*: discovery, result, conclusion.

fire *n.* The fire raged through the forest. *Synonyms*: blaze, flame, flare, inferno, holocaust.

fit (1) *adj.* The fit runner won the marathon. See **healthy**.

fit (2) *v.* All the pieces of the model airplane fit together. *Synonyms*: conform, blend in, dovetail, harmonize, correspond with, mesh. *Antonyms*: clash, jar.

fix *v.* You need a new pane of glass to fix that broken window. *Synonyms*: mend, patch, adjust, repair, replace, restore, correct. *Antonyms*: demolish, **break**, shatter.

flashy *adj.* The flashy red car had huge chrome bumpers and white leather seats. *Synonyms*: showy, garish, spectacular, extravagant. *Antonyms*: somber, plain, modest, sensible.

flat *adj.* You can see for miles along a flat highway. *Synonyms*: **smooth**, level, horizontal. *Antonyms*: **upright**, hilly, uneven.

flimsy *adj.* No one believed his flimsy excuse. *Synonyms*: frail, fragile, feeble, inadequate, shaky. *Antonyms*: sturdy, tough, well-built.

flow *v.* Water will always flow downhill. *Synonyms*: pour, gush, surge.

fly *v.* Many birds fly south in the fall. *Synonyms*: soar, glide, flutter. *Antonyms*: **crash**, ground, come down to earth.

fold *v.* Please fold your clothes neatly before you put them away. *Synonyms*: **crease**, crimp, tuck, pleat, double over. *Antonyms*: iron, flatten, smooth.

follow *v.* Follow me if you don't know the way. *Synonyms*: be behind, chase, pursue, stalk. *Antonyms*: **guide**, beckon, steer, pilot, conduct.

food *n.* Spaghetti is my favorite food. *Synonyms*: refreshments, fare, provisions, edibles, victuals, sustenance, nourishment.

forbid *v.* My parents forbid me to stay up late on school nights. *Synonyms*: prohibit, ban, suppress. *Antonyms*: **permit**, allow, encourage, incite, induce.

forever *adv.* We hope to live in this house forever. *Synonyms*: eternally, endlessly, continuously, permanently, constantly, immortally, perpetually.

forgetful *adj.* Jane is never forgetful; she always remembers my birthday. *Synonyms*: negligent, inattentive, absent-minded, heedless. *Antonyms*: mindful, unforgetting, attentive.

forgive *v.* Please forgive me for leaving early, but I have a headache. *Synonyms*: pardon, excuse, make peace, have pity. *Antonyms*: condemn, be vengeful, blame.

form *v.* Form the clay into any shape you wish. *Synonyms*: **shape**, construct, configure. *Antonyms*: destroy, undo, damage, smash.

free *adj.* The birds are free to fly all over the countryside. *Synonyms*: independent, at liberty, unrestrained.

fresh *adj.* After a rainstorm, the air is fresh and clear. *Synonyms*: **new**, original, renewed, unspoiled. *Antonyms*: stale, wilted, withered, decayed.

friend *n.* I share everything with my best friend. *Synonyms*: pal, partner, companion, confidant. *Antonyms*: enemy, foe, opponent.

friendly *adj.* The friendly people smiled at the new neighbors. *Synonyms*: amiable, kind, intimate. *Antonyms*: hostile, frigid, aloof.

full *adj.* Start your trip with a full tank of gas. *Synonyms*: complete, loaded, crammed with. *Antonyms*: hollow, void, vacant, **empty**, deserted, uninhabited.

fun *n.* We had fun at the beach last summer. *Synonyms*: enjoyment, pleasure, amusement, sport, revelry.

funny *adj.* The comedian told many funny jokes. *Synonyms*: comic, joking, droll, witty, humorous, ridiculous, wry, quizzical. *Antonyms*: **sad**, **serious**, somber.

fuss *n.* The children made a fuss about sharing their toys. *Synonyms*: commotion, disturbance, worry, ado.

fussy *adj.* The fussy dresser shined his shoes twice a day. *Synonyms*: particular, finicky, choosy. *Antonyms*: sloppy, careless, slovenly.

G g

game *n.* Chess is my favorite game. *Synonyms*: hobby, amusement, recreation, sport, diversion, pastime.

gather *v.* Birds gather on the shore, where food is plentiful. *Synonyms*: collect, assemble, concentrate, unite, congregate, heap, pile up. *Antonyms*: distribute, scatter.

get *v.* Can you get two good seats for the concert? *Synonyms*: receive, acquire, inherit, accumulate.

get rid of *v.* They will get rid of old toys at a garage sale. *Synonyms*: discard, eliminate, remove.

give *v.* They will give free samples of the new cheese. *Synonyms*: grant, issue, bestow, donate, furnish, contribute, sacrifice, relinquish, impart, endow, render. *Antonyms*: take, seize, repossess.

give up *v.* We must give up our plans to cross the river without a boat. *Synonyms*: **abandon**, discontinue, relinquish, yield. *Antonyms*: grasp, **cling** to, persevere with.

go *v.* Let's go to the movies. *Synonyms*: **move**, travel, advance, proceed, press on, scat, **leave**. *Antonyms*: **stop**, halt, come to a standstill.

go away *v.* I might go away and never come back. *Synonyms*: **leave**, depart, disappear. *Antonyms*: **stay**, remain, last, persist, abide.

go back *v.* After vacation, students go back to school. *Synonyms*: return, turn back, restore. *Antonyms*: **leave**, depart, run away, escape.

go toward *v.* The hungry animals go toward food. *Synonyms*: advance, draw near, seek out, approach. *Antonyms*: retreat, escape, avoid.

goal *n.* Becoming an astronaut is my goal. *Synonyms*: target, intention, purpose, aim, **end**.

good *adj.* Everyone is satisfied with the good work of the committee. *Synonyms*: excellent, upright, **pure**, terrific, valuable, satisfactory, dandy, genuine, respectable, favorable, reputable, virtuous. *Antonyms*: **bad**, **awful**, horrible, malicious.

good at *adj.* They were good at working out their differences. *Synonyms*: able, capable, efficient.

grab *v.* You must grab the rope and scramble up the wall. *Synonyms*: seize, snatch, grasp, clench, cling to.

grand *adj.* The grand ballroom was bigger than a football field. *Synonyms*: royal, noble, majestic, aristocratic, splendid, regal. *Antonyms*: puny, piddling.

gray *adj.* Rain fell from gray clouds. *Synonyms*: grizzled, drab, ashen, overcast, gloomy.

greasy *adj.* Their hands got greasy from fixing the bike. *Synonyms*: oily, slippery, lubricated. *Antonyms*: **dry**, rough, scratchy.

great *adj.* Thomas Jefferson was one of the nation's great leaders. *Synonyms*: noted, eminent, remarkable, terrific, superb, impressive, outstanding, spectacular. *Antonyms*: **awful**, poor, terrible, horrible, wretched.

green *adj.* The grassy green hills rolled toward the river. *Synonyms*: olive, emerald, hazel, lime, jade.

group *n.* A group of people stood outside the theater. *Synonyms*: cluster, aggregation, gathering, crowd, bunch, batch.

grow *v.* The seeds we plant will grow in the spring. *Synonyms*: sprout, develop, thrive, flourish, increase, enlarge.

grown-up *adj.* A grown-up kitten is a cat. *Synonyms*: adult, mature. *Antonyms*: childish, babyish, childlike, immature.

guide *v.* The ranger will guide us through the canyon. *Synonyms*: steer, navigate, escort, precede, maneuver, lead.

H h

happy *adj.* This birthday celebration makes me very happy. *Synonyms*: glad, jolly, merry, joyful, joyous, **cheerful**, joking, contented, gay, gleeful, perky, overjoyed, rejoicing, frolicking, zestful, blissful, ecstatic, jubilant, rapturous, elated. *Antonyms*: **sad**, gloomy, glum, bitter, down in the mouth, melancholy.

hard (1) *adj.* The bread is too hard to chew. *Synonyms*: bony, crisp, **solid**, sturdy, rigid, firm, rugged, stony. *Antonyms*: **soft**, crumbly, plush, slushy.

hard (2) *adj.* The test was hard, but I passed it. *Synonyms*: difficult, complex, tough, puzzling. *Antonyms*: **easy**, simple, facile.

head *v.* The mayor will head the city council. *Synonyms*: lead, direct, supervise, control.

healthy *adj.* The healthy children exercised daily. *Synonyms*: hale, vigorous, hearty, possessed of a sound constitution. *Antonyms*: wan, sickly, frail, ill, feverish, ailing.

help *v.* The young people help each other with the hard work. *Synonyms*: aid, **save**, enable, assist, cooperate with, benefit. *Antonyms*: hamper, hinder, obstruct.

helpful *adj.* The helpful guest did the dishes. *Synonyms*: useful, usable, cooperative, willing. *Antonyms*: harmful, **useless**, selfish.

hero *n.* Paul Revere was a hero of the American Revolution. *Synonyms*: champion, star, idol, role model, paragon.

heroic *adj.* The heroic lifeguard rescued the drowning person. *Synonyms*: **brave**, courageous, fearless, noble, gallant. *Antonyms*: villainous, despicable, cowardly.

hide *v.* The dog dug a hole to hide the bone. *Synonyms*: conceal, mask, disguise, screen, camouflage. *Antonyms*: **show**, reveal, expose, disclose.

hill *n.* It was a short climb to the top of the hill. *Synonyms*: mountain, mount, peak, dune, volcano, butte, heights. *Antonym*: **valley**.

hit *v.* The batter hit a home run. *Synonyms*: paddle, pound, punch, drive, slap, strike, whack.

hold *v.* You must hold the hot pan with a padded glove. *Synonyms*: grip, **grab**, clasp, clench, **cling** to, retain, hoard.

hole *n.* A groundhog lives in a hole in the ground. *Synonyms*: **pit**, crater, opening, chasm. *Antonyms*: **hill**, heap, dune.

holiday *n.* School is closed during Thanksgiving holiday. *Synonyms*: vacation, celebration, carnival, festival, festivity, fiesta.

hope *v.* I hope to visit Japan someday. *Synonyms*: wish, **trust**, desire, **want**. *Antonyms*: **fear**, reject, despair, give up, **doubt**.

hopeless *adj.* It is hopeless to think we can raise enough money in only one week. *Synonyms*: vain, useless, futile, irreparable, desperate.

hot *adj.* Wash the dishes in hot water. *Synonyms*: warm, heated, molten, sizzling, tropical, balmy. *Antonym*: **cold**.

house *n.* There was new furniture in every room of the house. *Synonyms*: dwelling, residence, shelter, home, abode.

hungry *adj.* Everyone was hungry when we sat down to eat dinner. *Synonyms*: starving, ravenous, voracious, famished. *Antonyms*: fed, sated, well-nourished.

hunt *v.* Help me hunt for the shoe I lost. *Synonyms*: look for, seek, stalk, chase, prowl, pursue. *Antonyms*: dodge, elude.

hurry *v.* Hurry to the store before it closes. *Synonyms*: rush, dash, race, speed, hasten, accelerate. *Antonyms*: lag, poke along, dawdle, dilly-dally.

hurt (1) *v.* Her muscles hurt after the long hike. *Synonyms*: suffer, ache, pinch, sting, bruise, be in agony. *Antonyms*: soothe, **comfort**.

hurt (2) *v.* Poor grades hurt his chances of entering medical school. *Synonyms*: ruin, spoil, destroy, injure, mar, harm, wreck, damage. *Antonyms*: fix, construct.

Thesaurus

I i

icy *adj.* The car skidded on the icy road. *Synonyms:* frozen, frigid, cold, freezing, frosty, slippery.

idea *n.* Your idea could lead to a new invention. *Synonyms:* notion, theory, theme, scheme, speculation, inkling, concept.

ignore *v.* Try to ignore the person who is teasing you. *Synonyms:* disregard, overlook, pay no attention to, snub, neglect.

imagine *v.* I try to imagine what I will do when I am an adult. *Synonyms:* envision, fantasize, picture, suppose, visualize.

important *adj.* Choosing a career is an important decision. *Synonyms:* crucial, **great**, momentous, significant, **serious**, critical, profound. *Antonym:* trivial.

include *v.* The photograph will include all my classmates. *Synonyms:* incorporate, combine, enclose. *Antonyms:* **ignore**, exclude, eliminate.

influence *v.* Reading about Marie Curie influenced my decision to become a scientist. *Synonyms:* motivate, induce, affect, inspire, persuade, sway, prompt, convince.

informed *adj.* An informed citizen is the best voter. *Synonyms:* educated, knowledgeable, learned. *Antonyms:* ignorant, gullible, naive.

information *n.* The library is a storehouse of information. *Synonyms:* facts, data, evidence, news, knowledge, facts.

interested *adj.* All interested parties should attend the next planning meeting. *Synonyms:* concerned, enchanted, fascinated, spellbound, riveted, absorbed, engaged. *Antonyms:* bored, indifferent.

interrupt *v.* We now interrupt this program for a special bulletin. *Synonyms:* stop, break in on, delay.

invent *v.* Researchers must invent new ways to solve problems. *Synonyms:* discover, create, devise, make up, develop.

404

J j

jab *v.* He tried to jab me with his elbow to get my attention. *Synonyms:* **push**, poke, thrust, probe, goad, prod.

jealous *adj.* The jealous actor envied the actress's success in the play. *Synonyms:* envious, resentful, covetous, protective. *Antonyms:* generous, content, openhearted, indifferent.

jerk *v.* I felt a fish jerk the fishing line. *Synonyms:* tug, yank, pull, twitch.

jewel *n.* A diamond is a very expensive jewel. *Synonyms:* gem, gemstone.

job *n.* A carpenter's job is building things. *Synonyms:* occupation, chore, task, work, craft, career, profession, skill, function, vocation.

join *v.* We join hands and form a circle. *Synonyms:* attach, braid, entwine, fasten, glue, knit, knot, sew, tape, tie, untie, weave, fuse together. *Antonyms:* undo, partition, sever, **divide**.

joke *n.* Tell me the joke so that I can laugh, too. *Synonyms:* jest, gag, wisecrack, anecdote.

judge *v.* They will judge who has done the best job. *Synonyms:* decide, assess, determine, appraise, referee, evaluate, reach a verdict about.

jump *v.* Mountain goats jump from rock to rock. *Synonyms:* leap, hop, skip, vault, hurdle, dive, plunge, plummet.

junk *n.* What are you going to do with all that useless junk? *Synonyms:* trash, garbage, rubbish, clutter, rummage, scrap. *Antonyms:* treasure, valuables.

K k

keep *v.* Please keep all the pieces of the puzzle in this box. *Synonyms:* preserve, retain, protect, store. *Antonyms:* discard, evict, dispose of.

kick *v.* The football player will kick the ball. *Synonyms:* punt, boot.

L l

laugh *v.* I like to laugh at a good joke. *Synonyms*: chuckle, giggle, cackle, chortle, guffaw, snicker.

lazy *adj.* The lazy dog slept in the shade all day. *Synonyms*: shiftless, idle, slack. *Antonyms*: active, hardworking, diligent.

lead *v.* You must be in front of the band to lead the parade. *Synonyms*: precede, command, pilot, guide, direct, set an example, spearhead.

leave *v.* You must leave now to catch your bus. *Synonyms*: depart, evacuate, **go**, disembark, withdraw. *Antonyms*: arrive, **enter**.

leftovers *n.* We couldn't eat all the food, so there were leftovers for the next day. *Synonyms*: ashes, scraps, remains, residue, remainder, remnants, parings.

let *v.* Let the smaller children get in line first. *Synonyms*: allow, **permit**, admit, grant, tolerate. *Antonyms*: ban, **forbid**, restrict.

lie *n.* Whenever Pinocchio told a lie, his nose grew longer. *Synonyms*: falsehood, bluff, exaggeration, perjury, fraud.

lift *v.* Two strong people can lift this heavy carton. *Synonyms*: hoist, raise, elevate, boost.

light *n.* Turn on the light so we can see. *Synonyms*: illumination, brightness, radiance, luminosity, lamp, beacon. *Antonyms*: darkness, shade, shadow, gloom.

like (1) *v.* Those performers like to sing and dance. *Synonyms*: enjoy, fancy, care about, be fond of, prefer, relish, favor, appreciate. *Antonyms*: hate, detest, scorn, loathe, have contempt for, disdain.

like (2) *prep.* The sisters look like twins. *Synonyms*: similar to, identical to, synonymous to. *Antonyms*: **different** than, opposite to.

limit *n.* There is a limit on the number of fish that can be taken from this lake. *Synonyms*: restriction, bounds, boundary, restraint, ceiling.

limp *v.* A blister caused the hiker to limp. *Synonyms*: shuffle, hobble.

liquid *n.* Each of the following is a common liquid: water, milk, juice. *Synonyms*: fluid, beverage, drink. *Antonym*: **solid**.

list *n.* Make a list of items we need to buy. *Synonyms*: catalog, index, inventory, census.

little *adj.* A pony is a little horse. *Synonyms*: tiny, miniature, **small**, puny, microscopic, minute. *Antonyms*: **big**, huge, immense, giant, mammoth.

live *v.* I would rather live in the country than in the city. *Synonyms*: dwell, abide, exist, survive, reside.

load *n.* He shoveled a load of dirt into the wheelbarrow. *Synonyms*: burden, freight, cargo, baggage.

lonely *adj.* The new students in the class were lonely until they made friends. *Synonyms*: deserted, lonesome, forlorn, friendless, solitary. *Antonyms*: crowded, popular, teeming.

look *v.* We like to look at our snapshots. *Synonyms*: watch, peek, stare, gaze, glance, glare, peer, examine, **search**. *Antonyms*: **ignore**, disregard, close one's eyes to.

loss *n.* The team suffered a great loss when three players moved out of town. *Synonyms*: defeat, setback. *Antonyms*: win, victory, triumph.

lost *adj.* The lost dog wandered the streets for several days. *Synonyms*: missing, wayward, mislaid, off-course. *Antonyms*: found, returned, rescued, recovered, discovered, replaced.

loud *adj.* The fire siren made a loud noise. *Synonyms*: **noisy**, booming, deafening, thundering, resounding.

lucky *adj.* It was a lucky day when I found money on the street. *Synonyms*: favored, provident, fortunate. *Antonyms*: unfortunate, ominous, ill-fated, ill-starred.

Thesaurus

M m

machine *n*. This sewing machine makes buttonholes. *Synonyms*: device, equipment, gadget, apparatus, engine, motor, mechanism.

main *adj*. Skiing is my main interest. *Synonyms*: chief, principal, foremost, leading, primary. *Antonyms*: insignificant, trivial, secondary, minor.

make (1) *v*. Do you know how to make applesauce? *Synonyms*: create, invent, fashion, assemble, contrive, construct, build, concoct, conjure up, generate, manufacture, devise.

make (2) *v*. Your arguments will not make me change my mind. *Synonyms*: **influence**, force, compel, require, decree that.

make-believe *adj*. The make-believe world of cartoons can be entertaining. *Synonyms*: pretended, imaginary, magic, legendary, mythical, fabulous. *Antonyms*: real, actual, believable, true.

many *adj*. There were many cars in the big parking lot. *Synonyms*: countless, numerous, considerable, abundant, manifold. *Antonyms*: few, none, rare.

march *v*. The bands will march from one end of town to the other. *Synonyms*: parade, hike, stride, **walk**.

mark *n*. That mark on the wall can be washed off. *Synonyms*: marking, stain, flaw, defect, blemish.

marked *adj*. The marked items are all on sale. *Synonyms*: labeled, stained, scuffed, smudged, speckled, dappled.

maybe *adv*. Maybe you can come to my house after you finish your homework. *Synonyms*: perhaps, possibly, depending on, potentially, feasibly, tentatively.

mean *adj*. The mean dog had to be muzzled. *Synonyms*: cruel, unfair, low, spiteful, menacing, bad-tempered. *Antonyms*: kind, gentle, good-natured, merciful.

measure *v*. We could measure the room to see if both the desk and the bookcase will fit. *Synonyms*: survey, gauge, pace off, **figure**. *Antonyms*: estimate, approximate.

medicine *n*. Many kinds of medicine are made from plants. *Synonyms*: cure, remedy, treatment.

meeting *n*. There was a meeting of the team in the gym. *Synonyms*: conference, appointment, rendezvous.

memory *n*. History students can recall from memory many famous dates. *Synonyms*: remembrance, recollection. *Antonyms*: absent-mindedness, forgetfulness, amnesia.

mess *n*. How can you find your shoes in this mess? *Synonyms*: disorder, chaos, confusion, turmoil. *Antonyms*: order, organization, tidiness.

messy *adj*. The scattered newspapers made the room look very messy. *Synonyms*: littered, sloppy, jumbled, disheveled, cluttered, chaotic, dusty, polluted, bedraggled. *Antonyms*: **neat**, **clean**, ordered.

middle *adj*. The pencil is in the middle drawer. *Synonyms*: central, intermediate, mid.

mistake *n*. It was a mistake to walk in the rain without a coat. *Synonyms*: error, blunder, slip, delusion, defect.

model *n*. She was a model of integrity. *Synonyms*: ideal, mold, paragon, archetype, pattern.

money *n*. I didn't have enough money to buy the tickets. *Synonyms*: cash, currency, coins, capital, wealth, fortune, treasure.

more *adj*. There are more cherries than I can eat. *Synonyms*: additional, **extra**, greater.

move *v*. Please move the boxes from the kitchen to the closet. *Synonyms*: **push**, **pull**, **go**, **leave**, set out, **flow**, scatter, migrate, depart, budge, shift, transport, act, ease, progress, mill about, dislodge, travel.

muddy *adj*. The muddy boots left tracks across the clean floor. *Synonyms*: sodden, **murky**, slimy, **dirty**.

murky *adj.* It was impossible to see the bottom of the murky pond. *Synonyms*: dim, **dark**, unclear, opaque, obscure. *Antonyms*: **clear**, glassy, transparent.

N n

narrow *adj.* The cat slipped through a narrow gap in the fence. *Synonyms*: slender, slim, **small**, cramped, confined, close. *Antonyms*: broad, wide, ample.

natural *adj.* In parts of Africa, you can see lions in their natural surroundings. *Synonyms*: normal, native, unrestrained, instinctive, inborn, innate.

near *adj.* I'll meet you on the near corner, not across the street. *Synonyms*: close, impending, neighboring, nearby. *Antonyms*: **far**, distant.

neat *adj.* It is easy to read his neat handwriting. *Synonyms*: tidy, orderly, trim, clean. *Antonyms*: sloppy, **messy**, careless, disorganized.

nervous *adj.* Everyone seems nervous on the first day of school. *Synonyms*: uneasy, tense, excitable, sensitive, anxious. *Antonyms*: **calm**, poised, collected.

new *adj.* The new house smelled of fresh paint. *Synonyms*: modern, young, unused, current. *Antonym*: **old**.

next *adj.* You are the next one in line to see the movie. *Synonyms*: succeeding, successive. *Antonyms*: previous, former, preliminary.

nice *adj.* There is a nice overstuffed chair by the fireplace. *Synonyms*: pleasant, cozy, charming, delightful, amiable, sympathetic, gracious, agreeable, affectionate, suitable. *Antonyms*: naughty, **awful**, dreadful, ghastly, horrid, hateful, fierce.

noise *n.* The noise from the car engine disturbed the whole street. *Synonyms*: racket, uproar, blare, bustle, jangle, din, commotion, outcry, hubbub.

noisy *adj.* The music was so noisy that we could not hear each other talking. *Synonyms*: **loud**, deafening, shrill, gurgling, booming, crashing, thunderous, resounding, strident,

ear-splitting, rowdy, boisterous. *Antonyms*: **quiet**, **calm**, **peaceful**.

now *adv.* Let's talk about this problem now, before it gets worse. *Synonyms*: immediately, instantly, momentarily.

nuisance *n.* A dog that is not housebroken is a nuisance. *Synonyms*: pest, annoyance, irritation, affliction.

O o

obey *v.* A well-trained dog will obey its master. *Synonyms*: heed, follow orders, mind, be governed by, submit to. *Antonyms*: defy, revolt, rebel, mutiny, be insubordinate.

odd *adj.* The warthog is an odd animal. *Synonyms*: **different**, **unusual**, unlikely, peculiar, unexpected, unfamiliar; **special**, exotic, anachronistic. *Antonyms*: **common**, usual, expected, predictable, typical.

often *adv.* I often eat lunch with my friends. *Synonyms*: frequently, continually, repeatedly, constantly, usually, habitually. *Antonyms*: occasionally, sometimes, rarely, infrequently, seldom.

okay *adj.* He was okay after a night's sleep. *Synonyms*: all right, adequate, acceptable, appropriate.

old *adj.* The old house needed paint and a new roof. *Synonyms*: aged, ancient, historic, quaint, antique. *Antonyms*: **new**, up-to-date, modern.

only *adv.* There was only one way to get across the rushing river. *Synonyms*: solely, merely, uniquely, singly.

orange *adj.* One by one, the orange pumpkins were sold. *Synonyms*: gold, ocher, tangerine, apricot, peach.

order *v.* The umpire will order the player from the game. *Synonyms*: command, direct, bid, **rule**, dictate, compel.

ordinary *adj.* On an ordinary weekday, I get up, eat breakfast, and go to school. *Synonyms*: customary, standard, routine, regular, typical, pedestrian, conventional. *Antonyms*: **odd**, outlandish.

ooze *v.* Mud will ooze between my toes when I step into the stream. *Synonyms*: emanate, seep. *Antonyms*: accumulate, **absorb**.

other *adj.* Put your weight on the other foot. *Synonyms*: opposite, alternate, competing, rival.

outdoors *n.* I enjoy the outdoors during the summer months. *Synonyms*: wilderness, nature, countryside, scenery.

P p

pain *n.* I told the dentist about the pain in my tooth. *Synonyms*: ache, discomfort, distress, suffering, soreness. *Antonyms*: pleasure, amusement, enjoyment.

part *n.* Can you find the missing part of this puzzle? *Synonyms*: **piece**, fragment, ingredient, fraction, portion, element, quality, vestige, segment.

peaceful *adj.* It was peaceful in the mountains. *Synonyms*: **calm**, safe, serene, still, tranquil, secure. *Antonyms*: **dangerous**, **noisy**, tumultuous.

peculiar *adj.* There was a peculiar smell in the old barn. *Synonyms*: strange, distinctive, **odd**. *Antonyms*: **ordinary**, expected, predictable, commonplace.

people *n.* The people who lived in the town were very proud of the park. *Synonyms*: humans, folk, population.

permit *v.* The guard will permit you to enter if you have a pass. *Synonyms*: grant, allow, let, regulate.

person *n.* Every person deserves enough food to eat. *Synonyms*: human, individual, mortal.

picture *n.* Gilbert Stuart painted a famous picture of George Washington. *Synonyms*: drawing, photograph, design, display, portrait, diagram, etching, illustration, outline, silhouette.

piece *n.* Please look for the missing piece of jewelry. *Synonyms*: shred, slice, patch, strip, scrap, share, fragment, morsel, quantity, portion, **bit**.

pit *n.* We dug a pit and buried the trash. *Synonyms*: cavity, **hole**, abyss, hollow, crater, depression.

pitiful *adj.* The frightened puppy made a pitiful whimper. *Synonyms*: piteous, forlorn, woebegone, pathetic, heartbreaking, mournful, poignant. *Antonyms*: happy, contented, merry, glad.

place *n.* This looks like a good place for a picnic. *Synonyms*: point, space, area, position, scene, locality, location, section, region, spot.

plan *n.* Our club made a plan for raising money. *Synonyms*: method, scheme, proposal, design, strategy. *Antonyms*: impulse, improvisation, spontaneity.

plant *n.* A tomato plant needs plenty of sunlight to grow. *Synonyms*: shoot, sprout, weed, vegetation, shrub, flora.

play *v.* Let's play a game of checkers. *Synonyms*: have fun, romp, amuse oneself, frolic.

plenty *n.* We have plenty of gas for the rest of our trip. *Synonyms*: abundance, sufficiency, ample amount, enough. *Antonyms*: scarcity, shortage, dearth.

plod *v.* The oxen slowly plod along the dusty road. *Synonyms*: slouch, lumber, lurch, straggle, shuffle, trudge.

polite *adj.* Polite people say "please" and "thank you." *Synonyms*: respectful, decorous, mannerly, well-mannered, tactful, civil, courteous. *Antonyms*: impolite, **rude**, arrogant, pompous, outrageous, offhand.

poor *adj.* Jane Addams helped poor people in the slums of Chicago. *Synonyms*: destitute, impoverished, needy. *Antonyms*: **rich**, affluent, wealthy, well-off.

practice *v.* Pianists practice playing scales several hours each day. *Synonyms*: drill, train, rehearse.

praise *v.* Her friends praise her for winning the swimming race. *Synonyms*: flatter, congratulate, commend, **compliment**, acclaim. *Antonyms*: condemn, blame, denounce, belittle.

pretty *adj.* New curtains made the room look pretty. *Synonyms*: attractive, pleasing, beautiful, delicate, charming, comely. *Antonyms*: plain, **ugly**, hideous, grotesque.

private *adj.* No one overheard our private conversation. *Synonyms*: confidential, exclusive, personal, secret. *Antonyms*: **public**, open, unconcealed, known.

problem *n.* Smog is a problem in every major city. *Synonyms*: plight, difficulty, predicament. *Antonyms*: solution, answer, resolution.

promise *v.* I promise that I will always tell you the truth. *Synonyms*: swear, vow, assure, pledge, guarantee.

proper *adj.* They took lessons to learn the proper way to swim. *Synonyms*: correct, appropriate, suitable, accurate, accepted, acceptable. *Antonyms*: **wrong**, misjudged, ill-timed, inaccurate.

proud *adj.* Our team is the proud winner of the trophy. *Synonyms*: pleased, happy, satisfied, filled with pride. *Antonyms*: humble, ashamed, ignoble, apologetic.

prove *v.* You can prove there are two hundred beans in the jar by counting them. *Synonyms*: verify, certify, document, attest. *Antonyms*: disprove, refute, reject.

public *adj.* All children can attend public school. *Synonyms*: civic, popular, common, open, shared. *Antonyms*: **private**, closed, restricted, exclusive.

pull *v.* You will pull all the weeds out of the garden. *Synonyms*: drag, **jerk**, pluck, yank, tug, tow. *Antonyms*: **push**, shove.

punishment *n.* The Constitution of the United States forbids cruel and unusual punishment. *Synonyms*: penalty, sentence.

pure *adj.* Pure water came from mountain springs. *Synonyms*: refined, clear, unpolluted, wholesome, distilled.

purple *adj.* Irises, pansies, gladiolas, and crocuses often have purple flowers. *Synonyms*: violet, lavender, lilac.

push *v.* We had to push the car to get it started. *Synonyms*: shove, press, drive, force, prod, nudge, propel. *Antonym*: **pull**.

put *v.* Put the dishes on the table, please. *Synonyms*: set, place, rest, position, deposit. *Antonyms*: remove, misplace, raise.

put up with *v.* The bus driver will put up with a lot of noise, but no horseplay. *Synonyms*: tolerate, endure.

Q q

question *v.* A lawyer must question every witness. *Synonyms*: interview, consult, interrogate, inquire, **ask**.

quick *adj.* We only have time for a quick visit. *Synonyms*: fast, hasty, rapid, swift, speedy, sudden. *Antonyms*: **slow**, plodding, **lazy**, **dull**, **boring**.

quiet *adj.* The library is a quiet place. *Synonyms*: silent, hushed, muffled, placid, subdued, mute, speechless, noiseless, mum, still, motionless. *Antonyms*: **noisy**, loud, talkative.

quit *v.* The car quit when it ran out of gas. *Synonyms*: stop, resign, cease. *Antonym*: continue.

R r

race *v.* I had to race to school because I was late. *Synonyms*: **hurry**, rush, **run**, dash, speed. *Antonyms*: **wander**, saunter, graze, browse.

rain *n.* Clouds gathered, and rain began to fall. *Synonyms*: drizzle, shower, cloudburst, torrent, downpour, deluge, sprinkle. *Antonyms*: drought, dry spell.

rare *adj.* Condors became so rare, they almost died out. *Synonyms*: **unusual**, unexpected, uncommon. *Antonym*: **ordinary**.

real *adj.* These gloves are made of real leather. *Synonyms*: authentic, genuine, actual. *Antonyms*: **make-believe**, pretend.

reason *n*. You have no reason to blame me. *Synonyms*: cause, motive, grounds, explanation, rationale. *Antonyms*: mystery, question.

rebel *n*. King George III tried to punish every rebel in his American colonies. *Synonyms*: malcontent, mutineer, revolutionary, traitor. *Antonym*: loyalist.

red *adj*. His face turned red when he blushed. *Synonyms*: cherry, pink, rose, coral, crimson, scarlet, ruby, cranberry, ruddy, maroon, vermilion.

refuse *v*. They refuse to clean up because they didn't make the mess. *Synonyms*: scorn, spurn, shun, reject, decline, oppose. *Antonyms*: **agree**, assent, conform to, concur.

rescue *v*. The mountain patrol will rescue the injured skier. *Synonyms*: **save**, aid, liberate, deliver from. *Antonyms*: capture, endanger, abandon.

respect *v*. I respect you for your honesty. *Synonyms*: esteem, revere, look up to, honor. *Antonyms*: **ignore**, disregard, pay no attention to, scorn.

return *v*. Throw a ball against a wall and it will return to you. *Synonyms*: come back, reappear, retreat, restore. *Antonyms*: depart, desert, flee.

rhythm *n*. The rhythm of the drums kept us marching in time. *Synonyms*: beat, cadence, cycle, frequency.

rich *adj*. Rich people used to cross the Atlantic on ocean liners. *Synonyms*: well-off, wealthy, affluent, moneyed, prosperous. *Antonyms*: **poor**, impoverished.

right *adj*. Who can tell me the right answer to this problem? *Synonyms*: **proper**, correct, accurate, just. *Antonyms*: incorrect, unfit, untrustworthy.

rock *n*. The continents rest on a layer of dense rock. *Synonyms*: stone, pebble, cobblestone, boulder, gravel, ore, mineral, crystal.

round *adj*. A round wall circled the garden. *Synonyms*: circular, curved, spherical, oval. *Antonyms*: straight, flat, angular.

rub *v*. You can rub your hands together to keep them warm. *Synonyms*: stroke, chafe, massage.

rude *adj*. I will not put up with rude remarks. *Synonyms*: inconsiderate, impolite, impudent, offhand, discourteous, bad-mannered. *Antonyms*: **polite**, courteous, considerate.

ruins *n*. The ruins of the old castle were covered with vines. *Synonyms*: remains, rubble, relics, devastation.

rule *v*. Elected officials rule a democratic nation. *Synonyms*: command, direct, **order**, instruct, require, govern, reign, have jurisdiction over, regulate, enforce.

run *v*. The sprinters run around a practice track. *Synonyms*: jog, dash, dart, gallop, **race**, trot, zoom, bolt, scurry, stampede, rampage, lope, flee, romp, scamper, scuttle, sprint, canter.

S s

sad *adj*. It was a sad day for the losing team. *Synonyms*: gloomy, unhappy, miserable, discouraged, **disappointed**, grim, sorrowful, pitiful, wistful, regretful, lamenting, tragic, homesick, melancholy, moping, rueful, woeful, anguished, dejected, tearful, bleak, dismal, desolate, forlorn. *Antonyms*: **happy**, **cheerful**, enjoyable.

said *v*. I said I would go. See **say**.

save *v*. Please save these newspapers for the paper drive. *Synonyms*: keep, put aside, store, reserve, hold on to. *Antonyms*: discard, throw away, spend.

say *v*. Did you say it was time to study? *Synonyms*: speak, remark, state, express, utter, announce, declare, **demand**, **tell**, pronounce, mention.

saying *n*. ''The early bird gets the worm'' is an old saying. *Synonyms*: proverb, motto, adage, maxim.

scare *v*. Loud noises scare away the birds. *Synonyms*: frighten, terrify, startle, make afraid, alarm, intimidate. *Antonyms*: **comfort**, embolden, soothe, reassure.

search *v.* The family went to search for pine cones in the woods. *Synonyms*: examine, ransack, hunt, seek, forage for.

second *n.* The doctor will be with you in a second. *Synonyms*: moment, minute, flash, instant. *Antonym*: eternity.

secret *adj.* I hid my money in a secret place. *Synonyms*: buried, hidden, private, mysterious, masked, concealed, disguised, undercover, stealthy, furtive, covert, obscure, camouflaged. *Antonym*: **public**

see *v.* You can see the mountaintop on a clear day. *Synonyms*: discern, notice, sight, spot, discover, view, recognize, **understand**, comprehend. *Antonyms*: overlook, wink at.

selfish *adj.* The selfish boy kept all the popcorn for himself. *Synonyms*: stingy, greedy, grudging. *Antonyms*: openhanded, generous, hospitable.

sell *v.* I might sell the extra vegetables from my garden. *Synonyms*: peddle, vend, market, auction off.

send *v.* Let's send a postcard to our friends. *Synonyms*: post, mail, transmit, dispatch, direct.

sense *v.* I can sense a change in your mood. *Synonyms*: detect, distinguish, perceive, feel.

serious *adj.* The serious faces show the importance of the occasion. *Synonyms*: grave, solemn, earnest, sober, somber. *Antonyms*: amused, **carefree**.

shake *v.* We will shake apples off the tree. *Synonyms*: shiver, vibrate, **wiggle**, wobble, sway, waver, quiver, totter, undulate.

shape *v.* You can shape the clay into a ball. *Synonyms*: form, arrange, mold, model, fashion. *Antonyms*: destroy, disintegrate, jumble up.

share *v.* We can share our remaining apple between us. *Synonyms*: **divide**, allocate, split, cooperate. *Antonyms*: hoard, stockpile.

sharp *adj.* The sharp scissors easily cut the paper. *Synonyms*: keen, honed, razor-edged, acute. *Antonyms*: **dull**, blunt, blunted, unsharpened.

shining *adj.* The star twinkled with a shining light. *Synonyms*: gleaming, **bright**, radiant, glowing, sparkling. *Antonyms*: **dull**, **dark**, muddy.

shout *v.* The fans of the winning team always shout the loudest. *Synonyms*: **call**, cheer, exclaim, scream, yell.

show *v.* Show the new student where to find the cafeteria. *Synonyms*: indicate, reveal, point out, display.

show up *v.* Our cats disappear during the day, but they always show up for dinner. *Synonyms*: appear, attend, arrive, be present, make an entrance. *Antonyms*: **leave**, exit, disappear, vanish.

shy *adj.* As a new student, she was very shy in the classroom. *Synonyms*: timid, bashful, skittish, modest, withdrawn, introverted; **ashamed**. *Antonyms*: outgoing, sociable, sophisticated, extroverted, arrogant, confident, boastful.

sick *adj.* The doctor healed the sick patient. *Synonyms*: ill, feverish, aching, itchy, diseased, infected, weak, ailing, injured, stricken. *Antonyms*: healthy, hale, vigorous.

silence *n.* The silence was broken by the sound of laughing children. *Synonyms*: **calm**, quietness, peace, stillness, lull. *Antonyms*: **noise**, sound, pandemonium.

silly *adj.* The comedian told a silly joke. *Synonyms*: absurd, ridiculous, stupid, inane. *Antonyms*: serious, profound.

simple *adj.* The problem looks complicated, but the solution is simple. *Synonyms*: uncomplicated, plain, basic, rudimentary, elementary, unadorned. *Antonyms*: elaborate, complex, intricate.

skill *n.* It takes skill to use a potter's wheel. *Synonyms*: art, craft, ability, cleverness, capacity, prowess.

sleep *v.* Many people snore when they sleep. *Synonyms*: doze, slumber, nap, snooze.

slide *v.* Let's slide down the water chute. *Synonyms*: glide, slip, slither, lunge, skid.

Thesaurus

slow *adj.* The slow truck delayed traffic. *Synonyms*: gradual, lingering, sluggish, static, slothful, indolent. *Antonyms*: lightning-fast, rapid, speedy, swift, **quick**, accelerated.

sly *adj.* With a sly wink, the magician made the scarf disappear. *Synonyms*: crafty, cunning, stealthy, mischievous, furtive. *Antonyms*: open, direct.

small *adj.* Only two hunters could stay in the small cabin. *Synonyms*: **little**, narrow, short, thin, tiny, dainty, minute, wee, midget, compact, infinitesimal. *Antonyms*: **big**, large, giant, gigantic.

smaller *adj.* We bought the smaller table rather than the large one. *Synonyms*: dwindling, ebbing, reduced, shriveled, contracted, diminished, waning, excerpted. *Antonyms*: **bigger**, extended, waxing.

smart *adj.* The smart shopper takes advantage of sales. *Synonyms*: able, brainy, **clever**, gifted, intelligent, thoughtful, wise, cunning, shrewd, ingenious, brilliant.

smash *v.* The egg smashed when it dropped on the floor. *Synonyms*: break, shatter, demolish, crack.

smell *n.* The smell of roses filled the air. *Synonyms*: scent, aroma, odor, fragrance, perfume.

smile *n.* The smile on her face was sincere. *Synonym*: grin. *Antonyms*: wince, frown, grimace.

smooth *adj.* The smooth water reflected the sky like a mirror. *Synonyms*: flat, **calm**, even, slick, polished. *Antonyms*: bumpy, rough, ragged.

snap *v.* If you stand on that board, it will snap in two. *Synonyms*: break, crack, fracture.

snow *n.* The rain turned to snow when the temperature dropped below freezing. *Synonyms*: frost, blizzard, sleet, ice.

soak *v.* Soak your tired feet in warm water. *Synonyms*: steep, drench, douse, quench.

soft *adj.* The soft clay was easy to shape. *Synonyms*: pliant, slack. *Antonyms*: **hard**, firm, rigid.

solid *adj.* They stopped digging when they hit solid rock. *Synonyms*: dense, sturdy, concrete, substantial, hard, firm, durable. *Antonyms*: liquid, gaseous, **soft**.

sometimes *adv.*. Sometimes I forget to feed the dog; then my parents forget my allowance. *Synonyms*: periodically, randomly, occasionally.

song *n.* The robin's song is cheerful in the spring. *Synonyms*: music, tune, melody, rhythm, carol, incantation, lullaby, refrain.

sound *n.* The sound of cheering came from the stadium. *Synonyms*: **noise**, din, racket, clatter. *Antonyms*: **silence**, stillness, peace, quiet.

special *adj.* Staying up late was a special treat. *Synonyms*: particular, **rare**, choice, delightful, precious.

spirit *n.* The cheerleaders showed their school spirit. *Synonyms*: temper, mood, disposition, personality.

squeeze *v.* I like to squeeze fresh orange juice for breakfast. *Synonyms*: press, pinch, compress, wring, draw out.

start *v.* Even junior high school students may start planning their careers. *Synonyms*: begin, originate, initiate, activate, commence, set in motion. *Antonym*: **stop**.

stay *v.* Please stay in your seats until the bell rings. *Synonyms*: wait, continue, remain, linger, persist. *Antonyms*: **leave**, depart, flee.

stoop *v.* Stoop down and pick up the newspaper. *Synonyms*: kneel, squat, slump, bend down, slouch, crouch down, hunch over.

stop *v.* Stop, look, and listen at railroad crossings. *Synonyms*: brake, halt, pause, suspend, hesitate, **quit**, stifle, forbid, stall, falter, cease, interrupt, block, hinder, cancel, immobilize, subside.

story *n.* The author wrote a mystery story. *Synonyms*: tale, narrative, account, fable, anecdote.

strange *adj.* That mask gives you a strange appearance. *Synonyms*: peculiar, freakish, freaky, odd, unusual. *Antonyms*: **common**, normal.

strict *adj.* Strict laws governed the Roman Empire. *Synonyms*: harsh, stern, severe. *Antonyms*: easygoing, casual, nonchalant, mellow.

string *n.* We used yards of string to fly the kite. *Synonyms*: cord, lace, rope, thread, yarn, strand, tassel, twine, fiber.

strong *adj.* Exercise builds a strong body. *Synonyms*: powerful, hardy, athletic, staunch, robust, muscular, impregnable. *Antonyms*: weak, feeble, fragile, vulnerable.

stubborn *adj.* The stubborn mule refused to move. *Synonyms*: obstinate, **determined**, headstrong, willful, persevering. *Antonyms*: flexible, wishy-washy, docile.

stupid *adj.* I wasn't paying attention and made a stupid mistake. *Synonyms*: backward, dim, **dull**, foolish, silly, idiotic, scatterbrained. *Antonyms*: **clever**, thoughtful, intelligent.

suggest *v.* Can you suggest a different title for my story? *Synonyms*: propose, recommend.

sulky *adj.* My sulky friend would not attend the party after his feelings were hurt. *Synonyms*: sullen, resentful, huffy. *Antonyms*: **cheerful**, willing, helpful.

sure *adj.* You are a sure winner because you have practiced so hard. *Synonyms*: certain, inevitable, unfailing.

surprising *adj.* The novel had a surprising end—the hero lost. *Synonyms*: unforeseen, unexpected, astonishing, stunning, startling. *Antonyms*: predictable, standard, routine.

surprise *v.* My friends surprised me with a birthday party. *Synonyms*: amaze, astonish, astound, dumbfound, take aback, stun, startle. *Antonyms*: bore, lull.

suspect *v.* Astronomers suspect that other stars may have planets. *Synonyms*: imagine, conjecture, believe, think, presume, suppose, guess.

swamp *n..* Cypress trees grow in the shallow water of a swamp. *Synonyms*: bog, mire, marsh, mud flat.

sweet *adj.* The baby gave us a sweet smile. *Synonyms*: agreeable, nice, pleasant, dear, lovable. *Antonyms*: disagreeable, nasty, unpleasant, **mean**.

swim *v.* A lifeguard can swim through the breakers. *Synonyms*: paddle, float, bob.

T t

take (1) *v.* What clothes should we take on the camping trip? *Synonyms*: transport, tote, deliver, **carry**, lug. *Antonyms*: **return**, bring back.

take (2) *v.* Did you take a book from the shelf? *Synonyms*: remove, grab, get, seize, capture. *Antonyms*: restore, give back, surrender, **give**.

take care of *v.* Who will take care of the garden while we are away? *Synonyms*: tend, attend to, mind, nurture. *Antonyms*: neglect, **abandon**, overlook, not bother with.

talk *v.* She likes to talk with children about their hobbies. *Synonyms*: chat, chatter, gossip, speak, recite, jabber, drone on, preach at, lecture, babble.

tasty *adj.* That was a tasty sandwich that you made yesterday. *Synonyms*: delicious, luscious, flavorful, savory. *Antonyms*: bitter, stale.

teach *v.* A geography book can teach us many things about the earth. *Synonyms*: instruct, explain, demonstrate, enlighten, educate.

tease *v.* Bullies often like to tease. *Synonyms*: taunt, mock, threaten, scorn, jeer, sneer at, mimic, ridicule, scoff at. *Antonyms*: **praise**, **compliment**, encourage.

tell *v.* A traveler can often tell interesting stories. *Synonyms*: declare, relate, narrate, recount, announce, remark, inform, notify.

Thesaurus

tend *v.* Plants tend to grow toward the light. *Synonyms*: prefer, lean toward, incline. *Antonyms*: avoid, reject.

test *v.* Test the temperature of the water with a thermometer. *Synonyms*: examine, measure, investigate, check. *Antonyms*: **ignore**, assume.

thankful *adj.* The thankful parent was happy to find the child safe from harm. *Synonyms*: grateful, appreciative.

thick *adj.* Thick fog made it difficult to see the road. *Synonyms*: dense, **solid**, broad, heavy. *Antonyms*: **light**, flimsy, **soft**, **thin**.

thin *adj.* Violin strings are very thin. *Synonyms*: slim, skinny, slender, slight, spindly, lanky. *Antonyms*: wide, **thick**, broad, fat.

thing *n.* What is that thing you found in the attic? *Synonyms*: object, utensil, artifact, article, item, device, specimen, substance, possession, belonging. *Antonyms*: nothing, vacuum, void.

think *v.* Do you think about what you will do with your life? *Synonyms*: ponder, reflect, deliberate, **wonder**, imagine, mull over, analyze.

threat *n.* The dark clouds held a threat of rain. *Synonyms*: danger, menace, **warning**. *Antonyms*: promise, reward.

throw *v.* Please throw the ball back to the players. *Synonyms*: heave, hurl, launch, chuck, fling, lob, pelt. *Antonyms*: **catch**, snare, snag.

throw out *v.* Spring cleaning is a time to throw out old junk. *Synonyms*: discard, eject, reject. *Antonyms*: conserve, **keep**, retain, recycle.

tight *adj.* The string is so tight that it's ready to break. *Synonyms*: tense, taut. *Antonyms*: loose, slack.

time *n.* The time for wearing winter clothes will end soon. *Synonyms*: term, episode, period, interval.

tired *adj.* The tired swimmers have finished the race. *Synonyms*: worn out, exhausted, weary, run-down, listless. *Antonyms*: brisk, frisky, sprightly, alert, peppy.

together *adv.* Please keep all the silverware together. *Synonyms*: collectively, jointly, in unison, simultaneously.

tool *n.* A drill is a handy tool for making holes. *Synonyms*: equipment, machine, device, instrument, invention, apparatus, **machinery**, contrivance, gadget, implement.

top *n.* We walked to the top of the hill and looked down. *Synonyms*: surface, crest, summit, pinnacle. *Antonyms*: bottom, base, foundation.

touch *v.* The runner did not touch the base. *Synonyms*: brush, rub, pat, tag, tap, tickle, handle, stroke, caress, nudge.

trick *v.* That's an old way to trick people, but no one will fall for it. *Synonyms*: outwit, puzzle, fool, betray, play a prank on, hoax, ambush.

trip *n.* The trip to the mountains was fun. *Synonyms*: tour, journey, flight, voyage, cruise, expedition, excursion, odyssey, wanderings, migration, safari.

trust *v.* I trust you to repay me. *Synonyms*: believe, depend on, have confidence in. *Antonyms*: distrust, suspect.

truthful *adj.* A truthful person never tells lies. *Synonyms*: frank, honest, candid. *Antonyms*: lying, cheating, deceitful.

try *v.* Try to do your best work. *Synonyms*: attempt, persist, strive, endeavor, aim, essay. *Antonyms*: give up, surrender, desist.

turn *v.* Turn the dial to another channel. *Synonyms*: twirl, crank, spin, whirl, rotate, revolve, gnarl, twist, swivel, coil, veer, pivot.

two *adj.* Beginners should use two hands to catch a ball. *Synonyms*: both, dual, twin, double.

U u

ugly *adj.* The ugly house became beautiful with a fresh coat of paint. *Synonyms*: bad-looking, hideous, unbecoming, disgusting, repellant. *Antonyms*: **attractive**, beautiful, handsome, **pretty**, comely.

under *adv.* The struggling business almost went under. *Synonyms*: **below**, beneath, down. *Antonyms*: **above**, over, aloft.

undercover *adj.* The undercover operation was known by a code name. *Synonyms*: concealed, **secret**, top-security. *Antonyms*: **public**, acknowledged.

understand *v.* I try to understand many scientific theories. *Synonyms*: comprehend, grasp, interpret, fathom. *Antonyms*: misjudge, misconceive.

understanding *adj.* The teacher was very understanding about the mix-up. *Synonyms*: compassionate, reassuring, soothing, sympathetic. *Antonyms*: intolerant, insensitive, unfeeling.

undo *v.* Undo your shoelaces before you take off your shoes. *Synonyms*: untie, unfold, unwrap. *Antonyms*: fasten, secure, strap down, restrain.

unusual *adj.* We had an unusual amount of snow last winter. *Synonyms*: **odd**, **rare**, **strange**, remarkable, extraordinary, unbelievable. *Antonyms*: **common**, everyday, down-to-earth.

upright *adj.* The upright piano was against the wall. *Synonyms*: vertical, perpendicular, erect. *Antonyms*: flat, horizontal.

upset *v.* The loss upset the team. *Synonyms*: bother, disturb, dismay, disconcert, ruffle, confuse. *Antonyms*: calm, reassure, soothe, pacify.

use *v.* I use my computer to play games. *Synonyms*: employ, utilize, handle, manipulate. *Antonyms*: discard, reject, shun, let sit idle.

useless *adj.* Many acres of land are useless for raising crops, but good for grazing cattle. *Synonyms*: futile, unhelpful, inadequate, unusable, ineffective. *Antonyms*: useful, productive, profitable, practical.

V v

vain *adj.* A vain person is forever looking in the mirror. *Synonyms*: conceited, proud, self-satisfied. *Antonyms*: modest, humble, meek.

valley *n.* The valley ran between two mountain ranges. *Synonyms*: canyon, gully, gorge, arroyo, ravine, gulch. *Antonyms*: hill, peak, mountain, mountain range.

value *v.* I value the gift of my grandmother's necklace. *Synonyms*: prize, cherish, treasure. *Antonyms*: disregard, be contemptuous of.

vanish *v.* The dew will vanish when the sun comes up. *Synonyms*: dissolve, evaporate, disintegrate, disappear. *Antonyms*: appear, materialize, become substantial.

vast *adj.* The vast forest covered hundreds of square miles. *Synonyms*: large, huge, extensive, enormous, boundless, **great**. *Antonyms*: **small**, limited, narrow.

villain *n.* The villain was punished at the end of the story. *Synonyms*: scoundrel, rascal, fink, knave, trickster, scamp. *Antonym*: **hero**.

W w

wait *v.* I will wait for the next bus. *Synonyms*: stand, rest, be still, perch, settle in, remain, bide one's time.

waiting *adj.* He stepped into the waiting cab. *Synonyms*: lingering, remaining, tarrying.

walk *v.* Don't drive—let's walk to the park. *Synonyms*: **march**, strut, pace, stride, step, hike, **plod**, stroll, prance, skitter, tread, sidle, promenade.

wander *v.* I wander through the meadow on sunny afternoons. *Synonyms*: drift, roam, stray, dawdle, stroll, amble, saunter.

want *v.* Do you want a glass of water? *Synonyms*: desire, long for, wish for, need, crave.

warning *n.* The blinking red light is a warning of danger. *Synonyms*: advice, caution, omen, **threat**, tip-off.

water *n.* The water was clear and cool. *Synonyms*: flood, rain, stream, tide, wave, river, lake, ocean.

wavy *adj.* There are wavy lines on the screen when your TV is not adjusted. *Synonyms*: sinuous, serpentine. *Antonyms*: straight, direct, unwavering.

weird *adj.* Weird noises were heard coming from the old, deserted house. *Synonyms*: **strange**, awesome, creepy, eerie. *Antonyms*: normal, **common**, average, regular, everyday, explainable.

well-dressed *adj.* At noon, the streets of the big city were crowded with well-dressed people. *Synonyms*: dressy, natty, dashing, classy, smart, chic. *Antonyms*: sloppy, frumpy.

wet *adj.* The wet sidewalk glistened after the rain. *Synonyms*: damp, melting, moist, humid, slippery, sodden, drenched. *Antonyms*: **dry**, arid, parched.

whisper *v.* I will whisper a secret in your ear. *Synonyms*: mumble, mutter, murmur. *Antonyms*: **shout**, yell, exclaim.

white *adj.* White snow covered the fields. *Synonyms*: ivory, pearl.

wiggle *v.* Waiting for recess, the students started to wiggle in their seats. *Synonyms*: squirm, fidget, writhe.

wild *adj.* Wild dogs roam this part of the forest. *Synonyms*: untamed, unruly, feral. *Antonyms*: tame, domesticated, **calm**.

wind *n.* Wind scattered the leaves. *Synonyms*: breeze, gust, twister, whirlwind, tornado, cyclone.

winning *adj.* The winning team got the trophy. *Synonyms*: successful, victorious, triumphant. *Antonyms*: failing, defeated, ruined, outdone.

wipe *v.* Wipe up the spilled milk. *Synonyms*: **clean**, polish, swab, mop.

wish *v.* Did you ever wish for a million dollars? *Synonyms*: want, hope, desire, request.

wonder *v.* I wonder if it will rain tomorrow. *Synonyms*: **question**, **doubt**, be uncertain.

wonderful *adj.* We saw a wonderful dinosaur exhibit at the museum. *Synonyms*: marvelous, fantastic, wondrous, miraculous.

worn-out *adj.* The worn-out shoes fell apart. *Synonyms*: **tired**, used up, damaged. *Antonyms*: brand-new, untouched.

worried *adj.* The worried coach hoped for a victory. *Synonyms*: concerned, alarmed, anxious, dismayed, distressed, fretful, apprehensive, troubled. *Antonyms*: relieved, carefree.

wrap *v.* Wrap yourself in a warm blanket. *Synonyms*: drape, encase, enclose.

writing *n.* She uses expressive words in her writing. *Synonyms*: prose, poetry, composition, report, essay, script, inscription.

wrong *adj.* We took a wrong turn and arrived late. *Synonyms*: incorrect, erroneous, mistaken, false, improper. *Antonyms*: **right**, correct, true, **proper**, suitable.

Y y

yellow *adj.* The yellow sun shone in the clear sky. *Synonyms*: blond, lemon, canary, saffron.

Z z

zero *n.* The score of the game was zero to one. *Synonyms*: nothing, naught. *Antonyms*: everything, infinity.

zone *n.* It is hot in the zone around the equator. *Synonyms*: region, area, belt, sector.

Writing Handbook

Type of Writing: Personal Narrative

A **personal narrative** has these characteristics:

◆ It tells about a real or imaginary incident that happened to the writer or narrator.
◆ It usually describes the events in the order they happened.
◆ It mentions the time, place, and people involved.
◆ It is told from the writer's point of view and uses words such as *I*, *me*, and *my*.
◆ It relates the writer's or narrator's thoughts and feelings about the experience.

In writing personal narratives, writers draw from their experiences to create true or imagined personal stories. When reading effective personal narratives, readers often identify with a writer's feelings and recognize that they are not alone in their experiences.

Writing About Personal Narratives

1. What can you, as a writer, possibly gain by sharing with a reader a story about some incident in your life? Explain your answer in a paragraph.
2. Recall something funny that happened to you. Describe the incident in a brief paragraph. Then write a few sentences telling what you learned from the experience.

Reading More Personal Narratives

Koehl, Ilse. <u>Mischling, Second Degree: My Childhood in Nazi Germany.</u> New York: Greenwillow Books, 1977.
In this moving personal narrative, the author describes how her half-Jewish father separated from her and her mother in order to protect them from the Nazis.

North, Sterling. <u>Rascal.</u> New York: Dutton, 1963.
This is the true story of the author's childhood in Wisconsin. As an eleven-year-old boy, he biked everywhere in his small village. He was accompanied by his favorite pet, a racoon named Rascal, who rode in the basket.

Type of Writing: Biographical Sketch

A **biographical sketch** has these characteristics:

◆ It gives information about the life of a real person.
◆ It usually tells important events in the person's life.
◆ It describes the person's most important achievements.
◆ It tells what events shaped the person's life.

The writer of a biographical sketch may be just as important as the person being written about. This is because the writer is the one who selects all the physical descriptions and all the incidents that are included in the sketch.

1. Suppose you wrote a biographical sketch about a friend you liked very much. If you wrote about this friend again after the two of you had an argument, how would your sketch be different? Which of the following do you think would change: the physical description, details of incidents, comments about your relationship? Or would your sketch not be different at all? Summarize your thoughts in a paragraph or two.

2. An interview is a way of getting information for a biographical sketch. Think of a person you admire. Then write five questions you would ask this person. Remember, a biographical sketch usually focuses on one major incident or one period of time in a person's life.

Reading More Biographies

Tassin, Myron. Bob Mathias: The Life of the Olympic Champion. New York: St. Martin's Press, 1983.
  Bob Mathias tells how he trained for and won the decathlon, at age 17, in the 1948 Olympics.

Wilson, D.C. I Will Be a Doctor! The Story of America's First Woman Physician. Nashville, Tenn: Abingdon Press, 1983.
  When Elizabeth Blackwell was a child, her father encouraged her to become a physician. At the time, there were no women doctors in America.

Type of Writing: Book Report

A **book report** has these characteristics:
◆ It names the title and author of the book.
◆ It identifies the main characters and the setting.
◆ It summarizes the story without giving away the ending.
◆ It tells why the writer of the book report liked or disliked the book.

People read book reports and reviews when they want to know something about a particular book before they actually read it. The writer of a book report decides whether or not a book is appealing. The next task is to explain that decision to the reader. The writer should provide short summaries or examples from the book to back up his or her judgements.

Writing About Book Reports

1. If you were traveling into space for two years and could take any five important books, which books would you take? List and explain your choices.

2. Biographies are one type of nonfiction book. Write the names of ten well-known people you would like to know more about. Your list may include historical or political figures, athletes, inventors, scientists, and music or movie stars. In a sentence or two, tell how you would find out if a biography has been written about one of the people on your list.

Reading for Book Reports

Blos, Joan W. <u>A Gathering of Days: A New England Girl's Journal, 1830-1832; A Novel.</u> New York: Scribner, 1979.
   By reading Catherine's journal, the reader learns how she and her new stepmother overcome their initial reserve and eventually become friends.

Neville, Emily Cheney. <u>It's Like This, Cat.</u> New York: Harper & Row, 1963.
   Dave Mitchell, growing up in New York City, tells of his relationships with his parents and neighbors. A stray tom cat helps him make new friends and learn more about himself.

Type of Writing: Business and Friendly Letters

A **friendly letter** has these characteristics:
- It shares news with a friend or relative.
- It is written in casual language.
- It has a heading, greeting, body, closing, and signature.

A **business letter** has these characteristics:
- It requests information, orders merchandise, or makes a complaint.
- It is written in formal language.
- It has a heading, inside address, greeting, body, closing, and signature.

Letters speak for their writers. They express thoughts that can be read and reread by the people who receive them. Writers of friendly letters are able to share their feelings in a permanent way when they are apart from others they care about. A business letter is a formal communication. It allows the writer to explain, inform, inquire, request, or complain to a company or another individual.

Writing About Letters

1. Are there ways to begin a friendly letter that are more imaginative than "How are you? I am fine. The weather here is nice?" Are there ways to end a friendly letter that are more imaginative than "Well, I guess I'd better go now?" Write a good opening sentence and a good closing sentence for a letter to each of the following:
   a. a friend who has moved out of town
   b. a relative in another city
   c. a former teacher who has transferred to a different school
2. What kind of an impression will your business letter make if you have not corrected errors in capitalization, punctuation, spelling, and usage? What might happen to your letter if it is illegible? Explain your answers in a few complete sentences.

3. Why should you get right to the point of your message in a business letter? Explain your answer in a few complete sentences.

4. A business letter is a formal communication. Should you try to use your most advanced and complex vocabulary, or is it all right to use simple vocabulary? Explain your answer in a few complete sentences.

Reading More Letters

Sometimes the letters of famous people reveal more about them than a biography. A letter can describe a person's innermost feelings at a particular moment or capture a unique insight, both of which might be forgotten later.

Conford, Ellen. Dear Lovey Hart, I am Desperate. New York: Little Brown, 1975.

Using the name Lovey Hart, Carrie writes a column of advice to the lovelorn for her school paper. Her classmates write for answers to their problems, and Carrie provides solutions. When her letter writers take her seriously, trouble follows.

Lewis, C.S. Letters to Children. Edited by Lyle W. Dorsett. New York: Macmillan, 1985.

Readers who loved the Narnia stories wrote to C. S. Lewis with their questions about his stories. In his answers, Lewis comments on his books, discusses his plans for future adventure stories, and encourages would-be writers.

O'Neill, Cherry Boone. Dear Cherry: Questions and Answers on Eating Disorders. New York: Crossroad Continuum, 1985.

The author answers letters she has received and gives practical answers to people with bulimia and anorexia. You learn that both illnesses can be treated successfully. Because the author herself suffered from these problems, she understands and cares about others with the same disorders. Included are lists of sources where more information and help can be found.

421

Type of Writing: Descriptive Writing

Descriptive writing has these characteristics:
- It describes a particular person, place, or thing.
- It describes details that appeal to one or more of the five senses: sight, sound, touch, taste, and smell.
- It paints a vivid picture with precise and imaginative words.

Descriptive writing is an important part of almost all forms of written work. In creating descriptions, a writer tries to help the reader experience the subject just as if the reader were there.

Writing About Descriptive Writing

1. Imagine you are looking at yourself in a mirror. Choose one overall impression about yourself that you want to convey. Are you, for example, fun-loving, studious, worried, athletic, delicate? Write a one-paragraph description of yourself that uses specific details to create a particular impression.
2. Vivid verbs strengthen descriptive writing. For each of the underlined verbs, suggest two more vivid ones.
   - a. <u>walked</u> down the street
   - b. <u>ate</u> his food
   - c. <u>thought</u> about her future
   - d. <u>talked</u> on the phone
   - e. <u>drove</u> around the curve
   - f. <u>cut</u> the meat

Reading More Descriptive Writing

Taylor, Mildred. <u>Roll of Thunder Hear My Cry</u>. New York: Dial, 1976.

This historical novel features a black farming family during the Depression. The story is told by a character named Cassie. Readers experience the warmth, humor, and dignity of this family as it struggles to maintain independence and keep the farm despite difficult circumstances.

Yep, Laurence. <u>Child of the Owl.</u> New York: Harper & Row, 1977.

Sent to live with her grandmother in San Francisco's Chinatown in the early 1960s, Casey learns about her Chinese heritage and resolves her confusion about her sense of identity.

Type of Writing: Research Report

A **research report** has these characteristics:
◆ It gives information on a particular topic.
◆ The topic may be divided into several main ideas.
◆ Each main idea is supported by facts or details.
◆ All information in the report is true and based on research.

When seeking information for a research report, the writer may consult a variety of sources, including books, magazines, and newspapers. The writer has the important task of deciding which facts, statistics, examples, or other details to include in order to present an unbiased, balanced account of the subject.

Writing About the Research Report

1. Each of the popular magazines listed below might be a source of information for a research report.
   Omni, featuring science articles with futuristic themes
   Popular Mechanics, featuring articles about electronics and new technology
   Sports Illustrated, featuring information about sports competitions, athletes, and training
   Time, focusing on national and world events and issues
   Young Miss, featuring articles and stories for girls ages 12 to 17
   If you were writing research reports on the following topics, which of the magazines would you consult for each? You may list more than one magazine for each topic.
   a. information about Jimmy Carter's presidency
   b. instructions for installing a car stereo
   c. the latest trends in swimwear for girls
   d. using robots as house servants
   e. underwater homes
   f. the baseball teams in the World Series
2. If you want to use a card catalog to locate a book on your research topic, but cannot find one, what should you do next? Write your answer in a few complete sentences.

3. If the topic you choose for a research report is too broad, you could spend the rest of your life in a library collecting information! Instead, you will want to narrow your topic until it is limited enough to manage. At the same time, however, you want your topic to be broad enough, so that information will be available. Narrow each broad topic that follows to a more specific topic.

a. water sports
b. the planets
c. hobbies

d. mammals
e. the Civil War
f. Australia

Reading More Research Reports

The books listed below are examples of good research. They are also sources you might use for your own research on the topics they discuss.

Macaulay, David. Pyramid. New York: Houghton Mifflin, 1975.
    The author speculates on the methods that were probably used to construct the Egyptian pyramids. Detailed line drawings accompany the step-by-step analysis of each method. You will be impressed by the enormous human effort that was required to complete the pyramids.

Schlein, Miriam. Project Panda Watch. New York: Atheneum, 1984.
    Although there have been many attempts to study pandas, scientists still know little about them. The author describes the life of these animals in zoos in America, Mexico, and Europe. She also discusses an expedition to China to study pandas in their native environment.

Yue, Carlotte and David. The Tipi: A Center of Native American Life. New York: Knopf, 1984.
    The authors describe the many forms and uses of the tipi (teepee). They also discuss the way of life of the Blackfoot, Crow, Sioux, and other Native American tribes of the Great Plains.

Type of Writing: Persuasive Essay

A **persuasive essay** has these characteristics:
- It states an opinion about a particular topic.
- It aims to persuade readers to accept that opinion.
- A statement of the opinion appears at the beginning of the essay, and a restatement appears at the end.
- The opinion is supported by facts or examples.

There are many examples of persuasive language in everyday life. Consider, for example, advertising brochures, movie reviews, or politicians' speeches. Students use persuasive language when they try to convince their friends, parents, or teachers to think the way they do about a particular issue.

1. Are you good at convincing people? Choose one of the situations listed below. Write your "excuse" in one or two paragraphs. Remember, to be persuasive you need as many reasonable facts or examples as possible to support your side of the story.
   a. You forgot to do a homework assignment. Present your reasons to the teacher.
   b. You would like an increase in your allowance. Persuade your parents that this is a reasonable request.
   c. You have found a stray animal. Persuade your family to let you keep it.

2. People can be persuaded in different ways. Suppose you were writing a letter to persuade a group of people to vote either for or against the construction of a nuclear power plant in their neighborhood. For each of the people listed below, think about the kind of information that might persuade them to accept your point of view. Then write a sentence to describe the information you would stress in order to convince each person.
   a. a young parent with a new baby
   b. a store owner with five children
   c. the manager of a local convenience store
   d. a nuclear engineer
   e. sixth graders

425

3. What kind of information would be helpful to have about someone before you try to persuade them of your views on a particular topic? Write your answer in a few complete sentences.

4. "Every public-school student should be required to learn to play an instrument. Then every student could be in the school band. Every student in Japan is required to learn to play two musical instruments. So Japanese teenagers like music more than American teenagers."

This argument is not very persuasive. List all the things you think are wrong with the writer's reasoning.

Reading More Persuasive Essays

Each of the books below aims to persuade its readers to adopt a particular point of view. The authors back up their arguments with solid facts and logical reasoning.

Hendrich, Paula. <u>Saving America's Birds.</u> New York: Lothrop, Lee and Shepard Books, 1982.

The author's goal is to persuade the reader that it is important to preserve and protect the many species of birds that are becoming extinct. The author is convincing in her position that chemical pollution and careless human behavior are the greatest dangers to bird populations.

Meltzer, Milton. <u>The Human Rights Book.</u> New York: Farrar, Strauss and Giroux, 1979.

The author argues that human rights are being violated in many countries, such as Iran, South Africa, and the Soviet Union. He discusses how many governments imprison those people who disagree or agitate for political freedom. This work includes many historical documents that have guaranteed civil rights in some nations and also gives the historical background of particular violations.

Watson, Jane Werner. <u>Deserts of the World: Future Threat or Promise?</u> New York: Philomel Books, 1981.

The deserts are spreading, and fertile land is disappearing. Famines result. The author explains how and why this is happening and what must be done to reverse the global problem. Many photographs, maps, and diagrams help describe and explain the situation.

Type of Writing: Short Story

A **story** has these characteristics:
- It has a plot, or a series of events that occur.
- It has characters, or people and animals that take part in the events.
- It has a setting, or the time and place of the events.
- The introduction describes the characters and setting.
- The problem tells what difficulties a character faces.
- The solution attempts are the ways the characters try to solve the problem.
- The outcome tells how the problem is solved.

In creating short stories, writers share the special world of their imaginations. The stories may be about new places or familiar ones. They may include characters who are lovable or detestable, ordinary or extraordinary. The use of descriptive and narrative writing helps tell the story so the reader can easily enter the writer's world.

Writing About Short Stories

1. Rather than simply stating the setting of your short story, you can reveal time and place by giving details about clothing, technology, and the activities your characters engage in. For example, a character who has a home computer clearly lives in the 1970s or later. Decide on a setting, such as a Midwestern farm in the 1890s, or a spaceship in the year 2015. State the time and place. Then write one paragraph that suggests the setting to the reader. Use sensory details, especially sights, sounds, and smells.

2. Symbolism is the use of a person, place, thing, or event to represent an idea or a concept. For example, in a short story about the wild west, an unbroken horse might symbolize freedom. Look at the list of concepts and characters below. If you were to write short stories about them, name an object you could use to symbolize the concept for each character.

   a. What could symbolize independence to a teen-ager?

   b. What could symbolize freedom to a sailor?

   c. What could symbolize friendship to a student entering a new school?

3. Including dialogue in your short story is an effective way to let the reader know what the characters are like. Imagine two twelve-year-olds meeting on the playground after school to discuss how they plan to spend the weekend. Each speaks only three times. Your task is to write their brief conversation in such a way that the reader learns something about each of their personalities. Try to make your dialogue sound natural.

4. When you read a good short story, it may stay in your memory a long time. Perhaps a particular character, theme, or action has impressed or surprised you. First, write the title of the best short story you have ever read. Then, in a paragraph, tell what it is about the story that makes it so memorable for you.

Reading More Short Stories

Do you have a book of stories that you liked a few years ago, but have outgrown? A nice gesture would be to share that book with someone younger than you so that person can have a good book to read. Perhaps one of the following books of stories will become your new favorite.

Ecke, Wolfgang. The Midnight Chess Game. Englewood Cliffs, New Jersey: Prentice Hall, 1985.
Do you like playing detective? These fifteen mini-mysteries are rated from easy to difficult. You can solve them by carefully sifting through the clues.

Hamilton, Virginia. The People Could Fly: American Black Folk Tales. New York: Borzoi Books, 1985.
Here are 24 Black American folk tales and several stories of slaves who long for freedom. A glossary explains words that appear in the unfamiliar Gullah dialect.

Hitchcock, Alfred. Sinister Spies. New York: Random House, 1966.
Alfred Hitchcock has chosen these ten stories of espionage that take you into the daring world of spies, counterspies, and international intrigue.

The Steps of Writing:
When Time Matters

Such everyday writing as an essay test answer and a quick letter to a friend are examples of writing done within a limited time. The writer must write clearly and accurately without spending too much time planning and revising. In the classroom, you may be given a set period of time to write an essay. Even though time is limited, you will write better if you use the steps of writing described below.

Planning Your Time

Know exactly how much time you have to write. Spend the first five or ten minutes brainstorming ideas about the topic. Write your essay without pausing too often. Finally, take five minutes to read through your paper. Be sure it makes sense. Add or delete words or phrases as needed, and correct errors in punctuation and spelling.

Understanding Directions

First, read the directions carefully. Pay attention to the words and phrases that name the type of writing that you are to do, your purpose, and your audience. Here are some examples of important words and phrases: *Describe, Compare, Inform, Create a story, your classmates, a young child,* and *Tell how to.* Also . . . focus on your topic, including any details that explain it.

Planning

Once you have a clear understanding of your writing task, brainstorm ideas about the topic. You may want to use a cluster diagram or list words and phrases. Decide on the best order for presenting your ideas. If you cannot make notes on your paper, spend a few minutes thinking about your topic.

Composing

Always keep your purpose and your audience in mind as you write. You should write a clear beginning that shows you understand the topic. The body of your paper should support the main ideas. Use specific details and reasons to show the reader what you mean. The conclusion should show the reader that you have developed your thoughts on the topic. Check the clock occasionally to make sure that you will finish in time.

Revising

Save at least five minutes of your time to read your paper. Are all the ideas clear, and do all the sentences make sense? Add or delete words if necessary. Quickly correct any spelling, punctuation, or capitalization errors.

Practice

A. Write a descriptive essay in 40 minutes. Read the directions below; then follow the writing process steps.

Directions: Food is part of everyone's life. Sometimes food is associated with entertainment. Think of the foods you have eaten at picnics, at birthday parties, or at family holiday dinners. Write a descriptive essay. Choose one of your favorite foods; describe it to someone who has seen but never tasted the food. Use vivid sensory details.

1. Notice the key phrases that tell you what your writing task is: "descriptive essay," "someone who has seen but never tasted the food," and "vivid sensory details."
2. Brainstorm ideas about the topic. Concentrate on words that describe the taste, smell, feel, and look of the food. What size and color is the food? How does it sound when you bite into it and chew it? Decide how to organize your description.
3. As you write your draft, try to use as many sensory details as you can. If you are writing an effective description, you should almost be able to taste the food as you write. Let the reader experience the food through your vivid description.
4. Use the last few minutes to revise your essay. Correct any spelling or punctuation errors.

B. *Directions:* Some people believe that it is wrong to keep a wild animal as a pet. Others say it is all right if the animal is given the kind of food it would find in the wild. Some people rescue wild animals that have been hurt. After they nurse the animals back to health, they release them into the wild. Your classmates have found a wild animal and want to keep it. Decide how you feel about this, and write a persuasive essay to convince the others to agree with you. Be as persuasive as you can. Write your essay in 40 minutes.

The Steps of Writing: When You Use a Computer

Using a computer to write is a special way to use the writing process. A computer allows you to combine the different steps of writing. You can save time because you see right away on the screen what you have written.

A computer is useful for brainstorming. Type ideas as you think of them. You can let your thoughts flow freely because it is easy to move words and phrases around. You may want to put similar ideas together in word clusters or in lists. Save your ideas when you have finished brainstorming. You may also want to print them to use for the next step.

When you write your draft on a computer, you will not be slowed down by having to write everything by hand. Instead, you can concentrate on the meaning and organization of your paper. You can also revise your writing as you work. You can add or delete words and phrases easily. You can also improve the organization of the paper by moving whole sentences or paragraphs.

After completing your first draft, you may find it useful to print it. You may want to have a classmate read your paper to help you find ways to improve it. When you are satisfied with the changes that you have decided to make, you can make them on the computer. Remember to correct spelling, punctuation, capitalization, and usage errors. Special computer programs can help you do this. Find out if one is available for your use.

When all the changes and corrections have been made, you will be ready to print your finished paper.

431

Letter Forms

Friendly Letters

heading —
greeting —
body —
closing —
signature —

> 1837 Cabaret Court
> Hopkins, Minnesota 55344
> June 20, 19—
>
> Dear Mr. Powell,
>   You have helped to make this school year the best ever. Your stories and jokes made math class interesting and a lot of fun.
>   Next year I will be attending Gibson Jr. High School. Perhaps I could come back to visit you some time and peek in on your new class.
>
>   Sincerely,
>
>   *Wendy Nielson*

A **friendly letter** has the following features.

* The **heading** gives the writer's address and the date. There is a comma between the city and state and between the day and the year. The heading is placed in the upper right-hand corner.
* The **greeting** says "hello" to the reader of the letter. It begins with a capital letter and is followed by a comma. The greeting is placed next to the left margin.
* The **body** of the letter contains the writer's message. Each paragraph of the body is indented.
* The **closing** says "goodbye" to the reader. It begins with a capital letter and is followed by a comma. The closing is placed in line with the heading.
* The **signature** is the writer's signed name. It is placed in line with the closing.

Practice: Use the steps in the writing process you have learned to write a friendly letter to someone you know. Label the heading, greeting, body, closing, and signature.

Business Letters

```
                              526 Fairfax Road
                              North Bend, Oregon 97459    ─── heading
                              October 25, 19—

Pen-Pal Club of America
132 32nd Street                                           ─── inside
New York, New York   10034                                    address

Dear Pen-Pal Club of America:                             ─── greeting
     Several of my classmates and I would like to participate
in your "Sister Cities" program, which brings citizens of
an American city in contact with citizens of a city in the
Soviet Union. Please send me any information you have    ─── body
regarding this program.
     My classmates and I would also be interested in seeing
a complete list of the various countries with which your
club is affiliated.
                              Sincerely yours,            ─── closing
                              Philip Remmer                ─── signature
                              Philip Remmer
```

A **business letter** has the following features.

- The **heading** gives the writer's address and the date in the upper right-hand corner.
- The **inside address** gives the name and address of the reader of the letter. It is placed next to the left margin.
- The **greeting** begins with a capital letter and is followed by a colon. It is placed next to the left margin.
- The **body** of the letter contains the writer's message.
- The **closing** begins with a capital letter and is followed by a comma. The closing is placed in line with the heading.
- The **signature** contains the writer's full name, both printed and signed. It is placed in line with the closing.

Practice: Use the steps in the writing process you have learned to write a business letter to Chapman Publishing Company, an imaginary business. Request a catalog of the books they sell. Their address is: 1202 Fletcher Lane, Billings, Montana 59105.

Spelling Strategies

1. You may learn to spell a word in three different ways. Discover which way works best for you.
   - Look at the word. Picture the letters in your mind.
   - Say the word aloud. Listen to the sounds.
   - Write the word. Practice spelling it many times.
2. When you proofread, always check your spelling.
   - If you are unsure how to spell a word, check in a dictionary. First look up the spelling you think is correct. If it is not listed, try another spelling. Keep checking until you locate the correct spelling.
   - Keep a record of words you misspell. Write them correctly in a spelling notebook. Organize the notebook like a dictionary. Devote one page to each letter of the alphabet. Review your words weekly.
3. Some words share the same letter pattern. Knowing a letter pattern can help you spell many words.
   - These words contain the -ank letter pattern:
     bank   clank   rank
   - These words contain the -ire letter pattern:
     attire   desire   retire
   What other spelling patterns do you know?
4. Some words can be broken into word parts. Knowing a word part can help you spell an entire word.
   - These words begin with the word part pre-:
     preheat   precook   preview
   - These words end with the word part -ful:
     hopeful   joyful   peaceful
   What other word parts do you know?
5. Many words can be broken into syllables to help you spell.
   - If a long word is difficult for you to spell, break it into syllables. The spelling may then become easier.
     spontaneous ⟶ spon ta ne ous
   - You may have trouble remembering whether a word ends in -ant or -ent. If so, say the word while stressing the syllable that gives you difficulty.

hydrant (say "hy DRANT")
violent (say "vio LENT")

6. Sometimes a memory hint can help you spell a word.
Which spelling is correct, *separate* or *seperate?*
Memory hint: There is *a rat* in *separate.*
Invent a memory hint to help you spell a difficult word.

Commonly Misspelled Words

1. accident	26. cough	51. molasses	76. shovel
2. ache	27. courage	52. necessary	77. similar
3. address	28. court	53. obvious	78. sought
4. aisle	29. cousin	54. occasion	79. sponge
5. angle	30. deceive	55. opposite	80. success
6. answer	31. definite	56. ought	81. sugar
7. anxious	32. doughnut	57. patient	82. sum
8. approve	33. earn	58. piece	83. teammate
9. ascend	34. eerie	59. pier	84. terrific
10. assign	35. embarrass	60. pleasure	85. thorough
11. balance	36. especially	61. possess	86. tongue
12. balcony	37. fascinate	62. proceed	87. tour
13. beginning	38. February	63. profession	88. tournament
14. bough	39. foreign	64. reassure	89. treasure
15. brief	40. grief	65. receive	90. trough
16. broad	41. height	66. rein	91. truly
17. business	42. independent	67. restaurant	92. unusual
18. calendar	43. interrupt	68. route	93. vacuum
19. cell	44. jealous	69. salad	94. view
20. cemetery	45. jewelry	70. sausage	95. villain
21. coarse	46. knowledge	71. schedule	96. waste
22. colonel	47. license	72. search	97. weigh
23. column	48. lieutenant	73. separate	98. whether
24. committee	49. machinery	74. sergeant	99. whom
25. congratulate	50. misspell	75. sew	100. worse

Handwriting Model

Sharing your ideas is simpler when people can read them easily. One way to allow this is to be sure that your handwriting is readable. The letters on this page are a model of legible handwriting. If your handwriting is not as clear as this model, it will be a helpful guide for you.

GRAMMAR DEFINITIONS AND PRACTICE

Sentences I

- A **sentence** is a group of words that expresses a complete thought. A sentence begins with a capital letter and ends with an end mark. *(page 42)*

   The computer is counting numbers.
- A **declarative sentence** makes a statement about something. It ends with a period. *(page 42)*

   Computers are useful machines.
- An **interrogative sentence** asks a question. It ends with a question mark. *(page 42)*

   Can computers count quickly?
- An **imperative sentence** gives a command or makes a request. It ends with a period or an exclamation mark. *(page 42)*

   Enter your information on the keyboard. Please hurry!
- An **exclamatory sentence** shows surprise or strong feeling. It ends with an exclamation mark. *(page 42)*

   What a fantastic computer this is!
- A **fragment** is a group of words that does not express a complete thought. *(page 42)*

   The memory of the computer.

A. Practice Identify each sentence as *declarative, interrogative, imperative,* or *exclamatory*. Then write the sentence, using the correct end mark.

1. Have you ever worked on a computer
2. The idea of computers is hundreds of years old
3. Charles Babbage built an early computer
4. How large computers once were
5. Have computers gotten smaller over the years
6. Now a computer can fit on a desk
7. Use the computer program correctly
8. What a good lecture on computers it was
9. Turn off that computer immediately
10. Does your school have a computer

B. Practice Write each group of words. If it is a sentence, write *sentence*. If it is a fragment, write *fragment*.

11. How useful computers are!
12. How often will Fran use her computer?
13. The teacher and the students together.
14. Computers help students with homework.
15. Fran and Dennis play games on the computer.
16. Ken's assignment for tonight.
17. Find out about the new computer.
18. Fran's computer, with a monitor and disk drives.
19. Please help me unpack it.
20. Runs without a programmer.

♦ The **complete subject** of a sentence is all the words that tell whom or what the sentence is about. *(page 44)*

> The captain of a spaceship uses a computer.

♦ The **complete predicate** of a sentence is the verb and all the other words that tell what the subject does, has, is, or is like. *(page 44)*

> The computer assists in the ship's operations.

Practice Write each sentence. Underline the complete subject once and the complete predicate twice.

1. A few authors write wonderful stories about computers.
2. One imaginative tale became the basis for a fine movie.
3. The name of the film was *2001: A Space Odyssey*.
4. A short story inspired the film.
5. Arthur C. Clarke wrote this original story.
6. Mr. Clarke worked on the script for the movie also.
7. A large spaceship explores outer space in the movie.
8. A special computer guides all the systems.
9. Scientists named the remarkable computer Hal.
10. Hal is very useful throughout the film.
11. This special machine assists the ship and its crew.
12. A strange thing happens to Hal during the long trip.
13. The machine disobeys a human's orders.

14. A member of the crew disconnects many of Hal's circuits.
15. The computer can only perform simple functions.

♦ The **simple subject** of a sentence is the main word or group of words in the complete subject. The simple subject is a noun or a pronoun. *(page 46)*

> The computer in the spaceship helps the crew.

Practice Write each sentence. Underline the simple subject.

1. Most works of science fiction take place in the future.
2. The theme of space exploration often arises.
3. Many characters in science fiction stories travel in space.
4. They encounter strange environments on other worlds.
5. Authors sometimes explore social concerns in science fiction.
6. Other stories serve simply as entertainment.
7. Fantastic inventions appear in much science fiction.
8. A background in science helps science fiction writers.
9. *Star Trek* was a popular science fiction series on TV.
10. It attracted many loyal fans.

♦ The **simple predicate** of a sentence is the main word or group of words in the complete predicate. The simple predicate is always a verb or a verb phrase. *(page 46)*

> The large computer guides them on the trip.

Practice Write each sentence. Underline the simple predicate.

1. The early Greeks told science fiction stories.
2. *Gulliver's Travels* was a major work of fiction of the 1700s.
3. The book stimulated much debate.
4. Authors thought about new ideas.
5. American writers have produced many works of science fiction.
6. H.G. Wells wrote many fine science fiction stories.
7. Other people created new science fiction novels.
8. The novels have become very popular since World War II.
9. Some very innovative films appeared in the 1960s and 1970s.
10. *2001* is one of our most famous science fiction films.

♦ In an **imperative sentence**, *you* is understood to be the subject. The word *you* is not written in the sentence, however. *(page 48)*

(You) | Tell the story, please.

♦ In an **interrogative sentence**, the complete subject often comes between parts of the predicate. *(page 48)*

Is | the class | reading a science fiction story now?

Practice Write each sentence. If the sentence is imperative, write (*You*). If the sentence is not imperative, underline the simple subject.

1. Do you like science fiction stories?
2. Please read some of the stories in this book.
3. Try the one on page 85.
4. Has anyone heard this story before?
5. Are the stories in this book very long?
6. Choose some from the last half of the book.
7. Can your younger sister read yet?
8. Does Susan have a favorite story?
9. Give this book a try also.

♦ In sentences that start with *here* or *there*, the simple subject usually appears later in the sentence. *(page 50)*

There is | our library.

Here is | the main desk.

Practice Write each sentence. Underline the simple subject.

1. There is the best collection of science fiction in the library.
2. Here is a review of several science fiction stories.
3. There is my favorite bookshelf.
4. Here is the librarian.
5. There is the new shipment of books.
6. There is the map of a space station.
7. Here are two descriptions of life in the future.
8. There is the schedule for the conference.
9. Here is the most recent update.

Nouns

◆ A **common noun** names any person, place, thing, or idea. It begins with a lowercase letter. *(page 80)*

    writer   river   game   holiday

◆ A **proper noun** names a particular person, place, thing, or idea. Some proper nouns have more than one word. Each important word in a proper noun begins with a capital letter. *(page 80)*

    Mr. Aaron   St. Louis   Eiffel Tower   Monday

Practice Write each sentence. Underline the common nouns. Capitalize the proper nouns.

1. The team played a big game last saturday.
2. The students sold tickets during the entire year.
3. Some players come from iowa, nebraska, and wyoming.
4. Fans from the area crowded into kennedy stadium.
5. The band from jefferson high school played first.
6. The coach and Mr. aaron encouraged the members of the team.
7. The athletes played very well on saturday.
8. The best athletes, phillip, jerome, and mario, led us to a victory.
9. Our teacher, Ms. chavez, congratulated us after the contest.
10. We took a tour down the plains river on tuesday.
11. The passengers on the boat were in a good mood.
12. The scenery near jefferson city was beautiful.

◆ A **singular noun** names one person, place, thing, or idea. *(page 82)*

    student   village   echo   belief

◆ A **plural noun** names more than one person, place, thing, or idea. To form the plural of most nouns, add *s*. Add *es* to nouns that end in *s*, *ss*, *ch*, *sh*, *x*, or *z*. For nouns that end in a consonant + *y*, change *y* to *i* and add *es*. For nouns that end in a vowel + *y*, add *s*. *(page 82)*

shirt/shirts	bus/buses	dress/dresses
ash/ashes	fox/foxes	waltz/waltzes
lobby/lobbies	bay/bays	pouch/pouches

441

◆ For other nouns, there is no set rule to follow to form the plural. For some nouns that end in *f* or *fe*, change *f* or *fe* to *v* and add *es*. For other nouns that end in *f* or *fe*, add *s*. For most nouns ending in a vowel + *o*, add *s*. For most nouns ending in a consonant + *o*, add *es*. For other nouns ending in a consonant + *o*, add *s*. Some nouns have irregular spelling changes or no spelling changes when the plural is formed. (*page 82*)

half/halves	patio/patios	goose/geese
chief/chiefs	echo/echoes	woman/women
	cello/cellos	sheep/sheep

A. Practice Write the plural form of each singular noun.

1. knife
2. toy
3. cliff
4. waltz
5. belief
6. potato
7. mouse
8. child
9. monkey
10. diary
11. sandwich
12. radio
13. mosquito
14. ox
15. trout
16. bus
17. man
18. auto
19. deer
20. shelf

B. Practice Write each sentence. Use the plural form of each noun in parentheses.

21. Jaime shopped in five (store) yesterday.
22. Louise bought two (salmon) for her family.
23. Mr. LaRosa travels to three (rodeo) every year.
24. Calvin heard (echo) in the canyon.
25. The farmer sold all the (tomato) at the fair.
26. He also bought many (sheep) for his farm.
27. Jim showed his paintings of nearby (ranch).
28. He packed the paintings in (box).
29. He bought refreshments at the (cafe).
30. The (photo) of the vacation are beautiful.

◆ A **possessive** is a word that tells who or what owns or has something. To form the possessive of a singular noun, add 's, even if the singular noun already ends in s. *(page 84)*

Christopher's compass   Luis's ship

Practice Decide which noun in the first sentence should be a possessive. Write that noun as a possessive in the second sentence.

1. Christopher Columbus dreamed of a voyage to China.
_____ dreams led him from Italy to Spain.
2. Columbus sought help from the king of Spain.
Columbus needed the _____ help.
3. Columbus used a compass on his voyage.
The _____ needle indicated the correct course.
4. Queen Isabella asked about the voyages of Marco Polo.
Columbus told her about _____ trips to China.
5. China had great wealth and riches.
Queen Isabella wanted some of _____ riches.
6. A sailor was afraid during the voyage.
Columbus calmed the _____ fears.
7. The trip across the ocean was difficult.
The _____ waves crashed over the ship.
8. The long journey finally ended in the New World.
The _____ end brought joy to the sailors.

◆ A **plural possessive** shows ownership by more than one owner. *(page 86)*
the sailors' hopes
◆ If a plural noun ends in s, add only an apostrophe (') to form the possessive. *(page 86)*
the explorers have boats   the explorers' boats
◆ If a plural noun does *not* end in s, add an apostrophe and an s ('s) to form the plural. *(page 86)*
the men have loyalty   the men's loyalty

Practice Write each sentence. Use each noun in parentheses as a possessive.

1. The (explorers) achievements led to the colonization of the New World.
2. The (colonies) survival was a matter of hard work, chance, and perseverance.
3. The (pioneers) lives were often difficult.
4. Most of the (colonists) homes were very simple.
5. The (women) tasks were never easy.
6. The (men) duties were sometimes dangerous.
7. Many of the (settlers) towns disrupted Native Americans.
8. Sometimes they destroyed the (deer) winter shelters.
9. Some of the (cities) names came from places in Europe.
10. The New World fulfilled many (people) dreams.

♦ An **abbreviation** is a shortened form of a word. Many abbreviations begin with a capital letter and end with a period. *(page 88)*

Dr.   Ave.   a.m.   U.K.

Practice Write each item. Abbreviate the underlined part.

1. Doctor Elizabeth Blackwell
2. President James Monroe
3. Senator Margaret Chase Smith
4. 413 Sanabel Terrace
5. 18 Allen Court, Apartment 6
6. Washington, District of Columbia
7. Monday before noon; Tuesday afternoon
8. 400 Beletier Boulevard
9. Mister Calvin Hodnett, Junior
10. Union of Soviet Socialist Republics
11. Professor Joan Whitman
12. 516 Union Place, Corbell City, California
13. 3626 Overlook Avenue, Yorktown, New York
14. Environmental Protection Agency
15. United Nations
16. Friday, October 30, 1991

Verbs I

◆ A **verb** is a word that expresses action or helps to tell what the subject is or is like. An **action verb** expresses action and tells what the subject does. Action verbs may describe physical or mental action. They may also show ownership. The verb *have* is often used as an action verb to show ownership. *(page 126)*

> Accountants <u>use</u> calculators in their work. (physical action)
> They <u>memorize</u> important regulations. (mental action)
> That accountant <u>has</u> an office downtown. (ownership)

Practice Write each sentence. Underline each action verb. Write whether it shows physical action, mental action, or ownership.

1. Pilots fly airplanes all over the world.
2. Doctors study their patients' symptoms.
3. Forest rangers prevent dangerous forest fires.
4. Teachers decide on assignments for students.
5. Chefs have many wonderful implements.
6. Some composers wait years for recognition.
7. Farmers grow a variety of vegetables and fruits.
8. Many artists possess natural artistic talent.
9. Journalists report news and other information.
10. Nurses value a patient's positive attitude.

◆ A **linking verb** connects the subject of the sentence with words that describe or identify it. Linking verbs usually help to tell what the subject is or is like. The most common linking verbs are forms of the verb *be*. *(page 128)*

> Jane's mother <u>is</u> an accountant.

◆ Other verbs can serve as linking verbs. Some of these are verbs that involve the senses, such as *look, sound, smell, taste, feel, seem,* and *appear*. Others express change or a lack of change, such as *become, remain, grow, stay,* and *turn*. *(page 128)*

> Her new office <u>seems</u> larger.

> The business <u>remains</u> profitable.

Practice   Write each sentence. Underline the verb. Write *LV* if it is a linking verb or *AV* if it is an action verb.

1. Aunt Shirley is an architect.
2. She designs houses, office buildings, and hospitals.
3. She makes many precise measurements.
4. Aunt Shirley became an architect only last year.
5. Her work grows better all the time.
6. An architect works hard for her clients.
7. People care a great deal about their homes.
8. Architecture remains an important profession.

♦ A **verb phrase** is made up of a main verb plus one or more helping verbs. A **main verb** expresses the action or tells something about the subject. A **helping verb** works with the main verb to make the meaning more specific. Forms of the verbs *be, have*, and *do* are often used as helping verbs. *(page 130)*

　　She has been working as an accountant for five years.
　　She really does enjoy her work.

Practice   Write each sentence. Underline each helping verb once and each main verb twice.

1. Geometry can be important in navigation.
2. Navigation does require a knowledge of angles.
3. Mr. Ortiz has taught at our school since 1975.
4. Teachers must study for many years for their jobs.
5. Did you know that?
6. Do you like your classes at school?
7. Would you help me with my homework?
8. We have not read all the assignments yet.
9. Mr. Ortiz is giving us plenty of help.

♦ **Tense** is the time expressed by a verb. A verb in the **present tense** tells about something that is happening now. A verb in the **past tense** tells about something that happened in the past and is now over. A verb in the **future tense** tells about something that will happen in the future. *(page 132)*

　　Sonia and Bill watch the game. (present tense)
　　They watched yesterday's game, too. (past tense)
　　They will watch the game tomorrow. (future tense)

Practice Write each sentence. Write the correct tense of the verb.

1. Cecilia (arrive) at Sonia's house at 2:15. (past)
2. The game (start) at 2:30. (past)
3. Sonia and Bill (walk) to the couch with popcorn. (past)
4. The batter (check) with the coach. (present)
5. The pitcher (play) tomorrow also. (future)
6. Who else (pitch) today? (present)
7. The umpire (signal) "foul ball." (past)
8. It (appear) fair to the runner. (past)
9. We (learn) in a minute. (future)
10. They (show) the instant replay immediately. (present)

♦ The **present perfect tense** tells of an action that took place at an indefinite time in the past or that began in the past and is still going on. The **past perfect tense** tells of an action that took place in the past before some other point in time. *(page 134)*

   Maurice <u>has read</u> many books. (present perfect tense)

   Anna <u>had finished</u> her book first. (past perfect tense)

Practice Write each sentence. Write the verb in parentheses. Use the perfect tense indicated.

1. Patrick (learn) many Greek myths. (present perfect)
2. He (list) some of his favorites. (present perfect)
3. He (prepare) a list once before. (past perfect)
4. He (finish) a story about Hercules. (present perfect)
5. He (listen) to that story as a child. (past perfect)
6. Patrick (enjoy) many stories about ancient Greece. (present perfect)
7. The teacher (make) the stories come alive. (present perfect)
8. We (ask) the teacher many questions. (present perfect)
9. She (answer) almost all the questions yesterday. (past perfect)
10. She (continue) the answers during class today. (present perfect)

♦ A verb has four forms, or **principal parts**: the present, the present participle, the past, and the past participle. The present participle is used with forms of *be*. The past participle is used with *has*, *have*, or *had*. The spelling of some regular verbs changes from the present to the past, the present participle, and the past participle. *(page 136)*

Present	Present Participle	Past	Past Participle
start	starting	started	(have) started
bake	baking	baked	(have) baked
carry	carrying	carried	(have) carried
admit	admitting	admitted	(have) admitted

Practice   Write each sentence. Use the principal part of the verb indicated in parentheses.

1. My class has (plan) a trip to the theater. (past part.)
2. The class has not yet (select) a play. (past part.)
3. Students have been (take) a survey. (present part.)
4. Sarah has been (suggest) *Macbeth*. (present part.)
5. She had (watch) it on television once. (past part.)
6. He (like) new French plays. (present)
7. John has been (support) this idea. (present part.)
8. We (decide) on a vote. (past)

♦ An **irregular verb** is a verb that does not form the past tense and past participle by adding *ed*. *(pages 138 and 140)*

Verb	Past	Verb	Past Participle (with *has*, *have*, *had*)
be	was, were	be	been
become	became	become	become
bring	brought	bring	brought
choose	chose	choose	chosen
come	came	come	come
eat	ate	eat	eaten
find	found	find	found
give	gave	give	given
grow	grew	grow	grown
hide	hid	hide	hidden
keep	kept	keep	kept

Verb	Past	Verb	Past Participle (with *has*, *have*, *had*)
let	let	let	let
make	made	make	made
mean	meant	mean	meant
read	read	read	read
run	ran	run	run
see	saw	see	seen
speak	spoke	speak	spoken
spread	spread	spread	spread
take	took	take	taken
tell	told	tell	told
write	wrote	write	written

◆ Three particular pairs of verbs cause trouble for many people. They are: *lie* and *lay*, *rise* and *raise*, and *sit* and *set*. *(page 140)*

Verb and Meaning	Past	Past Participle
lie (to put oneself or to be in a lying position)	lay	(have, has, had) lain
lay (to put or place something)	laid	(have, has, had) laid
rise (to go up or to get up)	rose	(have, has, had) risen
raise (to move something upward)	raised	(have, has, had) raised
sit (to put oneself or to be put in a sitting position)	sat	(have, has, had) sat
set (to put or place something)	set	(have, has, had) set

Practice   Write each sentence with the correct past or past participle of the verb in parentheses.

1. Jules has (come) down with the measles. (come, came)
2. Has he (give) them to me? (gave, given)
3. My mom (take) me to the doctor. (took, taken)
4. My doctor (write) a prescription for me. (wrote, written)
5. I have (eat) nothing but soft foods all week. (ate, eaten)
6. Today, Mom (choose) all my favorite foods. (chose, chosen)
7. She has (make) a wonderful dinner for me. (make, made)
8. I (lie) on the couch all evening. (lay, laid)
9. Dad had (raise) the TV up from the floor. (risen, raised)
10. Marissa (sit) on the armchair. (sat, set)
11. She (set) a book on the table for me. (sat, set)

Verbs II

◆ A **direct object** is a noun or a pronoun that follows an action verb in a sentence and receives the action of the verb. The direct object answers the questions *whom?* or *what?* after the verb. There may be several words found after the verb. The direct object is the one noun or pronoun that answers the question *whom?* or *what?* *(page 168)*

Rachel uses watercolors.

The teacher helped her with the painting.

A. Practice Write each sentence and underline the direct object. Write the question you would ask to find the direct object.

1. Many people admire the dreamlike art of Marc Chagall.
2. Chagall painted scenes from his Russian childhood.
3. He added fanciful details to his art.
4. Many of Chagall's pictures feature imaginary creatures.
5. Chagall often portrayed people in midair.
6. This unusual artist loved bright colors.
7. Chagall moved his home from Russia to France.
8. Marc Chagall illustrated some beautiful books.
9. He designed colorful windows for a hospital.
10. In 1964, he completed a giant picture for the ceiling of the Paris Opera House.

B. Practice Write each sentence and underline the direct object.

11. People draw cartoons for many reasons.
12. A comic strip tells a funny story.
13. Many newspapers publish comics.
14. Political cartoons have a serious purpose.
15. A political cartoon gives an opinion about an event.
16. Political cartoonists often use symbols.
17. Benjamin Franklin published a cartoon in 1754.
18. It criticized the quarrels among the American colonies.
19. Most cartoonists draw an outline in pencil.
20. They use ink for the final version.

◆ An **indirect object** is a noun or a pronoun that follows an action verb and tells *to whom* or *for whom* the action is done. When you are trying to find the indirect object, do not be confused by other words such as adjectives or adverbs. If the word that tells *to whom* or *for whom* already has *to* or *for* in front of it, the word is *not* an indirect object. *(page 170)*

Zeke told <u>Laura</u> about an idea for a story.

He also gave <u>her</u> his typewriter.

Practice Write each sentence. Underline the direct object once and the indirect object twice. If there is no indirect object, write *none*.

1. Abe showed the class a book about cave paintings.
2. The book described paintings to the class.
3. The artists probably used brushes for the paintings.
4. The teacher gave the class more information.
5. Cave artists drew outlines for their paintings with black carbon from their lamps.
6. They mixed materials for the paint.
7. Abe lent the teacher his book.
8. The book tells us many facts about early art.
9. The art teacher showed Mary the best drawings.
10. She gave her a good grade on her report.
11. Mrs. Nkobe told Mr. Dane some African tales.
12. She sang him a few traditional songs.
13. Mr. Dane read some unusual folktales to the children.
14. He wrote his sister a letter about them.
15. The letter gave his sister an idea.
16. She suggested her idea to Mrs. Nkobe.
17. She offered Mrs. Nkobe a contract with her company.
18. Mrs. Nkobe recorded the folktales for her class.
19. The company used the traditional songs for the record.
20. Later, a group awarded the record a prize.

◆ A **transitive verb** is a verb that is followed by a direct object. An **intransitive verb** is a verb that is not followed by a direct object. Many verbs can be either transitive or intransitive. When you are identifying a transitive verb, do not be confused by words other than the direct object that may follow the verb. *(page 172)*

The artist <u>painted</u> a picture. (transitive verb)
The artist <u>worked</u> quickly. (intransitive verb)

Practice Write each sentence. Underline the verb once, and write whether it is transitive or intransitive. If there is a direct object, underline it twice.

1. Artists work with many materials.
2. Painters have brushes of different sizes.
3. They usually paint on canvas.
4. A painter tacks a canvas onto a wooden frame.
5. Ancient artists applied colors to stone walls.
6. Many sculptors carve in marble and granite.
7. In Navajo ceremonies, the artist sprinkles sand in beautiful designs.
8. Some artists experiment with materials like string.
9. Early painters made colors from earth.
10. Paint with an egg base dried quickly.
11. Many artists preferred oil as a base.
12. Oil colors last for a long time.
13. Several other kinds of colors fade.
14. Many modern artists use oil for that reason.
15. Some people draw with charcoal.

◆ A **predicate noun** is a noun that follows a linking verb in a sentence and identifies the subject of the sentence. To find a predicate noun, ask: *Who or what is (subject)? (page 174)*

Crystals are tiny <u>cubes</u>. (What are crystals?)

◆ A **predicate adjective** is an adjective that follows a linking verb and describes the subject of the sentence. To find a predicate adjective, ask: *What is (subject) like? (page 174)*

Many buildings are <u>rectangular</u>. (What are buildings like?)

A. Practice Write each sentence. Underline each predicate noun once. Underline each predicate adjective twice. Write the question you would ask to find the predicate noun or the predicate adjective.

1. Katie has always been a good student.
2. She is also a lover of nature.
3. The air was warm, but breezy.
4. It felt cool against her skin.
5. The grass looked greener than before.
6. Her cat remained motionless on the lawn.
7. That is certainly a large grasshopper.
8. Suddenly the sky became dark.
9. The shadow on the ground was a huge circle.
10. It was only a cloud.
11. The roses in her garden smelled sweet.
12. The flowers were objects of beauty.
13. The garden was a picture of loveliness.
14. Finally, Katie felt lonely.
15. The noise in the kitchen was laughter.

B. Practice Write whether each underlined word is a predicate noun (PN) or predicate adjective (PA). If it is a predicate noun, write the noun it identifies. If it is a predicate adjective, write what it describes.

16. Many boxes are <u>cubes</u>.
17. The sun appears <u>round</u> in the sky.
18. The sun is really a <u>sphere</u>.
19. Sometimes the sun is a fiery, orange <u>ball</u>.
20. A pyramid sometimes looks <u>triangular</u>.
21. Some buildings are <u>circular</u>.
22. A half-moon is <u>semi-circular</u>.
23. Most books are <u>rectangular</u> in shape.
24. The globe is also a <u>sphere</u>.
25. From space, the earth is a big, blue <u>marble</u>.

Pronouns

◆ A **pronoun** is a word that takes the place of a noun or nouns in a sentence. A **subject pronoun** is a pronoun that is used as the subject of a sentence. The subject pronouns are *I, you, he, she, it, we, you,* and *they. (page 222)*

The <u>students</u> prepared for the exam.
<u>They</u> prepared for the exam.

◆ A **subject pronoun** is also used to replace a noun that follows a linking verb. A **predicate nominative** is a noun or pronoun that follows a linking verb and identifies the subject. *(page 222)*

The best student was <u>James</u>. (predicate nominative)
The best student was <u>he</u>. (predicate nominative)

A. Practice Write each sentence. Replace the underlined subject with the correct subject pronoun.

1. <u>Alan</u> finished the report early.
2. <u>James and I</u> also completed the assignment.
3. The <u>student</u> in front of the room is <u>Ted</u>.
4. The person at the chalkboard is <u>Nan</u>.
5. <u>Mrs. Johnson</u> asks many questions.
6. <u>One question</u> confuses James.
7. <u>Alan and James</u> stayed late at school.
8. <u>Rashid and I</u> left early.

B. Practice Write each sentence. Replace the underlined word or words with a subject pronoun. Label it either *subject* or *predicate nominative*.

9. <u>Jeremy</u> writes a report about Mexico.
10. The man with many books about Mexico is <u>Mr. Garcia</u>.
11. <u>Mr. Garcia</u> travels to Mexico every year.
12. <u>Raphael and Maria</u> gave Jeremy some information.
13. <u>Jeremy and I</u> work together often.
14. The student with the highest grades is <u>Maria</u>.

15. Mrs. Bringham told the class about Mexico City.

16. My good friend from Mexico City is Lola.

◆ An **object pronoun** takes the place of a noun or nouns used as a direct object or an indirect object. The object pronouns are *me, you, him, her, it, us, you,* and *them. (page 224)*

 Ed heard the musicians. Ed heard them.

◆ A **direct object** is a noun or pronoun that follows an action verb and receives the action of the verb. *(page 224)*

 Robert bought the book. Robert bought it.

◆ An **indirect object** is a noun or pronoun that follows an action verb and tells *to whom* or *for whom* the action is done. *(page 224)*

 Robert sent Susan a book about Mozart's music.

 Robert sent her a book about Mozart's music.

Practice Write each sentence. Replace the underlined word or words with an object pronoun.

1. Our teacher told Amy and me a story about Tchaikovsky.
2. She brought Phyllis a book about Tchaikovsky.
3. Peggy sent Jason and Jon to the music room.
4. Jason showed Mr. Meyers the Mozart piece.
5. Today we will hear a lecture on Mozart.
6. People all over the world study Mozart's music.
7. Mr. Meyers asked Phyllis a question.
8. Phyllis answered Mr. Meyers quickly.
9. Robert knew the answer, too.
10. Howard gave Donna a musical score.
11. Donna played the music beautifully
12. Mr. Meyers told Jon and Aaron the answer.
13. They needed Peggy and Claude for assistance.
14. Peggy walked Phyllis home from school.
15. Peggy asked Phyllis and me about Mozart.

◆ Subject and object pronouns are used in different ways in sentences. Subject pronouns are used as subjects in sentences or as predicate nominatives. Object pronouns are used as direct objects or as indirect objects. *(page 226)*

> He makes the recipe. The cook is <u>he</u>. (subject pronoun)
> <u>Ed</u> helped <u>them</u>. (object pronoun)
> Ed sent <u>her</u> the recipe. (object pronoun)

Practice Write each sentence. Replace each underlined word with the correct form of the pronoun.

1. <u>The recipe</u> came from an old native American meal.
2. John gave <u>the students</u> copies of the recipe.
3. <u>Olivia and Karen</u> bought fresh corn.
4. <u>The girls</u> cooked the corn briefly.
5. They gave <u>Jeremy</u> a small taste.
6. The cooks sliced <u>vegetables and meat</u>.
7. <u>Susan</u> prepared some soup stock.
8. <u>Olivia</u> told Karen a story about the recipe.
9. <u>Olivia and I</u> tasted the corn soup.
10. <u>The soup</u> was excellent.
11. <u>Jeremy</u> read a book about Native American food.
12. John sent <u>Karen and I</u> a new recipe.
13. <u>Olivia and Teresa</u> tried other recipes.
14. We all tasted <u>the meals</u>.

◆ The noun to which a pronoun refers is called its **antecedent**. A pronoun must agree with its antecedent. *(page 228)*

> The girl sold <u>Marta and me</u> several books.
> She sold <u>us</u> several books.

◆ Be sure a pronoun's antecedent is clear. If it is not, the sentence may be confusing. *(page 228)*

> Jake asked his father a question. <u>He</u> was annoyed.
> (*Who* was annoyed, Jake or his father?)

Practice Write each pair of sentences. Underline the pronoun. Underline the antecedent twice.

1. Dad and Jake discussed the issue. They had a solution.
2. Jake and I rode to school. We raced down the hill.

3. Mrs. Torres read a story. She answered questions.
4. Juliet and Calvin asked many questions. Mrs. Torres told them the answers.
5. The class played a game today. It was lots of fun.
6. Mr. Kim explained a new rule to Jake and Calvin. He watched them carefully throughout the game.
7. Julie and Mrs. Torres laughed at Calvin's joke. They smiled after the game.
8. Michael and Anna practice often. They are the best players.
9. Mrs. Torres watched the players. She was proud.
10. The class enjoys volleyball. The students play it well.

◆ Possessive forms of pronouns show ownership or possession. They may appear before a noun or may stand alone. Those that are used before nouns are *my, your, his, her, its, our, your,* and *their*. Those that stand alone are *mine, yours, his, hers, its, ours, yours,* and *theirs*. *(page 230)*

His books are new. This library card is mine.

◆ Some possessive forms and contractions sound alike. Do not confuse the two. *(page 230)*

Your sister is an eager reader. (possessive)
You're very kind to your sister. (contraction)

Practice Write each sentence. Choose the correct word.

1. (My, Mine) brother enjoys books.
2. (He, His) favorite book is *The Phantom Tollbooth*.
3. The authors wrote (they're, their) books quickly.
4. (They're, Their) excellent writers.
5. Susan brought (she, her) book to school.
6. (It's, Its) title was very long.
7. The other book was also (her, hers).
8. The magazine is (my, mine).
9. (Your, You're) books are in poor condition.
10. (Your, You're) in need of some new books.
11. (Their, They're) covers are dirty.
12. Those library books on the table are (him, his).
13. The new dictionary on the desk is (our, ours).
14. (Its, It's) pages are very thin.

Adjectives

♦ An **adjective** is a word that tells about a noun or a pronoun. *(page 264)*

The <u>young</u> woman ate the apple under a <u>shady</u> tree.

♦ **Articles** are special kinds of adjectives. The **definite article**, *the*, identifies a specific person, place, or thing. The **indefinite articles**, *a* and *an*, identify any person, place, or thing in a group. Use *an* before words beginning with a vowel sound. *(page 264)*

<u>the</u> boy   <u>the</u> tall boys   <u>a</u> dog   <u>an</u> egg   <u>an</u> old boat

Practice Write each sentence. Underline all the adjectives, including the articles. Write *definite* or *indefinite* above each article.

1. The six campers ran across the hot sand to the ocean.
2. The cool waves washed over twelve bare feet.
3. A girl plunged into the cold, blue water.
4. The three boys built a castle in the yellow sand.
5. A small motorboat and an enormous rowboat stood nearby.
6. A young woman and two little children played ball.
7. One thirsty boy drank an icy lemonade.
8. They carried a delicious snack back to the big blanket.
9. Two hungry children shared an apple and a sandwich.
10. The children had a wonderful day at the beach.
11. The bright sun glistened above the blue ocean.
12. A noisy seagull swooped and hollered in the clear sky.
13. Big waves crashed against the sandy shore.
14. We chose a lovely spot for the picnic.
15. The foamy sea pounded below us.

♦ **Proper adjectives** are adjectives formed from proper nouns. Like proper nouns, proper adjectives are capitalized. Many proper adjectives are formed by changing the spelling of proper nouns. *(page 266)*

Mexico   Mexican   Japan   Japanese

♦ Some proper adjectives have the same form as proper nouns. This is usually the case with the names of states and cities. *(page 266)*

Texas chili   New York steak

Practice   Write each sentence with the proper adjective.

1. For lunch we served ____ spaghetti. (Italy)
2. I used ____ sardines in the salad. (Portugal)
3. Clam chowder is a famous ____ meal. (Boston)
4. My cousin eats an unusual ____ yogurt. (Israel)
5. Many ____ restaurants serve southern dishes. (Atlanta)
6. My sister enjoys ____ food of all kinds. (Spain)
7. ____ foods include shrimp and rice. (Louisiana)
8. My grandfather makes delicious ____ dishes. (Mexico)
9. ____ dishes often include fish. (Japan)
10. Many ____ countries have fine cooks. (Europe)
11. ____ dishes are famous throughout the world. (France)
12. Some ____ restaurants serve seafood. (San Francisco)
13. ____ oranges are famous worldwide. (Florida)

♦ A **predicate adjective** is an adjective that follows a linking verb and describes the subject of the sentence. *(page 268)*

The dog feels <u>ill</u>.   His owner is <u>sympathetic</u>.

Practice   Write each sentence. Underline the linking verb once and the predicate adjective twice.

1. The dog's bark sounds sad.
2. His behavior seems unusual.
3. He remains quiet all day long.
4. His eyes appear dull even in bright daylight.
5. Sue's father looks anxious about the dog.
6. Sue becomes nervous at the veterinarian's office.
7. Her mother is not afraid at all.
8. She feels certain of the dog's recovery.
9. Sue slowly grows calm.
10. Dr. Wexler's explanations sound logical.
11. Everything seems fine to Sue's family.
12. Their pet is healthy at last.

♦ Use the **comparative** form of an adjective to compare two people, places, or things. Use the **superlative** form of an adjective to compare three or more people, places, or things. *(page 270)*

♦ Add *er* to most one-syllable adjectives and to some two-syllable adjectives to form the comparative. Add *est* to these adjectives to form the superlative. You must change the spelling of some adjectives to add *er* or *est*. *(page 270)*

California is a <u>large</u> state.
Texas is <u>larger</u> than California.
Alaska is the <u>largest</u> state of all.

♦ Use *more* to form the comparative of most adjectives of two or more syllables, including those ending in suffixes like *ful*, *less*, *ous*, and *able*. Use *most* to form the superlative of these adjectives. *(page 270)*

Mittens are <u>more useful</u> than sunhats in Nome.
Down coats are the <u>most useful</u> garments of all.

Practice   Write each sentence with the correct form of the adjective in parentheses.

1. Summers are (cold) in northern Alaska than in southern Alaska.
2. The climate of Sitka is (wet) than the climate of Nome.
3. Alaska is the (close) state of all to Asia.
4. The (early) sunsets of all occur in December in Alaska.
5. Huge Alaska has a (small) population than tiny Delaware.
6. Anchorage is a (big) city than Fairbanks.
7. Alaska was the (attractive) vacation spot of all.
8. The Inuit villages were (peaceful) than big cities.
9. The sun at midnight was the (unusual) sight of all.
10. Mt. McKinley is (beautiful) than Mt. Hamilton.
11. Malaspina Glacier is the (gigantic) glacier of all.
12. The bears were (agile) than the caribou.
13. Sunsets in Alaska are (colorful) than sunsets at home.
14. This trip was the (wonderful) vacation of all!

◆ Some adjectives have special comparative and superlative forms. *(page 272)*

Adjective	Comparative	Superlative
good	better	best
bad	worse	worst
much, many	more	most
little	less	least

Practice Write each sentence with the proper form of the adjective in parentheses.

1. Cloudy nights are (bad) than clear nights for astronomers.
2. A city is the (bad) place of all for an observatory.
3. Big cities have the (little) space of all for a huge telescope.
4. City skies also provide (little) visibility than skies elsewhere because of bright city lights.
5. The (good) observatories of all are at high altitudes, far from city lights and haze.
6. Telescopes in space relay the (much) information of all about the sky.
7. Modern astronomers spend (little) time at the telescope than at a computer.
8. The ancient Greeks were (good) astronomers than the ancient Romans.
9. Copernicus was the (good) European astronomer of all in the sixteenth century.
10. Modern telescopes can show (many) planets than early telescopes.
11. Williamina Fleming found (many) stars than Copernicus.
12. Annie Cannon classified the (many) stars of all.
13. Red stars generate (little) light than blue stars.
14. The constellation Orion contains (many) stars than the constellation Delphinus.
15. The star Arcturus gives (much) light than Denebola.

◆ A **preposition** relates a noun to another word in the sentence. Some common prepositions are *in, with, on, at, to, about, of, for,* and *around*. The noun or pronoun that follows a preposition is called the **object** of the preposition. *(page 274)*

I read the last chapter of the book.

◆ A **prepositional phrase** contains the preposition, its object, and all the words that describe the object of the preposition. A prepositional phrase can act as an adjective by describing a noun. It answers such questions as *"which one?"* or *"what kind?" (page 274)*

The book's back cover shows a picture of the author.

Practice Write each sentence. Underline the prepositional phrase once. Underline the preposition twice. Write the noun that the prepositional phrase describes.

1. Louisa May Alcott was the author of many books.
2. Her family later had a home in Massachusetts.
3. Alcott started a small school for children.
4. She told them stories with unusual characters.
5. These stories became the basis of her first book.
6. *Little Women* is the story of four sisters.
7. The main character in this book is Jo March.
8. *Little Men* is another book with these characters.
9. It is a book about the girls' adult life.
10. Alcott's sincere style was the key to her success.
11. Penny wrote a guidebook about her town.
12. It describes many buildings in the area.
13. The book's cover shows a picture of the town.
14. Visitors to our community find the book useful.
15. Penny autographed my copy of the book.
16. That house with white trim is a landmark.
17. It is the birthplace of a famous artist.
18. The fence around the house is iron.
19. This office building was once a factory for bicycles.
20. The statue at the crossroads shows the town's founders.

Adverbs

♦ An **adverb** is a word that describes a verb, an adjective, or another adverb. An adverb can answer the questions *how?*, *when?*, or *where?* about an action. *(page 314)*

The large whale moves <u>slowly</u>.
<u>Sometimes</u> the water covers the whale.
The whale swims <u>away</u>.

♦ One way to find an adverb that describes an adjective or another adverb is to ask a question with the word *how* right before the adjective or adverb. *(page 314)*

An <u>extremely</u> large whale swims near us.
  (How large? *extremely* large; modifies adjective)
Another whale dives <u>very</u> quickly.
  (How quickly? *very* quickly; modifies adverb)

Practice Write each sentence. Underline each adverb, and draw an arrow to the word it describes.

1. We can scan the distant whitecaps eagerly.
2. We look everywhere for whales.
3. Some whales suddenly appear near our boat.
4. One very beautiful whale looks at me.
5. The animal seems quite friendly toward us.
6. I quickly grab my camera for a picture.
7. My movements very nearly ruin my chances for a shot.
8. The big whale swims nearby.
9. The rather graceful creature glides through the water.
10. I thoroughly enjoyed my conversation with a whale.

♦ The **comparative** form of an adverb compares the actions of two people, things, or groups. Add *er* to adverbs of one syllable and to *early* to form the comparative. Use *more* to form the comparative of most adverbs that end in *ly* and other two-syllable adverbs. *(page 316)*

Our boat arrives <u>earlier</u> than their boat.
This boat moves <u>more quickly</u> than any other.

♦ Add *est* to adverbs of one syllable and to *early* to form the superlative. Use *most* to form the superlative of adverbs that end in *ly* and of other two-syllable adverbs. *(page 316)*

    Of all the whales, that one swims <u>fastest</u> of all.

    It also moves <u>most gracefully</u> of all the whales.

♦ The adverbs *well* and *badly* have special comparative and superlative forms. *(page 316)*

Adverb	Comparative Form	Superlative Form
well	better	best
badly	worse	worst

A. Practice Write each sentence. Write the correct form of the adverb in parentheses.

    1. Mona swims (skillful) of all the swimmers.
    2. She dives (beautifully) than the other champion.
    3. Mona tries (hard) of all the athletes.
    4. Mona's team ranks (high) among all the teams.
    5. Mona will win a trophy (soon) than Wanda.
    6. Wanda leaves practice (early) than Mona.
    7. Mona practices (long) than Charlotte, too.
    8. Inez swims (gracefully) than Mona.
    9. Mona swims (quickly) of all the team members.
    10. Jo listens to the coach (attentively) of all the swimmers.

B. Practice Write each sentence. Write the correct form of the adverb in parentheses.

    11. Pablo cooks (well) than his sister Inez.
    12. I cook (badly) than Inez.
    13. I cook Chinese food (badly) of all.
    14. Pablo works (well) of all in his own kitchen.
    15. Joanne cooks vegetables (well) than meats.
    16. Kevin makes eggplant (well) of all.
    17. He prepares chili (badly) than Inez.
    18. Maria cooks spicy foods (well) than mild foods.
    19. Kevin baked bread (badly) yesterday than today.
    20. Our class did (well) of all in the Chefs' Contest.

- An **adjective** describes a noun or a pronoun. An **adverb** describes a verb, an adjective, or another adverb. *(page 318)*

Adjective	*Adverb*

    Rachel has a <u>soft</u> voice.   Rachel speaks <u>softly</u>.
    (*soft* describes *voice*)   (*softly* describes *speaks*)
- Adjectives are most often confused with adverbs when they come after linking verbs. An adjective is often used after a linking verb to describe the subject. Adverbs are usually used with action verbs. *(page 318)*

    Jon is <u>quiet</u>. (adjective—describes *Jon*)
    Jon walks <u>quietly</u>. (adverb—describes *walks*)

Practice   Write each sentence. Underline adjectives once and adverbs twice. Do not underline articles.

1. The courageous Vikings sailed from northern Europe.
2. Their ships were excellent.
3. Storms were often dangerous.
4. The skillful sailors handled the rough seas very well.
5. The Atlantic Ocean is still hazardous.
6. Some Vikings quickly traveled to Iceland.
7. Others then explored the huge island of Greenland.
8. The Vikings were brave explorers.
9. Finally, they sighted a rocky coast.
10. The happy Vikings proudly called this new land Vinland.

- An **adverb phrase** is a prepositional phrase that works like an adverb to describe a verb. An adverb phrase can answer the question *how?*, *where?*, or *when?* about a verb. *(page 320)*

    Bartolomé de Las Casas was born <u>in Seville</u>, <u>Spain</u>.
       (*Where* was he born?)
    He sailed west <u>with great courage</u>.
       (*How* did he sail?)
- An adverb phrase often appears right after the verb it describes. But it can also appear in other places in the sentence. *(page 320)*

    Las Casas desired peace and freedom <u>with all his heart</u>.
    <u>In 1502</u>, Las Casas left his native Spain.

Practice   Write each sentence. Underline each adverb phrase once. Underline twice the word or words it describes.

1. Bartolomé de Las Casas worked beside Native Americans.
2. He treated the Native American workers with respect.
3. Many Spaniards treated the slaves with great cruelty.
4. Las Casas spoke about the Native American's plight.
5. In 1516, he traveled home.
6. There he spoke before the king.
7. The king believed Las Casas's stories at once.
8. Through Las Casas's efforts, Native Americans gained new rights and freedoms.
9. Las Casas helped Native Americans for many years.

♦ A **negative** word expresses the idea of "no" in a sentence. The adverbs *not* and *never* are negatives. Other common negatives are *no, none, nobody, no one, nothing, nowhere, neither,* and *nor.* *(page 322)*

    Rachel never raises her voice.

Contractions formed from *not* and a verb are also negatives.

    Rachel isn't a loud girl. (is not)

♦ It is incorrect to use two negative words in a sentence when only one is needed. This error is called a *double negative.* *(page 322)*

    Incorrect: Kyle couldn't never play baseball.
    Correct: Kyle could never play baseball.

Practice   Write each sentence. Choose the word or words that correctly form a negative sentence.

1. Cynthia doesn't (never, ever) act shy.
2. Company (doesn't, does) bother her at all.
3. She has (no, any) problems meeting people.
4. Carl almost (never, ever) talks to strangers.
5. (Nobody, Anybody) invites him to large parties.
6. He (never, ever) feels comfortable in crowds.
7. He doesn't show (no, any) shyness with friends, though.
8. Cynthia never says (nothing, anything) about his shyness.
9. It does not harm (no one, anyone).

Sentences II

♦ A **preposition** is a word that shows a relationship between a noun or a pronoun and other words in a sentence. Some common prepositions include *about, above, across, after, against, around, at, before, between, by, down, during, for, from, in, into, like, near, of, off, on, outside, over, through, to, toward, until, up, with, without,* and *within. (page 362)*

Emilio waits <u>near</u> the telephone.

♦ A preposition is usually followed by a noun or a pronoun called the **object of the preposition**. The preposition and its object together form a **prepositional phrase**. *(page 362)*

He also paces <u>around the entire house</u>.

Practice Write each sentence. Underline the prepositional phrase. Circle the preposition. Put another line under the object of the preposition.

1. This call is important to Emilio.
2. He wants a part in a new play.
3. The director will call during the evening.
4. Emilio has acted in many plays.
5. In school he played many important roles.
6. He has always learned lines with great ease.
7. In one production, Emilio portrayed a bold and vigorous pirate leader.
8. Later, he played the role of George Washington.
9. Once, Emilio worked with a famous actor.
10. Now, he plans his schoolwork and his weekends around his rehearsals.
11. He eagerly waits for his big chance.
12. Emilio grabs the phone from the hook.
13. He shouts happily at the director's decision.
14. Emilio's mother cheers at the good news.
15. The young actor is finally on his way!

◆ A **conjunction** is a word that joins other words or groups of words in a sentence. The most common conjunctions are *and*, *but*, and *or*. *(page 364)*

> Oceanographers study oceans <u>and</u> rivers.
> They work with marine life <u>but</u> study land plants, too.

◆ An **interjection** is a word or expression that is used to convey feeling. It has no close connection with the rest of the sentence. Some common interjections are *oh*, *goodness*, *hey*, *well*, *hurray*, and *wow*. *(page 364)*

◆ An interjection that expresses a strong feeling is followed by an exclamation mark and stands alone. An interjection can also express mild feeling. When it does, it is followed by a comma and is part of a sentence. *(page 364)*

> <u>Wow!</u> This is the fastest boat ever.
> <u>Oh,</u> I hope our boat floats.

Practice Write each sentence. Underline each conjunction once and each interjection twice. Write whether each interjection expresses strong or mild feeling.

1. Oceanographers study sea plants and animals.
2. An oceanographer's work is difficult but enjoyable.
3. Oh, so oceanographers are specialists in ocean science.
4. Undersea study and laboratory experiments are important parts of an oceanographer's life.
5. Wow! Sometimes they must live on a boat for months.
6. Some oceanographers specialize in whales or dolphins.
7. Others study the ocean floor and its secrets.
8. Well, can oceanographers give us information about earthquakes?
9. We won't learn about that next year or the year after.
10. The sea reveals some secrets but keeps many others.

◆ The **complete subject** of a sentence may contain more than one simple subject. A **compound subject** is made up of two or more simple subjects that share the same predicate. Sometimes the complete subject contains words besides *and* and the simple subjects. *(page 366)*

> Grains and beans are good sources of protein.

> Brown rice, fresh eggs, and tofu are other healthful foods.

Practice Write each sentence. Underline each simple subject in the compound subject.

1. Mr. Bell and the students plan a vegetarian meal.
2. Pictures and posters of appropriate foods hang on the bulletin board.
3. Each boy and girl chooses one item.
4. Hilary, Susan, and Luis decide on whole-wheat spaghetti.
5. Fresh mushrooms and red onions were ingredients in their special sauce.
6. Ginger and Martha bake a loaf of banana nut bread.
7. Herb and the teacher toss a fresh vegetable salad.
8. Black bean soup and brown rice simmer on the stove.
9. Fancy apples, sweet pears, and fresh strawberries are part of a delicious dessert.
10. The teacher and the students enjoy a delicious and healthful meal.

♦ The **complete predicate** of a sentence may have more than one simple predicate. A **compound predicate** is made up of two or more verbs that share the same subject.

> The chef baked and served whole grain rolls.

> The customer ordered, waited, and ate.

♦ A complete predicate may include words besides *and* and the simple predicates. *(page 368)*

> Joseph washed the pots quickly and dried them.

Practice Write each sentence. Underline each simple predicate in the compound predicate.

1. Mr. Lee plans a party and decides on a menu.
2. He lists and counts all the necessary food items.
3. The kitchen crew arranges and sets the tables for the party.
4. Deonne Lee checks and reviews the guest list.
5. The waiters and waitresses arrive and prepare for the evening.
6. The decorators discuss and examine the decorations.
7. The chef mixes, bakes, and slices the bread.
8. Deonne works hard through the night and hopes for success.
9. She glides quickly through the hall and announces the guests.
10. She opens the doors and smiles at the first arrivals.

◆ A compound sentence is a sentence that contains two simple sentences joined by a comma and one of the conjunctions *and*, *but*, or *or*. *(page 370)*

> Joyce made a bean salad , and Leone baked bread.

Practice Write each sentence. Write *simple* or *compound* to identify it.

1. A healthful diet provides energy for your body, and it keeps your mind alert.
2. Eat more whole grains, but eat fewer fatty foods.
3. Fresh fruit tastes delicious and promotes health.
4. Pocket bread is great for a quick sandwich or a tasty snack.
5. A pocket bread sandwich with guacamole and sprouts is a wonderful and healthful treat.
6. Angela improved her diet, but she still eats too much sugar.
7. She needs help with her nutrition, or she may become ill.
8. Jacob gave Angela a fabulous book on nutrition and health.

9. Angela and Jacob read the book, and they asked many questions of the health teacher.

10. We must all eat right, or we will not do our best.

◆ A **run-on sentence** is two or more sentences that are not separated by correct punctuation or conjunctions. To correct a run-on sentence, form two separate sentences or a compound sentence with a comma and a conjunction. *(page 372)*

Run-on: Maya Angelou is a famous black writer she is a singer, too.

Correct: Maya Angelou is a famous black writer. She is a singer, too.

Correct: Maya Angelou is a famous black writer, and she is a singer, too.

Practice   Read each sentence. If it is a run-on sentence, correct it by writing two simple sentences or by adding a comma and a conjunction. If it is correct, write *correct*.

1. Maya Angelou grew up in Arkansas she lived with her brother and her grandmother.

2. Maya loved her grandmother's general store, and she enjoyed visits there.

3. The store was popular, and it was the center of the town's social life.

4. People sang songs they strummed homemade guitars.

5. Maya's grandmother worked hard she listened to her grandchildren's problems.

6. Maya was an excellent student she graduated at the top of her class.

7. She worked during the day she studied dance at night.

8. Maya and her brother loved and respected their grandmother very much.

9. Grandmother did her best for the children she was happy with their success.

10. Maya Angelou gained recognition as a lead dancer in the musical *Porgy and Bess*.

Mechanics Rules and Practice

Capitalization and End Punctuation

Use a period (.) at the end of a statement or a command. (*page 36*)	As the noise died down, we all relaxed. Never do that again.
Use a question mark (?) at the end of a question. (*page 36*)	How can I be of help? Did you like the movie?
Use an exclamation mark (!) at the end of a statement or a command showing strong emotion or surprise. (*page 36*)	I can't believe this is happening! What good luck we had! Stop that, Spot!

Capitalize the following:	
the first word in a sentence (*page 36*)	He examined the situation.
names of people (*page 36*)	Helena Tanya Lutov Paco
first and all important words in titles of books, stories, poems, and songs (*page 120*)	*David Copperfield* (book) ''Ode on the Spring'' (poem) ''Out of my Dreams'' (song)
addresses (*page 160*)	538 Park Ave. 13 Moonlight Lane
calendar words and holidays (*page 160*)	Friday May Dec. Thanksgiving
titles and initials (*page 160*)	Ms. Rollins President J. F. Kennedy
the first word in the greeting and closing of a letter (*page 160*)	Dearest Grandma, Dear Mr. Presley, Sincerely, Yours truly,
places or nationalities as adjectives (*page 266*)	Canadian rivers Japanese restaurant

A. Practice Write each sentence using the correct end punctuation and capitalization.

1. Did you know that william shakespeare was born in 1564

2. he died in 1616 and is buried in Stratford, England

3. shakespeare wrote some of our greatest plays and poems

4. You must read his play about hamlet, prince of Denmark

5. I can't believe you've never read *romeo and juliet*

6. In *romeo and juliet,* there are two rival families, the montagues and the capulets

7. romeo is from the montague family, and juliet is from the capulet family

8. Did you know that mercutio and benvolio are also characters in the play

9. Was "a rose by any other name would smell as sweet" said by Juliet

10. as the prince declares, "For never was a story of more woe than this of juliet and her romeo," the play ends

B. Practice Write the letter using proper capitalization.

872 thorn street
bremen, ohio 43130
june 3, 1987

dear Kelly,

Washington, d.c., is fun. Today we saw the Smithsonian institution. The dinosaurs were amazing! Then we walked to capitol hill to visit senator Glenn and our congresswoman, but they were meeting the spanish delegation. One senator's aide gave us tickets for a debate in congress. i'm certainly glad we took this trip! I'll see you thursday.

sincerely,
Pat

P.S. I bought you a book called *washington in a day.*

Commas

Use a comma:	
between words in a series *(page 74)*	Stella brought a camera, some film, and flashcubes.
in a compound sentence before *and, but,* or *or (page 74)*	I wanted to visit Arlington Cemetery, but we didn't have time.
after introductory phrases *(page 74)*	In a few weeks, we will visit France.
to set off phrases that explain or clarify nouns *(page 74)*	They visited the White House, a residence for presidents.
after greetings in friendly letters *(page 160)*	Dear Lester, Dear Aunt Pauline,
after closings in letters *(page 160)*	Sincerely, Yours truly,
between the day of the month and the year *(page 160)*	I was born on May 9, 1979. Today's date is March 2, 1992.
between a city and a state or country *(page 160)*	Honolulu, Hawaii Rawalpindi, Pakistan
to set off expressions like *yes, well, however, though,* and *of course (page 210)*	Yes, dinner is ready. The flight, however, was late. I will be there, of course.
to set off the name of a person spoken to directly *(page 210)*	Look at this, Jim. Ingrid, what are you doing?
between a last name and a first name when the names are reversed *(page 258)*	Emerson, Ralph Romero, Patricia

A. Practice Write each sentence. Add commas where they are needed.

1. Roberto Clemente was born in Puerto Rico but he played for the Pittsburgh Pirates.
2. Clemente gave time money and energy to charities.
3. Clemente spoke for human rights especially those of Latin players.
4. Clemente was an all-star and he helped the Pirates win two World Series.
5. On December 31, 1972 a tragedy occurred.

6. On that day Clemente died while flying earthquake relief supplies to Managua, Nicaragua.

7. Sportswriters voted Clemente into the Baseball Hall of Fame and you can now read about him in the encyclopedia under Clemente, Roberto.

B. (8.—19.) Practice Write the letter. Add commas where they're needed.

September 16 1989
Florence Italy

Dear Mom Dad and Chris

Art school is going just fine. Mary and I especially like ancient Greek sculpture. Abstract art is my other favorite but Mary hates it. She keeps saying, "I don't understand it Peggy." I told her about the colors geometric shapes and strange scenes in the paintings of Pablo Picasso.

I'll always remember 1989 as the year I started to study art seriously. I always dreamed of it but I didn't think I would really make it. Well I better get back to my books!

Sincerely

Peggy

C. Practice Write each sentence, adding commas where they are needed.

20. The gold rush Juanita started in 1848 at Sutter's Mill.

21. San Francisco was the first place many prospectors saw when they arrived in California.

22. Yes life was full of difficulties.

23. However they had "gold fever" and could not be stopped.

24. Writers Edwin Markham, Bret Harte, and of course Mark Twain described the miners' lives.

25. In the encyclopedia, they are listed as Markham Edwin; Harte Bret; and Twain Mark.

26. Naturally newspapers in the East carried the stories, and many people dreamed of heading west for adventure.

27. For most however it was only a dream.

Other Punctuation

Use this punctuation:	
underline titles of books, newspapers, plays, movies, and magazines (*page 120*)	<u>Oliver Twist</u> (book) <u>Romeo and Juliet</u> (play) <u>The New York Times</u> (newspaper) <u>E.T.</u> (movie)
quotation marks around titles of songs, poems, stories, essays, and articles (*page 120*)	''Goodnight, Irene'' (song) ''The Raven'' (poem) ''The Necklace'' (story)
period after most abbreviations (*page 160*)	Mr. Rodriguez John F. Kennedy Oct. a.m. p.m.
colon after greetings in business letters (*page 160*)	Dear Ms. Rogers: Dear Sir:
semicolon between sentences not joined by a conjunction (*page 210*)	Emma loves dogs; Rosita prefers cats.
apostrophe in contractions in possessives (*page 308*)	he's they've can't Mary's cat students' notebooks
hyphen to form a compound adjective to form a compound noun (*page 308*)	mud-spattered double-decker father-in-law Senator-elect
quotation marks around direct quotations (*page 356*)	My friend wrote, ''I'm having a wonderful time.''

A. Practice Write the sentences using correct punctuation.

1. Detective stories like The Speckled Band have been popular for more than 100 years.
2. I wrote an essay about Sherlock Holmes called The Best Detective.
3. The first Holmes novel, A Study in Scarlet, was a great success.
4. A Scandal in Bohemia is a Holmes short story.
5. Holmes often read The Times for crime news.

6. Thomas Edison made a silent film called Holmes Baffled.
7. Basil Rathbone played Holmes in A Scandal in Bohemia.

B. Practice Write the sentences using correct punctuation.
8. I had an appointment with Dr Jones at 10:00 am
9. The date in her records read "Oct 5."
10. Mrs Chavez says she waited until 7:00 pm to see her.
11. She studied at the John F Kennedy Medical Center.
12. Mr Epstein says she is a skilled heart surgeon.
13. They are trying to make a better artificial heart this research may take a long time.
14. Ms Hing says they've got to find better ways to help the body accept mechanical hearts.
15. The mechanical heart's power source is unwieldy people's movements are greatly restricted.
16. It seems likely that scientists will work out the problems solutions are being actively pursued.

C. Practice Write the sentences using correct punctuation.
17. Ludwig Van Beethovens birthplace is in Bonn, Germany.
18. Beethovens birthdate is December 17, 1770.
19. His grandfather, whose name he bore, was a well known singer.
20. Although he wasnt a prodigy like Mozart, Beethoven had a more stable career.
21. Hed mastered the piano and violin at age 11, and his teacher wrote, He would surely become a second Wolfgang Amadeus Mozart were he to continue as he has begun.
22. When Mozart heard Beethoven play, he predicted, He'll give the world something worth listening to.
23. Although Beethoven began to lose his hearing in the 1790s, it wasnt until much later that he became totally deaf.
24. Nevertheless, his deafness didnt prevent him from composing.
25. When Beethoven died at age 57, hed composed many symphonies, piano concertos, and overtures.

Punctuating Conversation

Use quotation marks (" ") before and after the exact words of a speaker. (*page 356*)	"Lift the hatch," Dad said. "Hold it open," he added, "while I put the trees in."
Use a comma (,) to separate the speaker's words from the rest of the sentence. (*page 356*)	"When you closed the hatch," Jo said, "the treetop got caught."
Put this end punctuation inside quotation marks: period (.") exclamation mark (!") question mark (?") (*page 356*)	She said, "Put the tree in carefully." "Watch out!" Jo shouted. "What's wrong?" Dad asked.
Capitalize the first word of a quotation but not the first word of a continued quotation. (*page 356*)	Jo said, "That tree was too tall for the car." "That tree," Jo said, "was too tall for the car."
indent each time a new speaker begins (*page 356*)	Dad said, "Next year, I will buy a truck so we won't have this problem." "Sure, Dad," said Joe. "You said that last year."

A. Practice Write each sentence using correct punctuation.

1. I like collecting stamps said Luis.
2. He continued stamps can be a window on the world.
3. I asked Isn't there a country in which the main industry is stamps
4. Yes said Luis there are several small countries that earn a lot of money by selling stamps to collectors
5. Can you tell me the names of those countries I asked.
6. Well he replied one is Andorra
7. Andorra I exclaimed I've never heard of Andorra
8. Luis laughed and said it's on the border between France and Spain
9. As Luis showed me a map, I said, what an incredibly tiny country
10. It may be small Luis said but it is a very beautiful and peaceful country

B. Practice (11.–20.) Write the following, using correct punctuation. Indent to form new paragraphs where necessary.

> There are several small countries in Europe, said my geography teacher, Mr. Zeglarski. I know one I said. It's called Andorra. That's right said Mr. Zeglarski.
> "Andorra is a small country of about 180 square miles on the border between France and Spain. It is situated in the Pyrenees, a mountain range along that border." "What are some other small countries?" I asked. "Two others," Mr. Zeglarski said, are Monaco and Liechtenstein; they are both principalities. That means they are ruled by princes. Monaco has 368 acres, and Liechtenstein has 62 square miles.

C. Practice Write each sentence, using correct punctuation.

21. Tell me something about Monaco, said Luis.
22. Well, responded Mr. Zeglarski, its official language is French, and its citizens are called Monégasques.
23. How is Monaco ruled asked Luis.
24. A French minister of state, under the authority of the prince, heads the government.
25. Do the French have a lot of power in Monaco Luis asked.
26. Yes, they do Mr. Zeglarski replied And if Monaco's royal family has no male heirs, Monaco will be ruled by France.
27. Who is prince there now asked Luis.
28. Prince Rainier III is the current ruler.
29. Wait a minute exclaimed Luis. I've heard of him.
30. You have asked Mr. Zeglarski.
31. Sure explained Luis Didn't he marry a famous movie star
32. Yes, indeed replied Mr. Zeglarski. He married Grace Kelly.
33. Right said Luis I just saw her in a really good, old movie directed by Alfred Hitchcock called *Rear Window*.
34. I don't think I've ever seen it said Mr. Zeglarski.
35. Great exclaimed Luis Now it's my turn to lecture you.

Diagraming

A **diagram** of a sentence is a set of lines showing the relationships among all of the words and phrases in that sentence. Diagraming sentences can help you learn to identify the different parts of speech and their functions.

Simple Subjects and Simple Predicates

To diagram a sentence, begin with a base line. On the left half of this line, write the simple subject of the sentence. Then find the simple predicate, and write it on the right half of the base line. Separate the simple subject from the simple predicate with a vertical line that crosses the base line.

Here are diagrams for the four kinds of sentences.

Declarative: Lisa races.

Lisa | races

Interrogative: Will she win?

she | Will win

Exclamatory: Gina won!

Gina | won

Imperative: Hurry.

(You) | Hurry

Although the imperative sentence has no stated subject, the subject is understood to be *you*. Show this in your diagram by using parentheses.

Practice Diagram these sentences.

1. Joe ran.
2. I will go.
3. Did he leave?
4. Sara shouted.
5. Wait!
6. We hurried.
7. Manny rested.
8. Can I stop?
9. Run.
10. I will walk.

Direct Objects and Indirect Objects

The direct object receives the action of the verb. The indirect object tells to whom or for whom the action is done. On your diagram, write the direct object on the base line, to the right of the verb. Separate it from the verb with a vertical line that does not cross the base line. Write the indirect object on a horizontal line beneath the base line. Connect the indirect object to the verb with a slanted line.

They will bring us dinner.

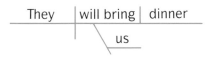

Adjectives and Adverbs

Adjectives, including articles, modify nouns. Adverbs can modify verbs, adjectives, or other adverbs. To diagram adjectives and adverbs, place them on slanted lines under the words they modify.

The young doctor very eagerly offered me advice.

Possessives

Possessives and possessive forms of pronouns modify nouns. Add these to your sentence diagrams by writing them on slanted lines below the nouns they modify.

Fiona's father gave me her paper.

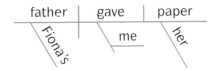

Practice Diagram these sentences.

1. My best friend threw me a big party.
2. The many guests arrived promptly.
3. Some guests quietly gave me their presents.
4. Jack's delicious pizza disappeared quickly.
5. We happily ate the fresh pineapple.

Predicate Nominatives and Predicate Adjectives

Predicate nominatives and predicate adjectives follow linking verbs. To diagram predicate nominatives and predicate adjectives, write them on the base line, to the right of the verb. Separate them from the verb with a line slanted toward the subject. This line should not cross the base line.

The cockatiel is an Australian bird.

It is rather small.

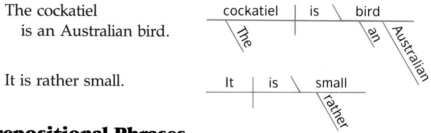

Prepositional Phrases

To diagram a prepositional phrase, write the preposition on a slanted line below the word the phrase modifies. Then write the object of the phrase on a horizontal line. Diagram modifiers of this object in the same way you would diagram other modifiers.

We keep the cage for our cockatiel in the kitchen.

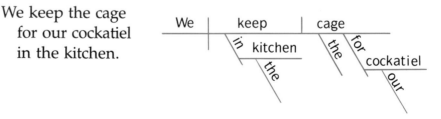

Practice Diagram these sentences.

1. Chile is a country in South America.
2. Santiago is the capital of Chile.
3. Valparaiso is a city on the coast of this country.
4. The Chileans are a proud people.
5. Spanish remains the official language in Chile.

Compound Subjects, Compound Objects, and Compound Predicates

To diagram a sentence with a compound subject or compound direct object, use one horizontal line for each noun in the subject or direct object. Connect these lines with a vertical dashed line, and write the conjunction on that line.

Newspapers and magazines
employ writers and reporters.

Diagram compound predicates like compound subjects.

Newspapers inform and
entertain their readers.

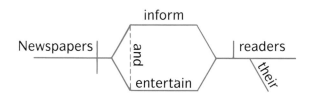

Compound Sentences

Diagram each clause in a compound sentence separately. Place the conjunction on a horizontal line between the clauses, and connect it to each clause's verb with vertical dashed lines.

Reporters research the news,
and later they write about it.

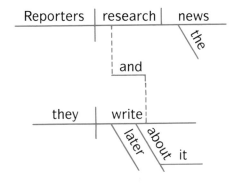

Practice Diagram these sentences.
1. "Cinderella" and "Snow White" are famous tales.
2. Cinderella danced and laughed at the ball.
3. The Grimms also published "Rumpelstiltskin" and "Tom Thumb," and these stories remain famous today.

Troublesome Words

◆ **Homophones** are words that sound alike but have different spellings and meanings.

Word	Meaning	Example
its it's	belonging to it it is	The dog wagged its tail. It's closing time.
their there they're	belonging to them in that place they are	Their grades are excellent. The list is there. They're on the bus.
to too two	in the direction of also; more than enough one plus one	I'm sending you to Paris. That's too expensive. I see two tigers.
your you're	belonging to you you are	Your entry won. You're kidding!

Practice Write each sentence. Choose the correct word in parentheses.

1. (Their, There) is a lot of trash on the floor.
2. (Too, Two) much paper falls on the floor.
3. (It's, Its) time to pick it up.
4. Please bring the large wastebasket that is near (your, you're) desk.
5. Bring the broom and dustpan, (to, too).
6. (Their, There) isn't much time.
7. We should be able to finish the work in only (two, too) minutes.
8. Even trash has (it's, its) proper place in a clean classroom.
9. (You're, Your) doing a fine job.
10. The other students are doing (they're, their) part in the cleanup.
11. They appreciate (your, you're) work.
12. (They're, Their) nearly finished now.
13. Take the trash (to, too) the large can beside the building.

◆ Some pairs of words are confusing because they sound similar
  but have different meanings.

Word	Meaning	Example
lie	to put oneself in or to be in a lying position	We'll lie by the pool.
lay	to put or place something	First, lay down your towel.
rise	to go up or to get up	Please rise from your seat.
raise	to move something upward	We will raise the flag.
sit	to put oneself in or to be in a sitting position	I can sit and talk now.
set	to put or place something	Set the book over there.

Practice Write each sentence with the correct word.
1. You may (lie, lay) your pencil and paper aside.
2. Now (set, sit) your materials on the desk.
3. Please (rise, raise) your hand if you have a question.
4. (Set, Sit) up straight in your chair.
5. Later you may (lay, lie) on the bed and rest.

The following pairs of verbs are often confused.

Word	Meaning	Example
can	to be able to	I can run ten miles.
may	to be permitted to	May I go with you?
lend	to give temporarily	Please lend me a dime.
loan	something lent (noun)	I will return the loan.
let	to allow	He will let me visit.
leave	to go away from	You must leave soon.

Practice Write each sentence with the correct word.
1. Could you (loan, lend) me a scarf for the dance?
2. Please (let, leave) me help you get ready.
3. What time will you (let, leave) for the dance?
4. I (can, may) be ready in ten minutes if necessary.
5. (Can, May) I walk with you to the dance?

Index

Abbreviations, 88
  in addresses, 88
  of days and months, 88
  on envelopes, 160
  in letters, 160
  for parts of speech, 52
Accent marks, 52
Acrostic poems, 216
Action verbs, 126
Addresses
  abbreviations in, 88
  inside of business letters, 154
Adjective phrases, 274
Adjectives, 264-275, 458-461
  or adverbs, 318
  comparisons with, 270
  irregular comparisons, 272
  predicate, 174, 268
  prepositions and adjective phrases, 274
  proper, 266
  strategy
    for comparing with *good* and *bad*, 272
    for comparisons with, 270
    for possessive or proper adjective, 266
Adverb phrases, 320-321
Adverbs, 314-323, 463-466
  adjectives or, 318
  avoiding double negatives, 322
  comparisons with, 316
  strategy for comparisons with, 316
Advertisements, 382-385
Alliteration, 204
Almanac, 246
Antecedents, 228
Antonyms, 90, 276-277, 324
  and synonyms, 276-277, 324
  in thesaurus, 90
Apostrophes, 308
  in plural possessives, 86
  in possessives, 84
Articles, 264
Atlas, 246

Base words, 142
Bibliography, 244, 258-259
Biographical sketch, 60-77

characteristics of, 61
  conducting interview for, 68
  preparing for interview, 66
Body
  of business letter, 154
  of friendly letter, 164
  of persuasive essay, 302
  of research report, 244
Book, parts of, 248
Book reports, 106-123
  characteristics of, 107
  facts supporting opinion in, 114
  introductions and summaries, 112
Brainstorming (*see* Thinking skills)
Business abbreviations, 88
Business letters (*see also* Letters)
  characteristics of, 151, 154
  punctuating, 160
  writing, 156
Bus schedule, reading, 144-145

Capitalization, 36, 120, 160, 356, 472-473
  in abbreviations, 88-89
  proper nouns, 80
Card catalog in library, 110
Cause and effect, 354
Character sketch, 348
Characters of story, 333, 348
Closing,
  of business letter, 154
  of friendly letter, 152, 164
Colons, 258
Combining sentences
  linking words describing subject and action, 158
  using *and*, *but*, or *or*, 34, 118
  with words showing cause and effect, 354
  with words showing time-order, 354
Commas
  in abbreviations, 88
  in bibliography, 258
  in compound sentences, 370
  in conversation, 356
  in correcting run-on sentences, 372
  in letters, 160
  punctuating with, 74
  review of general rules, 474-475

and semicolons, 210
Common nouns, 80
Comparisons
  irregular, 271
  with adjectives, 270
  with adverbs, 316
Complete predicates, 44
Complete subjects, 44
Composition
  biographical sketch, 61-77
  book report, 107-123
  business letter, 151-163
  descriptive paragraph, 195-212, 219
  friendly letter, 164-165
  personal narrative, 19-39
  persuasive essay, 295-311
  poem, 213-219
  research report, 241-261
  story, 333-359
Compound predicates, 368
Compound sentences, 370
Compound subjects, 366
Computer, writing on, 431
Conclusion
  of persuasive essay, 302
  of research report, 244
Conjunctions, 364-365, 372, 468
Connotation and denotation, 374-375
Context clues, 324-325
Contractions, 230
Conversation
  punctuation of, 356, 478-479
Cooperative learning (*see also* Presenting and sharing)
  action verbs, subjects, and direct objects, 169
  adjectives, 265
  adverb phrases, 321
  comparing with adjectives, 271
  comparing with adverbs, 317
  compound and simple predicates, 369
  compound sentences, 371
  context clues, 325
  direct and indirect object pronouns, 225
  end marks on sentences, 43
  filling out forms, 178
  fragments and sentences, 45
  helping verbs, 131
  homophones and homographs, 233
  informal dialogue and formal sentences, 223
  interrogative and declarative sentences, 49
  invitations using abbreviations, 89
  irregular verbs, 139, 141
  negatives, 323
  perfect tenses, 135

plural nouns, 83
possessives, 85
predicate nouns and adjectives, 175
prefixes and suffixes, 143
pronouns of different types, 227
proper adjectives, 267
synonyms, 91, 277
verbs, 127
words with many meanings, 53

Days and dates, abbreviations of, 88
Declarative sentences, 42
Definite articles, 264
Definitions in dictionary, 52
Denotation and connotation, 374-375
Descriptive writing, 194-219
  avoiding repetition in, 208
  characteristics of, 195
  figurative language in, 204
  organizing sensory details in, 200
  poetry, 213-218
    acrostic poems, 216
    free verse, 214
    rhyme, 213
    rhythm, 214
    tanka, 216
  precise details in, 202
Details
  precise, 202
  sensory, 200
  supporting, 30
Dewey Decimal System, 110
Diagraming, 480-483
Dictionary skills, 52-53
  entry words, 52
  pronunciation, 52
Direct objects, 168, 224
Direct quotation, 68
Directions
  following, 180
  giving, 234-235
Discussing (*see* Speaking and listening)
Discussion strategy (*see* Speaking and listening)
Double negatives, strategy to avoid, 322

Editor, letter to, 184-187
Effect, cause and, 354
Encyclopedia, 246
End punctuation, 472-473
English language, history of, 56
Entry words, 52
Envelopes, addressing, 160
Essay (*see* Persuasive essay)

Essay questions, 378
Example and opinion, 300
Example sentences or phrases in dictionary, 52
Exclamation marks, 36, 42, 356
Exclamatory sentences, 42

Facts supporting opinion, 114, 300
Feature section of newspaper, 92
Fiction books, 110
Figurative language, 204
First draft, writing a, 32, 70, 116, 156, 206, 254, 304, 352,
Formal language, 154
Forms, filling out, 178-179
Fragments, 42
    strategy for imperative sentences or, 48
Free verse, 214
French, English words from, 146
Friendly letters (see Letters)
Future tense, 132

Grammar and mechanics handbook, 437-485
    adjectives, 458-461
    adverbs, 463-466
    commas, 474
    conjunctions, 468
    diagraming, 480-483
    end punctuation, 472
    grammar definitions and practice, 437-471
    interjections, 468
    mechanics rules and practice, 472-479
    nouns, 441-444
    other punctuation, 476
    prepositions, 462, 467
    pronouns, 454-457
    punctuating conversation, 478
    sentences, 437-440, 467-471
    troublesome words, 484
    verbs, 445-453
Greeting,
    of business letter, 154
    of friendly letter, 152, 164
Group discussion, 54-55

Handwriting, 436
Heading
    of business letter, 154
    of friendly letter, 152, 164
Helping verbs, 130
History of language, 56
    animal words, 328
    history of English, 56
    words from French, 146

words from place names, 236
Homophones and homographs, 232-233
Hyphens, 308

Imperative sentences, 42, 48
Indefinite articles, 264
Indenting, 36, 258
Index of book, 248
Indirect objects, 170, 224
Inside address of business letter, 154
Interjections, 364-365, 468
Interrogative sentences, 42, 48
Interviews
    conducting, 68
    preparing for, 66
Intransitive verbs, 172
Introduction
    of book report, 112
    of persuasive essay, 302
    of research report, 244
    of speech, 376
    of story, 333, 350
Irregular comparisons with adjectives, 272
Irregular verbs, 138, 140

Journal (see also Thinking skills)
    adverbs, 315
    conjunctions, 365
    interjections, 365
    irregular adjectives, 273
    nouns, 81
    present, past, and future tenses, 133
    pronouns, 229
    sentences with here and there, 51

Key words, 246

Language in action
    filling out forms, 178-179
    giving directions, 234-235
    giving an oral report, 278-279
    giving a speech, 376-377
    group discussion, 54-55
    reading bus schedule, 144-145
    reading newspaper, 92-93
    recognizing propaganda, 326-327
Learning log (see Thinking skills)
Letters, 150-165
    business, 154-163
        characteristics of, 151
        combining sentences in, 156
        planning, 154
        to editor, 184-187

488

envelopes, 160
friendly, 164-165
    characteristics of, 151
letter forms, 432-433
punctuation of, 160
Library
using, 110
using reference materials, 246
Linking verbs
distinguishing from action verbs, 128
expressing change, 128
expressing the senses, 128
forms of *be*, 128
strategy for predicate adjectives following, 268
Listening strategy (*see* Speaking and listening)
Literature
"An April Kite," 215
"Aspirations," Emily Dickinson, 293
from "Auguries of Irinecause," William Blake, 105
"Autumn Evening," M. Daniel Hoff, 215
"Committee, The," Ellen Conford, 20-24
"Connections," Margaret Tsuda, 17
"Dream Woman, The," Patricia Hubbell, 124
"Eleanor Roosevelt: First Lady of the World," Doris Faber, 62-64
"Eletelephony," Laura E. Richards, 78
from *Endless Steppe, The*, Esther Hautzig, 196-197
"Escape from the City," Barbara Klinger, 214
"Falling Star, The," Sara Teasdale, 213
from the speech "I Have a Dream," Dr. Martin Luther King, Jr., 296-298
from *Letters to Horseface*, F.N. Monjo, 152
"Metamorphosis," May Sarton, 198
"Peabody Bird, The," Rachel Field, 40
"Raymond's Run," Toni Cade Bambara, 334-346
from "Road Not Taken, The," Robert Frost, 193
"Springtime," D. Heath, 216
"Summer Storm, The," 215
"There Are So Many Ways of Going Places," Leslie Thompson, 166
"Traveling Home," 216
"Waiting for Spring," M. Batchelder, 214
from "Walrus and the Carpenter, The," Lewis Carroll, 360
"Wasp, The," William Sharp, 312
"White Rabbit's Verse, The," Lewis Carroll 220
from *Wind in the Willows, The*, Kenneth Grahame, 262
"Winter Seems Forever," M. Batchelder, 214
from *Wizard of Oz, The*, L. Frank Baum, 113
Literature connection
adjectives, 262
adverbs, 312

nouns, 78
pronouns, 220
sentences, 40, 360
verbs, 124, 166

Main idea, 28
Main verbs, 130
Making All the Connections
advertisement, 382-385
historical play, 284-287
letter to editor, 184-187
news feature, 98-101
Metaphor, 204
Months, abbreviations, 88

Narrative (*see* Personal narrative)
Narrowing topic, 26
Negatives, avoiding double, 322
Newspaper, reading, 92-93
Nonfiction books, 110
Notes, taking
for an oral report, 278
for a research report, 250
for speech, 376
from an interview, 68
Nouns, 80-89, 441-444
abbreviations, 88
common and proper, 80
possessives, 84, 86
predicate, 174
singular and plural, 82
strategy
    for apostrophe in possessive, 84
    for common or proper, 80
    for identifying predicate nouns, 174
    for plural nouns and plural possessives, 86
    for plurals of, 82
    for using abbreviations, 88

Objects
direct, 168
indirect, 170
of prepositions, 274, 362
Object pronouns, 224
Onomatopoeia, 204
Opinion supported by facts, 114, 300
Oral report, 278-279
Order (*see* Sequence)
Organizing
advertisement, 384
historical play, 286
letter to editor, 186
news feature, 100

research report, 244
sensory details, 200
Outcome of story, 333, 350
Outline for research report, 252

Paraphrasing, 68
Parts of Speech (*see* Adjectives; Adverbs; Nouns;
    Pronouns; Verbs)
Past tense
    of irregular verbs, 138-139
    of regular verbs, 132
    spelling of, 132, 136-138
Perfect tenses, 134
Periods
    at end of abbreviation, 88, 476
    at end of sentence, 36, 42, 472
    in a bibliography, 258
    in quotations, 356, 386
Personal narrative, 18-39
    characteristics of, 19
    main idea and topic sentence in, 28
    narrowing topic for, 26
    supporting details in, 30
Personification, 204
Persuasive essay, 294-311
    characteristics of, 295
    order of presentation, 306
    structuring, 302
    supporting opinion, 300
Phrases
    adjective, 274
    adverb, 320
    as examples using entry words in dictionary, 52
    beginning sentences with, 72
    explanatory, 52, 324
    prepositional, 274, 362-363
    verb, 130
Planning
    advertisement, 384
    biographical sketch, 61-69
    book report, 107-115
    descriptive writing, 195-205
    historical play, 286
    letter, 151-155
    news feature, 100
    persuasive essay, 295-303
    research report, 241-253
    short story, 333-351
Plot
    of book, 112
    of story, 333, 350
Plural nouns, 82

Plural possessives, 86
Poetry (*see* Literature)
Possessive forms of pronouns, 230
Precise details, 202
Predicate adjectives, 174, 268
Predicate nouns, 174
Predicates
    complete, 44
    compound, 368
    simple, 46
Prefixes, 142-143, 358
Prepositional phrases, 274, 362-363
Prepositions, 362-363, 462, 467
    and adjective phrases, 274
    strategy for remembering, 362
Presenting and sharing
    biographical sketch, 77
    book report, 123,
    business letter, 163
    descriptive writing, 219
    friendly letter, 165
    news feature, 101
    personal narrative, 39
    persuasive essay, 311
    research report, 261
    story, 359
Present tense, 132
Principal parts
    of irregular verbs, 138
    of regular verbs, 136
Problem of story, 333, 350
Pronouns, 222-231, 454-457
    and antecedents, 228
    in contractions, 230
    correct use of, 226
    object, 224
    possessive, 230
    strategy
        for clarity of antecedent of, 228
        for contractions or possessive pronouns, 230
        for correct pronoun, 222
        for placement of, in sentences with *here* or *there*,
            50
        for subject or object, 224, 226
    subject, 222
Pronunciation key, 52
Proofreading, 36-38, 74-76, 120-122, 160-162, 210-212,
    258-260, 308-310, 356-358
Propaganda, recognizing, 326-327
Proper adjectives, 266
Proper nouns, 80
Publishing (*see* Presenting and sharing)

Punctuation
  apostrophes
    in plural possessives, 86
    in possessives, 84
    contractions, 308, 476
  of bibliography, 258
  colons, 160, 476
  commas
    in a bibliography, 258
    in conversation, 356, 478-479
    in letters, 160
    review of general rules, 474, 478
    and semicolons, 210
    in sentences, 36
    with transition words, 256
  of conversations, 356, 476-479
  exclamation marks, 36, 42, 364
  hyphens, 308
  of letters, 160
  periods
    at end of abbreviation, 476-477
    in a bibliography, 258
    in quotations, 356, 476
    at end of sentence, 36, 42, 472
  question mark
    ending interrogative sentences, 36, 42
    in quotations, 356, 478-479
  quotations marks
    in conversations, 356, 476-479
    in titles, 120
  semicolons, 210
  of sentences, 36
  of titles of works, 120

Questions
  essay, 378
  for interviewing, 66
Quotation marks, 120, 356
  in conversation, 356, 476-479
  in titles, 120
Quotations,
  direct, 68
  punctuation of, 356-357, 476-479

Readers' Guide to Periodical Literature, 246
Reference books and materials, 110, 246
Regular verbs, 136
Repetition, avoiding, 208
Report, oral, 278-279
Research report, 240-261
  bibliography in, 258
  characteristics of, 241

first draft, 254
historical play, 284-287
listing sources for, 251
oral report, 278-279
organizing, 244
outline, 252
taking notes for, 250
using reference materials, 246
Revising, 33-35, 71-73, 117-119, 157-159, 207-209, 255-257, 305-307, 353-355
Rhyme, 213
Rhythm, 214
Run-on sentences, 372

Schedules, bus, 144-145
Semicolons, 210
Sensory details, 200
Sentences, 42-51, 366-373, 437-440, 467-471
  (*see also* Topic sentences)
  avoiding run-on, 372
  combining (*see* Combining sentences)
  complete subjects and predicates, 44
  compound, 370
  compound predicates in, 368
  compound subjects in, 366
  as examples, in dictionary, 52
  finding subjects in, 48
  imperative, 42, 48
  interrogative, 42, 48
  kinds of, 42
  punctuating, 36
  simple subjects and predicates in, 46
  strategy
    for adjectives in, 264
    for adverbs or adjectives in, 318
    for avoiding fragments, 42
    for correcting run-on sentences, 372
    for finding adverbs in, 314
    for finding direct objects, 168
    for finding indirect objects, 170
    for identifying compound sentences, 370
    for not overusing interjections, 364
    for varying, 274, 320
  topic, 28, 378
  varying, with phrases, 72
  with *here* and *there*, 50
Sequence, 30
Series, commas separating words in, 74
Setting of story, 333, 350
Sharing (*see* Presenting and sharing)
Simile, 204
Simple predicates, 46

Simple subjects, 46
Singular nouns, 82-83, 441-442
    possessive form of, 86-87, 443
Solution attempts in story, 333, 350
Speaking and listening
    conducting a meeting, 54
    discussion strategy, 33, 71, 117, 207, 255, 305, 353
    giving an oral report, 278
    giving directions, 234
    group discussion, 54
    interviewing, 66, 68
    Making All the Connections, 99, 185, 285, 383
    making a speech, 376
    speaking and listening strategy, 39, 77, 123, 163,
        219, 261, 311, 359
Speech,
    making a, 376
    parts of, 52 (*see also* Adjectives;
        Adverbs; Nouns; Pronouns; Verbs)
Spelling strategy, 434-435
    breaking word into syllables, 122
    memory hints, 162
    for principal parts of verbs, 136
    remembering spelling rules, 260
    speak word aloud, 76
    using dictionary, 38
    visualize word, 76
    word families, 212
    words ending in *-el*, *-al*, or *-il*, 310
    words with prefixes, 358
    write word, 76
Sports section of newspaper, 92
State abbreviations, 161
Story, 332-359 (*see also* Literature)
    characteristics of, 333
    creating characters for, 348
    parts of, 350
Studying for test, 94
Study skills
    dictionary skills, 52
    outlining, 252
    parts of a book, 248
    skimming and scanning, 248
    taking notes, 250
    test taking, 94, 180, 280, 378
    thesaurus skills, 90
    using the library, 110
    using reference materials, 246
Subjects
    agreement with verbs, 132
    complete, 44
    compound, 366
    in sentences, 44-49
    simple, 46
Subject pronouns, 222

Suffixes, 142-143
Summary in book report, 112
Superlative form
    of adjectives, 270
    of adverbs, 316
Supporting details, 30
Syllables, 52, 122
Synonyms, 90, 276-277, 324
    and antonyms, 90, 276-277, 324
    in thesaurus, 90, 208, 393-416

Table of contents, 248
Tanka, 216
Tenses
    of irregular verbs, 138, 140
    perfect, 134
    present, past, and future, 132
Test taking
    answering essay questions, 378
    following directions, 180
    planning your time, 280
    studying for test, 94
Thesaurus, 90, 393-416
    using to avoid repetition, 208
Thesaurus skills, 90
Thesis statement, 302
Thinking skills
    brainstorming, 26, 99, 185, 285, 383
    fact and opinion, 114-115, 300-301
    journal, 51, 81, 133, 173, 229, 273, 315, 365
    learning log, 39, 47, 77, 87, 94, 123, 129, 137, 163,
        171, 180, 219, 231, 261, 269, 280, 311, 319, 359, 367,
        373, 378
    organizing information, 26, 100, 186, 200, 244, 252,
        286, 302, 384
    recognizing fallacies, 326
    sequencing, 306
    summarizing, 112
Time
    abbreviations in, 88
    planning, in test taking, 280
    planning, when writing, 429-431
Time order, 354
Title page of book, 248
Titles
    of people, abbreviations of, 88
    of works, punctuating, 120
Topic, narrowing, 26
Topic sentences, 28
    for essay question, 378
Transition words, 256
Transitive verbs, 172
Troublesome words, 484-485
Turning points, 193

Underlining titles, 120

Verbs, 126-141, 168-175, 445-453
  action, 126
  contractions, 230
  direct objects, 168
  helping, 130
  indirect objects, 170
  irregular, 138-141
  linking, 128-129, 174
  main, 130
  perfect tenses, 134
  present, past, and future tenses, 132
  principal parts of irregular, 138
  principal parts of regular, 136
  strategy
    for agreement with compound subject, 366
    for *be* as linking or action, 128
    for compound predicates, 368
    for correct tense, 132
    for forms of *be* in predicate, 44
    for *have* as main or helping verb, 134
    for identifying action, 126
    for more than one word in simple predicate, 46
    for past participles, 140
    for principal parts of irregular, 138
    for spelling of principal parts, 136
    for transitive and intransitive, 172
    for verb phrases, 130
  transitive and intransitive, 172
Verb phrases, 130
Verse, (*see also* Descriptive writing, Poetry)
  free, 214

Word roots, 176-177

Words
  base, 142
    prefixes and, 142
    suffixes and, 142
  commonly misspelled, 435
  finding, in dictionary, 52
  guide, in dictionary, 52
  key, 246
  strategy
    for finding, in dictionary, 52
    for homophones and homographs, 232
    for meaning of, 142, 176, 324
    for using synonyms, 276
    for using thesaurus and dictionary, 90
  transition, 256
  troublesome, 484-485
Writing (*see* Composing)
Writing Connection
  adjectives, 263
  adverbs, 313
  nouns, 79
  pronouns, 221
  sentences, 41, 361
  verbs, 125, 167
Writing handbook, 417-436
  commonly misspelled words, 435
  handwriting models, 436
  letter forms, 432-433
  spelling strategies, 434
  steps of writing, 429-431
  types of writing, 417-428

You, understood in imperative sentence, 48

ZIP codes, 160

Illustrations: Donna Corvi, 42–43, 64, 74–75, 79, 126–127, 243, 294–295, 312; Susan David, 81–82, 115, 169, 202–203, 218; Marie De John, 155, 159, 246–247, 264, 274–275; Mary Young Duarte, 60–61, 303, 332–333; Mike Eagle, 34–35, 304–305; Cameron Eagle, 123, 157, 200–201, 208–209; Jack Freas, 47, 99, 264, 274–275, 285; Steve Henry, 28–29, 41, 49, 106–109, 125, 167, 240–241, 249, 255, 308 361, 383; Jane Kendell, 18–24; Pat Lindren, 123; David Lindroth, 185; Jim Ludtke, 27, 30, 44, 71–73, 86–87, 135, 153, 224, 252–253, 257, 271, 349, 351, 358, 363, 366, 371, 374; Diana Magnuson, 334–345; Kathy Mitchell, 115, 118–119, 173; Sandy Rabinowitz, 18–24; Claudia Sargent, 50–51, 141, 206–207, 210, 216–217, 221, 227, 263, 319–320, 364, 373.

Photographs: 36–37 Montage by Ken Karp/Omni-Photo Communications, Inc. Postcards courtesy of the New York Historical Society; **62–63** The Bettmann Archive; **64** The Bettmann Archive; **68** John Lei/Omni-Photo Communications, Inc.; **128–129** John Lei/Omni-Photo Communications, Inc.; **136–137** Lee Bolton; **150–151** Ken Karp/Omni-Photo Communications, Inc.; **164–165** John Lei/Omni-Photo Communications, Inc.; **194–195** John Lei/Omni-Photo Communications, Inc.; **196t** D.W. Hamilton/The Image Bank; **196b** Peter Schaaf; **197** Henri Cartier-Bresson/Magnum Photos; **196–197** Montage by Ken Karp/Omni-Photo Communications, Inc.; **204–205** John Lei/Omni-Photo Communications, Inc.; **214–215** John Lei/Omni-Photo Communications, Inc.; **227t** Culver Pictures, Inc.; **227b** The Bettmann Archive; **230** Ken Karp/Omni-Photo Communications, Inc.; **240–241** John Lei/Omni-Photo Communications, Inc. Quick Reference Word Atlas © Copyright 87-S-171 by Rand McNally & Company, R.L.; **245** John Lei/Omni-Photo Communications, Inc.; **266–267** John Lei/Omni-Photo Communications, Inc. Antique map courtesy of Library of Congress; **274** Culver Pictures, Inc.; **275** Jack Mitchell; **297** Matt Heron/Black Star; **298** Ivan Messar/Black Star; **317** John Lei/Omni-Photo Communications, Inc.; **319** The Bettmann Archive; **320–321** The Granger Collection. Montage by Ken Karp/Omni-Photo Communications, Inc.; **322** Culver Pictures, Inc.; **352–353** John Lei/Omni-Photo Communications, Inc.; **356–357** Ken Karp/Omni-Photo Communications, Inc.; **363** Don Perdue/Gamma-Liaison.

Acknowledgments

For permission to adapt and reprint copyrighted materials, grateful acknowledgment is made to the following publishers, authors, and other copyright holders:

Atheneum Publishers for "The Dream Woman" from *The Apple Vendor's Fair* by Patricia Hubbell. Copyright © 1963 by Patricia Hubbell. Used by permission of Atheneum Publishers.

Bantam Books, Inc., for "I Have a Dream" from *Listen Children — An Anthology of Black Literature* by Martin Luther King Jr. Copyright © 1963 by Martin Luther King, Jr. Reprinted by permission of Joan Daves. All Rights Reserved.

Thomas Y. Crowell Company for "The Endless Steppe" from *The Endless Steppe* by Esther Hautzig. Copyright © 1968 by Esther Hautzig. Used by permission of Thomas Y. Crowell Company, an imprint of Harper & Row, Publishers, Inc.

Dodd, Mead & Company, Inc., for "The Wasp" from *Collected Poems* by William Sharp.

Doubleday & Co. for "The Peabody Bird" from *Taxis and Toadstools* by Rachel Field. Copyright © 1926 by Doubleday & Company. Used by permission of the publisher.

E. P. Dutton for "There Are So Many Ways of Going Places" by Leslie Thompson from *Another Here and Now Story Book* by Lucy Sprague Mitchell. Copyright © 1937 by E. P. Dutton & Co., Inc. Used by permission of the publisher.

Farrar, Straus & Giroux for "Soap Bubble" by Valerie Worth, excerpted from *All the Small Poems*. Copyright © 1987 by Valerie Worth. Used by permission of Farrar, Straus & Giroux; for "Sun" by Valerie Worth, exerpted from *All the Small Poems*. Copyright © 1987 by Valerie Worth. Used by permission of Farrar, Straus & Giroux.

Harcourt Brace Jovanovich, Inc., for seven lines from "Serve Me a Slice of Moon" from *Serve Me a Slice of Moon* by Marcie Hans. Copyright © 1965 by Marcie Hans. Reprinted by permission of Harcourt Brace Jovanovich.

Little, Brown & Co., Inc., for "The Committee" from *Me and the Terrible Two* by Ellen Conford. Copyright © 1974 by Ellen Conford. All Rights Reserved; for "Eletelephony" from *Tirra Lirra: Rhymes Old and New* by Laura E. Richards. Copyright © 1955 by Little, Brown & Co. Used by permission of the publisher.

Macmillan Publishing Company for "The Falling Star" from *Collected Poems* by Sara Teasdale. Copyright © 1930 by Sara Teasdale Filsinger, renewed 1958 by Guaranty Trust Co. of New York. Reprinted by permission of Macmillan Publishing Co., Inc.

W. W. Norton & Co., Inc., for "Metamorphosis" by May Sarton from *Selected Poems of May Sarton* edited by Serena Hilsinger and Lois Byrnes. Copyright © 1978 by May Sarton. Used by permission of W. W. Norton & Company, Inc.

Puffin Books for "Eleanor Roosevelt: First Lady of the World" from *Eleanor Roosevelt: First Lady of the World* by Doris Faber. Copyright © 1985 by Doris Faber. Used by permission of Puffin Books, a division of Viking Penguin, Inc.

Viking Penguin, Inc., for "The Prodigy" adapted from "Mantua, Milan, Milan" from *Letters to Horseface* by Ferdinand N. Monjo, copyright © 1975 by Ferdinand N. Monjo and Louise L. Monjo, published by Viking Penguin, Inc.

Vintage Books for "Raymond's Run" from *Gorilla, My Love* by Toni Cade Bambara. Copyright © 1960, 1972 by Toni Cade Bambara. Used by permission of Vintage Books, a division of Random House, Inc.